WALTER
CITRINE

WALTER CITRINE

FORGOTTEN STATESMAN OF
THE TRADES UNION CONGRESS

DR JIM MOHER

JGM BOOKS

To my wife, Ruth,
for her thoughtful comments
and support throughout

PRAISE

'This fascinating biography sets the record straight on a giant of the Labour movement who helped create the modern TUC. It is a wonderful personal story and contains many lessons for us today, not least the need for unity, hard work and organisation.'

　– Frances O'Grady, General Secretary, Trades Union Congress

'Like many trade unionists, Walter Citrine was crucial to my education. A major political figure of the 20th century, Citrine deserves the great biography that Dr Jim Moher has given him.'

　– Alan Johnson, former Home Secretary and union leader

'A lively account and sparkling analysis of the life of an under-appreciated great trade union man of the 20th century. At last, Citrine has the biography he deserves.'

　– Lord John Monks, former General Secretary of the
　Trades Union Congress

'An important and much-needed book. Walter Citrine was the most influential trade unionist in Britain between the wars. He made the TUC into a powerful industrial and political force. Churchill admired him, Roosevelt was grateful for his help and trade unionists honoured his leadership. This is the fascinating biography that Citrine deserves.'

　– John Edmonds, former General Secretary of the GMB
　union and President of the Trades Union Congress

Walter Citrine: The Forgotten Statesman of the Trades Union Congress is an important, long-overdue study of a key but neglected figure in 20th-century British history. As TUC general secretary through the interwar and wartime years, Citrine combined with Ernest Bevin to lead British trade unions to their post-war public influence. As Moher shows, Citrine was also an international labour statesman who saw off the totalitarian threat to free trade unions. His biography is rich with new insights into the mainstream moderate labour movement.

> – Professor Peter Ackers, Emeritus Professor in the History
> of Industrial Relations, Loughborough University

'Jim Moher's highly readable and expert work on Walter Citrine reveals much that is new about Citrine's TUC trade union work from the general strike to the end of the Second World War. But he also, uniquely, reveals much of Citrine's hitherto unnoticed seminal work as a Merseyside regional official for the Electrical Trade Union in and after the First World War. An excellent work that does complete justice to a great trade unionist.'

> – Dr John Lloyd, author of *Light and Liberty: A History of
> the EEPTU*

'Jim Moher's lively biography places Citrine at the heart of many of the major political debates concerning the class struggle, Labour's socialism and Anglo-Soviet relations. It is a valuable source of information that greatly furthers our understanding of one of the most important trade unionists of the twentieth century.'

> – Jonathan Davis, Associate Professor in Modern European
> History, Anglia Ruskin University

CONTENTS

Acknowledgements xv
List of illustrations xvii
Foreword xix

INTRODUCTION 1

Walter Citrine, as General Secretary of the Trades Union Congress (TUC) from 1926, was a prominent national and international union figure throughout the 1930s and during the war until he left office in 1946. According to Churchill, Citrine was as important for the country during the war as most government ministers. Yet he became a 'forgotten statesman' for the Labour government of 1945, without a commensurate role.

CHAPTER 1 – CITRINE'S MERSEYSIDE 7

We explore Citrine's early childhood and sickly youth, leaving school at age twelve to work in a dusty mill in Liverpool at the turn of the twentieth century. Born into a sea-faring Mersey artisan family, with a strict Presbyterian upbringing, he trains as an electrical worker. Through self-education and heavily influenced by very left-wing (Independent Labour Party) socialist views, Citrine pushes himself to the fore to become the leading Electrical Trades Union (ETU) district official on Merseyside and on the Liverpool Trades Council. This chapter examines his formative years.

CHAPTER 2 – THE MILITANT ELECTRICIAN 18

A more detailed examination of Citrine's work and the strikes he led, official and unofficial, from 1912 to 1914, before becoming the first elected ETU District Secretary. We explore his previously shrouded war-time activities as well as his support of his electricians against the exploitative dilution of skills and conscription campaigns of the War Office during the First World War. His leading role in wider union campaigns on the Liverpool Trades Council, notoriously in support of the turbulent Liverpool police strike of 1919, is revealed.

CHAPTER 3 – A NATIONAL UNION FIGURE 33

Citrine moves to the ETU's headquarters as an elected national official in 1920, only to find the union close to bankruptcy during a great depression and because of amateurish branch control of funds. Citrine takes on a reforming administrative role and 'saves the union'. Clashes with the syndicalist-controlled London District Committee over funding abuses for political ends. Also writes The Labour Chairman, *a guide to the conduct of meetings for all unions. Persuaded to apply for, and gets, a Trades Union Congress (TUC) administrative role as assistant general secretary in 1923.*

CHAPTER 4 – THE TUC AND THE FIRST LABOUR GOVERNMENT 50

Citrine arrives at the TUC in 1924 during the first Labour government and a growing mood for militancy in the unions. Serves an expanding TUC keen to involve itself and even to 'coordinate' large-scale industrial actions. The causes of the poor relationship between the two sides of the Labour movement, which led to diverging paths, imperilling the fragile first minority Labour government, are explored. The

TUC (and Citrine's) involvement in the confrontation with the Conservative govern-
*ment in 1925 (*Red Friday*), causing the government to concede, is examined.*

CHAPTER 5 – IN THE GENERAL STRIKE, 1926 67

This most powerful display of union power is an attempt by the TUC to use
the considerable industrial muscle of all the major unions to achieve a political
objective. The experience marks a watershed for the TUC and union leaders,
especially for Walter Citrine (then acting general secretary) and Ernest Bevin,
in learning the limitations of exercising such power when not intent on a
revolutionary challenge. The course of the nine-day strike and the 'human
factor' is charted.

CHAPTER 6 – CITRINE AND
THE COMMUNIST MOVEMENT 92

We explore the Communist International's attempt to use the General Strike for
revolutionary purposes and their extreme rage with the TUC for calling it off. We
examine Citrine's exposé of the role of the communist front National Minority
Movement. Citrine's emergence as President of the International Federation of
Trade Unions (IFTU) is assessed and why it made him the target of commu-
nist and far-left vituperation from there on.

CHAPTER 7 – 'ABOVE THE LAW'? 110

The unique position of British unions of legal 'immunity' from prosecution
during industrial actions is considered. The Conservative government's restrictive
Trade Disputes and Trades Union Act 1927, *conceived as a vindictive*
response to the General Strike, is examined for its impact and the strong TUC/
Citrine-led campaigns against it.

CHAPTER 8 – COMING TO TERMS WITH 'THE CAPITALIST SYSTEM' 121

We examine the now-very-different union response to an employer's post-Strike initiative for peace talks known as the 'Mond-Turner Talks'. We assess the historical significance of its recommendations. The complementary, but rivalrous, nature of the Citrine–Bevin partnership is examined.

CHAPTER 9 – THE TUC AND THE SECOND LABOUR GOVERNMENT 137

The TUC perspective on the failure of the second Labour government of 1929–31 is examined. The failure to deliver the promised repeal of the 1927 Act is highlighted. We also examine other internal factors driving the TUC to oppose the government's austerity proposals of 1931 and government failure to consult the unions adequately. The TUC's total opposition is considered as a cause of the break-down of a divided Cabinet, the defection of the Labour leadership and a gravely weakened Labour parliamentary position after the general election of 1931. Citrine's subsequent insistence on totally new arrangements for consultation and liaison with the Labour Party, the National Council of Labour, is considered.

CHAPTER 10 – AN ANTI-FASCIST PIONEER 159

The significance of Citrine's detailed reports from the IFTU Executive meetings in Berlin to the 1933 General Council and Trades Union Congress, entitled Dictatorships, and the Trade Union Movement, *is considered. The TUC's influence through the National Council of Labour in persuading the Labour leadership to change its policy on rearmament is explored. Citrine's prominent role in assisting Jewish groups and union refugees through the Anti-Fascist Council is highlighted. His active leadership of the TUC lobby to* aid the Spanish Republicans and his membership of the Moyne Commission to actively assist West Indian trade union leaders are also described.

CHAPTER 11 – CITRINE'S 'SEARCH FOR TRUTH' IN RUSSIA 183

We examine Citrine's quite complex attitude to the early Soviet Union as the 'first workers' state'. His second visit after ten years, in 1935, would encapsulate that ambivalence in a book of his diaries about the trip, entitled I Search for Truth in Russia. We also consider Citrine's decision to accept a knighthood in 1935 and the hostile reaction of some in the Labour movement.

CHAPTER 12 – AT WAR: CITRINE AND BEVIN 201

As TUC general secretary and a Privy Councillor from 1940, Citrine's involvement in the war effort on behalf of the trade unions is explored. He had ready access to the prime minister, all Cabinet ministers and all government departments. We examine the difficulties which arose between Citrine and Bevin after an initial period of close consultation.

CHAPTER 13 – THE DREAM OF INTERNATIONAL WORKERS' UNITY 231

The significance of Citrine's international union diplomacy in support of British efforts to counter American isolationism in 1940, and his trips to Moscow and Washington in 1941 to set up an Anglo-Soviet-American Trade Union Committee, are explored. The difficulties he encountered due to American union divisions and the lack of support on account of Foreign Office, Washington Embassy and Ministry of Labour hostility are examined. His subsequent involvement with the World Trade Union Committee and the TUC's exclusion *from the inaugural conference of the United Nations Organisation in 1945 by the coalition government are considered.*

CHAPTER 14 – CITRINE AND PUBLIC OWNERSHIP: COAL AND ELECTRICITY 266

We consider the reasons for Citrine's departure from the TUC in 1946, and his move to a very different role at the newly nationalised National Coal Board. We consider how effective he was in overseeing the huge challenge involved in the generation and supply of the country's electric power during his ten years as chair of the British Electricity Authority. His relations with his ministers, especially Hugh Gaitskell MP, and the senior managers of the industry highlight the challenges faced in the newly nationalised industries as a whole.

CHAPTER 15 – IN THE HOUSE OF LORDS 286

Citrine made important contributions to House of Lords debates from October 1959, usually on economic and industrial relations issues, until his health deteriorated in the early 1970s. We also examine his continuing interest and views about union affairs.

EPILOGUE: HIS PLACE IN HISTORY 299

Many of Citrine's achievements are recalled. It is argued that his outstanding contribution to the creation of the modern Trades Union Congress and to the rise of the trade unions to a prominent place in society from the late 1930s deserves fuller recognition.

Notes 311
Index 360

ACKNOWLEDGEMENTS

This book owes much to the kind comments of my colleagues in the History & Policy Trade Union and Employment Forum, in particular Tom Wilson, Professor Peter Ackers, John Edmonds and Dr Alastair Reid. A special thanks to Tom Wilson, a former assistant general secretary at the TUC, for our many discussions and his valuable insights into the workings of the General Council. His stamina in staying with and commenting on every chapter as it went along was most helpful. Also, to John Lloyd for his generous access to his early Electrical Trades Union papers and discussions, including our trip to Warwick University, where he has preserved that union's records. I am also grateful to Jonathan Davis, John Lloyd, Neil Riddell and Robert Taylor, whose previous work on Citrine I have built upon and who have been most helpful with their comments on my draft chapters. Robert sadly passed away in August 2020 after a long illness. So, a special dedication to him also.

Thanks also to Jeff Howarth at the TUC Library, and the staff at the LSE archives, the College of Arms, Maugham Library, Kings College, London, the British Library, the National Archives, the Churchill Archive Centre, Girton College Library, the University of Cambridge Library and the Warwick Modern Records Centre. Without their access to primary and secondary sources, this work could not have been written. Also to local librarians at Liverpool City Library and Brent, Harrow and Torquay Libraries for most helpful assistance on Citrine's early career and last days in Devon. Harrow Weald Cemetery was most helpful in identifying the Citrine grave plot.

This work rests especially on Walter Citrine's autobiographical gems *Men and Work* and *Two Careers*, which I have interrogated critically and generally found accurate and reliable. They should be brought back to print as in them Lord Citrine tells his story 'as though he were living each stage of it again' (*The Times*). My reliance on other historians who have noticed Citrine seriously – Bullock, Clegg, Cole, Lloyd, Marquand, Middlemas, Martin, Morgan, Phillips, Reid and others – will also be evident from the endnotes. To all who have ploughed these furrows, many thanks.

I'm most grateful to Chris Wold, Caroline McArthur and Gabrielle Johnson of whitefox who have assisted greatly in bringing my complicated manuscript to this shape.

ILLUSTRATIONS

1. *Modern Liverpool 1907* by Walter Richards, National Museums Liverpool.
2. Picton Library Reading Room, Hornby Library, c.1910. Reproduced by kind permission of Liverpool Record Office, Liverpool Libraries.
3. The ETU banner and membership card, courtesy of John Lloyd.
4. Citrine's ETU journal column, 'Talks with Our Officers', 1920–21, Warwick Modern Records Centre.
5. *The Labour Chairman*, Express Co-operative Printing Co. Ltd., Manchester, 1920.
6. *ABC of Chairmanship*, published by the TUC, the Fabian Society, The Co-operative Party and numerous unions, 1939.
7. Citrine with the ETU leadership before he left for the TUC, 1923, LSE Library, Citrine Archive 12/1 and 12/3.
8. Citrine at his office, 1927, LSE Library, Citrine Archive.
9. TUC General Council, 1926, in *The Encyclopaedia for the Labour Movement*, vol. III, 1928, p. 239.
10. Pugh and Citrine leave Downing Street. Courtesy of Topical Press Agency / Stringer.
11. Meeting of ARJAC, 1925 , Citrine Archive.
12. Citrine preparing a report at Transport House, 1945, LSE Library, Citrine Archive.
13. Bevin with Citrine in 1937, 'an involuntary partnership'. From the TUC Library Collections.
14. Citrine in his hospital bed. From Citrine, *Men and Work*.
15. IFTU Executive Council, 1930. From LSE Library, Citrine Archive 12/1 and 12/3.

16. Places visited during the Citrines' trip. From his book *I Search for Truth in Russia* (London: George Routledge & Sons Ltd., 1936).

17. Doris Citrine with a group of peasant women. From Citrine, *I Search for Truth in Russia*.

18. 1933 TUC Congress at Brighton with Bevin and Alec Walkden (president). From LSE Library, Citrine Archive 12/3.

19. Map of Citrine's US and Canadian tour, 1940, from Citrine's booklet of his tour, *My American Diary*.

20. The Soviet trade union delegation on its return visit to Britain, being received by Churchill at 10 Downing Street, late 1941– January 1942. From Citrine, *Two Careers*, p. 129.

21. Opening meeting of the World Trade Union Conference in Paris in 1945, with General de Gaulle and the Soviet leader, V. Kuznetsov. From Citrine, *Two Careers*, pp. 224–25.

22. Lord Citrine of Wembley's coat of arms. College of Arms MS Grants 109, p. 167. Reproduced by permission of the Kings, Heralds and Pursuivants of Arms.

23. Cover of book by Leslie Hannah showing Citrine with the king and Gaitskell at the opening of a new power station at Kingston. Leslie Hannah, *Engineers, Managers and Politicians: The First Fifteen Years of Nationalised Electricity Supply in Britain* (The Electricity Council, London, 1982), p. 7.

24. Lord Citrine, chair of the British Electricity Authority, opens a new headquarters near Leeds, 1950. From the LSE Library, Citrine Archive 12/1 and 12/3.

25. Addressing the TUC in 1975, aged eighty-eight, with Marie Patterson, chair general council, and Len Murray, general secretary. From the LSE Library, Citrine Archive.

FOREWORD

~

As Robert Taylor wrote in his history of the TUC,[1] 'The modern TUC is very much the personal achievement of Walter McClennan Citrine'. He was at thirty-nine the youngest man to be the TUC general secretary and he became 'one of the most important figures in the formation of the mid-twentieth century labour movement'.[2]

Yet unlike Lord Reith, who built the BBC, and unlike Ernest Bevin, who built the Transport and General Workers' Union and was later highly effective as the wartime minister of labour and national service and as the post-war foreign secretary, his contribution is known to relatively few today, a fate he shares with another favourite of mine, Frank Pick, who built up London Transport to be the foremost public transport authority in the world when he was in charge.

Citrine, where he is remembered, is primarily known as a trade union bureaucrat, an effective administrator, expert at filing and shorthand. Aneurin Bevan remarked sarcastically, 'poor fellow, he suffers from files'. Yet he was so much more than a top administrator. His book *ABC of Chairmanship* remains in use in the Labour movement and perhaps more widely.

He built up a cadre of bright staff in the TUC and developed among them an ethos of dedication to the Labour interest, high-minded public service and a largely selfless commitment to hard, professional work. It was an ethos I keenly appreciated when I worked at the TUC from 1969 to 2003 and I am pleased to say that it still continues under the able leaderships of my successors – Brendan Barber and now Frances O'Grady.

Citrine emerged from a working-class background to be an official in the Electrical Trades Union on Merseyside, a turbulent education. He was self-taught, a teetotaller and a rather austere man. He became TUC general secretary in 1926, always arguing strongly for a more centralised TUC and one more capable of laying down a united path for the British trade unions. At that time, he was a syndicalist, although not a revolutionary one, believing that centrally directed disciplined strike action was essential to working-class advance. While he had misgivings about the TUC's lack of preparation for the strike, he was fully committed to it while foreseeing clearly the difficulty that would arise when the miners' leaders refused to allow the TUC to negotiate a compromise settlement. The result, as he probably feared, was defeat. It fell to Citrine, by now the new general secretary, to pick up the pieces, and with others chart a way forward for trade unionism after the huge setback for organised labour. In this endeavour, he adopted certain principles. He favoured collaboration with the Labour Party but insisted on TUC independence. Getting that relationship to be mutually beneficial remains a challenge for every trade union leader. He was a key instigator of the so called Mond-Turner process in the late 1920s which sought to establish a less confrontational, more co-operative approach with employers to industrial relations – a holy grail we still seek today. After the General Strike he continued to press for more authority to the TUC so as to deal with any elected government on any subject to of relevance to trade unions. And he supported the efforts of the relatively new Ministry of Labour to establish his Joint Industrial Councils and industry-wide collective bargaining. This was to cover most of the private sector by 1939.

While this process was continuing, Citrine abandoned a rather tolerant approach to the Communist Party when it started to promote the National Minority Movement and sought to undermine the established leaderships of unions. He was to remain a staunch critic of communism for the rest of his life while keeping amicable relations with certain communist leaders, for example, Harry Pollitt. Citrine (and Bevin) went on to develop a strong hostility to the emerging dictators of both right and left, although he was always interested in developments in the Soviet Union and, in his capacity as President of the International Federation of Trade Unions, travelled widely in Europe and North America. His interest in international matters and his frequent visits abroad, often by long sea journeys, were supported by the TUC and he became widely acknowledged as an expert on international matters. Particular interests, among many others, were a commitment to building trade unionism in the Caribbean and his support for the Finns in 1934–40, when Finland was invaded by the Soviet Union after the Molotov–Ribbentrop Pact. But perhaps most importantly he almost saw a recovery of the TUC's influence with government (he was even consulted by the prime minister on the Abdication crisis). And this was to be cemented by Ernest Bevin's decisive influence in the wartime Cabinet when the trade unions became a major pillar of the British effort in the Second World War. Serious tensions were to arise between Bevin and Citrine under the pressures of wartime conditions, but they were outstanding wartime figures in British trade union history and more widely in British history generally.

What a record! I am grateful to Jim Moher, an old friend and trade union colleague, for dusting off the archives and writing in a lively and entertaining fashion the story of a remarkable man who deserves to be better known and very widely appreciated.

Lord John Monks
General Secretary of the TUC, 1993–2003

INTRODUCTION

At the very lowest point of morale in Britain during the Second World War – the Blitz in London, Birmingham and Liverpool and the almost total destruction of Coventry in 1940 – a Liverpool trade unionist, Walter Citrine, General Secretary of the TUC, was invited by his friend and fellow union official Bill Greene to New Orleans to address the American Federation of Labour Convention. It was a time when many thought Britain would fall to Nazi German conquest. Citrine was to give 'first-hand, accurate and definite information ... about the labour situation in Britain under war conditions.'[1] Even though it meant Citrine would be away for some months, his General Council insisted that he go, appreciating the significance of his visit at that time.

Before he went, Citrine was invited to lunch by the prime minister on 24 October in the heavily devastated Downing Street area, which the main occupant had refused to leave. Churchill extended every faculty Citrine needed from the embassy in Washington to assist the TUC visit.[2] At that time, in late 1940, Churchill was most anxious that the Americans should come into the war at the earliest possible moment. In his letter of introduction to President Roosevelt, he wrote that Citrine, worked with me 3 years before the war in our effort to arouse all parties in the country to the need of rearmament against Germany. At the present time he fills a position in the Labour Movement more important to the conduct of the war than many Ministerial offices ... He has the root of the matter in him, and I most cordially commend him to your consideration.[3]

Citrine's key role since 1933 in warning about the threat posed by the fascists was appreciated by Churchill.

Citrine's speech and tour of America and Canada turned out to be a huge success. Not normally a 'tub-thumping' speaker, his oratory had many of the union delegates weeping openly. As one American newspaper reported, he 'painted for his audience a picture of the horrors confronting his people, told of the amazing courage and resistance displayed by the British, and pointed to the vital war role of British Labor'.[4] The speech was reported to a Cabinet meeting of the president, who asked for a copy and invited Citrine to the White House. Citrine had, in fact, struck many of the notes Roosevelt had wanted his people to hear, and not the defeatist reports that Britain was 'on her last legs' that were then quite common in the United States. The TUC leader went on to address audiences of thousands and small luncheon groups in fifty-two other meetings. He broadcast on radio throughout his tour of industrial America. His request was for 'planes and planes and more planes', which, now that Roosevelt had been re-elected, would be delivered.[5] After they met at the end, the president wrote to Churchill 'telling him how much we admire the British people and the stand they are taking.'[6]

Citrine finished that arduous and dangerous 2,800-mile, twenty-six-hour journey across the Atlantic in a flying boat by late February 1941. He had hardly been united with his wife, Doris, and two boys, Norman and Ronnie, at their home in Wembley Park before he was off again, this time to Russia, braving the extreme conditions (not to mention the German U-boats) of the North Sea and the Arctic in winter.[7] This was hardly a time for a union conference, as Hitler was approaching Moscow. But Citrine was there to revive the link between the British and Soviet trade unions they had experienced in the 1920s. The presence of the TUC delegation strengthened a new alliance between Britain and the Soviet Union, as the Russian's valiant resistance to the German war machine became a ray of hope to Britain in late 1941. The Soviet trade unions made a return visit soon after, touring the war industrial works with Citrine to maximise the production of arms, planes and tanks for the Soviet allies.[8]

Who was this Sir Walter Citrine KBE? Why have we not heard more about his exploits? The purpose of this book is to answer these questions.[9] If Citrine is known at all outside union circles, it is for his *ABC of Chairmanship* on the procedures in the conduct of meetings, an arcane if important subject for all democratic clubs and societies, such as trade unions (see Chapter 3). Such a grammar-like production could leave one with the impression of a narrow technician mainly interested in the 'nuts and bolts' of things. They would be so wrong in Citrine's case. As with his other accomplishments, such activities were always undertaken to serve a wider purpose. He had applied himself to acquiring shorthand so that he would be chosen to attend TUC and Labour Party conferences as the one who could take a proper record and report back to his electricians' union.[10] It was a 'career move'. But Citrine was far from being a man of narrow vision or just a careerist, as our account will show.

Strangely for someone who spent more than thirty years involved in the Labour movement and more than twenty in the top TUC position, Walter McLennan Citrine (1887–1983) is now little known, even within the trade union movement. This is partly because Citrine was overshadowed by his much better-known contemporary, Minister of Labour and Foreign Secretary Ernest Bevin. Bevin has had many biographies, another just out by Lord Andrew Adonis.[11] (This is Citrine's first.) Also, Citrine left the TUC in 1946 for the nationalised coal and electric power industries.[12] But he was, too, deliberately left out of the Labour story. The influential international communist movement and far left of the Labour Party, whose influence Citrine had countered all his career, gave him a 'bad press'. Citrine's adversaries, who dominated many academic labour history faculties, either minimised Citrine's contributions or denied them a place altogether. Nye Bevan's jibe about the 'card-indexed mind of Walter Citrine' and 'poor fellow, he suffers from files' was typical in conveying the image of Citrine as an arch-bureaucrat and apparatchik.[13] Yet Citrine had as good a union and socialist pedigree as most. The fact that he also created an efficient and loyal 'bureaucracy' of professional TUC officials, equipped with modern systems, should be seen as part of his success.

Even Citrine's 'anti-communism' was a far more subtle and complex response to the great international challenges for unions in those days than has been appreciated. How many on the left could match his six missions to the Soviet Union? At first, like so many, he regarded the Russian Revolution as a beacon of hope – Lenin's *Electric Republic*. But he wasn't afraid to recognise the reality that emerged from that 'communist' experiment as a form of state capitalism. In this he was well ahead of his time. His defence of democracy against dictatorship and marshalling of the case for rearmament in the Labour movement in the 1930s is arguably on a par with Churchill's prescience. His international role for the TUC as president of IFTU since 1928 prepared him to make a major diplomatic contribution for the Allies during the Second World War, though it ultimately failed to create an international presence for the unions in the shaping of post-war global union conditions.

Citrine's own two-volume autobiography, *Men and Work* (1964) and *Two Careers* (1967), provides the best starting point to restore his reputation. In a sense, he has written his own history of his times, which has endured long after his critics have faded. These memoirs could be reprinted on their own as testimony to a remarkable career and man. They have stood up to much academic scrutiny and have become a major source for historians. The voluminous archive of his unpublished papers in the LSE Library Archives is also a mine of information that sheds much light on Citrine and his times. However, much care has been taken to 'go behind' them and to place them in their proper context. The writer has also built on the foundations of those historians who have given Citrine full credit, notably Jonathan Davis, John Lloyd, Neil Riddell and Robert Taylor.[14] At the same time, the classic histories of the British trade unions, such as Hugh Clegg's monumental three-volume work, have been fully consulted. This study will hopefully help to continue that interest in restoring the reputation of a truly extraordinary figure in trade union and Labour history.

This book is not just about doing justice to Citrine, important as that is. Through the lens of his life over such a long period, it is hoped to shed fresh light on historical controversies, some still current. Although the writer has not been an institutional academic, he does have those qualifications as well as direct experience of the Labour movement. So, this biography aims to meet the most rigorous academic standard, though being mainly intended to contribute towards the exploration of the reasons for the rise and decline of trade unionism in the twentieth century, which Citrine's careers spans.

Modern Liverpool 1907 by Walter Richards.

CHAPTER 1

~

CITRINE'S MERSEYSIDE

I loved the Mersey and the ever-moving spectacle of the vessels, large and small, ploughing its surface, bound for all parts of the world. When in later life it was decreed that I must leave the area I missed it more than I can say.

Lord Citrine, 1964[1]

Walter McLennan Citrine was born on 22 August 1887 at 65 Eastbourne Street, Liverpool, second-youngest of six, three sisters and two brothers.[2] Thirty years on, Walter Richards' painting of the city captures 'the abundant signs of illimitable expansiveness and invincible virility' of the Edwardian docks and smoke-stack metropolis.[3] This would be Citrine's 'beat' from the 1910s to the 1920s.

Liverpool was among the earliest places to face acute social challenges characteristic of the industrial city. It had grown rapidly as a modern global city, based around new systems of international trade and capital during the eighteenth and nineteenth centuries.[4] The port city had a population of just under 800,000, and the Wirral about 200,000, in 1900.[5] As one police officer noted in 1919, 'trams rattled through the city streets and the Overhead Railway plied its trade along a continuous line of docks with filled ships from every nation in the world'.[6] It was also the gateway to the 'New World', although many immigrants stayed. However, though the name Cirtini was of Italian origin, Walter Citrine's great-grandfather had been married in London and his grandfather, Francisco Cirtini, had been born there in 1816. His father, Alfred, had been born in Liverpool in 1852 with that name but changed it to Citrine upon marrying.[7] Of sea-going artisan stock, his family were always poor on account of his father's irregular work pattern as a ship's rigger/ Mersey pilot and his heavy drinking. However, 'he had long spells of sobriety, and during those periods our home life was supremely happy'.[8] Seeing him 'in drink' – 'a big powerful man of six feet' – and 'the worry and sorrow' caused to his little mother, 'I resolved never to let drink get a hold over me'. So Citrine didn't take any strong drink until he came to the TUC and then only to be sociable at professional receptions.[9]

The family moved to Seacombe, Wallasey, in the Wirral, two years later and so Walter grew up in that area.[10] They were living at 17 Lucerne Road at the time of the 1901 census, when he was thirteen.[11] He and his wife, Doris, and son, Norman, lived at Poole Road, Egremont in 1918 until he moved to Manchester.

The young Walter attended Poulton Board school in Secombe until the age of twelve. He started work in a very dusty flour mill.[12] He contracted inflammation of the lungs and kidneys due to exposure to the dust.[13] A 'delicate and sensitive child', he was fortunate in being 'lavished with home love and kindness'. He was a quite nervous child, and 'because I was a weakling there is no doubt that I was spoiled and became headstrong and self-willed.'[14] This self-analysis and self-awareness was one of Citrine's strong characteristics throughout his life. He was frequently critical in private notes about how he had handled himself in TUC committee meetings.[15] His mother, Isabella, trained as a hospital nurse at the Royal Infirmary, Liverpool, and became a visiting private nurse,[16] so she was away at times to supplement the family income. In her absences, her younger sister, Catherine McLellan, who lived with them, 'made me her special care'.[17]

Walter's mother, born Isabella McLellan in 1847, was a staunch Scottish Presbyterian from Arbroath and so he grew up in a very strict religious family environment, which may account for his noted self-discipline and hard work in later life. However, Walter didn't become very religious, though he attended Sunday school and Bible class at the Oakdale Presbyterian Mission school.[18] When, as the Labour candidate, he was 'charged with being an Atheist' (and therefore a Bolshevik), during the 1918 general election campaign in Tory Cheshire, Citrine took the trouble to get the *Liverpool Echo* carefully to correct the report, saying, 'Mr Citrine has for many years been identified with the work of the Oakdale Presbyterian Mission'.[19] He had joined the Anti-Cigarette League at Sunday school and so never acquired that habit.[20] His mother also impressed on him 'the wickedness of gambling'. But there was a tragic story behind this, for his mother (who died in 1913), sister and an uncle died of tuberculosis – which he called the 'the scourge of the Citrines'.[21] Cold baths and sleeping with the windows open was a common anti-TB sanatorium regime. He said, 'I knew the dangers of my incurring this dreadful disease and framed my habits as much as I could to keep it at bay.'[22]

When he recovered from his childhood illness, Citrine grew up in his father's robust sea-faring tradition of the Mersey (his brothers and uncles were connected with the sea – which 'was in our blood').[23] He had sought to start in that occupation as a cabin boy going to sea, but could not get taken on. His father then set him up to be trained as an electrician, one of the modern trades of that new power source, then being applied all round the Mersey.[24] Walter does not seem to have been much influenced by the sectarian traditions of the strongly Orange and Green city.[25] The family moved again to nearby Egremont, in Wallasey, where he lived at home until adulthood.[26] As a young man, he continued to live in Poole Road, Egremont, and married his long-term local girlfriend, Doris Slade, in 1913.[27] Their first boy, Norman, was born in 1914.

One of his later idiosyncrasies, even as a union official in adulthood, was an interest in palmistry and he told a story about visiting a Madame X in Warwick while waiting for a union meeting to start 'in the autumn of 1923'.[28] (Another popular fad in those days was phrenology and he used to study the facial characteristics of important people he met – such as Stalin in 1925 – to gauge their character.)[29] His interest in palmistry and phrenology remained with him throughout his life.

AN ELECTRICAL WORKER

Citrine was trained with a firm of electrical contractors in New Brighton at the top of the Wirral peninsula, sometime around 1900.[30] In 1903, he became an 'improver' on the electrical staff of New Brighton Tower Company.[31] Their tower, the largest of the kind, which were then 'all the rage' in Britain, was 621 feet high and had its own generating station. This powered the lights and a quite dangerous lift to the top, a key attraction, which he operated. Citrine spent three happy years there, until visitors to the once hugely popular northern seaside resort declined and he had to move on.[32] About 1906, he 'crossed the Mersey' to join a small

Liverpool contracting firm, still as an improver, at Colonial House, Water Street.[33]

Here Citrine came under the influence of an electrician workmate, one Tom Brett. Tom was an active member of the tiny but influential Marxist Social Democratic Federation (SDF), who 'deluged me with their pamphlets and arguments' and 'helped the process of political understanding with his daily diatribes'.[34] This early exposure to Marxist and syndicalist texts contributed to the shaping of Citrine's very analytical mind from a strong 'anti-capitalist' socialist perspective. About this time, a 'street social-ist' speaker captured his interest and persuaded him to come to a meeting of the Independent Labour Party (ILP).[35] The ILP was then strong on Merseyside and in the North-West and was the main ethical socialist 'ginger' group within the infant Labour Party. Citrine soon joined both bodies and became one of their key activ-ists in Wallasey at the age of eighteen.[36]

Citrine was greatly influenced by the socialist literature of the ILP, particularly Robert Blatchford's *Merry England* and *Britain for the British*.[37] Blatchford (1851–1943) had his own newspaper, *The Clarion*, and produced many such very clear and educative tracts on socialist topics. It had a huge circulation in the north of England at that time (annual sales of over three-quarters of a million), and was part of a Clarion Movement, which involved cycling clubs and touring socialist caravans.[38] His future TUC boss, Fred Bramley, a cabinetmaker from Bradford and official in the furniture trades union NAFTA, spent his early years driving one of these 'caravans for Socialism' all over the north of England.[39] Citrine found Blatch-ford's tracts 'a cogent and reasoned argument for Socialism'.[40] He was also impressed when two of the then left-wing stars of the ILP, Ramsay MacDonald and Philip Snowden, spoke at meetings in

Liverpool.[41] The ILP paper *Labour Leader* 'and a stream of socialist pamphlets' became his 'bedtime' reading. He would later remark, 'I didn't know so much about politics or human nature as I do today.'[42] He became active in his Wallasey area and was soon giving talks to ILP members and chairing the local branch. In 1907, they had him addressing open-air meetings in the popular Shiel Park in Liverpool.[43] However, from 1911, 'barely twenty', he joined the Electrical Trades Union (ETU) and became immersed in union activities. Now, 'politics receded more and more from purview'.[44] That was a significant time of industrial unrest in Liverpool, and he was swept up in his first strike, as we will see.

ELECTRICAL POWER AND PRACTICAL THEORY

After some months in Water Street, Citrine set off on his own across to the eastern edge of the city and the Cowley Hill plate glass works of the famous Pilkington's glass company in St Helen's.[45] He took lodgings nearby in a collier's cottage in Seddon Street.[46] At Pilkington's, the nineteen-year-old got a taste of the autocratic 'bossing' employer who dominated St Helen's at that time.[47] If he was late for the 6 a.m. start after the hooter went, he could be shut out until after breakfast and lose two hours' pay. He 'resented the way in which Pilkington's obtruded the doctrine that they were the bosses and that anyone who didn't like it could get out'.[48] He left after a row with his foreman over a sudden weekend work requirement.[49] Not even a union member, he was, however, already assertive, but he didn't have the experience or confidence to stay and organise the other workers into a union, to counter such poor managerial practices. So, as a fully fledged (though non-indentured) electrician, he returned to Egremont and worked locally around the Wirral for the next few years. He took seasonal work at the New Brighton Tower Company again and worked for a couple of years with a good-quality contractor, wiring houses for the better-off in the Wallasey district ('its amenities were still out of reach of working-class people').[50] Citrine thought: 'Someday I and other workers will have electricity just like these people', though, 'I was not infected with the class-war bug'.[51]

In the early part of 1910, 'work slackened' and, at the age of twenty-three, Citrine got his first taste of unemployment. Though he made the rounds of electrical firms in Liverpool, 'refusal followed refusal', and clerks treated him so 'cavalierly' that he felt humiliated and depressed.[52] After a substantial period out of work, 'almost in desperation' he went back to Pilkington's, which was pleased to take him back, as a bright young electrician.[53] Pilkington's was one of the first firms to go over fully to electrical power to drive its grinders and other plate-glass-making machines. Its staff had greatly increased 'because of the extensive electrification which had gone on ... The firm was installing some of the biggest direct-current electric motors in the country and heavy traction work was all new to me. I was deeply interested in electrical theory ...'[54] Here Citrine was 'at the cusp' of the technological development of the time and he seized the opportunity. He developed a method of study for 'reasoning out' the practical electrical problems which he encountered at work. He would write them down in a notebook in shorthand, and work out how to solve them at home. He filled many notebooks in this way and most of his evenings were spent doing this, instead of 'loitering about with companions or playing organised games'.[55] The girl he was courting, Doris Slade (his future wife), sat patiently 'knitting or sewing and never interjecting a disturbing remark', while 'I was struggling with these problems night after night'.[56] He and Doris were engaged 'in the spring of 1912', when he carved their names with a screw-driver on the obelisk at West Kirby, where he was wiring up a house.[57] This formative blend of technical and politico-economic learning would explain the considerable mental powers which Walter Citrine was developing and would bring to bear throughout his life as a union leader. In later years, he would recall, 'I applied exactly the same methods during my trade union days and right through my chairmanship of the British Electricity Authority'.[58]

CULTURAL DEVELOPMENT
AT THE PICTON LIBRARY

When out of work, Citrine had made good use of the time on his hands – looking for jobs in the morning but spending the afternoons in Liverpool City Council's magnificent Picton Reading Room.[59] Modelled on the British Library Reading Room, it is part of the Brown Free Library. Both facilities were 'intended principally for the working classes' by Liverpool City Council and provided access to anyone 'regardless of class to an opportunity for self-education'.[60] Incredibly, in the library booklet picture of the Reading Room in 1909 our young electrician, Citrine himself, can be seen sitting in the front row. There he was able to read the literary classics. George Bernard Shaw and W. S. Gilbert also 'were a real joy to me'.[61] He had developed 'a Dictionary habit' for learning the meaning of words. But he was now able to broaden his mind and develop his literary culture. In subsequent years, he would have 'many non-political cultural interests'. He loved Gilbert and Sullivan operas and was a keen student of Shakespeare's works, which influenced his thinking.[62]

Picton Library Reading Room, Hornby Library, c.1910.
Citrine sits third from left at the front table.

Citrine's time at St Helens was enlivened by debates with
the miners' sons at his lodgings in Seddon Street. 'They read
economics and philosophy and could argue intelligently. One was
a strong Socialist and between the three of us we had animated
discussions.'[63] He would recall those exchanges fondly in later life.
Citrine remained at Pilkington's until September 1911. A new and
'infinitely broader-minded' generation of directors had by now
taken over; they recognised trade unions and were pioneers in
the shorter-hours movement (cut to forty-four hours a week). He

probably got his first taste of trade unionism there before returning to Merseyside in 1911.[64]

JOINING THE ELECTRICAL TRADES UNION[65]

On 9 October 1911 Citrine joined the Liverpool branch of the Electrical Trades Union (ETU) as his fellow electricians on a job were all strong trade unionists. [66] Characteristically, he didn't just sign up, but soon took an active interest in its work, studying the constitution of the union and carrying a copy of the draft working rules around with him and attending the branch meetings every Monday evening (and even those of some of the other Merseyside branches – Birkenhead and Bootle).[67] Clearly, this was someone who had set his mind on a union career. In the early days of trade unionism, branch meetings were a vital centre of the unions' democracy, the ETU's more so than most unions, as the electricians were a bright and lively young group (average age about thirty).[68] The union branch was the place where news of the trade and job opportunities, progress (or lack of it) with wage claims and employers' responses could be learned. No ordinary activist, Citrine was soon writing very clear and informative monthly reports for the union's monthly *Electrical Trades Journal*. He scoured the second-hand bookshops of the city for books on the theory and practice of trade unionism and on socialism. He developed a fluent style of writing which distinguished his many writings from the average trade unionists' scribble throughout his life, in addition to his marvellous two-volume autobiography.[69] This indicated a clear and well-informed intellect.

His other love was music and he had begun his musical education from a young age as a member of the Oakdale Mission (brass) Band, playing both the tenor horn and cornet.[70] When he was later employed at New Brighton Tower he 'took lessons from one of the professional cornet players' and played in a variety of bands – the Seacombe Victoria, Birkenhead Borough, Moss Bank and the Nutgrove Band at St Helens.[71] Brass bands were then a huge attraction in working-class communities, especially in the north of England, with collieries, factories and offices competing fiercely for prizes before large audiences. His future boss at the TUC, Fred Bramley from Bradford, he regarded as a far better cornet player,[72] but, as we will see, Citrine also had a good tenor voice.

CHAPTER 2

~

THE MILITANT ELECTRICIAN

Walter Citrine recalled that 'at times I was just as militant in trade union aims as were any of our members'.[1] This was during a period of industrial unrest nationally which lasted until the First World War. Merseyside was a centre, having had a transport general strike in 1911 which closed the massive docks, rail and road transport of Liverpool with major disturbances.[2] In 1931, Citrine referred to his involvement in these events as 'in any strike I have had experience of, for example, Liverpool 1911', but gave no details.[3] *The Times* commented on the Liverpool strike, 'The present movement has much in common with the Syndicalist movement which paralysed France during its brief hour of success.'[4] This strike closed the huge docks area and paralysed the commerce of the city, leading to violent disturbances and deaths, in clashes with the police.[5] We know that the electricians at the largest Lister Drive power station walked out in sympathy, closing many of the electric-powered factories, but whether Citrine was involved we don't know.[6] He made no mention of this in his autobiography. The fact that he held onto his notebooks from that earlier period suggests that he did not wish to reveal the extent of his youthful militancy.[7]

In this heady atmosphere, active union militants were often moved by syndicalist philosophies of direct action and sympathetic action to achieve political ends. Citrine was undoubtedly of that disposition. Neil Riddell thought that Citrine accepted 'both the syndicalist belief in the need for industrial unionism – the amalgamation of sectional or craft societies into one single union for each industry – and the Marxist viewpoint that conflict between capital and labour was inevitable.'[8]

Citrine's syndicalist-sounding articles of 1912–13 seem significant in revealing the extent of his ideological influence.[9] He wrote, 'The workers are in much the same economic position as they were fifty years ago … education has caused them to discern the issues more clearly and has enabled them to utilise a medium which their longstanding grievances can secure a more or less adequate expression. The trade union is that medium and it has played a vital part in the conflicts between capital and labour.'[10] Entitled *Trade Unionism – its Rise, Development and Future*, Citrine argued that 'the industrial community had become segregated into two distinct classes' and that 'the interests of the employer and the worker are diametrically opposed'.[11] He concluded that in this conflict, 'present day [trade union] organisation is totally inadequate to effectively fight the organised force of capital'.[12] He advocated amalgamation of all unions into twelve to fifteen industrial groups, in line with classic syndicalism. He even had a jab at 'union officialdom', arguing that 'to guard against the possibility of officialdom dominating the activities of the group, it is suggested that no paid official shall be allowed to vote on any subject affecting its policy'.[13] The need for a 'general staff' to co-ordinate and direct all unions' efforts would be his constant theme from here on. In this 'bolshie' frame of mind, as chair of the local strike committee, Citrine led the Merseyside branches in the official national electricians' strike of June–July 1914.[14]

CITRINE'S DISTINCTIVE APPROACH

We cannot imagine Citrine as a vigorous agitator of the street-fighting type. He comes across more as the cerebral type, reading up on the issues and producing articles on current ones. His distinctive approach was applied science, always directed to find a solution to practical issues. He also studied wider trade union issues and the unions' lifeblood, *organisation*, attending a range of meetings and applying them to particular situations.[15] He devoured the Webbs' classic study *Industrial Democracy* from cover to cover, taking extensive notes so that it 'became my bible'. The eager student was particularly interested in their detailed dissection of how unions and their 'collective bargaining method' worked. [16] The other subject Citrine majored on was company finances, learning 'how to analyse a company balance sheet and about such things as reserve funds, bonus shared, and depreciation'.[17] These were the days before unions had research departments to assist negotiators and in arguments over whether a wage claim could be afforded, and so Citrine's skills would have been invaluable to his colleagues. Union finances were a subject all on their own, requiring some knowledge of actuarial practice in devising benefit payments.[18] This would become a specialism of his when he became a national officer, as we shall see. He also 'had a hankering after legal knowledge' and in those days unions needed practical guidance on the legal pitfalls to be avoided.[19] So if one can surmise that he was catapulted into the trade union movement on account of the militant culture of the Merseyside Labour movement in 1911 and syndicalist influences, now he was finding a constructive outlet for his energies in the ETU. But this young unionist was acquiring an all-round knowledge and ability to grasp complex issues, far beyond the ken of the average branch or district secretary.

Of course, 'trade unions couldn't just fix their rates of wages'.[20] They had to reach agreements with the employers. While workers of all kinds were then flocking into the unions, it was a real challenge to persuade employers to recognise unions as worth bargaining with, on their behalf.[21] Employers also combined to avoid cutting one another's throats by unrestricted competition. Such collective agreements as were reached between unions and employers 'were not in any sense legally binding on the parties'.[22] This actually suited both sides, giving a greater flexibility to alter things when, as was frequently the case in labour markets, the terms of trade changed.[23]

When Citrine joined the ETU in 1911, there was no collective bargaining for electrical workers in the Mersey area.[24] He was approached to join by his workmates, all strong trade unionists, which he did immediately. He thought that the union had fewer than 3,500 members in the whole country (less than 1,000 locally).[25] These were scattered around various enterprises and industries. The big shipbuilders Cammell Laird at Birkenhead (where Citrine worked for a while as an electrician) employed large numbers of electrical workers, skilled and semi-skilled. The ship-repairing sector also employed electrical engineers. As district secretary, he had a number of encounters with Cammell Laird's Chairman, Sir George Carter, who was also Chairman of the Port of Liverpool Employers' Association. Citrine described him as 'as rugged as they make them' but a 'straight-from-the shoulder type', with whom he got on.[26] In a related field, ship-repairing, the ocean-going shipping lines (Cunard and White Star) needed a growing number of electrical engineers as they switched from steam to electrical power. Electricity generation and distribution in power stations were municipally owned then. Domestic and commercial lighting also created a large number of small and large electrical contracting businesses. Yet 'there were no agreed wages or working rules in any of them' as the employers' associations in the Mersey-side Shipbuilding Employers' Federation were 'the hardest nut to crack'.[27] Each firm had to be applied to and so even where rates were agreed with the union, great variations developed. So, the union's aim was to harmonise these rates across the region and later nationally, through collective bargaining. This period saw 'the emergence of negotiating as the union's first line of approach'. [28]

His members on Merseyside were well organised. The three main branches – Liverpool, Birkenhead and Bootle – operated together through a District Committee. They sought to set codes of working rules, designed to keep hourly wages in each sector, approximately the same.[29] The old system of bargaining was for the general secretary to send the rules to all the employers on a card, with a view to negotiating an agreed rate. The small but key electrical members in each firm were then expected to press their employers 'to come in line'.[30]

Citrine was soon elected to the more important District Committee from his Liverpool branch, and was immediately in the thick of its activities. It decided 'to turn on the heat with the ship-owners and the repairing firms' with its first (unofficial) strike in December 1912.[31] This persuaded all the employers' associations to meet with the union in a joint conference and agree the union's codes of rules. [32] Cammell Laird now recognised the union and assented to the advances sought, as did the ship-repairers. Even the electrical contractors' association, the most poorly organised section (because

The ETU banner and membership card.

'there was much coming and going amongst electricians'), agreed to the new rates. The hours of work were very long, fifty-three per week in shipbuilding and ship-repairing and fifty in contracting. 'By July 1913 all three sets of rules were being operated.'[33] This significant victory for Merseyside branches took them to the top of the union's national scales. Citrine's part in this achievement was recognised as he was elected chair of the District Committee.

We catch an interesting glimpse of Citrine just before the outbreak of the First World War, from an item in the *Liverpool Echo* of July 1914. It reported a strike of Liverpool electricians in the contracting sector.

An 'Echo' reporter who called at 19 Frederick-street, the headquarters of the Strike Committee, found a large party of cheerful strikers gathered round a piano whilst a man with a really good tenor voice was warbling sentimental and ragtime melodies.[34]

This was Citrine, who told the *Echo* representative that 'the strikers were now taking on Contracts … and they would guarantee a saving of 25% on present prices'. He claimed that 'the funds coming in from the contracts undertaken by the strikers were ample to cover the expense, apart from the fact that the national organisation was at their back'.[35] Citrine's offer of electricians as direct labour to customers as a way to pressure the contractors into settling the dispute in their favour is interesting. It was a tactic which had been inspired at the time by 'guild socialists' who advocated workers' control of industry through the medium of trade-related guilds.[36] More immediately, this episode shows his early appreciation of the need for attention to media presentation and relations, describing the *Liverpool Echo* as 'my favourite evening newspaper'.[37]

So, here we have an imaginative use of radical ideas for the union's purposes, trying out tactics which he and his active colleagues had agreed. He was clearly quite a character then with his 'warbling tenor voice', keeping his members' spirits up during the strike in quite an imaginative manner. This is not at all the 'grey' image of Citrine that is usually portrayed. The dispute, which had started in April as part of a national ETU strike, was not just about pay. It was to resist the attempt by the contracting employers to require electricians to sign a 'Document' agreeing to work with non-unionists. It led to the locking out of thousands of electricians in London and Liverpool who would not sign. One hundred and forty-nine members were drawing unemployment benefit from the union on Merseyside.[38] At one point, the District Committee asked the executive council to take legal action against a local contractor 'for slandering the chairman of the district committee, Walter Citrine, by informing numerous parties that he is only a labourer'![39] This jibe suggests that he wasn't a time-served indentured electrician. He was clearly the contractors' *bête noir* then. By August, with the First World War looming, the contractors caved in and paid a ½d.-an-hour increase and abandoned their demand to sign the Document.[40] Union membership shot up from around 3,000 to over 8,000 by that time. At the ETU's annual conference, the union's leaders singled out the 'thoroughness shown in the management of the dispute' in Liverpool.[41]

MERSEY DISTRICT UNION OFFICIAL

In October 1914, Citrine was elected as the first full-time district secretary of the ETU nationally, over 'other candidates whose trade union experience exceeded my own'.[42] As the local members had to fund this post with a levy, he had to ensure that his efforts on their behalf met with their approval. His salary was just £2 10s. per week with a small travelling and expenses allowance. This salary was just a little over the district rate for electricians (and without their 'considerable overtime' earnings). A few months after, the ETU executive council gave the Merseyside branches a grant with which they took a small office in Don Chambers, Paradise Street, Liverpool. This was just over from the Albert Dock, which was part of Citrine's 'beat'.[43] He later installed a telephone and a second-hand typewriter on which he typed his own letters, with one finger of each hand. Still living in Egremont, this new role involved travelling the ferries and buses and walking all over the huge dock area to the dispersed workplaces wherever electricians were employed. With his weak ankles, this cannot have been easy. However, he was a workaholic. One of the members he met on the Wallasey ferryboat told him, 'you are going to kill yourself the way you are going on'.[44] It was hardly a well-paid or secure career path that this well-read and talented Merseyside electrical technician had now embarked upon, but his choice of it shows a bold and idealistic ambition.

LEARNING TO NEGOTIATE EFFECTIVELY

As a full-time official, Citrine quickly learned the art of negotiation with some of the toughest employers in different industries. Despite his theorising about 'the antagonistic interests of labour and capital', he found that by and large he got on well with the employers. He learned that negotiation was the essence of trade unionism.[45] This was a crucial thread in his development. In the *Electrical Trades Journal* he was very critical of the employer associations.[46] Years later, he admitted to having learned a good deal from the employers.[47] Above all, Citrine was clear 'that the process of collective bargaining between employers and trade unions must be based on good faith on both sides'.[48] If those legally unenforceable agreements were to be honoured and fairly interpreted, 'there must be reasonable confidence between all concerned'.[49] He was especially influenced by an encounter with Viscount Leverhulme, founder of the famous industrial village at Port Sunlight in the Wirral.[50] The electricians had been penalised for taking part in a strike in September 1918 by being excluded from the company's co-partnership arrangements for other staff. Having lost their first encounter, Citrine felt completely defeated and inexpert by comparison, even 'below his intellectual level'.[51] But having studied what went wrong, he came up with a different approach, which bested Leverhulme and got his members back in the co-partnership scheme. Citrine regarded it as a psychological victory for himself in 'a decisive phase in my life'.[52] Throughout his life, Citrine carried out such self-analyses after major encounters, saying, 'I invariably try to correct any defects which I can detect.'[53]

DURING THE FIRST WORLD WAR

As a full-time union official, Citrine was exempt from war service, as were most of his members. As the war wore on, with mounting losses, these exemptions were narrowed and electricians also began to be conscripted.[54] As an active ILP member, Citrine was opposed to the war.[55] The ETU conference denounced the war at its 1914 conference.[56] However, the union leadership instead subscribed to the joint union 'Treasury Agreement' in March 1915[57] in support of the British war effort. This Agreement and subsequent legislation suspended members' right to strike and introduced compulsory arbitration of wage claims for the duration of the war. The left in the union, especially the syndicalists in the London District Committee, attacked the executive council and senior officers vigorously for this.[58] Citrine may have had sympathy with that stance, though he did not articulate it in the union's journal. On more practical grounds, he was never happy with the compulsory arbitration system as he regarded the government-appointed Committee of Production as being 'miserable' with its awards. Once he warned that 'if they expect that trade union officials are likely to exercise a restraining influence … they are very mistaken … speaking personally, I have not the remotest intention of acting as an apologist for any Government tribunal'.[59] He described one 'miserable' award early in 1917 as 'still another nail in the coffin of compulsory arbitration'. This was not at all the official ETU line as General Secretary Jim Rowan was a clear supporter of it.[60] Nor did Citrine like the influx of dilutees to replace his members who were called up as the war went on. Dilutees were workers, including women, hired to perform the less-skilled aspects of engineering and electrical work during the war. On Merseyside, Citrine was keen to challenge the abuses of the dilution system such as taking girls to technical schools and then paying them fifteen shillings a week instead of the skilled rate of forty shillings. His monthly reports in the union journal are a rich source of detailed information about all these issues and Citrine comes across as anxious to defend the craft position against dilution of skills.[61] The compromise reached to enable the ETU to recruit the large number of dilutees entering the industry was the formation of an auxiliary section in 1914, with lower subscriptions but fewer rights and benefits.[62]

The operation of 'leaving certificates' also became a major source of contention. In April 1917, 'Walter Citrine reported with pride that the Leeds, Manchester, Mersey, and Sheffield districts had struck, presenting the spectacle of four of the largest districts in the Union acting jointly together.'[63] In August, Merseyside branches unanimously sought to cancel the 'Dilution Agreement', 'much to Walter Citrine's pleasure' as he said that 'as far as we in this post are concerned, no agreement, as to the acceptance of any form of diluted labour, exists'.[64] As Neil Riddell noted, 'In 1917 it [the ETU] was more involved in unofficial strikes than any other union apart from the engineers; something to which Citrine chose not to draw attention to in 1964.'[65]

Citrine was re-elected as district official in 1917 without a challenge.[66] He also became President of the Federation of Engineering and Shipbuilding Trades (FEST) for the Lancashire region that year. This was a joint union body to resolve inter-union demarcation disputes (largely unsuccessful) and to co-ordinate supportive action in disputes affecting common matters of principle (partially effective).

He became its secretary, as well as president, from 1918 until 1920. It was an important position for the ETU to hold, showing that it was now 'a recognizable part of the emerging collective bargaining system in Britain'.[67] It would have seen his emergence as one of the most prominent union leaders in the region.

Although Citrine had taken such an active role against conscription and dilution, and was no fan of compulsory arbitration, he was not aligned with the opposition forces against the leadership of the union. Lloyd's sub-heading 'Class War on the Executive Council 1915–16' gives a flavour of the London scene.[68] This was not Citrine's style, though he was clearly sometimes at variance with Rowan and Ball in the Manchester headquarters. Certainly, the pro-war leadership do not seem to have made any attempt to 'rein him in', as they would have known that his militant stances reflected widespread membership attitudes. He was generally quite positive about his relationship with Jim Rowan and Jack Ball.[69] Ball, the long-serving president, would later explain its attitude to this pushy but talented arrival. 'He did not always say and do things as we liked, but he was young in thought and deed ... a brilliant and clever exponent of the principles of trade unionism.'[70]

THE CHANGE TO NATIONAL WAGE BARGAINING

By the end of the war, with government backing, 'Whitley Councils'[71] spread rapidly, and to electrical cable-making, electrical contracting and electricity supply in 1919.[72] Despite some left opposition, Citrine supported participation, publishing a letter in the union journal.[73] This was to overcome the sheer lack of information about wages and conditions in myriad workplaces. So, he was one of the eight district officials who went to the inaugural meeting of the Electrical Contracting NJIC at Leeds in June 1919.[74] The NJIC reached agreement to reduce the working week in contracting from fifty-three to forty-seven hours, a major issue for the unions. Citrine's developing pragmatic approach would not have gone unnoticed by the union hierarchy, as a significant departure from his former strong left line.

THE SHOP STEWARDS' MOVEMENT

Citrine valued his shop stewards as a medium of communication with individual employers. One of the syndicalist/communist leaders of the Shop Stewards' movement, J. T. Murphy, recalled meeting Citrine 'at a shop stewards' conference during the First World War when he represented a branch of the Electrical Trades Union'.[75] In Liverpool, he devised a system of four permanent shop stewards, with employer-funded paid time off. He urged the union 'that shop stewards should be given full and cordial recognition by the unions … at the next rules revision conference'.[76]

CITRINE'S VENTURE INTO POLITICS

Citrine was persuaded by his Wallasey Labour Party branch to stand for Parliament in the safe Tory Cheshire seat of Wallasey, with the support of the ETU and FEST. He issued a most radical manifesto proclaiming, 'I stand for national ownership of the mines, railways, canals and all monopolies', for 'equal pay and equal rights for both sexes'.[77] Citrine came a respectable second.[78] However, he soon decided that 'from that time onwards I stuck to my trade union duties without any thought of entering Parliament'.[79] In this he was unusual, as in that union-dominated Labour Party many officials also became MPs. However, Citrine 'felt I could yield more political influence out of Parliament than in it'.[80]

THE LIVERPOOL POLICE STRIKE, 1919

By far the most serious strike that Citrine became 'immersed in' was the Liverpool police strike of August 1919.[81] After a solid strike of the 30,000-strong National Union of Police and Prison Officers (NUPPO) in 1918, the government brought in a bill to outlaw such strikes and to prevent police officers from joining a union. It also addressed many of the pay and conditions grievances which had given rise to the strike and so undermined the union's opposition to the loss of recognition as a union.[82] In Liverpool, where police pay and conditions were worst, there was a strong response to a new strike call by NUPPO in 1919. Over half the officers there at Birkenhead, Bootle and Wallasey stations refused to attend roll call from 1 August. However, this withdrawal of an effective police presence led to a major break-down in public order, and an orgy of looting and rioting ensued over a weekend.[83] There were a number of fatalities and more than 200 arrests.

Citrine was secretary of the police support committee as the FEST representative.[84] *The Times* says he summoned all other unions to a meeting to consider a general strike in support of the police.[85] He wrote to the home secretary promising the solidarity of his and other major unions for the police strikers. He said they took 'the strongest possible exception to the attitude of the Home Office and the Government in declining to recognize the Police Union'.[86] Instead, the home secretary denounced their call for a general strike as 'attempting ... to hand over the country to the mercy of the criminal classes'.[87] After the riots, many, including the powerful dockers' and rail workers' union leaders, were reluctant to contemplate a general strike. Citrine complained bitterly that 'trade unionists as a whole have badly let the police down'. The strike and NUPPO collapsed as the bill passed rapidly through Parliament and the authorities refused to re-admit a single policeman, all of whom also lost their pension rights. Citrine blamed 'the so-called trade union leaders', saying, 'I have seen in the last month enough of the defects of trade union machinery to make one despair.'[88] At the Glasgow Trades Union Congress soon after, he spoke for the first time as an ETU delegate criticising the Parliamentary Committee's handling of the strike. The big unions did not support that move, though Ernest Bevin complimented him on his speech.[89] Citrine showed amazing courage in siding with the Merseyside police so openly, being described as 'dangerous' by the police authorities.[90] There is no mention of this incident in his autobiography.

THE LEAVING OF LIVERPOOL

This deep involvement in such a controversial strike and the hostile response of the Liverpool authorities may have caused Citrine to think about 'moving on'. We don't know, as his papers are unusually silent about it. The Merseyside members were sorry to lose him, and he was given a tremendous send-off and the members presented him with a leather-bound set of his favourite Dickens novels and a cheque for £41 (about seven weeks' salary), which Merseyside members had collected in appreciation.[91] The District Committee also paid tribute, saying, 'without him during the past two or three years we would been somewhat left'.[92]

CHAPTER 3

~

A NATIONAL UNION FIGURE

The phenomenal membership growth which the Electrical Trades Union was enjoying showed no signs of waning by the summer of 1920, so the ETU executive council decided to appoint a second assistant general secretary, an elected national position.[1] Now well known around the union, Citrine topped the poll and easily defeated other experienced candidates from London and Glasgow.[2] However, soon after he was elected, a period of deep trade depression set in. He noted, 'Our membership, which at the end of 1920 had risen to over 57,000, fell to 31,000 by January 1923 and was to fall lower. Our finances were drained.'[3]

Manchester, the capital of the north, with its vibrant cotton manufacturing and machine-making/engineering industries, was just thirty-five miles north-east of Liverpool. The trade union and co-operative movements were strong and a number of key unions like the ETU were headquartered there.[4] Citrine did not move his family (which, as well as Norman, aged six, now included Ronnie, under two) for almost a year. He first commuted by bus, ferry and express train to the union offices at Withy Grove, near Victoria Station, Manchester, from the Wirral – an hour and a half each way. Some evenings, where meetings took place after office hours, he didn't get home until midnight. So, from August 1921 they rented a large flat in a former stately home, Crumpsall House, Crumpsall, off the Rochdale Road, for a couple of years.[5] Twenty minutes from the office, in such salubrious surroundings, he said, 'I felt I was becoming a member of the leisured class'.[6]

As a tiny union of fewer than 2,000 members in 1907, the ETU had moved from London to the centre of Manchester.[7] The governance of the union nationally had been left to local branch representatives (London), since its founding in 1889. Now it would become more representative of the union as a whole and be governed through an elected executive council of nine, from all over the country. This move from London owed much to the uneasy relations between activists there and the large Manchester branches. This division reflected basic differences over the purpose of the union: 'Was it to recruit qualified (i.e., time-served) electricians only and defend their exclusive craft interests, on the Engineers (ASE) model, or was it to represent all workers in the electrical industries, semi-skilled grades as well?'[8]

As the second assistant general secretary, Citrine had been recruited to put the administrative system in order, and he soon set about this unglamorous but vital role. Sorting out the poor state of correspondence between head office and branches was a first key task. In 1920, the ETU head office sent out about 26,000 letters to branches, with 176 letters arriving each day. The sheer amount of work involved for branches can also be seen from the paperwork they had to deal with – handwritten branch cash books, contribution books, benefit payment books, letter books, minute books, rule books, transfer forms, political levy exemption forms and so on (more than a dozen in all).[9] Their office needed a filing capacity for at least 50,000 letters a year at head office.[10] Citrine did this so well that one London branch secretary jokingly said, 'his members didn't like Brother Citrine meeting the postman at the top of the stairs and handing him the reply!'[11] In those days of letters and telegrams (even telephone availability was patchy), unlettered union officials were notorious for their poor paperwork and dilatory responses. A good secretary and shorthand typist was a lifesaver at head office. When Citrine asked where the filing system was, he was jauntily informed by the general secretary that 'the filing system is just putting her hat and coat on', as the secretary was about to leave for the evening.[12] Modestly, Citrine doesn't explain the scale of the administrative nightmare that greeted him in August 1920. He had to deal with a rising tide of chaos induced by the slump in employment of electricians, the collapse of the union in Ireland, a defeat at Penistone, Sheffield, and the steady decline in effective representation in the cinemas, mines and for sea-going electrical engineers. The ruling sub-executive council dealt with 700 separate issues between January and March 1921. So, Citrine's willingness and ability to drastically overhaul its systems made him a godsend.[13] He even asked branch officers to send all unimportant correspondence without sealing the envelopes, and so save the union a penny-halfpenny on each one![14]

BRANCH EXPENDITURE PRACTICES: FINANCIAL DRAIN

Citrine didn't mind being immersed in this administrative work, thinking 'someone had to stay in the office, and I was possibly the person best fitted for it by temperament'.[15] He soon instituted a new system of filing. The rather casual expenditure practices

of the boom years were now a source of serious concern for the
union. It occasionally had to take some branch officers to court
for stealing funds entrusted to them for members. A Sheffield
Magistrates' court case showed a branch officer had kept £20 for
himself out of the £70 he was sent as payments for locked-out
members during a dispute. The same branch officer appropriated
another £23 by 'fiddling' the branch and member entries in the
books. He got six months in jail.[16] So, economies were the order
of the day for survival and Citrine was the one in the front line
making them for the executive. 'Benefits had to be cut, and various
levies were decided upon by ballot vote to keep the union going.'[17]
The density of membership in a firm was then an 'important
determinant of its bargaining power'.[18] A loss of bargaining
power meant fewer would join. It was a vicious circle. Citrine
had a vested interest in steadying the ship, as his job depended
on it. With a young family, now uprooted from their home city,
he must have felt deeply anxious. Characteristically, he set about
devising a practical solution. After studying the methods of other
unions and business administration generally (his night-school
bookkeeping studies proving useful), he came up with a simple
but radical proposal, namely to centralise finances at headquarters. He thought that, 'Instead of allowing our branch officers to
hold sums running into a few hundred pounds, why not require
them to send these to head office? ... If they required money
to meet current branch expenses, they must apply for it to head
office.'[19] However, Citrine didn't just rely on bureaucratic power
to impose these hugely controversial changes. He was at pains
to justify them – serious deficiencies occurring under the existing branch-based system, at a time of major loss of revenue. He
made frequent visits to branches to discuss the changes, as well as

Citrine's ETU journal column, 'Talks with Our Officers', 1920–21.

providing detailed written guidance to branch officers in circulars and in the monthly journal on how the new system would work.[20] To this end, he started a monthly journal column, 'Talks with Our Officers', in January 1922.

Nonetheless, for the first time Citrine now became unpopular with branch officials, not least his old Merseyside ones. There was a long tradition of branch autonomy in all unions, especially with regard to their funds, which they guarded jealously.[21] Citrine was met with 'a wall of opposition' and 'howls of resentment', as branches objected to the very idea, despite evident 'leakage' from many branches.[22] Branch critics even asked if his services were not 'something of a luxury' and some called for his resignation. However, as an elected officer he had 'a certain measure of independence'.[23] Citrine stood his ground and the executive council kept its nerve and backed him. A national ballot of ordinary members narrowly approved the changes in the summer of 1922.[24] By 1923, when he was up for re-election, things had settled down so much that he was returned unopposed.[25] The changes were gradually introduced from there on and years afterwards they were seen as 'Walter Citrine's finest achievement' for the union.[26] The president at that time, Jack Ball, later publicly acknowledged that 'the system of centralised finance which Citrine introduced saved the union'.[27]

ABC OF CHAIRMANSHIP

Another of Citrine's seemingly mundane technical productions was a set of guidance notes on the effective conduct of branch and other meetings. Union meetings were very well attended in those days and were central to union communications and accountability to their members, as voluntary associations. The 'meat' of such gatherings involved discussions on reports about contribution levels and benefits from headquarters, reports on ongoing disputes with employers locally and nationally, job availability, wages and conditions in the area/region and for general social life (they usually met in pubs, but strictly controlled the intake of alcohol). John Lloyd captured the rich flavour of workers conferring and arguing – the themes which divided as well as united them, such as 'who was a typical ETU member and whom the union should admit to its ranks'.[28]

However, these meetings were often acrimonious and undisciplined and so, in 1917, Citrine addressed the problem by producing guidance notes on the conduct of meetings. These were so well received that the leadership incorporated them into the ETU rulebook. An expanded version known as *The Labour Chairman* was published in 1921 for the Labour and Cooperative movements and, in 1939, was expanded to become *ABC of Chairmanship*. The *ABC*, or 'Citrine' as it was known, came to be seen as the authority for all unions on meeting procedures, on a par with Erskine May for Parliament.[29] *The Labour Chairman* booklet was also full of useful advice. Its fourteen short chapters each contained a summary and clearly laid-out paragraphs on motions, amendments, points of order, closure and methods of voting, with all the technicalities of debate clearly expressed. It had a table giving 'branch procedure' at a glance 'for the harassed chairman' and even a glossary

The Labour Chairman, 1920.

of common Latin phrases commonly (mis)used, such as *bona fide*, *ex officio*, *facsimile* and so on. It also had an elaborate diagram of what can happen to any motion or amendment and a fourteen-page alphabetical index 'with the gist of the point', for quick reference. Jim Rowan, the general secretary, promoted this book enthusiastically in the *Electrical Trades Journal* in May 1921.[30]

This booklet had a foreword by one of the leading union leaders of the time, J. R. Thomas of the National Union of Railwaymen (NUR). It also carried the recommendation of many of

ABC of Chairmanship, 1939.

the rising figures of the Labour movement at the time, such as Ramsay MacDonald, Margaret Bondfield and J. R. Clynes. The author was clearly making himself known on the wider national scene. Many famous union officials, such as former home secretary Alan Johnson, once general secretary of the postal and telecom workers union (CWU), have since recalled that they had relied on Citrine as their 'handbook' to advance their careers.[31] It became the standard text on TUC and union education courses for generations of union officers and activists. The *ABC* is still in print and Citrine is probably better known for this little book than for all the other things he did for the trade unions.

SENIOR UNION RESPONSIBILITIES

As his reputation grew, Citrine was given broader duties negotiating with employers. When 5,000 ETU members were caught up in a bitter engineering industry confrontation concerning overtime working, and locked out with a quarter of a million AEU members,[32] the normally moderate ETU General Secretary James Rowan called on the TUC to 'consider a general down tool policy on a national basis'.[33] Citrine replied to criticism of that decision by a member in the union journal. He defended the general secretary 'for suggesting that a general strike is the most effective method to stop the attack on wages'.[34] He also went to Carlisle for a key meeting with the related Shipbuilding Employers' Federation[35] and to Birmingham for amalgamation negotiations with the 30,000-strong Enginemen, Firemen and Electrical Workers in autumn 1923.[36] In the absence of the 'indisposed' general secretary, Citrine regularly substituted at the weekly meetings of the key sub-executive committee, throughout the period March 1922 to July 1923.[37] It seems that he was coming to be regarded as the deputy general secretary of the union.

Citrine was now also on many union delegations to TUC and Labour Party conferences (they were joint affairs then). His reports in the union's journal showed a keen grasp of the broader political issues as he developed a wider perspective on Labour movement matters.[38] His reports from these conferences are frequently critical of those in charge, but more on account of their 'un-business-like nature', their empty rhetoric and lack of follow-up than their policies. He reported from the February 1921 Labour Party/TUC conference that he thought a conference decision not to strike was

nothing short of a confession of the utter futility of the stage
army of Labour. I realised, however, that the alternative of
Direct Action would be hopeless without the machinery to
carry it out. At present, the movement is simply deceiving
itself with its power. As a movement it has no machinery
which enables it to function efficiently. Instead of passing
pious resolutions at futile and wasteful conferences, we would
be better occupied by concentrating on the long awaited
'General Staff'. It is 'organised power' which 'counts' in the
long run, not eloquent speeches.[39]

Strong stuff! As far back as 1918 he had revealed an attitude to
politics as a secondary force, saying that it was 'fortunate that we
have the industrial weapon and are not solely dependent on the
political arm'.[40] His decision not to stand again for Parliament after
his 1918 outing at Wallasey may also have reflected that attitude.
This was very like a syndicalist viewpoint, which he retained as late
as 1921. His ideas for revamping the TUC as the central executive body which could act decisively on behalf of trade unionism
and the Labour movement should be seen in this light. He said, 'I
gave long consideration to this aspect of things and drew up what
appeared to me to be a thoroughly practical scheme for endow-
ing the T.U.C with greater powers. I thought it must evolve into
a general staff for labour and by labour I mean the trade unions.'
[41] Citrine sent his proposal to the *Daily Herald* and heard no more,
only to be 'staggered' months later 'to see proposals not very different from my own featured in the *Herald*, over the name of Ernest
Bevin'.[42] He said that he didn't mean to imply by this that Bevin had
appropriated his idea, but, by mentioning the incident, he leaves it
to the reader to draw his own conclusions.

Citrine with the ETU leadership before he left for the TUC, 1923.

THE SHORTHAND NOTE-TAKER

'Gregg shorthand has been my daily companion throughout fifty years'.[43] Readers may wonder why Citrine took the trouble to learn this skill (in those days one that shorthand typists and some male clerks were expected to have), but for Citrine it was entirely a 'career move'. His rationale for taking all this trouble is interesting. It was to encourage his colleagues at the ETU 'to make me a member of various delegations to meet employers and others', which they did regularly. 'I found myself installed as a reporter to almost every delegation that I was appointed. This gave me the sort of scope and experience I desired.'[44] Here is another illustration of the Citrines' domestic bliss – 'I learned the outlines and phrases easily, my wife dictating them to me

in the evenings, holding our little son (Norman) on her knee'!
[45] Citrine's facility for taking quick and accurate notes of decisions and key points from meetings gave him an edge over his
colleagues throughout his life.

LONDON DISTRICT vs
THE EXECUTIVE COUNCIL

London was the largest ETU region, with over 20,000 members
by 1914, and one of its biggest strikes occurred there that year
in the construction and electrical contracting industry over the
employment of non-union members. It would spread beyond the
capital and in Liverpool, Citrine (as district secretary) and his
branches became deeply involved, as we saw in the previous chapter.[46] The London branch activists and the District Committee
(LDC) they controlled were regularly in conflict with the official leadership at headquarters, who they called 'the Manchester
oligarchy'.[47] Many were dominated by very politically minded
activists, susceptible to the strong current of syndicalist ideas
and industrial militancy in the capital at the time.[48] Syndicalists
from outside the union viewed the new 'power of the electron'[49]
as having enormous potential for revolutionary purposes. H. A.
Clegg considered that 'during the war they began to invent for
themselves the idea of an "electrical industry" to fit their organisation into the theory of industrial unionism.'[50] C. H. Stavenhagen,
a leading exponent of these theories, was a London West branch
ETU member, president of the LDC and an influential executive
council member for a time.[51] As president of the LDC in January
1918, he published a fiery propagandist pamphlet, *Labour's Final
Weapon – Industrial Unionism*.[52]

A classic example of their activities occurred in late November 1918, when the London district secretary Bill Webb (another syndicalist/communist, but highly popular) and a group of members removed the fuses from the Albert Hall because of the cancellation of a post-war rally.[53] Webb 'told the management of the Kensington area's company that in the event of anyone replacing them, the whole of that area of west London would be blacked out.'[54] The Albert Hall gave in and the rally went ahead with every speaker praising the ETU for effectively using industrial power for political ends. This gesture was enough to cause 'hysteria' and such alarm at the Home Office that it summoned the entire ETU executive council to its offices and warned them that such political action about non-trade dispute issues was illegal and that the union could face massive fines or even imprisonment if it didn't 'impose some discipline on local activists'. The Cabinet papers show that leading London ETU militants were being watched.[55] In February 1919, the LDC (by a 5:4 majority, led by Stavenhagen) sought to bring out the entire London ETU membership in support of a forty-hours-a-week demand, without balloting the members, as the rules required. Harold Morton, representing the power station workers in London, objected strongly, saying that the 'decision to strike for forty hours was taken before the ink was dry on the forty-seven hours agreement for station men [down from fifty-three hours]'.[56] The newspapers were full of the union's threats to plunge London into darkness – but the station men knew nothing about it and complained that it 'caused our union to be known as a Bolshevik organization'.[57] Eventually, the executive was forced to ballot members and this resulted in a narrow vote against the strike. This led to the resignation of those executive members who had made the decision, though only

Stavenhagen stuck to his principles and left.[58] Stavenhagen was an extraordinary character who had been a sizable thorn in the side of the union leadership since he was elected to the national executive council just after 1910. He became an electrical contractor and lived to be ninety-two, dying in 1980.[59] Interestingly, 'he was admired by Citrine' for his technical writings and, as deputy editor, Citrine 'successfully campaigned for him to write articles for the union journal long after his flamboyant politics had exasperated the "Manchester oligarchy"'.[60]

The extreme loss of membership and revenue caused by the 1920–22 depression 'virtually bankrupted the union'.[61] Beatrice Webb noted, on 27 June, 'with the funds of every Trade Union fast disappearing, some of the wealthiest Unions – e.g. the Steel Smelters – being bankrupt … whilst other Unions are … denuded of money…'[62] This brought matters to a head between London and Manchester and Citrine would be at the centre of the clash.[63] In April 1921, the executive council's special auditor, Archie Stewart, looked at one London example of high expenditure on a strike at the Enfield Cable Company at Ponders End. He found one of the LDC's four organisers paying out benefits to non-existent members – after receiving strike benefit, they joined the Workers Union! So, under the guise of furthering the 'class struggle', Stewart found that the organiser had spent much of it in a pub![64] Citrine, the national officer with special financial expertise, was sent in support of the special auditor, investigating other abuses. They were met by 'obstruction and abuse' and 'a refusal to hand over the books' for examination as they were required by rule.[65] Citrine had to get a court order and eventually the LDC officers handed them over. In July, they reported to the executive council, having found that £1,300 (today's equivalent of about £58,000) had been paid out 'casually' during strikes and in support of solidarity with other groups.

Late in 1922, Stewart and Citrine were back in London to investigate 'the dubious finances of the London district committee's radical magazine *Electron*'.[66] For Citrine the key question was 'where got their money from to print it'.[67] It turned out that it all came from misappropriated union funds under the control of the LDC officers (£1,079; c. £48,000 today, when the union's funds were only £6,000 in total).[68] An inquiry committee was then set up by the executive council, which reported scathingly in February 1923, with nineteen recommendations.[69] However, not much followed by way of action against those responsible, apart from their being censured and a report sent to their branches. The LDC continued on its way as before, though the departure of Stavenhagen probably weakened its influence considerably. Although Citrine was only interested in its financial corruption (not the political ramifications such as its membership of the Red International and sending delegates to its conferences[70]), he would now be seen by some as part of the 'Manchester oligarchy'. There were demands in July 1922 for the second AGS post (his) to be abolished.[71] It was hardly a secure post in that fractious outfit. Citrine makes no reference at all to this first venture into London or very much about his period in Manchester generally in his memoirs. If they should ever turn up, his missing notebooks would make interesting reading.

LONDON BECKONS ONCE MORE

So Citrine had made quite an impression on this small but important union. It was even thought that his general secretary, Jim

Rowan, must have 'been looking over his shoulder' at his assistant as a potential replacement.[72] Citrine seems to have had no such aspirations, though he had clearly justified his own retention as 'second Assistant General Secretary' more than twice over. But now with a young family to consider, this uncertainty must have raised questions in his mind about what to do next.

It was hardly surprising, therefore, that when the Trades Union Congress advertised for an assistant general secretary in early November 1923, he was very interested. He was also 'strongly advised by my colleagues to apply'.[73] Though it meant moving to London, it clearly fitted in with his long-term aims. Curiously, as if a believer in blind fate, he thought a palmist had predicted that he would achieve a good outcome in the future.[74] From a field of more than 200 applicants, 'I was selected for interview, together with four others' and then appointed by the full General Council after a short ten-minute discussion, based on his CV. There were few questions – 'Was my health generally good?' and 'Did I write shorthand?'. After such a short interview, before he came in Citrine thought they had made up their minds against him. They *had* made up their minds, but in his favour; as John Hill of the Boilermakers told him later that evening, he had been 'elected' by an overwhelming majority of the General Council.[75] Clearly, his reputation had gone before him as the job – reforming and modernising the TUC's administration – was what he had done so effectively at the ETU. His future boss, Fred Bramley, the general secretary and a fellow northerner, was clearly impressed. This was just the man to sort out his chaotic administration at Eccleston Square in Victoria.

Citrine's two very different experiences, first as a militant district official on Merseyside and then as a national administrative officer in Manchester, with considerable organising/negotiating exposure, fitted him admirably for the wider national role he was about to assume. At thirty-six, Walter Citrine was ready for the much greater challenges that lay ahead.

CHAPTER 4

～

THE TUC AND THE FIRST LABOUR GOVERNMENT

Trade union membership had grown immensely during the First World War, from over 4 million in 1914 to over 8 million in 1920.[1] The larger union leaderships increasingly thought that what was needed for the now-more-common large-scale disputes was a centrally co-ordinated body, directed by a 'general staff', rather than the weak Parliamentary Committee of the Trades Union Congress.[2] The national railway strike of 1919 crystallised that thinking and discussions commenced among key leaders about creating a new body to replace the TUC Parliamentary Committee with a more industrially focused General Council.[3] Aspirants would be elected to seventeen electoral trade groups annually by the entire Congress and from a women's group.[4] This resulted in the TUC General Council of thirty-two from all the main unions, with two reserved places for women. A sub-committee system was devised to service the trade groups and sub-committees. Soon after, the number of specialist staff, including a number of graduates, was significantly increased. However, as they had to serve both the Labour Party and TUC's research, publicity and international department needs, the arrangement proved unsatisfactory for the TUC.

Perhaps the most effective change occurred in 1923, when the General Council decided to make the position of its executive officer, the general secretary, full-time. There was a specific stipulation that the person must not seek or hold political office, as had been the practice of previous holders. The post had traditionally been held by a part-timer, usually a Member of Parliament, who worked with the Parliamentary Committee in the Houses of Parliament.[5] Now Fred Bramley, who was elected at Congress in 1923 from six candidates, set about putting the General Council 'on the map', especially industrially. At the same time, it created the position of assistant general secretary, who would handle the TUC's growing administration (not Bramley's forte). It was that position that Walter Citrine was recruited to fill from January 1924, as Bramley also spent a considerable time away on international union affairs. This had become a quite important function of the TUC, since the International Labour Organisation was set up in 1919 to improve and spread good standards of labour welfare worldwide through its semi-legislative Conventions, such as on maximum hours of work.[6] If ratified by the national parliaments, these standards came into national law. Though governments and employers resisted the more radical union proposals, a number of important Conventions were ratified.[7]

So, the TUC was acquiring the staff and officers to pursue the interests of the 200 or so unions affiliated to it. An even more ambitious industrial role was being discussed by the large unions outside the TUC. This followed the failure of the Triple Alliance (miners, road and rail unions) to gel in 1921. It had spurred efforts to find a more effective 'Industrial Alliance'.[8] However, this attempt also failed because of the reluctance of many unions to give the constitutional commitment required to direct such a body in the case of a big strike.[9] However, resolutions carried at the Hull Congress of 1924 to strengthen the powers of the TUC General Council to enable it to 'co-ordinate' unions' industrial actions focused attention on this vehicle instead. The big union of the time, the million-strong Miners' Federation of Great Britain (MFGB), now turned to the TUC for assistance as its bitter post-war coal dispute reignited.[10]

It was against this background that Walter Citrine arrived at the TUC headquarters in Eccleston Square, Victoria, in January 1924, to take up the post of assistant general secretary. His role was to be a mainly administrative one, literally to assist the general secretary. But as Fred Bramley (1874–1925), as well as being regularly away on international union business, suffered from ill health, Citrine

Citrine at his office, 1927.

was soon involved in wider matters, at which he proved more than capable. As Beatrice Webb noted, 'Citrine, the assistant secretary, who owing to Bramley's bad health, counts considerably'. She added her perception that Citrine 'is communistic in sympathy'.[11] This was not the case, but, as we have seen, he was one of the keenest exponents of the view that the TUC should become the centre of the trade union movement as a 'general staff' of labour – note the military connotation. So his membership of the TUC's Special Industrial Committee, responsible for the mining dispute as acting general secretary from August 1925, strengthened the TUC's willingness (and ability) to take on this role.[12]

THE FIRST LABOUR GOVERNMENT

When Citrine arrived in London, the Labour Party had just taken office for the first time, led by the charismatic but remote Ramsay MacDonald. He was mainly concerned with post-war foreign affairs and negotiating with the other parties to stay in office. [13] Once the 'darling of the left' and the leading ILP figure of socialist ideas, he had played a central role in the creation and advance of the Labour Party since 1900. He had been a serious socialist theoretician, with an international perspective before the Great War.[14] In 1914, he became the leading anti-war Labour parliamentarian, resigning as Labour leader rather than support the war, to the delight of the ILP and pacifists. He resumed his leadership of the Labour Party when Arthur Henderson[15] deferred to him. By 1922, Labour had become the main opposition party in the British Parliament. The Liberals had been hopelessly split by the war and Lloyd George's assumption of the position of prime minister in a coalition with the Conservatives. Henderson became secretary of the Labour Party organisation and devoted himself to building the party as a grass-roots body in the constituencies. By 1924, MacDonald, now a very cautious reformist, was mainly intent on establishing the Parliamentary Labour Party as the main Opposition party and even the party of government. He saw militant unions, with their strikes and anti-capitalist rhetoric, as an obstacle to that aim. Labour 'won' the 1923 general election, though it had only 191 MPs out of 607. It had again ousted the Liberals (who had slumped to 158 MPs) from second position. Espousing free-trade policies, for a brief time Labour commanded the support of a majority of MPs from all parties in the House of Commons. The Conservatives, though still the largest party (258 seats), were divided on protectionism versus free trade and so their leader, Stanley Baldwin,[16] decided to allow Labour to take office as a minority government in January 1924.

Most Labour MPs then had union backgrounds, and MacDonald appointed a number of senior TUC General Council members to the government.[17] Some would hold senior Cabinet office, among them James H. Thomas,[18] general secretary of the NUR, as secretary of state for the Colonies, and Harry Gosling,[19] president of the T&GWU as minister of transport. Margaret Bondfield[20] stood down as chair of the General Council and the NUGMW's chief women's officer to become under secretary of Labour; Frank Hodges,[21] secretary of the Miners' Federation, 1918–24, became Civil Lord of the Admiralty. Another minister (of Labour) in MacDonald's government with a solid trade union background was Tom Shaw,[22] the secretary of the Colne weavers and other Lancashire textile workers' unions.

All these senior and representative union figures brought considerable experience to the Labour government. However, they were isolated politically from their left-minded replacements at the TUC leadership. In some cases, as with 'Jimmy' Thomas and Margaret Bondfield (who were close to MacDonald politically), they were hostile to the new TUC team. These 'TUC Lefts' (as they were called) were led by A. A. (Alf) Purcell MP,[23] who became chair of the General Council in January 1924, and close associate of the general secretary, Fred Bramley. [24] Purcell was a very forceful, 'deeply syndicalistic and communistic in a loose sense ...'[25] Both Purcell and Bramley held commanding positions, despite being from a tiny, very left-wing furnishing trades craft union (NAFTA). This was an indication of the left-wing orientation of most large union leaderships, who elected them annually at the TUC Congress. It was also a reflection of Bramley and Purcell's ability to manipulate the General Council trade group electoral system. This is likely to have been with the help of another of the 'TUC Lefts', George Hicks[26] of the construction trades union AUBTW, Purcell's 'closest political ally'.[27] Hicks was Purcell's political soulmate from their days in the Industrial Syndicalist Education League (ISEL).[28]

In his first two years at the TUC, Citrine says, 'I came a good deal in contact with George Hicks, who was a member of the General Council and a close friend of Alf Purcell.' [29] Whenever Bramley was away, more frequently now as a result of his trips to Amsterdam on the IFTU executive and worsening illness, Citrine says, 'I consulted Purcell on all important matters of policy.'[30] He saw Purcell as a dominant personality, 'a strong, forceful character, forthright in his opinions and incapable of finesse'. He became friends with both Hicks and Purcell when he first resided in Clapham, south London (Hicks' union location).[31] Purcell also became president of the International Federation of Trade Unions (IFTU) in 1924. The TUC had held this token presidency in deference to having the IFTU's largest membership, with J. H. Thomas as president, from 1919 to 1924. However, it was run by the continental union leaders at their Amsterdam headquarters. Bramley and Purcell would change that as regards relations with the unions of the Soviet Union. With Citrine's enthusiastic assistance, they would involve the TUC in very contentious exchanges with the German, French, Dutch and Belgian executive union leaders, over an All-Russian Central Council of Trade Unions proposal to merge with the IFTU for the cause of 'international workers unity'. Since 1919, the Amsterdam unions had been attacked scurrilously (called 'the Yellow International') by a Moscow-created rival Red (Communist) International of Labour Unions (RILU). So they were entirely opposed to any relationship, particularly a merger, with the Comintern-led body, as the new TUC leadership was advocating.[32] Although now a Labour MP and less fierce than his rhetoric suggested, Purcell's (and Bramley's) support for the Soviet Union and 'international workers unity' was total. He had been chair of the Hands Off Russia campaign against British intervention in the Russian civil war in 1919–20, visited Russia in 1920 and led a TUC/Labour Party delegation to the Soviet Union in November 1924. The Soviets' regard for his efforts was shown when they made him an honorary member of the Moscow Soviet in 1924.[33]

These 'TUC Lefts' were joined by others of a similar disposition – Alonso Swales[34] from the engineering union (AEU) became General Council vice-chair and George Hicks took over from Thomas as chair of the important International Committee. Equally significantly, Hodges' departure from the secretaryship of the powerful Miners' Federation created a vacancy which the hard left (Communist Party and Minority Movement – see Chapter 6) filled with the election of a firebrand, Arthur Cook.[35] It was this team which Citrine joined and, within a year, he would become their very effective executive officer.[36]

The TUC had not expected a Labour government. Its personal relationships with Labour leaders were poor. Bramley and Purcell were diverging from the traditional role of the TUC, which deferred to the Labour leadership on political matters.[37] MacDonald and his team were then trying to establish Labour's credentials as a government and parliamentarian party and so were adopting a very moderate social democratic stance. By contrast, the Bramley–Purcell leadership team now demanded far more substantial reforms of capitalism, and an international focus which would assist the young Soviet Union with recognition and generous trade terms. From a weak minority government position, dependent on the Opposition for his survival, MacDonald had little to offer this left-led TUC by way of social or industrial reform. Many leading union and Labour people had questioned whether they should enter such a minority government at all, but MacDonald, Henderson, Clynes,[38] Webb[39] and the other Labour members of his inner circle were set on doing so.[40] Despite the sprinkling of MPs with a union background in his government – he couldn't avoid it as most MPs then came from that background – MacDonald had a deeply dismissive attitude towards the new TUC leadership. In fact, like many Labour leaders since, he seems to have had a strong aversion to unions in their collective identity. This is suggested vividly in a letter he sent to Sidney Webb offering him the Ministry of Labour. He suggested that Webb should 'see Sir Allan Smith and get a programme from him, you can say that the interview has my approval.'[41] Smith[42] was the most anti-union employer representative then. Under his direction, the Engineering Employers' Federation had just (in 1922) locked out a quarter of a million engineers in a bitter three-month dispute and

hammered the unions. To propose him as the key adviser to the new
Labour government was not an auspicious start. As an ETU national
officer in Manchester, Citrine had represented 5,000 of their electrical engineers also locked out in that dispute. Like many other union
officials, he despised Smith, whom he called 'a cold-blooded fish'.[43]
Had they known MacDonald's attitude, it is not at all certain that
they would have agreed to him becoming prime minister!

So, despite the auspicious advent of the first Labour government, the TUC leadership had little incentive to 'rein in' their
affiliated unions pursuing 'the economic war' in wages demands, as
the economy revived. Foremost in this respect was Ernest Bevin,[44]
who in 1922 had formed a strong, militant mega-union, the Transport and General Workers' Union (T&GWU). Soon after the
Labour government took office in January 1924, Bevin, one of the
most aggressive trade-union leaders in the country, called a strike
of his 100,000 docker members, which closed all the country's
ports. A month later, in March, he called another, of his London
tram and bus members, which paralysed the capital's transport
system.[45] In his early forties, Bevin, who had come late to trade
unionism on the Bristol docks, had risen rapidly to become a major
transport union leader. He was a 'union boss' in the 'Gompers'
tradition. Gompers had been one of his heroes since his visit to the
US in 1916.[46] Though Bevin was 'ostensibly an adherent' of the
syndicalist philosophy which Gompers abominated, 'they got on
extremely well'. Bevin admired Gompers' control of his Convention and union. 'He had many of the qualities Bevin admired', 'a
shrewd, dogmatic leader, wily in bargaining and genial in his dictatorial handling of the affairs of his Union.'[47]

Although involved in creating the General Council, Bevin
initially had little interest in the TUC. He was instead attempt-

ing to form a looser Industrial Alliance, which would be more effective than the previous Triple Alliance which had collapsed on Black Friday in April 1921.[48] Faced by such a tough strike leader, MacDonald threatened to invoke the Emergency Powers Act of 1920, which would have brought out the troops to do their jobs. When MacDonald appealed to him to call off the London strike which was forcing Londoners to walk to work, Bevin threatened to close the underground as well! However, the dock's dispute was settled quickly in the dockworkers' favour and eventually also the London tram and bus strike, with a pay increase, without the need for the government to act. [49] The very threat from a Labour government to invoke such emergency powers caused shock and dismay in the Labour movement. Harry Gosling, as transport minister, had had to step down from the T&GWU presidency and there was some suspicion that Bevin wanted to take it on as well as the general secretaryship. However, Gosling was popular in the union, with a reputation going back to the dockers' strike of 1889. This ensured that he resumed the union presidency after the government fell.[50] The TUC leadership and the Labour Party's National Executive Council issued a joint resolution deploring the government's intention to invoke the Act.[51]

However, it was the fallout between MacDonald and Bevin which had the more lasting effect. Emmanuel ('Manny') Shinwell MP, then Secretary of Mines,[52] claimed that MacDonald and Bevin's actions during this dispute 'created a mutual pathological hatred' and 'the uncompromising hostility of the two most powerful men … sowed the seeds of future disaster, culminating in the General Strike and, indirectly, in the 1931 debacle'.[53] This comment was perhaps overblown, but Bevin never forgot MacDonald's threat and the feeling was mutual (MacDonald called him 'a swine'). Bevin even tried to get the 1925 Labour conference in Liverpool to prevent the party leader from ever entering a minority government again, in order to force his resignation. [54] However, there was little support for this move from the other unions. According to Lord Bullock, Bevin was unwilling to face the fact that 'once it came to power, (the Labour government) 'was bound to assume national responsibilities which might conflict with the immediate sectional interests of the trade unions. Bevin was unwilling to face this issue in 1924.'[55] Bullock traces his evolution from those early-1920s battles when 'the aggressive and assertive side of his character' was to the fore before his 'maturing of powers, a deepening of character and experience' in the 1930s.[56] Lord Adonis' recent work sides with his hero against the afterwards-discredited MacDonald, but this glosses over Bevin's real early character. Nor (unusually) did Citrine address the issue. They were all in the grip of an 'industrial unionist' psychology, which would be tested to the point of destruction in 1926.[57]

In fact, Bevin's attitude was typical of many in the union movement at the time. The docks and tram/bus strikes and the rash of other ones that year (railways, almost the mines) demonstrated the use of union power on a large scale. Here is Bevin:

A great deal has now been said during the past few weeks regarding the taking of industrial action now that we have a Labour Government, but I am of the opinion that if we rest on the industrial side for one moment it will be fatal to our progress and even to the Labour Government. It would be too great a price to pay and we must therefore go on with the economic war, waging it the whole time and utilizing every opportunity on behalf of the class we represent.[58]

There was a Marxist and syndicalist sentiment underlying this philosophy, though Bevin was neither. Francis Williams, in his *Ernest Bevin: Portrait of a Great Englishman*, thought his 'considerable suspicion of the Parliamentary Labour Party' throughout the 1920s 'was in part a heritage of the Social Democratic Federation days of his youth'.[59] It may have had more to do with his efforts to establish control in his new union, especially the bus group, who were then left-/communist-led.[60] However, as a result of the successful outcomes in both docks and tram disputes, Bevin's reputation as a tough and successful leader was made. It consolidated his position as his union's undisputed leader. In September 1925, after the TUC-led union victory on 'Red Friday', he eventually decided to join the General Council. Coincidentally, the other emerging union leader of the time, Walter Citrine, also stepped up to the General Council as acting general secretary.[61] Bevin contributed significantly to the mood towards concerted action by all the unions, culminating in the General Strike of 1926. Citrine had noticed 'Napoleon' Bevin (as Bramley and others called him) agreeing that 'the description was not far out, whether it related to features or character'. However, he went on to say that he 'regarded him from the first as one of the strongest, if not the strongest, personal forces in the trade union movement'.[62]

Surprisingly, Citrine has very little to say in his memoirs about that short, but intense, eight months of Labour government. It fell mainly because of Liberal objections to the terms of a trade treaty the government had agreed with the Soviet Union, which they alleged union representatives had influenced.[63] MacDonald had recognised the Soviet Union officially in January. Purcell, in his role as a Labour MP in the Commons, was able to lobby strongly for the best deal possible for their 'promised land'.[64] Citrine said that

the arrival of the Soviet trade delegation 'excited my imagination
most of all'.[65] He impressed Mikhail Tomsky and his All-Russian
Central Council union team, who were on that delegation, showing
them round his new office system at the TUC Eccleston Square
offices in Victoria.[66] He would afterwards become Secretary of
the Anglo-Russian Joint Advisory Committee (ARJAC).[67] But the
Liberals made an issue of the 'generous' terms said to have been
influenced by the unions. This triggered a defeat in Parliament and
caused MacDonald to call the general election of late October
1924. The Russian treaties and the forged Zinoviev 'Red Letter'
dominated the campaign.[68]

Citrine was clearly well aware of all this when he was invited to
address the Parliamentary Labour Party after that administration
had fallen.[69] His focus had naturally been on the office and the
rather chaotic state of administrative affairs at the TUC, which
he had inherited.[70] But with Bramley's increasing illness, Citrine
had to emerge from the back room. He became the officer to the
Special Industrial Committee dealing with the mining industry
crisis, and of the ARJAC dealing with the Russian unions, from
June 1925.[71] The Parliamentary Labour Party invited him to
address them, probably keen to see what the new man at the TUC
was like. Beatrice Webb's description of him as 'communistic in
sympathy'[72]was probably the leadership's view. But MacDonald's
universally recognised poor handling of the Zinoviev forged letter
affair and issues generally gave the Opposition a focus to bring
down his government.[73] Citrine would later blame MacDonald
for his mishandling of the Zinoviev letter, which he considered
one of the 'principal factors' in Labour's election defeat.[74] This
weak performance may have strengthened Citrine's mildly syndicalistic views about the respective benefits of industrial as opposed

to parliamentary action. However, he later concluded that 'trade unionism and political activity … were complementary', and he would show this throughout his leadership of the TUC in the following decades.[75]

In MacDonald's presence, Citrine made a strong statement for the independence of the TUC from the Labour Party, with a veiled criticism of their government.[76] He said, 'I took as my theme the necessity for a closer collaboration between the Labour Party and the T.U.C … I had noticed that this was somewhat lacking in 1924 when the Labour Party was in office.'[77] This was putting it mildly. Fred Bramley had claimed that, during the period the Labour government was in office, 'we were not taken into consultation at all by the Prime Minister'.[78] He had shocked a good many of those Labour MPs present, he thought, and he sat down deflated, but unrepentant. Yet he felt that it was desirable for the Party leaders to realise that they could not treat the TUC as though it didn't count.[79] Soon, he and Bramley would be making arrangements to separate the TUC's Research, Publicity and International departments at Eccleston Square from the joint arrangement, 'a fertile source of friction' with the party next door in Eccleston Square. This 'shaking free of the Party' crystallised the very different paths these two parts of the Labour movement were then taking.[80]

No wonder, then, that this first, short-lived attempt at Labour government failed, though it established the Labour Party's claim to govern. In the October 1924 general election, the Conservatives were returned with 413 seats and the Liberals were finished as a parliamentary force, down 118 seats to a mere 40. Labour, while losing 40 seats, still held 151. Ironically, their vote went up from 4.4 to 5.4 million in the enlarged electorate, which included women over the age of thirty.[81]

MORE POWER TO THE GENERAL COUNCIL?

An equally important issue for Bramley and Purcell had been
to strengthen the TUC's influence, if not authority, over unions
involved in major industrial disputes. Although it had always served
a strategic role for the unions since its foundation in 1868, this was
mainly as a political lobbying body focused on parliamentary affairs.
So, Bramley and the General Council sought more explicit authority from Congress to enable them to act for all unions on strategic
industrial matters. As we saw, Citrine was also keen to create

> a much more powerful body – to make it in fact, the centralized
> leadership for the whole trade union movement in industrial
> matters. We [Bramley and he] talked about this at the office
> from time to time and he soon found that I had long been a
> convinced believer in this.[82]

To achieve this, they needed to get the unions to agree it at annual
Congress, not an easy thing. They had to avoid giving the impression
that the jealously guarded autonomy of the individual unions was
being eroded. The new General Council's role had been designed in
1921 as a supplementary power and then only to 'co-ordinate' the
actions of individual unions or groups of unions that requested it.
Major unions – MFGB, AEU and T&GWU – had refused to give
the General Council more power at the 1922 and 1923 Congresses.
Citrine learned this when he put forward a radical plan. But 'wiser
heads than mine were convinced that this would be a mistake', as
the unions would not agree such 'a considerable transfer of power
to the General Council'.[83] So, 'a more gradual approach' just to
'enlarge its duties' immediately was decided upon. A vaguely worded

proposal on the extension of TUC powers sailed through the Hull Congress in September 1924, without opposition. It was moved by George Hicks, but this time seconded by the Miners' Federation, now in the person of the very left-wing Arthur Cook.[84] Although the actual change to the TUC's Standing Orders was not major, it reflected a significant mood change by important union affiliates.[85] The 'big three' – miners, rail and road transport/port workers – all now supported the move, and many other important unions, such as the AEU, ASLEF and ETU, did so too. Together they represented over 50 per cent of the TUC's 4.3 million members.[86] This was far more than 'an inexpensive gesture of solidarity'. [87] It symbolised a wider 'mood music'. This can be seen also from the other resolutions passed by acclamation, such as the very radical Industrial Workers' Charter.[88] The Communist-led Minority Movement also secured an instruction to the General Council to rationalise union structures along industrial lines.[89] Citrine was given the task of preparing a General Council report for the 1925 Congress.[90] So, already in 1924, the TUC was gearing up for enhanced authority and power.

Citrine's role at the Hull Congress as assistant to the general secretary was mainly to manage the 'behind the scenes' arrangements, but his obvious status as 'heir apparent' to Bramley, now evident by his close association with the chair of Congress, Alf Purcell, and his ally, George Hicks, meant he was no longer in 'the back room'. They would have introduced him to the key delegations at the social and political gatherings of those large union affiliates in the evenings. He was generally seen as a 'brilliant' addition to the TUC as it pushed itself to the head of the union movement.

Heads of department and key staff attended to service the many committees at Congress. Citrine gave this resource a new sense of direction and *esprit de corps*. This involvement also helped the staff's motivation and dedication back at Eccleston Square. Such senior staff as Alec Firth (acting assistant general secretary), Vincent Tewson (organisation), W. J. Bolton (international), Walter Milne-Bailey (research), Herbert Tracey (publicity) and his personal secretary, Frances E. MacDonald, would become key figures in the new TUC secretariat which Citrine was building. These were highly able, dedicated and committed civil servants of the union movement (some would later succeed Citrine as general secretary). Most served the union movement for much of their working lives, rather than market their undoubted skills in academia or business. With this support, Citrine impressed the General Council and delegations that a new team had taken over as the euphoria of 'Red Friday' created the mood to allow them to flex their muscles again.

CHAPTER 5

~

IN THE GENERAL STRIKE

'We must retreat … as an army, not as a rabble.'[1]

'We put the wind up these people.'[2]

Walter Citrine on the General Strike, 1926–27

These two sentiments expressed Walter Citrine's ambivalent views about the outcome of the General Strike in May 1926. The first was on day six (of nine), 9 May, as he nervously looked around the General Council in session, anxious about how it was going to end the strike. A year later, the second view was uppermost in his mind, as it faced the government's retribution. At a summer school of the Trade Union Defence Campaign against the trade disputes and trade unions bill 1927, he said,

> I am satisfied that, in spite of many who have said that the national strike was a failure, we put the wind up these people, and that they have been continually under it ever since. I am not an advocate of the General Strike. I *do* recognise that it was not a failure last May.[3]

Those ten days have entered union folklore. The General Strike
has a whole bibliography of its own now and there will be more to
come as its hundredth anniversary approaches.[4] Here we seek to
shed some fresh light through the eyes of a well-placed observer and
actor in the drama, Walter Citrine. Citrine's contemporary shorthand notes are a unique record which captures the atmosphere and
personalities in those important events – what he called 'the strike's
human factor'.[5] It must be appreciated how much faith was placed
by union activists in the efficacy of the withdrawal of the workers'
labour in strikes. They had

> a sense of power springing from a belief in the efficacy of the
> strike. That belief was a dominant element in trade union
> thought up to 1926. It centred on the notion that the unions
> held in their hands an ultimate weapon – the general strike.[6]

Bitter, protracted disputes, involving about 1 million workers in
the British coal-mining industry, had been occurring since 1911,

TUC General Council, 1926, the people who led the General Strike.
Citrine seated with President Pugh and Vice-President Swales.

involving the loss of millions of working days.[7] The main cause
was that the owners found themselves in an industry with declining
prospects for the sale of their product, and, as usual, their natural response was to 'force down money-wages'.[8] Citrine says that
Keynes' 1925 pamphlet *The Economic Consequences of Mr Churchill*,
which argued that the return to the Gold Standard that year at a
high level exacerbated the crisis, 'made a deep impression on me'.[9]
A serious obstacle to such plans was the militantly led and well-organised miners' union. The miners, living mostly in tightly knit pit
village communities, had a tradition of solidarity and struggle in
long strikes and lockouts.[10]

The Miners' Federation of Great Britain (MFGB) had lost the
last major battle in 1921, despite a thirteen-week-long strike.[11] It
blamed that defeat on the rail and road transport unions' failure
to honour its Triple Alliance membership promise of solidarity.
At the time, Citrine, then a still-militant national ETU officer in
Manchester, felt 'tremendous indignation' towards the other union
leaders responsible.[12] The 1921 battle was to be *the* general strike
long talked about in the Triple Alliance of miners, rail and road
leaders and all militant unionists, including Citrine. The government was considering continuing to keep the coal mines in public
control, so powerful was the MFGB. The threat of support from
the rail and road and port unions to prevent the movement of coal
was thought to be decisive. Beatrice Webb's diary captures what she
felt about 'the cancelling of the general strike'.[13]

> *April 16th.* – 'The strike cancelled': was the staggering news line
> of yesterday's evening paper. ... But the leaders clearly funked
> it: Thomas, Bevin and even Williams and a majority of the
> Executives of the N.U.R. and Transport Workers rode off on

the refusal by the Miners' Executive to ratify Hodge's unauthorised offer to give up temporarily the national pool and national
rate and discuss the district rates offered by the employers.[14]

Whatever the rights and wrongs of the leadership of that particular dispute, the subsequent failure of the miners' strike seared the
failure to support the miners into the memory of those union leaders
who came to decide on the General Strike in 1926. As Citrine said,
'We had visions of Black Friday, 1921 in our minds'.[15] Perversely,
Citrine and the TUC leadership got no credit for having expunged
that memory in May 1926.

After failing to revive an Industrial Alliance with Bevin and
other unions, the miners' leaders turned to the TUC in the middle
of 1925.[16] Faced with the issue of dismissal notices to all the miners,
the Miners' Federation pressed the General Council to exercise the
powers just given at the Hull Congress of 1924, to 'co-ordinate'
large-scale industrial action and force the government to restore
the subsidy and take over the industry.[17] The TUC set up a Special
Industrial Committee (SIC) in July 1925, with Alonso Swales, the
president, as chair and Citrine as secretary, to confer with the
government and the miners.[18]

The miners' leaders now had a sympathetic TUC leadership.
Significantly, before 'Red Friday', union leaders, 'in Bevin's mind as
much as anyone else's', had 'concealed doubts about the capacity of
the working-class to make its strength felt'.[19] Citrine worked closely
with his trusted and able head of publicity, Herbert Tracey, to use
all their industrial correspondents' contacts to brief the press on the
mining dispute.[20] Citrine now met its leaders, Herbert Smith and
Arthur Cook, a few times and they got on well.[21] At the same time, the
TUC sought a conference with the railway unions and the Transport

Workers' Federation for an embargo on 'black coal', to which its readily agreed.[22] The SIC committee members had a series of meetings with the prime minister, Stanley Baldwin, at which Citrine pressed Baldwin to publicly appeal to the mine owners to withdraw the notices, saying 'we could not allow the miners to be beaten on this issue'. Baldwin said he would do everything he could to get a peaceful settlement.[23] As a result, on Friday 31 July, at a meeting in the Ministry of Labour, the prime minister, looking 'tired and worn', 'walked in, accompanied by Winston Churchill and Lane-Fox … to announce that the coal-owners' notices would be suspended and financial assistance to the industry' given, until 1 May 1926.[24] One can imagine the jubilation with which this climb-down by the government was greeted by the whole trade union movement.

In fact, Baldwin had simply retreated to prepare for the full battle. However, the 'hawks' in his Cabinet − such as the home secretary, Sir William Joynson-Hicks − also saw it as 'a surrender' to naked union industrial power and the undermining of parliamentary democracy.[25] Churchill, as Chancellor of the Exchequer, would later tell the former TUC president Alf Purcell MP in the Commons that this 'settlement' was achieved 'over my blood-stained corpse'.[26] The interim deal also involved the setting up of a Royal Commission to examine the problems of the entire industry and make recommendations by the end of March 1926.[27] There was considerable hope vested in this inquiry as the chair, Lord Herbert Samuel, a former Liberal home secretary, was widely respected, as were his panellists.[28] It was regarded as such a huge victory for the unions' direct-action approach that it was dubbed 'Red Friday' in a *Daily Herald* headline in July 1925. The left-wing TUC president, Alonso Swales, captured the mood at that year's Congress in Scarborough, saying he was 'thrilled at the thought of a glorious week

– one that will ever be remembered'.[29] 'Red Friday' demonstrated 'that the General Council could organise successful sympathetic action in an emergency …'[30] It created a sense of euphoria that would be an important psychological factor in the unions' decision to go for a General Strike nine months later.

This achievement was a major turning point for the TUC, and an exciting, if very challenging, role for the de facto General Secretary. Apart from his role in the SIC, Citrine had to manage the TUC, due to Bramley's incapacity. It had a small staff of about thirty-five, and though many of them were enthusiastic socialist and union-minded people, they would have to service the many sub-committees of the General Council which would have to be energised.[31] Citrine frequently worked late into the evening, getting home to Wembley Park at all hours.[32] For he firmly believed that the victory of 'Red Friday' was but the beginning – a mere 'skirmish of outposts', he called it. 'I knew that our forces had not been tested.'[33] The transport unions had made it clear that they could not be expected to bear all the burden in supporting the miners again. The enormity of the task of involving the TUC in 'co-ordinating' supportive action of all the other 200 unions, if the Samuel Commission's recommendations were unacceptable, must have kept Citrine awake at night, but by his own account he seemed remarkably calm and business-like.[34]

LACK OF TUC PREPARATION

Citrine knew that little, if any, preparation was being made by the Special Industrial Committee (SIC) or the General Council for the possibility of conflict in the mining dispute and so was very uneasy.[35] They hoped talks would settle the dispute on the basis of the Samuel Commission recommendations, rather than require them to face the challenge of such a huge national strike.[36] However, the miners' leaders, now led by the fiery left-winger Arthur J. Cook, were emboldened by 'Red Friday' and TUC support and were making 'unbridled public prophecies of a general strike'.[37] Arthur James Cook was without a doubt the most controversial character of the General Strike.[38] From Somerset, with a background as a Methodist lay preacher, he went to work in the South Wales coal-field in the 1900s. He was one of the young miners educated at Ruskin College, Oxford, on a union scholarship, who were politi-cised there and at their Central Labour College in London, by the syndicalist Plebs League.[39] In the usual miners' union progression, Cook became a miners' agent in the Rhondda Valley coalfield from 1919 to 1924. He was elected to the South Wales Miners' Feder-ation (SWMF, known as 'The Fed') executive and to the Miners' Federation of Great Britain (MFGB) national executive also. He joined the British Communist Party (CPGB) at its formation in 1920, but left within a year, finding its discipline irksome, while remaining a firm Marxist in his outlook.

Cook was touring the collieries and labour movement centres, whipping up the 'long smoldering anger of the miners'. A huge momentum started to build at grass-roots level. Cook succeeded to such an extent that 'he was listened to and trusted more than any miners' leaders had ever been'.[40] The miners were not thinking of compromise. Nor were the coal owners, as they co-operated with the government's preparations, through the Organisation for the Maintenance of Supplies.[41]

In September 1925, Citrine tried to warn people that 'Red Friday', had not been a major test and that effective preparations for the full battle, if it came, were essential.[42] So, he called publicly

for better preparations by the TUC and all the unions. He did so in
a number of speeches and in one of the most remarkable articles
ever written by such a high-ranking union official (though couched
as 'my own personal point of view'). It appeared in the widely
read Labour Party and TUC journal *The Labour Magazine*, entitled
'Lessons from the Mining Dispute'.[43] Churchill's attention (he was
a leading member of the special Cabinet committee dealing with
the mining crisis) was drawn to Citrine's article by the minister
of labour, Arthur Steel-Maitland MP. He attached a note saying,
'both generally and from Mr Citrine's own position, it is well worth
reading'.[44] We do not have Churchill's response, but as a leading
Cabinet hawk it could only have strengthened his disposition to
see the TUC's involvement in the coal dispute as an expression of
union power, which he regarded as a challenge to the state.[45] Churchill probably shared this intelligence with Baldwin and the rest of
the Cabinet with relish, to confirm his worst fears of what the TUC
was now out for.[46] In his article, Citrine called for 'the development of an industrial strategy based on the principle of centralised
power and united leadership'.[47] He warned that it would be 'a
mistake to overrate the apparent success of the General Council's
efforts' on 'Red Friday', but acknowledged 'the effect on working
class psychology of the successful efforts of the General Council
to rally the forces of the unions'. However, he argued that nothing
would be more 'harmful and perhaps fatal than to engender a false
sense of security' or 'an inflated sense of victory' from reliance on
'the might of the trade union movement' on that occasion.[48]

Citrine was arguing for a complete overhaul of the ages-old
ramshackle union machinery. In some unions, the decision to call
industrial action rested with their executive council, but in many
others members controlled that decision through a ballot. Citrine

was urging all unions to alter their rules to give the power to their executives to call strike action 'in consultation with the TUC'.[49] This would fit them for an era when 'the large-scale industrial dispute will take the place of the sporadic and detached individual strike or lock-out'.[50] So, in view of the massive scale of strikes then, which required great coordination and single-minded direction, Citrine was in favour of national executive-led strikes by 'generals' rather than elemental 'grass-roots' upsurges. He wanted to take it a step further on general strikes. It was the Miners' Federation he had in mind, which was loath to share its sovereignty in the conduct of the strike, an issue which would run throughout the General Strike without being resolved. He anticipated also that 'rules might be swept aside in a spontaneous outburst, but union executives are usually wisely averse to that method'! [51] These were not 'usual' times, and there was not time to follow his 'wise' method once the last-minute coal industry negotiations broke down. So, the General Strike was called in a 'spontaneous outburst', though, interestingly, it was not challenged on legal grounds. Instead, the government was now determined 'on forcing a retreat by the TUC, while the latter remained confused and divided about its course of action'.[52]

By pointing out these difficulties, but couched in militant terms, was Citrine trying to slow the momentum towards the strike? Taylor concluded that 'he was reluctant and apprehensive about leading the TUC into a conflict with the government which he did not believe the trade unions could possibly win'. Was he 'trying to alert his general council colleagues to the realities'? [53] Maybe, but it was a very strange way to do it. Militaristic metaphors pervaded his article – 'The ['Red Friday'] struggle was won without bringing our guns into action', 'without firing a shot', it was only 'a skirmish of outposts' and 'our forces had not been tested'.[54] He saw as 'steadily emerging the desire for a body … which can in time of necessity organize the unions to fight as a single army'.[55] Was this the rhetoric of syndicalism, presumably pitched for those union leaders or activists amenable to it? Or was it the language that his left leader colleagues, Swales, Purcell, Hicks and Bromley, would approve of? That would not have been Citrine's style; he usually expressed his opinion openly, whoever he was with. He pointed out 'that in any future dispute of considerable magnitude', the government would again become involved. In that case, 'it may be that a capitalist Government next time will show no inclination to evade the issues but will be prepared to force matters to a conclusion on grounds of their own choosing'.[56] Citrine warned that they needed to get ready if they wanted to win any full-scale strike. Clearly, he was pitching it to an audience seized by the necessity of standing by the miners this time.

Citrine's article contained not a moment of hesitation as to the necessity to support the miners with action. Citrine even explored the possibility that the government would portray any such combined action 'as a denial of their right to govern and as the beginning of open war between society as at present constituted and the whole organized working-class movement'. Only Citrine (apart from the railway workers' NUR leader Jimmy Thomas) anticipated that possibility.[57] Most union leaders ignored or overlooked this danger.[58] As Bullock put it, even Bevin 'failed to grasp fully the political implications of industrial action on the scale of a general strike'.[59] Citrine concluded that, 'The Industrial Committee … saw Red Friday largely as a triumph of bargaining powers … They refused to regard this procedure as a challenge to the state.'[60] Citrine himself insisted that the TUC's objective was 'a purely Trade Union one, legally and morally justified'.[61] However, there is no question about his advocacy of a form of industrial unionism. It comes through clearly from that *Labour Magazine* article, though it wasn't an overtly revolutionary one.

This remarkable document shows a strategic thinker with the confidence to publish such strong 'advice' – a foretaste of Citrine's style of leadership for the future. The General Council would call it a 'National Strike' to avoid the syndicalistic connotation of the words 'General Strike'.[62] However, calling it something else didn't change the reality – 'the idea that the unions had the right – and the power – to bring the economy of the nation to a standstill and secure what they demanded by direct action ...'[63]

THE SCARBOROUGH CONGRESS, SEPTEMBER 1925

Citrine's *Labour Magazine* article was probably available to the delegates who jubilantly trooped to the annual Trades Union Congress at Scarborough from 7 to 12 September 1925. That conference has been described as 'the high-water mark' of trade union militancy.[64] President Alonso Swales' address calling for the 'overthrow of capitalism' set the tone and the communist-led Minority Movement delegates were prominently in evidence. A number of revolutionary-sounding resolutions were carried, but when it came to the unions agreeing a resolution which gave more power to the General Council to call for a levy and order a stoppage of work, even Swales' own Amalgamated Engineering Union (AEU) jibbed.[65] The motion was 'referred' to the General Council which decided not to adopt those extra powers. Even the left-dominated SIC had decided not to include Citrine's 'addendum' in the General Council report to that conference. In it, he had suggested that the SIC become a permanent committee with calendared meeting dates, meaning to address the issues more urgently. However, 'Much to my chagrin the Committee regarded this addendum as going too far, and it never appeared in the printed report of the General Council.'[66] He would be taken up with behind-the-scenes running of the conference, at which his boss, Fred Bramley, made just a brief appearance.

A differently composed Special Industrial Committee, after that Congress, would be even less inclined to step up preparations for a confrontation over the miners' dispute. The left-wing AEU president, Alonso Swales,[67] was replaced as chair by the more realistic Arthur Pugh, the steelworkers' leader, now chair of the General Council.[68] Pugh was joined on the SIC by the now right-wing, but one of the most experienced union leaders and a former government minister, Jimmy Thomas of the NUR.[69] Thomas had just returned to the General Council and SIC and would have considerable influence with Citrine during the strike.[70] This change in the composition of the SIC would have a significant impact on the conduct of the coal dispute negotiations.[71] At the same time, Ernest Bevin of the T&GWU joined the General Council and supported the more cautious approach of Pugh and Thomas. He made the decisive intervention at Scarborough to defeat the Minority Movement motion giving the General Council more power to 'call for a levy, to order a stoppage of work ...'[72] In Bullock's view, 'Scarborough marked the end rather than the beginning of the left-ward mood in the trade unions.'[73] Yet this would be the General Council which would lead the unions into the General Strike six months later.

Citrine, who was in Russia after the Congress,[74] had to rush back to take up the post as acting general secretary in October, after Fred Bramley's sudden death. He would have to adjust to that changed leadership mood. Looking to the Samuel Commission, the SIC and the General Council were preparing for a settlement of the coal dispute, rather than for a strike. Citrine now felt, 'I was carrying my advocacy for greater powers to an extent that was irritating to most of my colleagues'. He got a 'few words of appreciation from Arthur Cook', though! [75] The SIC and the General Council awaited the Samuel Report in March 1926, content to believe that the threat which succeeded on 'Red Friday' would retain its potency to encourage a settlement.

CITRINE'S 'MEMORANDUM'

In November 1925, Citrine, now in charge, was getting 'more uneasy'. He therefore crafted a much lengthier 'Memorandum' so that they would be 'far better equipped to face any emergency in 1926'.[76] He had genuine sympathy for the miners' situation, having worked as an electrician in the South Lancashire coalfield and lodged with miners in St Helens as a young man.[77] In 1908, he witnessed the grief of that community after an explosion killed seventy miners. It had all left a deep impression on him.[78] So, his memorandum, entitled 'The Impending Crisis', outlined thirteen 'questions of principle' of what needed to be done for 'coordinated action' of all unions, in support of the miners.[79] The key points were that they should press the government to continue the subsidy beyond April; prepare for the eventuality of a general strike; insist that the TUC have control of policy in consultation with the miners' leaders; and mount a vigorous 'platform' campaign.[80]

Citrine now sought to get his Committee to involve the General Council so that they could take 'responsibility for framing policy', as, in his view, 'the mining situation has ceased to be exclusively a miners' question'.[81] However, the SIC showed little inclination and after a 'prolonged discussion' on 19 January 1926, his paper was discussed again on 28 January and sent to the Miners' Federation.[82] Joint meetings followed on 12 and 19 February. However, the issues raised were never referred to the General Council, as Citrine's document was not proceeded with.[83] Although the miners' leaders, Herbert Smith (1862–1938)[84] and Arthur Cook, 'complimented him on the paper', even Smith said there was 'no need to rush things'.[85] Citrine said, 'it was clear to me that the [joint] meeting did not want to face the issues raised in my memorandum and would do anything to put off a decision'.[86] Put at its best, they wanted to avoid any action which might be seen as preparing for a strike, in case it might prejudice their attempt to negotiate a settlement. It was a fine balance, but, as things turned out, Citrine was proved right about the need to prepare for the eventuality of a strike. But it also shows that he, like Bevin, was still a firm believer in industrial action for political ends (i.e., to persuade the government to pressure the coal owners towards the miners' demands).[87]

Once the Samuel Report was received, it was found to be a curate's egg, good in parts. While rejecting the mine owners' key demand for an increase in hours from seven to eight per day, it concluded that 'some' reductions in wages (undefined, but much less than the coal owners were demanding) would be necessary immediately, pending a full reorganisation of the industry.[88] Of particular disappointment to Citrine was its call for an end to the government subsidy of the coal industry. Citrine had argued strongly that they should press that on the government ahead of the Samuel Report. This would have bought time for a reorganisation of the industry and the possibility of success in the negotiations.[89]

NEGOTIATIONS

Negotiations only got going in late April 1926 and then without much progress, as both the coal owners and the miners' leaders held entrenched positions.[90] The coal owners posted termination notices in all the districts telling the miners that their contracts would expire on Friday 30 April. The SIC team leading the negotiations equivocated about backing the miners' demand for 'not a penny off the pay, not a minute on the day'. They focused instead on Samuel's reorganisation proposal, to enable the industry to pay reasonable wages in a more efficient and competitive industry.[91] Pugh reported the situation to the conference of union executives at the Memorial Hall, Farringdon, on 29 April, without challenge. The hall was 'packed to suffocation', with 1,300 delegates adding to 'the excitement'.[92] Even Ramsay MacDonald made 'a glorious speech' in support.[93]

Pugh and Citrine leave Downing Street after
meeting with the prime minister.

Bevin presented the Ways and Means Committee report on how the strike would be conducted (Citrine says he seconded Thomas' motion), requiring all the union executives to hand over their powers to the General Council for 'the conduct of the dispute'.[94] One after another, leaders of the forty-three unions rose to authorise the TUC to call the strike on their behalf and Herbert Smith for the Miners' Federation indicated qualified acceptance that the TUC would now be responsible for the conduct of the negotiations and strike.[95] Bevin even defended the General Council's delay in making preparations.[96]

It was at this point that events took over. Baldwin agreed to further discussions by smaller negotiating teams (Citrine was secretary of the union side of three – Pugh, Thomas and Swales).[97] Much midnight oil was burned as they struggled to find 'a formula' which the miners' leaders might agree to, but which would assure the Cabinet it was not just another 'Red Friday' 'appeasement' of the unions. The government had taken the precaution of getting the king's approval for a proclamation under the Emergency Powers Act of 1920 on 30 April, while the TUC at the same time issued a formal call to strike for 3 May – both intended as 'precautionary' measures in case the negotiations again failed. Bevin called the proclamation 'a declaration of war', but at the same time ambiguously placed a caveat on the 3 May start date by adding, 'that is to say, if a settlement has not been found'.[98] It was a fluid situation and all these equivocations were understandable. Meantime, Churchill and his group of hawks wrongly saw the compositors' refusal to print the *Daily Mail* as the result of TUC instructions. So, they persuaded the Cabinet to discontinue the negotiations, demanding 'unconditional withdrawal of the threat of a general strike'.[99] The reconvened conference of union executives picked up this gauntlet and the TUC General Council then called the General Strike for 4 May.

The story of the strike has been pored over in great detail over the years since. There is still no final account, as much that happened was not recorded and the memories/diaries of the key players afterwards conflicted.[100] But key features emerge – lack of trust and suspicion on all sides, failures of communication, divisions in the unions and TUC, Cabinet hardliners' determination to confront the unions. All these went into the 'stew' which made the General Strike ineffectual.[101]

THE GENERAL STRIKE

The General Strike started on 3 May 1926 and lasted nine days. Citrine's 'Diary of the General Strike' remains a vivid daily account of the strike arrangements at the TUC.[102] In humorous, almost biblical language, Citrine describes Bevin, 'with the most becoming modesty' as 'offering to sacrifice himself on the altar of duty', to take the burden of running the strike off the shoulders of his colleagues. However, 'the lesser luminaries having communed with themselves and were wroth at the proposed usurpation, whereat Bevin was aggrieved'.[103] Yet there is no doubt but that the T&GWU leader was making his presence felt on the General Council. He became secretary to the Powers and Orders Committee (as it became), with Alf Purcell as chair, and they largely organised the conduct of the strike together (though Bevin typically later claimed all the credit!). When Citrine read more of Bevin's exploits, he commented wryly, 'If Bullock's history of the national strike is correct Bevin did some things behind the backs of the General Council. Most of them were not even known to me.'[104] Adonis again gives Bevin credit for seizing the initiative in getting negotiations 'going somewhere' by contacting Sir Herbert Samuel, though he was already in contact with Thomas.[105] But Bevin didn't let Citrine know and they seemed not to have been in close contact during the strike.

Citrine noted that Thomas was 'deeply distrusted by the miners' as he was in touch with government ministers and others.[106] But on the second day (5 May), he surprised them all by advocating an extension of the strike, saying, 'it should be settled as the constitutional issue got more dangerous … the Government thought they knew our power, but the strike exceeded their greatest expectation. The position is that they are staggered.'[107] Everybody, especially the government, was surprised by the huge response from the working class to the TUC's call. One and a half million workers came out on day one. The strike impacted on every city and major town in the country, though, with brilliant sunshine, the mood was light-hearted.[108] Citrine describes his own role at General Council meetings rather modestly: 'the acting secretary, making copious notes, peeping from behind a pile of papers, and pouring a steady flow of advice into the unheeding ears of the chairman.'[109] However, it is clear that, as secretary to the TUC negotiating team, Citrine was in a good position to judge the course of the dispute.[110] General Councilors' shifting moods are captured well in his diary, as news of the strike up and down the country came in for the nine days of the action. However, by day five, he was having serious doubts about the strike's effectiveness. For instance, there 'is practically open strife between [the transport workers] and the railwaymen' over their 'diametrically opposed views of policy about the transport of food'.[111] Bevin doesn't seem to have been able to influence that situation as instructions from T&GWU and NUR headquarters were not always obeyed.[112] 'Citrine, consistently unemotional and detached, wrote an assessment of the situation on day 7, full of foreboding.'[113] By day eight, he was 'swinging first to one view and then to another', as to how long it could go on.[114] The government's preparations to limit the impact of the strike were having increasing effect. By day eight, the General Council members, including Bevin, Purcell, Hicks and Bromley, 'were all convinced that if the General Council determined to call off the General Strike, [it] would not be an unpopular one.'[115]

So, the General Council was looking for a way out. Pugh made an impassioned appeal to Cook and Smith at a General Council meeting on 10 May, to no avail.[116] There was considerable bitterness in the General Council debates now, as most blamed the miners' leaders for refusing to engage with any of the compromise formulas which the TUC's negotiators came up with. Citrine believed 'that had the miners acted differently the Government would have approved the proposals'.[117] The feeling on the General Council was that 'the miners seemed oblivious to the sacrifices that other unions had made'.[118] There was no precedent anywhere for a general strike of that duration, except perhaps in the wildest of syndicalist dreams. So, the TUC concluded that it had no choice but to, as Citrine put it, 'retreat ... as an army and not as a rabble'.[119] Unfortunately, it wasn't very orderly.

The General Council called it off on 12 May in the belief that the government would get the mine owners to withdraw their lockout notices and that negotiations with the miners would resume. This was their understanding from Samuel, who they thought (wrongly) was acting in some informal capacity with Baldwin's approval. He had assured them this would happen, but he wasn't speaking for the prime minister.[120] Then, 'the decision of the Miners Federation to call a conference on Friday next, and not to resume work in the meantime', scotched that possibility.[121] The notion that the Miners'

Federation had handed over its power to conduct the strike to the TUC was dispelled. It was soon realised that there would be no honourable peace but what seemed more like Churchill's 'unconditional surrender'.

THE BITTER AFTERMATH AND LESSONS

Citrine had wanted the 'Inquest' to take place in July, so that they could answer the attacks on the General Council's decision before the critics' version took hold.[122] But the General Council understandably decided to postpone it while the miners' strike was going on and so it did not take place until 20 January 1927.[123] Then, at last, Citrine was able to rebut each of Cook's arguments at that conference.[124] He thought that the negotiations had failed 'more than anything else' because of the 'infernal, intolerable suspicion all through'.[125] He said that 'suspicion of the Council seemed to walk in the room at the same moment as the miners'.[126] For this he blamed Cook particularly, whose attacks on all and sundry 'renders intimate and practical negotiations nearly impossible'.[127]

Citrine had very mixed feelings about Cook throughout their short but intense acquaintance. Personally, they got on surprisingly well and had had many friendly discussions since they first met in June 1925. Citrine's *Labour Magazine* article of September 1925 and his memorandum of January 1926 were appreciated by Smith and Cook, for, although they were deeply suspicious and critical of the SIC and General Council leadership, they did not include Citrine. They nominated him as general secretary at the Congress of September 1926.[128] Citrine regarded Cook as an honest but easily led character; 'no doubt he was exploited by the Communists'.[129] He observed him in full flow at close quarters from his special vantage

point – the Council chamber. 'Excitable and fiery', he was a messi-
anic figure and a powerful orator.[130] However, Citrine thought that
his style of working 'himself up into a state bordering on hysterics'
didn't work on the General Council.[131] 'He made wild assertions
and accusations against almost everyone.'[132] They remained friends
until Cook's untimely death from cancer in 1931.[133]

Citrine never accepted that the General Strike had been a total
failure, as it was 'a sympathetic strike on a national scale'.[134] Lord
Bullock's observation about Bevin applied to most TUC leaders then:

> shaken … free of the syndicalist belief in Direct Action. He
> and the other union leaders would come to realize that there
> were limits not only to their power but also to the use they
> could afford to make of it unless they were prepared to risk
> being carried further than most of them meant to go.[135]

Citrine would ruefully acknowledge this reality, saying, 'Well it
is a hard business but experience sometimes has to be painful to
furnish an example from which we can profit.'[136] For both Citrine
and Bevin, those traumatic nine days of the General Strike were a
major turning point.

That fascinating strike is also crucial to understanding the
development of the unions in the twentieth century. It has been
described, without exaggeration, as 'the most important episode in
the history of British trade unionism'.[137] This is because it tested
to destruction many of the utopian and dogmatic ideologies which
had dominated militant thinking since the 1900s. 'Intellectually,
industrial unionism had held the stage in the British trade union
movement for twenty years.'[138] In the course of that traumatic
episode, the General Council of the TUC established itself as the

authoritative centre of the trade union movement in Britain.[139] It also started the 'rising political authority' of its new general secretary, for whom it was also a defining moment. [140] As Neil Riddell put it, 'Citrine's arguments for greater centralization and general council control were reinforced and he was able to redefine the objectives of the TUC.'[141]

HOW OTHERS SAW CITRINE

We have a contemporary criticism of Citrine and of the General Council's conduct of the strike, from within the Labour movement at that time, which sheds light on his thinking then. It is by Beatrice Webb (1858–1943) and her husband, Sidney, 1st Baron Passfield (1859–1947), who were influential (Fabian Society) socialist figures in the early Labour Party. They were also respected historians of the British trade unions, whose 'monumental' works *The History of Trade Unionism 1666–1920* (1894 edition) and *Industrial Democracy* (1897) had been regarded by Citrine as his 'bible' as a young ETU District Official.[142] The updated 1920 edition with its new chapters commenting on union developments since 1900 was also required reading for all those heavily involved in the Labour movement. Sidney was a leading active Labour Party executive council member and adviser to the Labour leadership. He had been one of the Sankey Commissioners of 1919 who had recommended nationalisation of the mines.[143] MacDonald and Henderson, although not openly critical of the decision to call the General Strike, made no secret of the fact that they regarded it as wrong-headed.[144] MacDonald had even denounced Baldwin in Parliament for backing down on 'Red Friday' in the face of union power. He said that 'He had fought the idea of a general strike since its reappearance in labour politics before the war, and he had fought the attitudes behind it since his twenties.'[145] Afterwards, MacDonald described it as 'one of the most lamentable adventures in crowd self-leadership of our labour history' and the mood of the Labour Party swung in favour of parliamentary methods.[146] Beatrice's diaries reveal the depth of the Webb's hostility to what she called 'a proletarian distemper; the last gasp of the workers' control dream' and 'a grotesque trage-dy'.[147] On 4 May, the first day of the strike, she wrote in her diary, 'we personally are against the use of a General Strike in order to compel the employers of a particular industry to yield to the men's demands, however well justified these claims may be'.[148]

So, when Citrine and his wife Doris spent the weekend with the Webbs at their cottage in Liphook, Hampshire, in July 1927, they 'wrangled vigorously hour after hour' about the justification for and outcome of the General Strike. Beatrice had come to like Citrine after being initially suspicious of what she saw as his 'communis-tic' tendencies in the TUC leadership.[149] She now thought he was 'the first really able Secretary the TUC has ever had', after his performance at the Strike Inquest TUC Conference the previous January, where he had ably rebutted all of Arthur Cook's charges against the TUC. Nonetheless, she left us a much-quoted, rather mixed portrait/caricature of him.[150] Interestingly, she thought he still 'believed in the future of the T.U.s as a great controlling force *through the weapon of the national and sympathetic strike*, or rather the threat of it'.[151] This was hardly the case in July 1927.

Beatrice described Citrine as 'an intellectual of the scientific type' caught up in a syndicalistic and Guild Socialist-inspired drama.[152] After describing his personal characteristics as a 'hygienic puritan in his daily life', 'with the manners and clothes and way of speaking of a superior bank clerk', she opined that Citrine's 'pitfall will be personal vanity and the sort of conceit which arises from continuous association with uneducated and unselfcontrolled official superiors'. 'I think he is very ambitious – expects too much relatively to his faculties' but with 'the integrity and loyalty characteristic of the better type of British mechanic'. Worst of all, she claimed that 'Citrine is contemptuous … of the members of his General Council and the T.U. Congress, and like all the other brain-workers who were in the inner circle of the TUM during 1926 he gives a picture of deplorable lack of grip – alike of intellect and character – among those who led the millions of Trade Unionists in and out of the General Strike – whilst the leaders of the Miners approach, according to his estimate, mental deficiency.'[153]

This latter observation seems totally out of character for Citrine, but it was a penetrating question as to his relations with his 'uneducated and unselfcontrolled official superiors'. He was not overimpressed by the Webbs on that first occasion either (they would become good friends in the 1930s), seeing them as cold fish, 'looking at me in much the same way as an entomologist might peer at a new species of butterfly safely impaled on a pin'.[154] They thought that 'when we come to write our book on Twentieth Century Trade Unions – if we ever get time – Citrine will be useful to us. And what he will make out of the Movement, during the next ten years, raises my curiosity.'[155]

Beatrice Webb was well known for her razor-sharp but often non-factual pen, but with her vast experience and writing ability her observations are sometimes very acute.[156] Citrine didn't take it seriously, allowing the editor Margaret Cole to publish 'this remarkable comment' in her diaries, and reproducing it in his own autobiography.[157] He said, 'I really cannot recognize myself at times' and 'some of her judgements as to my state of mind are rather fallacious'. However, as 'it was Mrs Webb's [she rarely used her title, Lady Passfield] candid opinion of me as she saw and judged me at the time ... it would be wrong for it to be deleted from her Diaries'.

Beatrice Webb's diaries are a fascinating contemporary 'gossip' about the period she covers (1912–32), and for her pen portraits of 'everybody who was anybody' in the government, Labour Party, unions and much else. Beatrice, who majored on wider social deprivation and destitution issues (repeal of the Poor Law and, with Sidney, the national minimum wage), comes across in her diaries as contemptuous of 'dull', 'wooden' union officials in the Labour movement, whose 'stupid untrained persons may pass up to the highest office if only they have secured the suffrages of the members of a large union'.[158] They weren't quite sure what to make of this former electrical worker, an 'intellectual' who had developed in the Labour movement as an electrician and union official, not the universities, but with the supreme confidence to humour her jottings. It's a pity they never completed their history of the unions in the twentieth century.

CHAPTER 6

~

CITRINE AND THE
COMMUNIST MOVEMENT

Citrine had greeted the October Revolution in Russia of 1917 enthusiastically, as indeed had most active British trade unionists and Labour people. He remained a fan even after the Bolsheviks took the revolution in October 1917 on a most extreme 'communist' journey, romanticising that Lenin's picture of an Electric Republic would deliver 'the advantages of a planned economy and the blessings of modern civilisation'.[1] The ETU *Electrical Trades Journal*, of which he was then assistant editor, published an article entitled 'The Electric Republic' in 1921. This saw 'the power of electricity as the helper of the new civilisation in Russia'.[2] As the new, clean power, electricity symbolised the promise of a brighter world.

So, soon after Citrine joined the TUC in 1924, the visit of a Russian trade union delegation was 'the one [topic] which excited my imagination ... I looked forward to it with eagerness ...'[3] It is difficult for us today, knowing how that experiment worked out, to appreciate the feelings and hopes that the Russian Revolution aroused worldwide. Citrine in his thirties was no dreamer, nor a communist, yet, he says: 'I accepted almost at its face value, without critical reservations, practically everything which emanated from

Russian official sources.'[4] He was sent to greet his boss, Fred Bramley, and Alf Purcell after their return from an official visit to the Soviet Union in December 1924 and they gave him a glowing account of their two-month official delegation there.[5] They would produce a massive, quality booklet on their trip, which was circulated widely in the Labour movement at home and abroad.[6] In discussions with Tomsky and senior Soviet trade union leaders, Bramley and Purcell had agreed to recommend that the General Council would set up an Anglo-Russian Joint Advisory Committee (ARJAC), to the consternation of their international colleagues in IFTU.[7] This Committee was formally set up in July 1925, with Citrine the enthusiastic joint secretary (in place of the very ill Bramley), along with the Russian union council chair, Mikhail Tomsky.[8]

IFTU was reborn in the midst of hostility from the Communist International who set up a rival Red International of Labour

Anglo-Russian Joint Advisory Committee in London
meeting, 1925. Citrine at back (left), Purcell, Wicks, Tillett
at back (right). Tomsky and Soviet delegation sitting.

Unions (RILU), trying to use working-class organisations for revolutionary purposes. Between 1924 and 1926, after the failure of all Comintern attempts to foment revolution in Germany and other parts of Europe, the Soviet leadership tried a softer tack, through their more emollient union leader, Tomsky. As we saw, the TUC, under Bramley and Purcell, tried to accommodate this move for 'international workers unity', i.e., the merger of the Soviet and IFTU unions.[9] However, the decidedly sceptical continental social democratic union leaders proved extremely unwilling to accept the 10 million or so Soviet 'union' members into their organisation on the Soviet leader's terms.[10] In pursuit of this dream, Bramley had been backwards and forwards to Amsterdam and other conference venues in Europe, trying to persuade the IFTU Executive colleagues, without success. When he returned from a General Council-suggested recuperative cruise to Latin America, Citrine found him still very ill.[11] He would die in Amsterdam in October 1925, while still trying. Citrine, his deputy, would fill the gap at home and as secretary of the ARJAC.[12] The well-organised Citrine proved more than capable of coping with the extra responsibility. Though a very different type from the traditional manual worker union leader, as we saw, he was equally experienced in all aspects of union activities.[13] Still, it was a daunting challenge, servicing the hundred or so affiliated unions (small, medium and large) while gearing up for the biggest industrial and political battle ever.[14] He had to manage the TUC through 'its finest hour'.

Tomsky was so impressed by Citrine that at the Scarborough Congress of September 1925 he invited both him and George Hicks (chair of the International Committee) to visit the Soviet Union. It seems amazing that the assistant general secretary could be spared for such a long absence at a time when the general secretary himself was seriously ill. Clearly, 'the powers that be' at TUC headquarters, Purcell and Swales (who succeeded him as chair of the General Council after the Congress), thought it appropriate that he should go, in order to cement the relationship. They went some weeks later in September.[15]

Ostensibly, this invitation was to advise the Soviet trade unions on how they could modernise their union administrative systems (the Russian trade delegates spent an hour and a half in Citrine's office admiring his new system[16]). But, of course, it was more likely Tomsky's shrewd attempt to woo the TUC's obvious 'heir apparent'. Bramley had been their 'best friend' at Amsterdam executive meetings of IFTU and in the trade negotiations with the MacDonald government.[17]

However, while there, Citrine proved to be his own man, asking awkward questions and arguing with them in the many discussions he and Hicks had with Tomsky and his union central council members.[18] Citrine was shocked to learn that they favoured Stalin for the succession to Lenin and not Trotsky, as many in the West expected.[19] Citrine pressed Tomsky about the unions' independence in the Soviet Union, but Tomsky was insistent that in 'their workers' state' they had no need of independence, as in capitalist countries. However, Citrine argued, from their recent negative experience with the Labour government in Britain, that unions should never 'sacrifice their independence to the State'.[20] When Tomsky protested 'we are the State', Citrine perspicaciously told him, 'you will find your trade unions will be sacrificed to the political expediency of the Government and your members will tell you that you are not performing the job of looking after their interests where they may clash with the State'.[21] Tomsky may have recalled that conversation a few years later when he and his colleagues on the executive of the All-Union Central Council of Trade Unions were removed.[22]

They were introduced to many of the Soviet and party leaders, including Stalin and Zinoviev. What Citrine saw in the Soviet Union and learned from these detailed discussions with top union officials must have helped cloud his rosy image of the *Electric Republic*. He had an interview with Zinoviev, president of the Communist International, who asked him about the recent Liverpool Labour Party conference decision to ban communists as delegates. Citrine explained that while 'we were not unfriendly to the Communists, at the same time we did not feel they were an inherent part of our movement'.[23] After that, the conversation became desultory and they parted. Hicks and Citrine were also struck by the cult of Lenin's personality since his death in 1924. Citrine remarked that 'certainly they had made him a god ...'.[24] Overall, the visit was quite successful and, though critical of some aspects, on balance they were impressed by the Soviet Union's progress since the Civil War had seriously disrupted the economy. After his recall to become acting general secretary in October, Citrine was immersed in the business of the General Council and so ARJAC matters and negotiations with IFTU did not progress. Then came the General Strike of May 1926.

The relationship started to go sour at the TUC's Bournemouth Congress in September 1926, when the General Council received a 'tirade of abuse' in a 3,000-word telegram from Tomsky.[25] They accused the TUC leadership of 'betraying' the miners in calling off the General Strike.[26] Tomsky's 'over the top' response dismayed Citrine and the Congress. A pamphlet by the secretary of the Red International of Labour Unions (RILU), Alexander Lozovsky, in January 1927 contained a bitter attack on the General Council, calling the former president, Arthur Pugh, 'a liar' and 'the General Council traitors'.[27] Citrine responded with an interview in the *Daily Herald*, warning that if this interference in British union affairs was endorsed by the Russian union council, they would be unable to continue with the Anglo-Russian Committee. The 'TUC Lefts' – Purcell, Hicks and Swales – once the darlings of the Soviet leadership, now became 'traitors, renegades and capitalist lackeys'.[28] In effect, they were abandoning the courtship and it would only be a formality for Citrine to announce the end of the engagement at the Edinburgh conference in September 1927.

What had gone wrong? Why was this British union matter so important to the Soviet leadership as to jeopardise their whole ARJAC initiative? It seems that it got caught up in the power struggle then reaching a climax in the Central Committee of the Communist Party in Moscow. Trotsky and the opposition had decided to make it one of the two key issues between them and the Stalin group leadership. Trotsky blamed Stalin for relying on the TUC left group rather than on the British revolutionists.[29] The Soviet government wanted to continue with the Anglo-Russian committee and Tomsky and his team met Citrine, Purcell, Swales and Hicks in Berlin on 29 March–1 April 1927 – the entire 'TUC Lefts' team! The TUC insisted that they agree explicitly not to interfere in each other's domestic affairs. Tomsky and his team acquiesced and reported to the CPSU Central Committee, claiming a major achievement in keeping the Anglo-Russian Committee alive and Citrine's promise to be more active.[30] However, a London *Times* story put an entirely different gloss on 'the Berlin accords', calling them 'the Russian Unions' Surrender'.[31]

That spin must have rankled in Moscow as the opposition now launched their attack on the government's handling of the whole affair. They declared it as 'kowtowing' to 'the notorious Citrine'.[32] At a CPSU Central Committee plenum on 13–16 April, Trotsky moved a resolution 'rejecting the Berlin agreements and scolding the men who had made them'.[33] He mounted a full attack on the TUC General Council, which he called 'a collection of well-placed strikebreakers'. He rejected the notion in the accords that the Soviets should refrain from interference in British union 'domestic affairs', as 'a betrayal of the first principles of proletarian internationalism'. To assume that the TUC 'could help create some fighting new trade union international was just ludicrous', Trotsky said. 'All one could expect from the likes of Hicks, Swales and Citrine was betrayal.' He argued that the agreements 'struck a particularly severe blow at the Minority Movement' as by boosting the General Council 'what excuse could the NMM present for recommending they all be ousted?' He wanted instead that they should back what 'revolutionary trade unionists in Britain wanted … an opportunity to wage direct war on the TUC's "left-wing": Trotsky demanded that 'the Committee should be liquidated forthwith'.[34]

At the July–August 1927 Central Committee meeting, Stalin included in his speech a chunk about 'The Anglo-Soviet Unity Committee'.[35] He denied ever having 'banked' on that committee or the TUC and British unions, which he called 'reformist trade unions, reactionary trade unions'. He sought to diminish the importance of ARJAC as simply the least important of three channels they had used to revolutionise the British working class (the other, more important ones being the Comintern, the Red International of Labour Unions (RILU) and, significantly, 'the revolutionary trade-union minorities', i.e., the NMM). He justified their decision in 1924 to befriend the 'reactionary' TUC in ARJAC, citing Lenin's advice on the need 'to resort to maneuvers, arrangements and compromises'.[36] So there could be no objection to their entering this committee with the 'reactionary' TUC. The reality was that neither the TUC nor the unions were now seen to have any influence with the Conservative government. The whole point of the committee for Stalin and his government was now redundant. In fact, they didn't care if the TUC pulled out of ARJAC. The General Council was also only too happy to oblige and Citrine's report to the Edinburgh Congress later that year would be adopted with minimal opposition. There was no war or intervention, but diplomatic relations with Britain were not restored until another Labour government came to office in 1929.

So, Citrine's encounter with the 'communism' of the 1920s was an eye-opener. How could they ever have imagined linking up with such a bizarre group? It was due to Bramley and Purcell's dream of international working-class unity, which Citrine fully signed up to. But the other reason was Tomsky. He had charmed them all since his appearance on the IFTU scene in 1923 and visits to Britain addressing the TUC in 1924 and 1925. Although superficially he was an orthodox Bolshevik, Citrine and Hicks got to know him well on their tour of the Soviet Union. They had the impression that he was more of a trade unionist than a politician. With his position as chair of the Soviet 'TUC', they might even have thought that the unions there might help to get post-revolutionary and civil war Russia to settle down to a more social-democratic model with the trade unions linked to IFTU giving them a degree of autonomy, if not independence.[37]

THE MINORITY MOVEMENT

Citrine's other brush with communist groups was with the National Minority Movement, or the MM as it was known, then the most important industrial militants' group in the British unions. It had replaced the Comintern's British offshoot, the Red International of Labour Unions, in 1924. RILU was entirely run from Moscow and openly pursued a revolutionary alternative for unions on the Communist International model.[38] The MM was a more sophisticated 'home-grown' British communist-led front organisation (though still under RILU direction).[39] Led by prominent communists in Britain, such as Harry Pollitt, John Campbell, Willie Gallagher, Arthur Horner and J. T. Murphy, it proved far more effective than RILU.[40] Pollitt (1890–1960) had been active in the Hands Off Russia campaign with Alf Purcell in 1919–20 and was regarded by Citrine as 'by far the most important member of the Minority Movement'.[41]He was an effective communist speaker at TUC and Labour Party conferences as a Boilermakers' Union delegate, for a few years. The MM was strongest in communist-dominated coalfield districts of South Wales, Lancashire and Scotland and also in the London Trades Council (including the ETU London District Committee militants). Though deeply hostile to most existing union leaderships, the MM presented itself as the greatest supporter of fundamental union aims and all actions, official or unofficial, including the TUC, with its slogan 'All power to the General Council'.[42] Their real operation was encapsulated in its other slogan, 'Don't Trust Your Leaders'.[43] It sought to mobilise 'rank-and-file' militant workers through the local bodies where activists attended without official union control – the Trades Councils and 'Councils of Action'.[44] Union leaders like Bevin, who knew how the CP worked in their unions through such bodies, were totally opposed to any increase in Trades Councils' official local status.[45] In the heady period running up to the General Strike, the MM also had significant support in other major unions such as the

Engineering Union (AEU) and in many of the smaller ones like Purcell's NAFTA.[46] As it was providing much energising support to the TUC's efforts, all was 'sweetness and light'. 'The TUC Lefts', including Citrine, had taken the TUC and the unions onto a parallel militant and hazardous path as the far left wanted.

As soon as 'the line' from Moscow changed, however, the MM became a menace. Now it led the recriminations in the trade unions over the 'betrayal' of the miners by the TUC. It began to campaign around the slogan 'Change Your Leaders' and attempted to exert 'influence in determining the official leadership and policies of the Trade Unions'.[47] Its activities began to cause considerable concern in the unions.[48] Evidence was emerging of secretive caucus activities in all unions. Copies of MM instructions to its delegates were found at many union conferences. Characteristically, Citrine gathered all the evidence together in a detailed dossier, which he published in his own name in *The Labour Magazine* late in 1927. He wrote,

> After two years of careful thought, observation and mature deliberation, I am convinced that it is the duty of all who have a sincere concern for the welfare of the trade union and Labour movement to abandon a negative attitude towards this problem of communist propaganda, and to make up their minds positively on the question of whether the cancer of Communist influence is to be allowed to grow.[49]

This was a very brave and controversial thing to do as general secretary. He was obviously having difficulty getting some left-wing union leaders to accept that the left-sounding MM activists should be exposed as communists. The communists, though a tiny force in the Labour movement of Britain, had an international dimension which was quite formidable, i.e., the Moscow-controlled and -funded Communist International, with its Red International of Labour Unions (RILU) offshoot. However, with strong support from the likes of Ernest Bevin and many other senior union leaders, Citrine's lead was followed by the General Council. It republished his *Labour Magazine* articles in 1928 as a pamphlet entitled, *Democracy or Disruption? – An Examination of Communist Influences in the Trade Unions.*[50] Now, 'the gloves were off' domestically as 'a definite and organized opposition within the unions faced the existing leadership'.[51] This led to a decision to launch a full-scale TUC committee inquiry in the unions, at the 1928 Swansea Congress.[52] This report fully endorsed Citrine's claims and recommended strong union action to counter the influence of the MM.[53] Previously, at the 1927 Edinburgh Congress the TUC had carried a strong denunciation of the Minority Movement by a crushing majority card vote (3,746,000 to 148,000).[54]

The National Minority Movement claimed to be just 'a ginger group' in the trade unions. However, in its reports to the Communist International Executive, it took full credit, as 'the biggest thing the Communist Party has done in Britain has been to inspire the creation of the Minority Movement. We are able in Britain for the first time … actually to move the workers …'[55] Its activities had convinced Citrine that it was 'definitely a disruptive force, inspired, assisted, or even completely controlled by Communist organizations, both within and outside this country'.[56] Citrine made it clear that he did not believe that most of the MM active members were involved in such plotting and he urged that the trade union leaders should be tolerant of differing views and militancy as such. In his revealing personal memoir, Arthur Horner, who had been an Executive Committee member of the CPGB since 1920, confirmed that 'The

Bureau of the R.I.L.U., together ... took a major part in the formation of the Minority Movement, and in its early work.'[57] It was just 'a subsidiary of the Communist Party', as some other communists had admitted.[58] Roderick Martin's study of the National Minority Movement concluded that it 'was an uneasy alliance between the Communist International and the extreme left-wing of the British trade union movement'.[59] This suggests that Citrine underestimated its 'home-grown' dimension.[60] But there could be no doubt about his claim that the communists aimed to make the MM a rival leadership of the British Trade Union Movement. If they had succeeded, it could only have split the British TUC, just as it had in Germany and the rest of the European Labour movement. Arthur Horner again made it clear that 'we were looking for ways to impose the organized power of the rank and file on the leaders of the Movement'.[61]

The first MM conference in 1924 attracted 270 delegates, claiming to represent about a quarter of a million union members.[62] Before the General Strike, such gatherings were not viewed with suspicion by the union leadership, as their criticism of the TUC was then muted.[63] By March 1926, with the publication of the Samuel Report, the MM could muster a conference of 883 delegates. It claimed to represent a million union members in rejecting the Samuel Report in its entirety. That policy was adopted by the Miners' Federation, preventing it from effective negotiations with the TUC General Council's team. With the leaders of the CPGB locked up in October 1925,[64] Horner was in charge of the Industrial Department of the party and he was prominent at that MM conference. He directed the CPGB efforts from his base in Mardy in the Rhondda (known as 'Little Moscow'), mainly by telephone, as the authorities were monitoring his movements.[65] Even in September and October he was calling for an intensification of the miners' strike. The South Wales Miners' Federation ('The Fed') supported him, and although there were signs that the strike was crumbling in some districts (Nottinghamshire), he managed to get the majority of the Miners' Federation executive lined up to intensify the strike in October. By 4 November, when the miners' delegate conference (including Arthur Cook) was mostly 'in favour of finding ways to calling off the strike', Horner and the MM urged them to stay out.[66] Even his South Wales Fed colleagues (including Aneurin Bevan) were for giving up and agreeing to negotiations district by district to get what terms they could. In the end, even Horner had to acknowledge that they were beaten. Following this 'unconditional defeat', the miners and their union would suffer the consequences.[67]

Horner's case epitomises the deep grip that the communist philosophy had on such men of considerable courage and character. Citrine described him and Pollitt as 'inherently decent fellows', 'except when Communist dogma bemused them'. Citrine's main charge was that 'the use which Communists are to make of these organizations is plainly to foment disruption'.[68] In his pamphlet, Citrine described the 'methods of working' of the MM. Although it elected a National Executive at its annual conference, he claimed that it was the 'working bureau' it appointed, 'which is the real executive organ'.[69] The National Executive on which sat 'the innocents', i.e., leading left-wing trade unionists and officials, did not control things, he maintained. 'That must be understood as fundamental.'[70] He argued that the pretence was maintained that it was they who were 'forcing upon a reluctant official [union] element' their programme of 'demands' – such as nationalisation of all utilities, banks and land, 'without compensation'. He produced extracts from the minutes of a meeting in 1924 of the Comintern bureau in Moscow dealing with the CPGB's work in the unions. It was about

how the communist nucleus[71] in a factory should secretly influence all other bodies, preferably using an 'influential non-party
skilled worker', as the most effective means. Citrine regarded 'the
nucleus' as the key to communist influence. 'Look for the communist nucleus' was his rule in spotting their operation 'surrounded by
innocents'. How the nucleus is to be enlarged and groups formed
'was all carefully prescribed from Moscow'.[72] He next describes the
time and effort put in by the MM into grooming delegates who
had been selected in union branches to attend policy-making union
conferences. This was a very intensive exercise and he surmised
that 'a great deal of time and money must be spent in coordinating
their work'. The 'sinister feature about the whole business is, that
the *principles* governing the instructions are ... definitely laid down
at the Conferences of the Red International in Moscow'.[73]

Turning to specific cases, he now pointed to the MM attacks on
miners' leaders, such as Herbert Smith. Things had turned around
in the Miners' Federation. The extreme tactics of the MM and
CPGB prevented last-ditch attempts at salvaging some settlement,
after five months of ineffective striking. Horner's hardline approach
– he quarreled even with his 'closest confidant' Arthur Cook (by then
'a broken man').[74] As a result, splits had developed, for example, in
Scotland, and the Miners' Federation had become highly critical
of the Miners' MM generally.[75] The Miners' 1928 Conference
resolved by 620,200 to 8,000 to place on record its 'strong condem-
nation of the Communists and the Minority Movement'.[76] In what
must have been a heartfelt personal note, Citrine described how the
Communist Party and the MM treated opposition.

They carry on a continuous campaign of innuendo and insin-
uation which leaves him no redress. The dissemination of

half-truths, distortion of facts and imputation of improper motive as part of the stock-in-trade of the exponents of the Communist cult. Many of the best types who have belonged to the Communist Party in this country have become disgusted and severed their connections with that body.[77]

Was Citrine overreacting to 'the nuisance but not really danger-ous' influence of the communists inside the trade unions? They were always a tiny party scattered around the country, concentrated in the mining districts and some engineering plants. Citrine had concluded that 'it was a menace which must be faced' and a 'cancer' which must not be allowed to grow. 'I knew that their disruptive tactics had split the trade union movement in several European countries, leaving it weak and its members confused and disillusioned.'[78]

Was he right? The best judges were, of course, his fellow trade unionists. He had the full support of Ernest Bevin and most other union leaders, who were experiencing similar MM attacks in their own unions.[79] Across the Labour and trade union movements, the activities of the Minority Movement and the CPGB were condemned and most now moved to isolate them. Action was taken against MM militants in the AEU, the Boot & Shoe Operatives, the Boilermakers, Iron & Steel Workers, Distributive Workers, General & Municipal, NUR, Painters, Shop Assistants, Tailor & Garment workers and the T&GWU.[80] As a result, 'the "political culture" of the trade union movement became increasingly anti-Communist and anti-MM' for a decade.[81] It was not a 'right-wing' union intol-erance or a theoretical rebuttal of a philosophical trend. They were just seen as a Moscow-inspired disruptive and divisive element.

With the release of the Comintern archives in the 1990s, it was disclosed that an International Lenin School was set up in Moscow in 1926 as 'a university of revolution'. While it was not focused exclusively on the trade unions, they would have been a prime target. They were trained 'not just in Marxist Leninist theory, but also the basics of party organization as well as how to acquire the skills a practical revolutionary might need ...'[82] Another study by sympathetic academics revealed that 'about 150 alumni of that Lenin School' became 'the most extreme of the intrusions by the Third International, the Comintern ... of trained, responsive and carefully vetted cohort of revolutionary activists.'[83]

Such tactics succeeded in other European countries, especially Germany (though it was only one factor there, as Citrine explained, as we will see). But the united British union centre led by Citrine, working closely with the union leaderships, 'nipped it in the bud' in Britain in 1928–29. The Minority Movement was isolated and shrank. Even the Communist International admitted in 1935 that

> the most glaring example of sectarianism in the trade union movement was provided in Great Britain where ... the Communists adopted such clumsy and sectarian tactics that the Minority Movement actually fell to pieces ... These mistakes were aggravated by the fact that the Communists regarded the Minority Movement as the germ of new trade unions.[84]

As a result, they were 'entirely isolated from the trade union movement, and the Minority Movement collapsed'.[85] *The Manchester Guardian* published the CPGB membership list which confirmed that it had about 10,000 in 1921 and 6,000 in 1926, then declining steadily to about 2,500 in 1930.[86] This extraordinary episode in the history of the British trade union movement has not been much dwelt on by labour historians, perhaps because it seemed illiberal to highlight such abuses by 'progressive' forces. But it is clear that Citrine and the union leaders were absolutely right to expose and defeat this attempt at a takeover/split.

Citrine's publication of *Democracy or Disruption?* must be considered a watershed in his relations with the left. Clearly, he was undergoing a major change in outlook due to his experience of the General Strike and relations with the Russian unions. He had always had serious ideological reservations about Marxism and its 'class war' and the Leninist 'dictatorship of the proletariat' doctrine (see Chapter 10). Yet he distinguished between 'Russian communists faced with real problems, and the irresponsible advocacy of world revolution by the British communists operating under the instructions of the Comintern'.[87] But now, as his pamphlet drew their fire onto himself, he would endure the strongest attacks and misrepresentation on the left for the remainder of his union and Labour movement career. Citrine believed that 'Scarcely had the first article appeared than the hounds were in full cry and I was assailed with all the standardized abuse which the Communists were able to organize.'[88] He also complained that 'no innuendo, no aspersion, no abuse was too scurrilous to be hurled at me'.[89] He was 'the subject of repeated attacks' in *The Worker*, *Workers' Life* and *The Sunday Worker*. He 'stood this for a long time', not wishing to be 'charged with trying to interfere with the right to free expression by suing them in the courts'. In February/March 1928 they accused him of (among other things) having the assistance of 'documents from Scotland Yard' and having been 'supplied by Government spies' for his *Democracy or Disruption?* articles. In fact, those documents were freely available, as the Home Office published them after the Arcos Raid in 1927.[90] Citrine now felt that he had no choice but to sue the communist press and their printers and publishers. The printers of both papers 'publicly apologized, dissociating themselves from any attacks on my honesty or integrity', which he accepted.[91] However, the company which owned the papers, Workers Publications Ltd, after a shareholders' meeting, transferred the assets to 'friends of the movement' and ceased publication. His legal advisers informed him that there was no person against whom he could obtain a judgement and he had to give up on those actions, though 'the attacks on me did not ease off'. Bevin was awarded the substantial figure of £7,000 damages from the publisher of the Workers Press for libel, but again he didn't receive a penny from them.[92] *The Daily Worker* appeared in 1930, initially as 'the official organ of the Communist Party', though it soon dropped that from the masthead and it continued the tradition of publishing distortive and libelous material about Citrine and the TUC leaders (see Chapter 13). It usually had to retract and apologise after a successful libel action by Citrine. And so it would continue. As we shall see, hostilities were renewed against Citrine following the publication of his *I Search for Truth in Russia* in 1936.

We see then how Citrine had changed his attitude to communists in the short time between his first visit to the Soviet Union in 1925 and 1927. From seeing them in 'not unfriendly' terms to being a 'cancer' in the Labour movement, was he articulating the views of most unionists? Certainly, this reflected the views of the trade union leaderships facing MM attacks and attempts to replace them. Their isolation was helped by the ultra-sectarian 'Class against Class' propaganda of the international communist movement, which categorized the union and labour leaders as 'social fascists', as we will see in Chapter 10.

CHAPTER 7

~

'ABOVE THE LAW'?

I always had a hankering after legal knowledge … Eventually
I felt competent to hold my own in the rough-and-tumble of
discussion with employers.[1]

British labour law is among the most complex and challenging
issues trade unionists have to contend with. But as it goes to the
heart of the labour contract and the dynamic activity of workers'
combining to exert their rights, their officers must give it a lot of
attention. Citrine seems to have had a keen interest in the law
affecting industrial relations and unions from his earliest studies.
Early on, he made it his business to master this subject, devouring
the Webbs' classics *History of Trade Unionism* and *Industrial Democracy*.[2] His defiant attitude to the trade disputes and trade unions bill
1927, when it was thought that the government was vindictively
reintroducing the pre-1906 restrictions on trade disputes, is more
than apparent.

The Trade Union movement is not, in the twentieth century,
going to be debarred by the attempt to limit its effective power
by legislation. The Trade Union movement has no evidence of

any machinery which can stifle a body of men exercising the legitimate purpose of ceasing work.[3]

To illustrate this defiant attitude, he gave the students an instance of a case he had conducted during the war. He had coached 500 shipyard electricians, who had struck unofficially for a day and were arraigned in a Liverpool court. He got them off by encouraging all 500 to leave work for another day and attend the court personally.[4]

Even in the days of the Parliamentary Committee, the TUC had a strong tradition of effective lobbying, since the time of the union legal reforms of the 1870s (which Citrine called 'the *Charter of British Trade Unionism*'[5]). In that case, they helped persuade a Gladstonian Liberal administration to ignore the majority report of the Erle Royal Commission of 1869.[6] Instead, with the Trade Union Act of 1871,

Citrine preparing a report at Transport House, 1945. He left numerous files on the Trade Disputes and Trade Unions Act.

that government granted unions charged with being 'in restraint of trade' their first protections from the unsympathetic common law rulings of judges.[7] As a result, unions came to be recognised as semi-corporate bodies, able to enter into normal commercial contracts, while not being liable to be sued for actions of their members and officials during strikes. The stain of criminal conspiracy was removed and some forms of peaceful communication with non-strikers, i.e., picketing, were allowed. However, these protections were whittled away again by judicial activism in the 1890s.[8] So, again in 1906, the Parliamentary Committee helped persuade another Gladstonian Liberal prime minister, Sir Henry Campbell-Bannerman (1836–1908), to overrule his Cabinet colleagues in favour of a more radical TUC-sponsored trade disputes bill.[9] It was the background Citrine studied carefully so as to guide the TUC in its advice and assistance to all unions throughout his career.[10]

The best illustration of how the law could impact on the activities of the trade unions was the *Taff Vale* House of Lords' judgement of 1901.[11] This was a case brought by a South Wales coal-supplying railway firm of that name, against the Society of Railway Servants (ASRS, predecessor of the National Union of Railwaymen and today's Rail and Maritime Transport Union, RMT). There were extremely poor labour relations in the company, with an aggressive manager facing an equally militant left-wing union organiser. It led to an unofficial strike, which the union headquarters didn't know about until the company took legal action. The general secretary, Richard Bell MP (1859–1930), then a very respected Lib-Lab union leader, tried to escape liability by withholding official approval for the strike, but he was overruled by his executive in London. The strike turned violent when the manager imported replacement labour, which led to 'robust' picketing, arrests and imprisonment.[12]

This was the sharp end of industrial relations – most strikes being peacefully conducted under the control of union officials. Most employers would settle disputes in a compromise, and everybody would go back to work. Not so the Taff Vale Railway Company's aggressive manager, who took legal action and pursued the union for huge damages for the losses. To everyone's surprise and shock, the House of Lords allowed it and awarded an enormous sum, which, with costs and other expenses, came to £41,893 in all (equivalent to nearly £5 million today). This, the Society of Railway Servants (ASRS) had to pay – equivalent to a year's income for the union.[13] This infamous judgement would have enormous consequences. The case also highlights the frail control unions have as voluntary associations during strikes, in the exercise of their authority over defiant lay officials or militant groups of members.[14]

The TUC Parliamentary Committee, then ably led by some formidable union leaders,[15] was the central organiser of the campaign to overturn the Lords' judgement and to strengthen unions' legal protection.[16] This case also spurred the development of a separate political party as the unions poured funds into the infant Labour Representation Committee, which in 1906 became the Labour Party.[17] Their efforts bore fruit with the return of a Liberal government in 1906, committed to reforming the law. The Trade Disputes Act 1906 restored union protections in a most radical fashion, as it restricted judicial intervention in trade disputes signifi-cantly. It laid the foundation for union freedom from prosecution or injunctions for much of the twentieth century. A short five-clause Act, it restored legal protection: i) to acts done 'in contemplation or furtherance of a trade dispute'; ii) to peaceful picketing; iii) against actions for breaches of contract of employment; iv) against injunctions to stop strikes. It made it crystal-clear that such claims 'shall not be entertained by any court', which judges could no longer ignore.[18] Clause V of the Act broadened the definitions of contentious legal words such as 'trade dispute', to prevent hostile judicial interpretation. Such protection would facilitate industrial actions by unions, free from judicial intervention for six decades thereafter. This new legal scenario undoubtedly provided a benign framework of law during the great industrial unrest from 1910 to 1914 and again from 1919 to 1926. It was this complete immunity which raised the accusation that the unions were 'above the law' during strikes. On Merseyside, the young militant Citrine, as chair of the ETU District Committee and as a full-time official from 1914, would avail of that legally uninhibited freedom to strike.

THE EMERGENCY POWERS ACT 1920

It must not be thought, though, that there were no legal inhibitions on union strike activity. There was a general power for government to intervene during disputes affecting 'essential' services or other emergencies: the Emergency Powers Act 1920 (The EPA). This Act gave the government power to declare a state of emergency for a month after a royal proclamation enabling ministers 'to take any steps necessary for the preservation of peace, for securing or regulating the supply of food and other necessaries (e.g. water, fuel or light also) for maintaining transport ... and for any other purpose vital to public safety'.[19] Citrine kept a copy in his desk and a note explaining that Act's origins and significance.[20] The EPA was enacted after the war-time Defence of the Realm Act (DORA) lapsed, to deal with protracted large-scale strikes affecting essential services, such as the national rail strike of 1919.[21] It gave ministers power 'to take possession of land, to commandeer goods, to arrest without warrant, to proscribe meetings and generally to control conduct'.[22] It was used during the big coal strike of 1921, when it was feared that the threat of Triple Alliance action would halt all coal transport. As we saw, MacDonald prepared to invoke it against the dock strike and London tram strike of 1924. It was used extensively during the General Strike of 1926.[23] It was the declaration of an emergency, then, which caused the TUC to issue its precautionary notices of strike action that May.[24]

THE TRADE DISPUTES AND TRADE UNIONS ACT 1927

After the General Strike there was great clamour in Conservative Party and employer circles to ban strikes for the future. Strictly speaking, the General Strike was illegal, as there was no 'trade dispute' between the TUC and the coal owners or government. This had been argued in the Commons' debates, but Baldwin and his Cabinet decided not to make a legal challenge, so as not to give the TUC a focal rallying point.[25] We saw Citrine's view that the strike was called outside the rules of many unions also. After much Cabinet debate, the Baldwin government enacted the Trade Disputes and Trade Unions Act 1927 which made it crystal clear that general or sympathy strikes across more than one industry were illegal. It spelled out that strikes designed or calculated at 'coercing the government' directly or indirectly by 'inflicting hardship on the community' or strikes for political or revolutionary objects were illegal.[26] While this sounds draconian, in reality it was not so. That Act did not repeal the vital Trade Disputes Act 1906 in normal disputes, which was what the main employers' association, the National Confederation of Employers' Organisations

(NCEO), and the Engineering Employers' Federation (EEF) want-ed.[27] Baldwin stopped short of that extremity and 'even Churchill argued that the Bill should be confined ... and should not attempt to deal with picketing or the 1906 Act'.[28] The 1927 Act did restrict picketing further, by redefining 'intimidation', but again fell well short of a ban on peaceful picketing. The attorney general, Sir Douglas Hogg (later Lord Hailsham), was also against making substantial changes as 'the [1906] Act was regarded by all Trade Unionists as their magna carta'.[29] In the end, the Cabinet 'finally desisted from tampering with the 1906 Act'.[30] However, to satisfy Conservative Party and employer outrage about the General Strike, they tacked on a 'hodgepodge' of other anti-union and anti-Labour Party measures to their bill. These changed the onus for payment of the political levy by union members and banned civil, public and local government staff unions from affiliating to the TUC and the Labour Party. This latter provision was thought to be a reaction by Conservative MPs to postal workers' involve-ment in the strike.

Historians still differ in their opinions about the significance of the 1927 Act,[31] but there is no doubt how trade unionists and the Labour Party saw it at the time. Citrine did a number of seminars in its campaign against the Act, as part of his organisation of 'the most comprehensive defence campaign ... within my trades union experience'.[32] At the Ruskin seminar, he highlighted 'the looseness of the language used' in the Act, which the Labour Party had been advised would enable hostile judicial interpretation against any strike.[33] At the same seminar, Sir Henry Slesser KC MP, the TUC legal adviser, took members through all the potential risk areas and vague wording, and reminded them of Arthur Henderson MP's Commons' debate comment:[34]

I have to warn you that this Bill ... will, in many respects, cripple the activities of the Trade Unions and what is more important, the basic right of individual citizens in which that freedom has not been crippled since the repeal of the Combination Acts just 100 years ago.[35]

Henderson was not normally given to such overstatement, but, as secretary of the Labour Party, he was probably genuinely worried that it would weaken union funding dramatically. It did so in some unions but most improved their administrative systems to mitigate those losses.[36] The TUC also lost the significant affiliation fees of the public service unions' 130,000 members. So Citrine, in full flow at the Ruskin College conference of 9 April in London, had every reason to denounce the bill. He really did wind up the union students there. At one conference, he said, 'Not since the repeal of the Combination Laws has the Labour Movement been faced with such a serious menace.'[37]

The impressive scale of the Trade Union Defence Committee (TUDC) campaign showed how concerned the General Council was about this bill. George Hicks chaired the National Trade Union Defence Committee, whose members included Alf Purcell MP, Alonso Swales, Ben Tillett and Ben Turner, with Citrine as joint secretary.[38] They divided the country into nine regions, making full-time officers responsible in each region, working with Labour Party counterparts (whose salaries the unions funded). In all, more than 1,150 meetings and demonstrations were organised, with one 'monster' demo on 26 June in London's Hyde Park as the bill went through Parliament. It was said to be 'the largest which has been held in the history of the Labour Movement'. A bugle was sounded at 5 p.m., after many speeches, and a Trade Union Covenant was read as a signal for 'tens of thousands of workers to raise their

right hands pledging themselves to stand by' the covenant.[39] The
TUC published twenty-seven leaflets and distributed 19 million of
them. It also printed *The British Worker* again, in 'the most expensive campaign that the Labour movement had ever undertaken'.[40]
Citrine was very active in this campaign and frequently just took
questions at his lively summer school sessions. He showed an
impressive grasp of this complex bill.[41]

Though that TUC campaign was to no avail in preventing or
seriously modifying the bill, the feelings it aroused were not wasted.
Firstly, it united the unions who had been demoralised by the defeat
of the General Strike and the bitter recriminations after it from
the miners, the communists and the Minority Movement. We saw
how the TUC leadership rallied once the Special Conference in
January 1927 had roundly defeated Cook and his supporters in the
unions. So, the campaign against the bill also helped in this respect.
It showed the government and the employers that the unions were
still a force and that any general onslaught on wages would still be
resisted. Finally, it restored the unity of both wings of the Labour
movement as the campaign focused on getting a Labour government which would repeal the Act. This seemed to bear fruit with
the return of a Labour government in June 1929, committed to
total repeal of that Act.[42]

In practice, the effect of the 1927 Act was far less serious than
feared. It established beyond doubt the illegality of general strikes
and sympathetic strikes in more than one industry and restricted
'intimidatory' picketing. Hardly any cases were brought, or injunctions obtained, by 1931 as regards 'ordinary' strikes about specific
industrial disputes. This had been the great fear of Citrine and the
union leaders.[43] A more sober Ernie Bevin later said that the Act
was 'more of an insult than an injury'.[44]

The Labour government of 1929–31 was elected on a manifesto pledge to repeal the Act in its entirety. But, because it did not have a majority in Parliament, decided instead to amend it, while keeping the general and sympathy strike illegality clause of the 1927 Act. This botched attempt (see Chapter 9) alienated the unions, who asked for the bill to be dropped. Interestingly, in view of their dependence on the Liberals, Citrine realised earlier on that they would not get the desired repeal and instead pressed for their other measures. He told the government, 'Now, you ought to bring in another Bill … In my opinion I would much prefer to see the Washington Convention [on maximum forty-eight hours per week] passed into law because of its international effects, if I had to make my choice of the two. … If we thought the Liberals would back a simple Bill, I would back it.'[45] The government did bring in an Hours of Industrial Employment bill[46] and also Factory and Workmen's Compensation ones, but these fell with the government in May 1931.

The 1927 Trade Disputes Act remained a source of serious union grievance over the next decade, with the really annoying features being the ban on civil service and public service unions affiliating to the TUC and Labour Party. Conservative Party resistance remained adamant, especially to reversing the onus of members' political contributions, for obvious party reasons.[47]

Citrine continued to raise the issue of amending the Act with governments at every opportunity. For example, he raised it with the new prime minister, Churchill, and the coalition government in September 1941 and it was discussed in the Cabinet.[48] At its suggestion, Churchill consulted the Conservative Party informally and the Liberals, but they were opposed even to reform of it.[49] A year later, Citrine raised it once more with Churchill, but he replied in the negative, pleading the 'critical period in the war'.[50]

Though disappointed that the spirit of coalition did not extend to civil and public servants' rights, Citrine and the TUC were not minded to bring down the coalition government over the issue. In 1943, the civil service (the clerks mainly) and postal worker unions (UPW) again pressed their grievance, lobbying Churchill directly for exemption to enable them to affiliate to the TUC at the least. However, Churchill insisted on enforcing the law, which, if defied, would remove civil service status with the loss of their pensions. The postal workers (UPW) were threatening to go ahead and seek affiliation, to which the TUC was minded to agree. Citrine had a very 'testy' meeting with Labour leader and deputy prime minister Clement Attlee in August 1943. Citrine pressed the Labour ministers in the government (Attlee, Bevin and Morrison and many more junior ministers) not to follow Churchill's threat in their own departments. He even told Attlee that it 'raised the question as to whether they should continue in the Government or not' (though it is hard to believe he was serious). However, Attlee, as deputy prime minister, refused to confront the Tories over the minor amendment sought, or to make an issue of it between the coalition partners – perhaps a first sign of Attlee's resistance to union demands, as he also had Bevin's support.[51]

So, the hated Act remained on the statute book intact, until the return of the majority Labour government after the war. The Act became one of the first issues that the TUC addressed, and so strong was the pro-union mood of the Labour Party that the government agreed to repeal the entire 1927 Act in August 1946, so restoring the full Trade Disputes Act 1906 immunities position.[52] Bevin now took full credit as 'the instrument by which the obnoxious Trade Disputes and Trade Unions Act 1927 was removed from the Statute Book in August 1946.'[53]

CHAPTER 8

~

COMING TO TERMS
WITH CAPITALISM

For the first time in history, the representatives of organized labour have been invited to meet a group of important industrialists to discuss the financial and management of industry. Things like the status and security of workers and methods of achieving the highest possible standards of living for all.

Ernest Bevin, 17 February 1927[1]

Bullock acknowledged that it was 'Bevin and Citrine who supplied the driving force on the trade union side from the beginning'.[2] This was indeed a remarkable turnaround, just a year after the unions shut down their industries and the employers clamoured for legislation to curtail union power. There had been 'soundings' of senior union leaders such as Ernest Bevin by leading employers like Lord Muir, inspired, it is said, by top officials in the Ministry of Labour.[3] However, the first public indication of what was afoot came in an article by the TUC general secretary for *The Manchester Guardian* in November 1927, entitled 'The Next Step in Industrial Relations'.[4] Citrine had previously trailed the idea through George Hicks, that year's TUC president, at the Edinburgh Congress. Hicks' address struck a more cooperative note and the reaction from the delegates was not unfavourable.[5] The 'Next Step' article spelt out in much greater detail what Citrine had in mind.

> Trade unionism has reached the end of a definite stage of evolution … It has become a power in the land, with a growing consciousness of purpose, to which increased responsibilities and obligations cannot fail to be attached.[6]

This was a very new way of putting things. The General Strike itself had in a sense demonstrated that power, but negatively, but now Citrine wanted to exercise it positively. He saw 'the next stage in the evolution of trade unionism' as a planned development, taking on more 'functions it is capable of exercising in the economic life of the country'. His article addressed changes taking place in industry 'in conditions of fierce international competition for markets'. It was called the rationalisation of industry with its guiding principles being standardised products, simplified processes, scientific planning of workshops, labour-saving machinery, improved technique of management.[7] But these were all happening without reference to the wage-earners who were the most affected by them. Citrine said that 'Up to then, unions had served … in bringing questions of wages, hours and conditions to an agreed settlement and reducing friction and conflict.' Now, however, they should 'assume much more important functions than those they have hitherto discharged'.[8] These would include the methods of wage determination and the system of unemployment insurance. Existing practices on 'the employment and dismissal of workers will be modified …'[9]

Citrine argued that as long as workers are allowed to remain under the impression that they have little to gain either materially or in status by the introduction of methods and measures designed to promote greater efficiency and economy, why should they bother? But if union co-operation could be secured through adequate safeguards,

> unions should actively participate in a concerted effort to raise industry to its highest efficiency by developing the most scientific methods of production, eliminating waste and harmful restrictions, removing causes of friction and avoidable conflict, and promoting the highest possible output so as to provide a rising standard of life and continuously improving conditions of employment.[10]

Citrine and his TUC team had been developing this new outlook for some time as he always questioned the Marxist conclusion that workers, standards could not be improved under capitalism.[11] It wasn't a new thought. The system of Joint Industrial Committees which sprung up after the First World War, known as 'Whitleyism',[12] were initially expected to develop into a similar broad forum for joint industrial relations generally, like the Mond-Turner National Industrial Council proposal. Whitley Councils did encourage wage bargaining in a large number of industries. We saw this in the electrical contracting and related industries from 1919, during Citrine's time as a District and National ETU officer.

These ideas would again not have got off the ground in the late 1920s but for an important development on the employers' side. The TUC received an invitation to talks in November 1927 from an informal but very representative group of twenty-four employers, led by Sir Alfred Mond of the chemicals' giant Imperial Chemical Industries (ICI).[13] Ben Turner (1863–1942), a veteran of the once buoyant textile industry workers and an MP, was TUC president that year and so this engagement became known as the Mond-Turner talks.[14] Citrine listed the standing of the signatories with 'directorships in 189 companies … 98 chairmen of those companies; 2 past presidents, 6 vice-presidents', as well as the chairman and past chairman of the National Confederation of Employers Organisations (NCEO).[15] These were the 'top brass' of most of the large companies in Britain at the time, but, significantly, the gathering did not include the operational directors or the NCEO as a body. Still, the impressive list was 'able to speak with authority as to the powers of their organisations'.[16] Citrine asked the NCEO to take part officially, but it declined. He learned that it was strongly opposed to any discussions of broader questions of industrial organisation, finance, technique and management with trade unions. This was due to objections from the Engineering Employers' Federation (EEF)'s key figure, Sir Alan Smith, and so the NCEO was deeply divided on how it should respond.[17] Citrine regarded Smith as the main obstacle, 'an expert on procrastination, whose icy-cold speeches were enough to freeze to death any warm impulses towards progress which his members might feel'.[18] Citrine believed that Smith was 'threatening even to break it [the NCEO] up', if it did join the talks.[19]

Mond/Muir and his employer colleagues hoped to gain union support for the rationalisations that were occurring following mergers at ICI, British Oxygen, Dunlops, Courtaulds, Richard Thomas and Dorman Long in the face of American and Japanese competition on the world market.[20] There was also a resentment of the 'parasitical' role of the banking and City system, which industry and the unions shared.[21] The General Council overwhelmingly agreed to enter the talks, despite the vocal opposition of a few, such as Arthur Cook, and the engineering union leadership. The very left-led

AEU's executive was totally opposed to what it saw as 'cross-class collaboration'.[22] Cook published a pamphlet called *Mond Moonshine* with James Maxton MP, the leader of the now far-left Independent Labour Party, but this proved a 'damp squib'.[23] Moreover, the Miners' Federation leadership disclaimed Cook's publication after a remarkable shift of opinion at its Llandudno conference the previous July.[24] It now strongly supported the talks. Cook was also condemned by the TUC General Council for the pamphlet, which it claimed was 'full of inaccuracy, misrepresentations and deliberate falsehoods ... obviously written for the purpose of discrediting and damaging the prestige and authority of the General Council.'[25] Citrine thought that the booklet had been financed by the CP or the MM.[26] Remarkably, Herbert Smith bemoaned its lost opportunity to refuse an offer of industrial participation in 1920.[27] Ironically, the AEU now led the opposition within the unions as well as Smith in the EEF/NCEO.[28]

THE MOND-TURNER REPORTS

The TUC leaders held a series of very constructive meetings with the Mond group, the first on 12 January 1928, to discuss a range of topics. These included the rational organisation of industry and trade, amalgamations, security and status of the workers, housing, health and unemployment insurance and so on.[29] An interim report was produced in July 1928, and this was expanded into a series of resolutions, including an agreed recommendation supporting union recognition, union representation and opposing victimisation. The main proposal was to set up a National Industrial Council for regular periodic discussions of broad industrial issues by representative employers and unions, with Joint Conciliation Boards machinery to resolve disputes. Although many employers 'did not agree with a word of this', especially the repudiation of victimisation, it was some achievement to get so many top industrialists to do so, laying the ground for better industrial relations in the future. [30] This progress was reported by Citrine to the Swansea Congress in September 1928. Opening the debate, he said that 'it was desirable to avoid extravagance of optimism or pessimism as to what would happen', but it was encouraging that so many employers had agreed to talk with them. This was itself also an indication of public support, he said. He had justified the talks on the grounds of the trade union movement's long-held ambition to gain 'a voice in the control and administration of industry'. [31] By engaging, unions would be 'raising the status, security and standard of living of the workers'. [32] There followed a long debate on a hostile amendment from the AEU. It challenged the General Council's authority even to enter such discussions with 'unrepresentative' employers, let alone agree joint proposals. [33] Citrine responded that the 'tendency to endow the General Council with increasing authority has been unmistakable'. [34] If nothing else, the Mond-Turner initiative reinforced the TUC's standing in handling such matters on behalf of all unions.

The opposition put up its strongest team – Brownlie, Swales, Hicks (who had been 'got at' in his own AUBTW) and Cook. But Bevin, in responding to the debate for the General Council, now rammed home its rationale for engaging in the talks – the historic opportunity for unions to discuss the financing and management of industry. 'These are things the Trade Union Movement had been claiming for years to have some voice in, and for years it has been denied that voice.' [35] Bevin dealt with the AEU's objections, which centred on the proposal for the National Industrial Council. He chided its president, J. T. Brownlie, that his speech 'was awfully near that of Allan Smith' and 'the attitude adopted by the Engineering Employers' Federation'. That was a telling point. Bevin insisted, 'we have an organic body known as the Trades Union Congress. Its representatives are the General Council.'[36] Here Bevin was confirming the TUC (and Citrine)'s new-found authority and status in his eyes.

Now Bevin balanced his well-known view that the General Strike had been a disaster ('we have committed suicide'[37]) with a new assessment.

> A challenge is being made by the movement for more power.
> The fight went on right through the post-war period, one side
> trying to drive us back to conditions worse than 1914. I have
> claimed from the beginning, and I have never apologized for it,
> that the general strike was a culminating point of that conflict
> that had been going on for power, and in view of this invitation
> and subsequent development if it was not all that we desired it
> proved that we had not lost the fight after all.[38]

He had come around to Citrine's point of view. Following Bevin's closing speech, the General Council report was adopted by an overwhelming majority.[39] The Citrine–Bevin double act was now fully on show. Their remarkable cohesion, yet slight personal rapport, was in evidence.

The final joint gathering of the Mond-Turner conference in March 1929 focused especially on the rapidly deteriorating unemployment problem. Between a tenth and an eighth of the insured industrial population (over 2 million at one time) were out of work.[40] Events had overtaken their bold initiative. Despite overwhelming TUC support for the agreed report, a divided NCEO, on reporting back the proposals to its constituent employers, got a pretty hostile response. Articles began to appear in employer trade journals attacking the National Industrial Council and Joint Conciliation Boards proposals. Soon after the March interim report, the talks were 'suspended'. The employer organisations did, however, agree to meet the TUC in informal joint consultations on a regular basis from 1930 onwards.[41] This would set the pattern for the 1930s, despite the onset of the Great Depression. The Mond-Turner talks had 'broken the ice' in employer–union relations and would create the foundations for such 'corporate' liaison in the future.

THE CITRINE–BEVIN PARTNERSHIP

This may also be a useful moment to take stock of the extraordinary emerging 'involuntary partnership'[42] between two remarkable union leaders. The one, Ernest Bevin, from Somerset, a former carter and dock union official, was now leader of the very large and assertive Transport and General Workers' Union (T&GWU). He was 'a man swarthy of countenance and square of jaw, with the shoulders and chest of a heavyweight all-in wrestler'.[43] We have noticed his emergence as a tough 'union boss' in Chapters 4 and 5. The other, Walter Citrine, the tall but slim former electricians' union national officer from Merseyside, was now established as leader of the TUC. They had first met in Glasgow at the 1919 TUC Congress, when Bevin complimented Citrine on his maiden speech in support of the police strike. The two men arrived almost at the same time on the General Council in October 1925, though by different routes. They soon clashed openly there over Citrine's defence of his head of research, Walter Milne-Bailey. Bevin had 'brutally attacked' Milne-Bailey for publishing an article about the General Strike in an American journal, with which Bevin did not agree.[44] Faced with Citrine raising the issue on the General Council, Bevin stormed out, muttering that 'the Secretary has the knife in for me'.[45] Yet Bevin did not hold that against Citrine when it came to his nomination and election for general secretary at the September 1926 Congress. He said he had been impressed by Citrine's standing up to Arthur Cook and the miners' leaders during the General Strike, admitting that 'Citrine has courage. That has decided where our vote for the secretaryship will go.'[46] This shows Bevin in a better light, as he was generally thought to hold grudges for a long time. Nevertheless, Citrine always believed

Bevin with Citrine in 1937, 'an involuntary partnership'.

that this was the beginning of their difficulties. As general secretary and most influential union leader on the General Council respectively, they never seem to have hit it off. Citrine added, 'I was antagonized by Bevin's utmost bumptious habit of arrogating to himself the work of other men.'[47] He later concluded that Bevin 'genuinely imagined that he was exclusively responsible for most of the proposals and schemes he put forward. This was very irritating but was completely over-balanced by the creative character of his thinking.'[48] In reviewing Bullock's first volume in 1960, Citrine returned to this flaw: 'he would lead his hearers to believe that he was the author of work which had been prepared by others … it was invariably "I" and never "we".'[49] For all that, in the eyes of the public and those of their General Council and Congress colleagues, 'their combination of talents in pushing a policy through the TUC was invincible'.[50] It is particularly difficult to disentangle responsibility for union decisions altogether, as they tend to be part of a collective process and pool into which many streams flow. Bullock concluded of Citrine and Bevin's very different but 'unusually complementary' skills:

> Bevin was always conscious that Citrine was different from other elected General Council members. Even though Citrine's union pedigree was considerable, he came from a small, but important *craft* power production union.[51]

Citrine's electrical engineers were a very different group of workers from Bevin's much more general workers in docks and transport. Nor did the two have much in common as individuals. Although both were from humble backgrounds and had left school early to come into the trade unions through socialist

ideological influences, their cultural hinterlands were very different. As Citrine observed,

> We were different in many ways. Bevin read practically nothing
> about trade union theory or economics. He didn't need to. His
> native intelligence and flair taught him many things that were
> not to be found in textbooks or in dogma of economic theorists.
> He had great drive and a measure of ruthlessness which I did not
> possess. He was subjective in practically all he did: he person-
> alized almost everything ... He had a good reasoning mind but
> he also had flashes of insight which bordered on inspiration.[52]

Citrine wasn't at all religious, while one of Bevin's formative influences had been as a Baptist pulpiteer. You could never
imagine Bevin playing a cornet in a brass band. Nonetheless, he
would develop strong middle-class tastes and lifestyle (he drove 'a
big yellow Talbot Darracq', mixed in fashionable showbiz circles
and was a member of the Garrick Club). He married Florence, a
former *Daily Herald* journalist.[53]

Both were absorbed in building and developing huge, complex
organisations and neither had much time to be very 'clubbable'
personally, even if they were so minded. So, from the word go, their
relationship was always akin to that of an elected ('shareholding')
member of the board and the chief executive, engaged to run the
business. As Bullock put it, 'each being a masterful man himself,
accused the other of trying to dominate the General Council.
Citrine looked on his office as ... giving him a unique claim to
represent the views of the trade union movement. Bevin its most
powerful personality, enjoying the independent status of general
secretary of a big union yielded first place to no man.'[54]

In trade unions there is also often a cultural difference between those elected and officers appointed from outside the organisation. Bevin drew his authority from his origins and activity in the powerful 'T&G', as it was known, with its massive block vote (over a million and a quarter by the late 1930s),[55] whose resolutions initiated and shaped policy at TUC Congresses and on the General Council. Citrine had no such base, but, by dint of his ability to manage and speak for the entire General Council and Congress, he derived an eminence and superior authority with the unions, as well as with the outside world.

Inevitably, they were rivals as well as partners and never close, but Bullock and other historians have grasped the secret of their huge success at the TUC – they complemented each other's strengths.[56] Bullock saw 'the combination of Citrine's precise, lawyer-like mastery of the facts to present a case and Bevin's larger, sweeping strokes to sketch a policy proved once again its power to convince a trade-union audience'.[57] There was, of course, much more to Citrine than this, as this study shows, but the key point is their complementarity. In 1928, the TUC would move into Bevin's other creation, the magnificent new six-storey Transport House T&GWU offices in Smith Square, as tenants, round the corner from the Houses of Parliament.[58] This edifice would come to symbolise the Labour movement for much of the twentieth century, also housing the Labour Party and Cooperative Society.

Citrine recalled that despite having adjoining offices in this building, 'the occasions on which Bevin and I discussed policy outside the Council chamber might be counted on one hand, certainly on two'.[59] Yet, almost instinctively, they were in agreement on all the key issues. Looking back, Citrine declared, 'I cannot now recall a single issue of first-class importance on which we seriously differed. On tactics, yes, but not on basic policy.'[60] This coincidence of view must have owed much to Citrine and his high-calibre team of officers' careful examination of all issues before they came to the General Council from the Committee system. It worried Citrine lest 'the rest of the Council members would think that he and I had framed the whole policy together in private discussion'.[61] It was a delicate balancing act to be seen to be independent – his standing up to Bevin over Milne-Bailey in 1926 would have sent the right messages. What brought them together was a shared perception of the potential for the TUC, as Citrine concluded, 'without external collaboration, we worked together to increase the influence of the TUC, to establish its right to consultation in the national sphere, and to make it a centre with power to evolve policy and take decisions on general principles affecting the trade union movement as a whole'.[62]

Always generous with his praise for Bevin, Citrine credited him as 'one of the strongest, if not the strongest, personal forces in the trade union movement'.[63] Yet he also noted that Bevin 'had few close friends and still fewer intimates'.[64] They were two of the most intriguing characters of that inter-war era, 'harnessed' together during an exciting and tumultuous period, which would repay a study in power itself. The tragedy was that they became unfriendly rivals, mainly due to Bevin's ruthless pursuit of power, as will appear.

Citrine would put up with a lot from Bevin's idiosyncrasies to take advantage of those T&G strengths. This was crucial at both TUC *and* Labour conferences. Only Bevin could attend the latter and become the force that he did in public throughout the 1930s. But what wasn't seen (or acknowledged by himself) was the degree to which Bevin depended on his membership of the General Council and its committee discussions, from Citrine's (and his staff's) sharp analysis and contributions to the General Council debates and at the annual TUC congresses, before the Labour conferences.[65]As we shall see, the controversy over rearmament is the best illustration of this, with Citrine's decisive role rarely acknowledged. Bevin's primary biographer, Lord Bullock, gave much credit to Citrine in this respect, while naturally giving his subject pride of place. Other biographers less so. Francis Williams (a great admirer of Bevin's, and editor of the *Daily Herald* from 1936 to 1940, when Bevin was deputy chairman) was most uncritical of his hero, as, for him, his account was 'a Portrait of a great Englishman'. Yet, he too acknowledged that 'they together exercised an influence greater than either could have done', but hardly mentions Citrine's role, such as in the rearmament policy debates.[66] Lord Adonis' recent book, *Ernest Bevin, Labour's Churchill*,[67] considerably overstates Bevin's contribution, for instance, in the General Strike, the Mond-Turner initiative and their respective wartime roles. Citrine was regarded by most government and union leaders of the inter-war years as the key partner in that team. For the first couple of years of the war, Citrine was, as Churchill said to Roosevelt, more important than most ministers, as we shall see.

The unique source of Citrine's authority was the ability to pitch the union case, not as a sectional interest as it had previously been seen, but as the representative of a broader working-class interest to governments and political leaders. He was able to bring out the much wider social and national dimension of the labour view of current issues, which was keenly listened to. This we will see internationally as well, with his leading influence on the European-wide anti-fascist movement in the 1930s. We will find them both at the forefront of sorting out the Labour Party policies in the fight for rearmament and in stiffening British resistance to the fascist powers, but the vehicle for doing so, the National Council of Labour, was primarily Citrine's initiative and execution from 1932 onwards. It was a solution borne out of the union's experience of the two first Labour governments, in ensuring that the unions' voice was listened to, while they acknowledged the primacy of the Labour leadership in government.

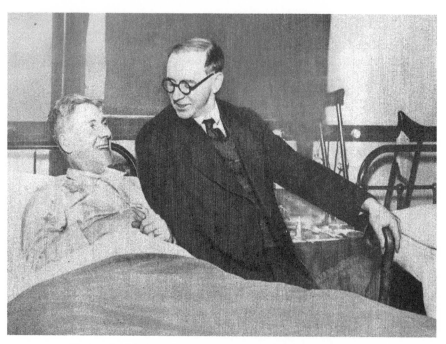

Citrine in his bed at Manor House Hospital in 1931,
visited by Arthur Cook.

CHAPTER 9

~

THE TUC AND THE SECOND LABOUR GOVERNMENT

Labour became the largest party in Parliament for the first time in June 1929, though it was again dependent on fifty-nine intensely rivalrous Liberal MPs.[1] Although a dwindling band in terms of seats, led by the formidable Lloyd George the main Liberal group was still a significant force in that Parliament. Accordingly, Labour was severely constrained as to what it could do. On the other hand, Labour and TUC conferences had committed firmly to restoring the unions' legal status, by repealing the 1927 Trade Disputes and Trade Unions Act. An ambitious TUC General Council optimistically devised a list of demands covering fifteen major areas of policy with high expectations.[2] Apart from a repeal of the hated 1927 Act, it wanted ratification of the ILO Convention for a maximum of forty-eight hours of work per week, the reform of unemployment insurance, a new factories bill and a new workmen's compensation bill.[3] A year into the government's term, however, little concrete had materialised in the government's legislative programme.[4]

For Prime Minister Ramsay MacDonald, whose primary focus was again on foreign affairs and Britain's position as a world power (especially in relation to the now more assertive United States of

America[5]), his primary domestic concern was to keep the Liberals 'on board'.[6] He even offered them electoral reform in return for a two-year commitment to keep Labour in office – a historic lost opportunity.[7] Citrine did appreciate the parliamentary arithmetic as to the limitations on what they could achieve, but shared his General Council members' annoyance that so little progress had been made.[8] When the trade disputes and trade unions (amendment) bill did finally arrive in late 1930, they found it to be gravely deficient. It retained the ban on general and sympathetic strikes entirely, repealing only the clauses on the political levy and the ban on civil service unions' affiliations. Worse was to come. When the bill went into its Committee stage in January 1931, the Liberals, with eager Conservative support, used their majority to amend it further as regards strikes in essential services. Citrine and his legal adviser, Sir Henry Slesser KC MP, reckoned that 'no large transport strike would be legal under the suggested Liberal amendment'.[9] He and the General Council committee responsible for the bill (the chair, John Beard, with Bevin and Swales), who attended the Commons, were infuriated by this.

Having seen the Committee in action, with even Labour MPs not following their whip, the TUC sub-committee (including Bevin) decided to get MacDonald to withdraw the bill.[10] Citrine was involved in a very heated argument with two Labour MPs, who ignored the party whip.[11] It got so heated that they nearly came to blows, so much did they resent what they saw as the TUC 'trying to dictate to the party'.[12] Annoyance at MacDonald's failure to 'square' the Liberals was intense. In one meeting with the prime minister, Citrine was shocked to see the reality of MacDonald's frailty (his eyesight was so poor he had difficulty taking the wrapper off a packet of cigarettes without glasses).[13] When they met on 29

January 1931, MacDonald told him, 'I am trying to run half a dozen departments' and 'I don't know how long we can go on'.[14] The Conservatives sensed that this division with the Liberals could bring down the government, and so the 'progress' of this bill in Committee had everybody's close attention.[15] MacDonald lacked confidence in his ministers' handling of the bill and so was monitoring the Committee progress himself through his office, while Citrine was there.[16] This early episode in the short life of the second Labour government is illustrative of the fragility of its position and of its relationship with the trade unions from the start.

Aware of their poor liaison and friction with the previous 1924 Labour administration, Citrine now sought a defined format of contacts between the TUC and the government. He jotted down a summary of its requirements – the 'need for consultation between Cabinet and T.U.C; Cabinet-making at Hampstead; Henderson suggests see Memoranda; we kept the Labour Party informed in 1946 [i.e., 1926], we want reciprocity; Cabinet seems to be afraid of connection with the TUC; if they don't get our Bills through we must take other means; Macdonald and Geneva Convention.'[17] These cryptic jottings tell us a lot about the TUC's concerns. The reference to 'Hampstead' was to MacDonald's home where the decision to go into government again was made exclusively by MacDonald and his inner circle, Clynes, Snowden, Thomas and Henderson.[18] Henderson suggested it could be shown 'Memoranda' at the early stages, if not the bills, but asked Citrine to confirm even this with the prime minister! In the end, Citrine concluded that at best it could only expect that any measures suggested by the TUC should be 'rapidly passed into legislation'.[19]

After the government had fallen in August 1931, Citrine drew up a fuller note headed 'What should be the relationship between the Trades Union Congress General Council and the Labour Party in Parliament' (both in office and 'during periods of opposition'), saying,

> I tried hard to get Mr Ramsay MacDonald to adopt some organised arrangement to avert the differences of 1924 when the Government was brought down because of friction with the Trades Union Congress over the Russian Treaty. Such an arrangement could readily be made and it should be continuous and official. I do not think that any advantage is gained by the Labour Party's denying its relations with the Trades Union Congress. Perhaps the National Joint Council idea with regular meetings could help to establish contact.[20]

This note was drawn up in light of MacDonald's defection leading to the fall of the Labour government and Labour Party slaughter in the October 1931 general election. It reflected the TUC and unions' natural expectation from a Labour government and party in Parliament. Though quite ambitious for a radical Labour administration, this was a far more cooperative TUC than in 1924. It felt entitled to be concerned about MacDonald's return to his remote style of government, with 'unfettered power'.[21] So 'consultation' was a key need, preferably in a formal NJC-type structure. But MacDonald would not agree such an arrangement, fearing it would lay the government open to criticism that it was 'being run by an outside body', or dictated to by the trade unions.[22] This was to be the perennial fear that Labour leaders in office (or, indeed, in Opposition) would be accused of. Far from seeking any improper domination by the unions, Citrine was urging a proper open relationship. The Labour leaders always underestimated the maturity of the union side, even when Citrine's moderating influence on behalf of the General Council was supreme. Predictably, the Conservative-dominated press, especially the *Daily Mail*, carried regular headlines about how the union 'bosses' were dictating to the Cabinet.[23] MacDonald and his ministers seemed ultra-sensitive to this charge. Margaret Bondfield, the minister of labour, confidentially advised Citrine not to write to MacDonald on TUC-headed paper, as this riled members of the Cabinet as 'dictation by Transport House' when circulated.[24] So no formal arrangement was established, leading to the lack of communication which would contribute to the fall of the government in August 1931.

MacDonald's primary focus as prime minister was again on foreign affairs[25] and Britain's position as a world power.[26] He had reluctantly appointed Arthur Henderson foreign secretary, but continued to run the show.[27] In the parliamentary power game, his primary concern was to keep the divided Liberals on board, but this was by no means easy with Lloyd George as leader of their main group.[28] The union relationship and its demands was a problem for him when it threatened his parliamentary dealings with the Liberals, which the Conservatives could then exploit.

Union relations with the new government had been better initially and, in November 1929, MacDonald appointed Citrine as the TUC representative to his Economic Advisory Council.[29] Citrine's appointment was an indication of MacDonald's original way of recognising the TUC on behalf of the unions. Soon after, Bevin also became the TUC nominee for the important Macmillan Committee on finance and credit. This was an indication of how important the TUC had become and Citrine and Bevin 'worked together to increase the influence of the T.U.C. to establish its right to consultation in the national sphere, and to make it a centre with power to evolve policy and take decisions on general principles affecting the trade union movement as a whole'.[30]

The Economic Advisory Council was to be a key advisory body for the prime minister, its membership being handpicked for this purpose. MacDonald himself would chair it. He wanted the EAC to counterbalance the Treasury's orthodox advice to the Chancellor of the Exchequer, Philip Snowden.[31] It included a number of top industrialists, bankers and economists, but also a number of known critics like Keynes, G. D. H. Cole[32] and Professor Richard Tawney.[33] Had it performed this function, the government could not but have tackled the financial crisis more effectively. However, its agenda was cluttered with minor issues from the start (perhaps deliberately so by senior civil servants not keen on such a conduit for influence by the unions and 'lefties'?[34]). At the few meetings he attended, Citrine expressed dissatisfaction with the EAC's weak, non-permanent, staffing.[35] A serious illness then prevented him from pursuing the matter. He was replaced by Bevin, who remained dissatisfied with the EAC's shortcomings and disorganisation.[36] Though the EAC met thirteen times between January 1930 and August 1931, fundamental differences between the diverse participants prevented any consensus recommendations emerging, which MacDonald might have adopted. After three meetings in the early months of 1931, as the economic crisis grew more serious, the EAC simply 'faded away' and the different views just polarised.[37] As the financial crisis of 1931 worsened, MacDonald, whose grasp of economics Citrine thought extremely 'woolly',[38] was left dependent on Snowden and Treasury orthodoxy.

In November 1930, on Henderson's recommendation, MacDonald also offered peerages to both Bevin and Citrine. This was to strengthen the Labour representation in the Lords, which was then very weak. Some have viewed this offer as an attempt by MacDonald to neutralise the two most powerful figures in the trade union movement.[39] Labour did have a serious problem of representation in the Lords, which Henderson, as foreign secretary, was concerned about, as this was the pool which his office looked to for junior ministers.[40] Perhaps MacDonald thought he could tempt Bevin – to whom a peerage was first offered – away from his base in the T&G? Bevin said, 'he would like to think the matter over'. However, after a few days he came into Citrine's office at Transport House to say he had decided not to accept a peerage.[41] Citrine had declined immediately, saying that 'it would be incompatible with my job'.[42]

The Macmillan Committee, on which Bevin sat from the start during 1930, proved a real inquiry into the whole financial system. The radical Liberal political economist John Maynard Keynes (1883–1946) was the reason for this success.[43] Its proceedings became renowned for his forensic interrogation of the top Treasury, Bank of England and City bankers, as well as for expounding his own theories about how the international financial system worked (or didn't, as was then the case).[44] Citrine had long regarded Keynes as 'Britain's foremost economist', since his 1925 pamphlet *The Economic Consequences of Mr Churchill* fastened the Conservative government with the blame for returning Britain to the Gold Standard at the pre-war level (£1=$4.80), which made exports, especially coal, uncompetitive, leading to the General Strike.[45] So the TUC was totally supportive of his current crusade to expose the role of the City and Bank of England over their focus on sterling in the international financial markets to the detriment of British trade and industry. Bevin, the TUC nominee on this committee, was completely taken by Keynes' insights into the mysteries of the credit system and benefited greatly from Keynes' 'mega tutorials'.[46] Citrine praised his dedication for his zealous attendance at the large number of meetings over eighteen months and for grappling with this most complex branch of economics, commenting, 'worthily did he acquit himself'. Keynes wanted to enlist the TUC's support to press his arguments against Treasury orthodoxy, and so 'went out of his way to woo Bevin'.[47] Bevin and Keynes kept Citrine informed, but he could hardly keep abreast of such an intense examination of the financial complexities when he was so seriously ill.[48] So Keynes primed the TUC, through Bevin, to fire the shots against the economic policies he sought to change. He could not have predicted how effective that would be, through the force he set going in Ernest Bevin.

The failure of the EAC to provide an antidote for MacDonald to Snowden's subservience to Treasury orthodoxy was compounded by Citrine's inability to oversee the TUC's conduct of these sensitive engagements with the government. This was due to a serious nervous breakdown, brought about by overwork and stress. The significance of this has not been fully appreciated. Citrine said, 'Towards the end of 1929 I was feeling badly rundown. So seriously did he [his doctor] regard my health that with my consent he saw the president and vice-president of the General Council, and then met the whole Council ... [who] ordered that I must take a sea voyage, accompanied by my wife.'[49] Citrine would be off for about six months; he probably did not fully recover his health during the entire crucial year of 1930. This left a vacuum of leadership at the TUC in Transport House at that vitally important time. Bevin now majored on key economic policy issues, through his membership of the General Council's Economic Committee.[50] He was greatly assisted by its officer, Walter Milne-Bailey (1891–1935), the 'ablest'

Head of the Research and Economic Department, who 'Bevin spent a good deal of time with'.[51] Milne-Bailey had also assisted Bevin on the Mond-Turner and Macmillan committees. He would have drafted the very strong TUC Economic Committee submission to the Macmillan Committee of May 1930 (when Citrine was away ill) 'on the lines of thought that Bevin developed in the latter's discussions'.[52] From the Economic Committee, Bevin's 'minority' reservation to the Macmillan Report probably derived.

No ordinary researcher, Milne-Bailey was a formidable political theorist and published author who had worked for the postal workers' union (UPW) and the TUC since 1920.[53] His mentor was Professor Harold Laski at the London School of Economics,[54] who supervised his PhD. They were so close personally that they lunched together weekly at the LSE.[55] So Milne-Bailey was a significant left influence on TUC General Council members and policies, especially on Ernest Bevin in 1930–31. Citrine mentions him often, once after his death, commenting that he was 'a very studious and thorough official though not a strong personality'[56] (hardly fulsome praise), whereas he describes his publicity officer, Herbert Tracey, with whom he worked closely on public relations, as 'fertile in ideas' and 'one of my most trusted and value colleagues throughout the whole of my secretaryship of the T.U.C.'.[57] Milne-Bailey died from cancer in December 1935 and was replaced by George Woodcock, a future general secretary.

Another significant left academic influence on Bevin at that time was (G. D. H.) Douglas Cole (1889–1959), Oxford economist and socialist theoretician, a left Fabian with strong former Guild Socialist (mild syndicalist) beliefs, like Milne-Bailey.[58] He was also on the Economic Advisory Council. He set up a Society for Socialist Inquiry and Propaganda (SSIP) in late 1930/early 1931, to achieve 'a more secure intellectual foundation for socialism', which Bevin agreed to chair.[59] Cole and Bevin published a pamphlet on 'The Crisis', which Cole drafted, casting 'into more systematic form many of the criticisms Bevin and he made of the Labour Government's policy', that year.[60] It was agreed to merge the SSIP with some of the ILP activists who were planning to leave the party and the merger became the Socialist League in 1932. Cole regretted that move, as he lost Bevin as chair when Sir Stafford Cripps' far-left supporters wouldn't have him for that position. This alienated Bevin from what he termed 'intellectuals' for evermore.[61]

In September 1930, Bevin presented all the major reports to Congress on behalf of the General Council (which Citrine would normally have done).[62] He reported sharply on the lack of progress to repeal the Trade Disputes Act of 1927 and that any failure would be 'deeply resented', showing his deep dissatisfaction with the Labour prime minister.[63] 'Manny' Shinwell (1884–1986), mines minister in the 1924 government, thought that 'the uncompromising hostility of the two most powerful men in the two movements – the Labour Party and the TUC – sowed the seeds of [that] future disaster'.[64] However, Bevin's biographer Lord Bullock was probably right in concluding that Bevin's long-held personal dislike of MacDonald was 'only a partial explanation' for his intransigent opposition to the government in August 1931.[65] It was his recently imbibed Keynesian economic philosophy which inspired him to challenge the validity of the government's economic analysis. It confirmed his gut instinct that the government's intention to switch to deflationary policies was biased against 'his people' and wrong. This confirmed him in his total opposition to the government and he would exert his considerable influence on the General Council and Economic Committee to strongly oppose Snowden's proposals for tackling the crisis based on the May Report. One can surmise that, had Citrine been well during that crucial 1930/31 period, Bevin would not have dominated the TUC response. A Citrine fully in command of his powers would have engaged Bevin's concerns, but tempered his anger with a more sagacious political judgement about how far to push things with that Labour leadership. Citrine, who got on with MacDonald personally, knew from his earlier discussions with the now almost blind prime minister, and his ministers' poor performance on the trade disputes bill, that it was an extremely rickety Labour government.[66] Similarly, the very able officer Milne-Bailey might not have been allowed to respond to Bevin's inclinations so readily, had he been more under Citrine's control. But, for a time, TUC economic policy and relations with the government were not totally under the usual direction of the general secretary, but were liable to be excited from inside and out.[67]

Towards the end of 1930, despite the offer of peerages, TUC relations with the government again became quite tense. This was because of the announcement in the King's Speech of the government's intention to set up a Royal Commission about unemployment insurance, without consulting the TUC. The minister responsible, Margaret Bondfield (ironically, a former TUC General Council member and chair), made things worse when she 'muffed subsequent moves to discuss the commission's terms of reference and to secure TUC representation on it'.[68] These moves were seen by the unions as 'a dastardly plot to strengthen support for reductions in unemployment pay'.[69] Robert Skidelsky concluded that her handling of the Royal Commission issue was inept. Citrine led a deputation to Downing Street on 2 January 1931 in protest, accusing the government of having 'conspired with the other two Parties to set up the Commission in order to "fix" a result, unfavourable to the unemployed'.[70] Skidelsky also confirmed Citrine's suspicion of a government deal with the Opposition. Bondfield had been meeting with the Liberals who wanted 'restoration of the insurance fund to a sound "actuarial" basis by separating those in insurance from those on the "dole"'.[71] Citrine had refused to be drawn into her offer of last-minute 'consultation' and MacDonald had to send John Clynes, the home secretary and respected former union leader, to the TUC 'to undo the damage'. Bondfield was blamed for her 'bad error of judgement', but it is inconceivable that she would have pulled such 'a stroke' without Prime Minister MacDonald's knowledge or approval.[72] The incident caused considerable anger on the General Council. Citrine told the prime minister that 'of late that cohesion [with our movement] has almost disappeared and as far as I am personally concerned scarcely exists'.[73]

THE SHOWDOWN

In February 1931, Chancellor of the Exchequer Philip, later Viscount, Snowden (1864–1937) made a major deflationary speech in the Commons debate on the economy. It went down very badly on the Labour benches but was greeted with jubilation by the Opposition.[74] Snowden made the case for serious cuts in expenditure as the only realistic option to assuage the foreign bankers and stop the run on the gold reserves and the pound. The Liberals obligingly moved for a Committee of Inquiry and Snowden hand-picked the members. That May Committee forecast a £120 million budget deficit for the year 1932–33,[75] with the TUC nominees writing a minority report disagreeing with their recommendations.[76] The May Report recommended cuts of £96 million, specifically targeted, 'two-thirds to come from unemployment benefit', the rest from teachers' salaries, police and the armed forces' pay.[77] That report was immediately adopted by MacDonald and Snowden, though the Cabinet Economy Committee set up to receive the report (including Arthur Henderson, the foreign secretary, and Willie Graham, president of the Board of Trade), after many meetings from 13 to 18 August, did not follow suit, and they would later oppose Snowden's recommendations.[78]

Snowden had been averse to consulting the TUC at all on budgetary matters or government financial policy.[79] It was only on Henderson's insistence that MacDonald agreed to call a special meeting for 20 August 1931, with the General Council and the Labour Party NEC, to address their concerns and to try and persuade them to support an austerity package.[80] As Citrine tells it, he welcomed this 'organized method' of consulting the unions, which he had called for. When they just received 'what purported to be a review of the financial position' from MacDonald, Citrine pointed out that they had not had 'a vestige of information' beyond what had appeared in the newspapers. He said, 'If this was an attempt at consultation it could only achieve its purpose by the Government placing the Council unreservedly in possession of information on which the Cabinet was to make a decision.' Otherwise, it would be impossible for them to express any opinion and could not support 'any future action taken by the Cabinet'.[81] That reasonable approach drew a more detailed response from Snowden, giving much more detail of the financial position. He said that the budget deficit was now nearer to £200 million (much higher than the £120 million disclosed by the May Report and rising with unemployment levels then being experienced). Therefore, he argued that the budget deficit could not be met by taxation alone or borrowing (already at their permitted limit of £50–60 million a year). It would have to come out of current revenue if they were to support the growing unemployment insurance fund deficit. They had considered increasing contributions from employers, workers and the Treasury and limiting payment of benefits to twenty-six weeks in a year but had decided against. There was some dispute later with Citrine as to whether he also stated that there would not be any reduction in benefits.[82] There would be other reductions in salaries for teachers, police and the armed forces, but that would only cover half the budget deficit. However, as Chancellor of the Exchequer, he would not disclose 'the sources of new taxation he had in mind'. So, Citrine accepted that this was the information they had sought and they prepared to adjourn to consider it.

At that point, Bevin had a go at MacDonald for dramatising the position with his interviews to the right-wing press, but not their *Daily Herald*, an indication that their personal rancour was not far below the surface.[83] This lack of respect for the prime minister can only have confirmed MacDonald in his defiance of 'the dictating' unions. The meeting broke up soon after four o'clock 'amid confused and angry argument'.[84]

The TUC group met separately from the Labour NEC (which left matters to its Cabinet colleagues) for four hours of 'animated discussions' (suggesting some considerable disagreement).[85] We are not told of the lines of those discussions, but nobody argued that they should accept the government's analysis or remedy. However, they agreed to put forward their own proposals to bridge the yawning budget deficit based on the principle of 'equality of sacrifice' by the whole community. These were a graduated levy on all sections of the community; to suspend payment of £50 million into the Sinking Fund (National Debt); and tax all fixed-interest-bearing securities. They were even prepared to consider revenue tariffs (which Citrine favoured, but over which Bevin hesitated).[86] These points implicitly accepted the reality of the crisis, but it was the lopsided nature of Snowden's focus on unemployment benefit cuts that was the TUC's main objection. However, it was precisely those type of cuts that the foreign bankers were insisting upon and so Snowden was only interested in those. So, when Citrine, Hayday, Bevin and Walkden met the Cabinet committee later that night on behalf of the General Council, Snowden didn't even consider the three TUC proposals. However, Citrine found him 'not at all dictatorial as I had sometimes seen him' and 'evidently oppressed by the weight of his responsibilities' as he believed that 'complete industrial collapse' would follow if they didn't act.[87] This brief encounter ended the government's reluctant 'consultation' with the trade unions. It had been a waste of time and only exacerbated union leader hostility.

MacDonald and Snowden then sought to rush a tough pro-gramme of unemployment benefit and public servant pay cuts through the Cabinet. Initially, the entire Cabinet accepted that a lesser cuts package (£76 million) would have to be made, but this was not seen as enough by the City, foreign banks or the Opposition parties. MacDonald and Snowden then tried to obtain further cuts from the Cabinet, but this was resisted strongly by nine members of the Cabinet. These were led by the foreign secretary, Arthur Henderson, who seems to have been impressed by Bevin's argu-ments,[88] and other leading ministers, such as Willie Graham, the president of the Board of Trade (who Citrine found 'much clear-er-headed on financial subjects than Snowden').[89] Henderson and Graham had been on the Cabinet Economy Committee which met the TUC and the strength of the union objections clearly

impressed them, particularly Henderson, the key figure.[90] All the
Cabinet had accepted that there was a real crisis and was prepared
to go along with the lesser cuts programme. But when the TUC,
supported by a large section of the Parliamentary Party and the
Labour Party, pressed its objections, nine Cabinet ministers, led
by Henderson, would not agree to the further cuts.[91] Seeing the
scale of their Cabinet, party and the TUC opposition, MacDonald and Snowden then concluded that they were politically unable
to carry through the austerity programme they thought necessary
to recover confidence and stem the run on the pound.[92]

The logical outcome should have been the fall of the Labour
government. Its party and TUC supporters were resigned to that,
rather than accept the deflationary measures now being proposed
by the leadership. What they had not considered was that
MacDonald and Snowden felt so strongly about the necessity for
their measures as to be prepared to lead a government from their
supporters and the Opposition parties. The TUC's refusal to countenance even the lesser cuts proposals, which the Cabinet would
have gone along with, created the impression that it was seeking
to dictate the government's economic strategy. Sidney Webb
expressed that view crudely: 'The General Council are pigs, they
won't agree to any "cuts" of Unemployment Insurance benefits
or salaries or wages.'[93] The unions would now also be accused of
'running away' from the problem, though they had clearly been
placed in an impossible situation by MacDonald and Snowden's
failure to consult them properly.

This failure to reach even an understanding, which would
have allowed the government to respond to the 'dread realities he
[MacDonald] must face',[94] was probably partly due to the personal
character of the protagonists. Citrine didn't rate Philip Snowden

highly (Bevin despised him) as Chancellor of the Exchequer, saying that he was 'not quite such an expert as he was reputed to be'[95] and describing him as 'pompous, rigid, devoid of imagination and frigidly orthodox'.[96] But Snowden had a substantial Labour pedigree and was once regarded, like MacDonald, as the darling of the activists as a left-wing ILP/Labour leader. But since Labour had come into government in 1924, as Chancellor of the Exchequer Snowden had changed considerably and was now a very orthodox disciple of 'the system'. He was actually hostile to the unions' influence in economic policy, seeing them as keeping up wages and resisting cuts in unemployment benefits, when they should be falling in orthodox economical terms. In January 1931, Citrine complained to MacDonald that 'the Treasury, Mr Snowden in fact, had written to the Banks suggesting that a movement should be undertaken by them for the purpose of reducing wages'.[97] But Snowden was also 'a sick, lonely man who confided his thoughts to nobody'.[98] He was just recovering from a prostate operation and was minded to retire to the Lords (as MacDonald wanted him to).[99] However, after his operation he 'dug in' dogmatically behind the Treasury, City and foreign banks' analysis of the crisis, clearly panicked by their insistence on cuts on pain of refusal of loans. MacDonald couldn't overrule him, as he would have resigned, which would have made things far worse in the financial markets.

The other main protagonist, Ernie Bevin, undoubtedly had a grudge against MacDonald, but it would not do justice to his standing to attribute his vehement opposition to the government solely to that personal factor. Cultivated and patronised by Keynes,[100] Bevin had come to believe that he knew better than the financial experts. The eighteen months he had spent on the Macmillan Committee were an 'important chapter in his education' but he 'was apt to believe too

easily that he "knew all about" banking and currency afterwards'.[101]
Skidelsky concluded that 'his opposition to the policy which the
bankers were trying to foist on to the Government stemmed ...
from an immense distrust of international finance' which he was
convinced was 'soaking industry for its own profit.' He referred to
the international money market as 'a system of collective usury' and
his anti-Semitic views are well known.[102] His remedy was 'to create
a regional grouping based on the Empire in which there would be
a rough balance between supplies of raw materials and foodstuffs
on the one hand and manufactured goods on the other, a group
of nations practicing Free Trade between themselves, but putting
up tariffs, if necessary against outsiders ...'[103] This imperial preference idea probably derived from similar recipes current at that time,
not least Mosley's nationalist 'vision'. Bevin was taken with Mosley's
Empire preference ideas to combat unemployment initially but
would vehemently have denied any Mosley influence for his ideas.[104]
In 1930, the press barons Lords Beaverbrook and Rothermere
attempted to commit the Conservative Party to Empire Free Trade.
This failed with the Conservative government as Baldwin, the prime
minister, opposed it. Significantly, Lord Adonis described this idea
as 'politically compelling if economically dubious'.[105] Under Bevin's
influence, Milne-Bailey had developed these ideas of a Common-
wealth bloc in a TUC economic strategy document for the Imperial
Conference in October 1930, but Snowden was unenthusiastic and
it got nowhere.[106] Bevin had more success with his views on coming
off the Gold Standard and devaluation of the pound. Despite 'the
vast majority of expert opinion' (including Keynes on the Gold
Standard issue) being against him on his call for devaluation in his
Macmillan Report reservation, Bevin's educated hunch was 'proved
right' about the need to devalue the pound.[107]

Bullock was quite equivocal about whether Bevin and the TUC were right in their stand, saying, 'This is not to argue that they were right – that is a question of opinion which every reader will answer for himself ...'[108] To appreciate Bevin's motivations fully for pressing so hard, we must take into account the fact that he was also in 'party politician mode' at that time. He had become 'an import-ant personality' at the Labour Conference in 1931 as a result of his opposition to the deserters.[109] He agreed to stand for Parliament for a solid Gateshead, Durham Labour seat, during the 1931 General Election. He would have been expected to become an MP, though his biographers play down this bid.[110] 'Bevin set about learning the rules of the political game but to obtain power in the way that had taken him to the top in trade unionism.'[111] He became chair of the left-wing Society for Socialist Inquiry and Propaganda (SSIP), a socialist propagandist body, from June 1931 and also chaired the board of Cole's weekly, *The New Clarion*. Most significantly, he was vice-chair of the Board of the TUC's *Daily Herald*, which pushed his distinctive view on the economic crisis throughout.[112] Skidelsky concluded that the *Herald*'s attitudes 'betray unmistak-ably the guiding intelligence of Ernest Bevin'.[113] So, Skidelsky rated Bevin as 'the dominant personality in the trade union movement, with an intelligence and breadth of vision far beyond those of his colleagues, with the possible exception of the general secretary, Walter Citrine, with whom he worked closely'.[114] Bevin's formida-ble presence undoubtedly drove the TUC to its uncompromising stance, but it is not clear what Citrine really thought about it, as he regained control after his nervous breakdown. However under-standable in view of the Snowden/MacDonald panic, Bevin's dominance may have driven the vehicle over the cliff! So it seems that a reluctant and superficial 'consultation' of the unions by a

beleaguered and poorly led 'physically and mentally exhausted'
Labour leadership[115] drew a Bevin-driven General Council refusal
to support government policy.[116] This split the Cabinet and Party
and led to the fall of the Labour government on 24 August 1931.

This complex and confused scenario has been pored over in the
voluminous commentary over the decades since. This fresh trawl
from the perspective of Walter Citrine during the whole of that
1929–1931 administration will hopefully have shed new light on
those historic events.[117]

AFTER THE DEBACLE

All are agreed that the defection of the MacDonald leadership
changed the dynamic at the top of the Labour movement. The
sixty-eight-year-old Arthur Henderson, the 'grand old man' of
Labour, who had built the party at the 'grass roots', as well as at
national and parliamentary levels with MacDonald, now took over
as interim leader. He had been a critical figure in leading the nine
Cabinet dissidents and he immediately accepted that the movement
needed a fundamental change in its relations with the unions if it
was to rejuvenate itself after the traumatic MacDonald leadership
defection.[118] So, a joint manifesto of the three Labour movement
bodies (the TUC, the Executive of the Parliamentary Labour Party
and Labour's National Executive Council) was announced by
Citrine on 27 August 1931, who became joint secretary of a revit-
alised National Joint Council.[119] The National Joint Council would
now get a meaningful role as the liaison body on policy between
the political and industrial sides of the movement. As Lord Bullock put it, 'During the course of the 1930s, the National Council
became the most authoritative body in the Labour movement in

formulating policy, especially on foreign affairs ...' [120] However, Bevin played no part in it until October 1932, when Henderson persuaded him of its importance.[121]

Although Citrine never aspired to be a party politician, as the creator and active partner in the NJC (which became the National Council of Labour from 1934), he then became a leading figure in the politics of the Labour movement. Given the weak party leadership (Lansbury, Attlee and Cripps) and Citrine's international perspective, the TUC side would become a dominant partner in the course of that decade. We can assume that the leading politicians were not comfortable with this arrangement. The pro-union veteran left-winger George Lansbury would not have minded, but, as we shall see, Major Clement Attlee MP and Sir Stafford Cripps KC MP would have jibbed at taking 'advice' from trade unions. However, in view of the previous Labour leadership's disregard of the union views in 1924 and 1931, they had little choice. The National Council of Labour would now be the vehicle whereby the more coherent practical, but equally progressive social, programmes of the TUC would inform the policies of the Labour Party in the 1930s, especially on defence and rearmament. They would also help shape the social and economic programme of the radical 1945 Labour government.

CHAPTER 10

~

AN ANTI-FASCIST PIONEER

As the recovery from the Great Depression began from 1934 onwards, the remainder of the decade was 'one of the most successful periods in the history of British industrial relations'.[1] Evidence of this was seen with the spread of union recognition and collective bargaining by large employers and the low level of disputes that resulted in strike action.[2]

Events in Europe during the 1930s would now involve Citrine closely, as president of the International Federation of Trade Unions (IFTU) at Amsterdam, Berlin, Paris and London.[3] The IFTU was the mainstream union federation and was aimed at influencing international bodies like the ILO and governments, on labour matters. Since 1920, the Communist International had created a rival body in Moscow, the Red International of Labour Unions (RILU), to use the unions for their 'revolutionary' purposes.[4] Thanks in no small degree to Citrine's strong leadership of the TUC and IFTU, they failed abysmally, particularly in Britain.[5]

IFTU moved its headquarters from Amsterdam to Berlin in July 1931, ironically at the insistence of its large German union federation affiliate, the Allgemeiner Deutscher Gewerkschaftsbund (ADGB).[6] In April 1933, it had to move again to Paris, to avoid

IFTU Executive Council, 1930. Seated L to R: Jouhaux (Fra.),
Sassenbach (secretary until 1931, Ger.), Citrine (president and chair,
UK), Schvenels (secretary 1931-45, Belg.), Leipert (Ger.). Standing L to
R: Tyerla (Checo Slovakia), Mertens (Belg.), Jacobson (Den.). All would
figure in the lead-up to Hitler's rise to power in Germany in 1933.

being raided by the Gestapo and having it records and funds seized.[7]
After an IFTU Executive meeting on 19 February 1933 in Berlin,
just after Hitler came to power on 31 January, Citrine reported to
his General Council on the dire situation it faced.[8] It is a unique
contemporary document describing what was happening, as it was
happening, in Germany.[9] The Nazis were seizing all the key levers
of power, like the police and army, who would have 'responsibility for maintaining order during the General Election. This clearly
means intimidation of the electorate by armed force. He [Hitler] has
further declared that the Nazis (Brown Army) will be turned into an
auxiliary police force, evidently of a permanent character, and will
be fully armed.'[10] A week or so later, Hitler exploited the burning
of the Reichstag (parliament) to consolidate his power, blaming
the communists for the fire. Opponents in all parties were taken
into 'protective custody'. Hermann Goering, now minister of the
interior, instructed the police to use their firearms 'without regard

to the effect of their shots'.[11] This happened daily all over Germany, but especially in the heartlands of the social democrat and communist movements, particularly Berlin. All socialist newspapers were suppressed. Public meetings were no longer free to say what they liked and 'even at private gatherings detectives must be present'. All 'demonstrations have been forbidden'. Citrine reported that 'the consensus of opinion' in Berlin was that 'the Nazis will sequestrate the property of the German trade unions and Socialist Parties at the first opportunity'. They were expected to remove the leaders, but not dissolve the trade unions. Instead, it was thought they would convert them into a 'form of State organisation', as Mussolini had done in Italy.[12] All Citrine's worst fears were realised after the elections of 5 March, even though the Nazis failed to secure a majority in the Reichstag. He reported that, 'The German Trade Union leaders talk guardedly of a general strike, but they point out that the declaration of a general strike with six million unemployed ... and with many of the workers sympathetic to the Nazis, is a precarious undertaking.' It 'must lead to bloodshed and civil war'.[13]

In early February 1933, the leader of the ADGB, the huge German union federation, Theodor Leipart, who sat on the IFTU Executive, assured them 'that all arrangements had been made to meet any contingency and that the leaders only had to give the word' (for a general strike, as had prevented a previous right-wing putsch in 1923).[14] However, it was clear that the ADGB leadership was hesitating: 'They had sent a deputation to Goering who had assured them nothing would happen against the trade unions ...'[15]

This 'pulled the rug' completely from IFTU's efforts to rally opposition to the Nazis. Citrine's reports to the General Council, the National Council of Labour and Congress elaborated on how the German unions sought to stifle criticism of the fascist regime internationally. The ADGB had been linked to the Social Democratic Party (SPD) since its formation in 1920. Now, the once powerful federation of unions was reduced to a state of impotence and supplication. Goering, the president of the Reichstag as well as minister of the interior, demanded that they 'disassociate themselves from the "Marxist" internationals'. This the ADGB leadership was apparently prepared to do and Leipart failed to turn up for a crucial executive meeting soon after. It would not avail them as he and many of his colleagues would soon be arrested and detained. There was considerable dissension within the ADGB about this move and 'a general strike was seriously being considered at the end of March 1933'.[16] However, the ADGB leadership was overawed by the tightening grip of Nazi control on the state machine, and concluded that 'a general strike would be suicidal'. Instead, it tried to reach an accommodation with the Nazis, and discouraged the other IFTU affiliates from organising boycotts of German goods and so on.[17] Citrine said that they had 'several times' asked the ADGB leaders how IFTU could help but they only sought financial help for the SPD in the (March) general election and agitation in the foreign press about the 'conduct of the German government'.[18] Citrine concluded, 'I do not disguise my opinion, that irrespective of … what the result of the Election is, Hitler intends to remain in power.'[19]

In other words, it was already a dictatorship in Germany and rapidly manifesting itself as one of the worst in history. He reported that the attitude of the regular army, the Reichswehr, was that 'the ranks are in the main sympathetic to the Nazis'.[20] There was disaffection in some of the German provinces, but no serious challenge. The aged president, Hindenburg, died in 1934 and Hitler assumed his powers as well. This ended in the suppression of the unions,

together with all the political parties of the left and the huge cooperative movement. The trade unions were replaced by the Nazi 'Labour
Front'.[21] In this disheartening scenario, Citrine said that the IFTU
Executive would be meeting in early April to consider its position in
Berlin – its phones were already being tapped and 'a minimum of
money' was being kept there. It didn't want to 'give the impression
that we were deserting the German Trade Union Movement', but 'if
the situation became more acute this might be imperative'.[22] Walther
Shevenels, IFTU general secretary, was given 'discretionary power to
act in any way he felt necessary'. Schevenels, a Belgian union official
who became assistant secretary and then secretary of IFTU from
1930, proved a very capable operator, working closely with the president, Citrine. He stayed at his post during the Nazi occupation of
Belgium and France in 1940, keeping up contacts and making all
arrangements for winding down IFTU's administration and funds,
before moving to the TUC in London.[23] At the April Executive
meeting it decided to remove to Paris, where the French government helped with accommodation. The TUC General Council now
instructed Citrine to make a full report to the annual Congress in
Brighton in September. In the meantime, all possible assistance was
provided to refugee trade unionists and Jews fleeing from Germany.

DICTATORSHIPS, AND THE
TRADE UNION MOVEMENT

Citrine's report to the General Council and to the 1933 Brighton
Congress was entitled *Dictatorships, and the Trade Union Movement*.
It was the highlight of that Congress and received widespread
press coverage.[24] It traced the now well-known causes of the rapid
rise of Hitler in Germany – the humiliating Treaty of Versailles

(1919), the hyperinflation of 1923 and the subsequent collapse of the German economy after the Wall Street Crash in 1928.[25] The huge unemployment (over 8 million) had severely weakened the once powerful union, cooperative and socialist movements. In the political sphere, Citrine also drew attention to the fact that the German Republic was a very 'immature' democracy, it being their 'first attempt' since 1918.[26] Its proportional representation system of election produced a multiplicity of parties unable to produce a stable government to tackle the multi-faceted crisis.[27] In the thirteen years of the Weimer Republic, Berliners went to the polls for seven national, five state and four municipal elections. This permanent election campaigning atmosphere fostered anti-democratic attitudes in the population.[28]

In his speech, Citrine drew special attention to the divisions in the working class as a major cause of the fascists' successful climb to power. The Social Democratic Party (SPD) had had its strength sapped by 'divisions, hostilities and bitterness', since the end of the war, especially by the unrestrained hostility of the Moscow-led communist movement. Citrine was convinced 'the Communists bore a considerable responsibility for the divisions which made possible the Nazi victory'.[29]

Eric Hobsbawm, a leading British communist of Jewish Austrian extraction, lived in Berlin from 1931 to 1933 and was active in the German Communist Party, the KPD, during these heady years. In his memoir, Hobsbawm explained the rationale of the communist leaders and confirmed the accuracy of Citrine's judgement:

it is now generally accepted, that the policy the KPD pursued, following the Comintern line, in the years of Hitler's rise to power, was one of suicidal idiocy.[30]

He went on to explain, 'It rested on the assumption that a new round of class confrontation was approaching ... and that the chief obstacle to the necessary radicalization of the workers under communist leadership was the domination of most Labour movements by the moderate social democrats.'[31] As a young Marxist, Hobsbawm had been attracted to the exciting mass communist movement, 'visible everywhere on the streets'.[32] Its membership had tripled from 125,000 in 1929 to about 360,000 by 1932, mainly from the unemployed youth. In the November 1932 general election, it (the KPD) polled more than 6 million votes and 'put a hundred Communist deputies into the Reichstag'.[33] It attracted 'thousands upon thousands of workers onto the streets'. There the Nazis 'locked horns' with them 'in constant street battles, bar-room brawls, and rowdy, violent political meetings.'[34] Hobsbawm confessed how much they underestimated the Nazi danger. He says, 'We thought that, if they got into power, they would soon be overthrown by a radicalized working class under the leadership of the KPD, already an army of three or four hundred thousand.'[35] The 'rationale' for this policy, which Hobsbawm also accepted, 'bordered on political insanity',[36] captured in the communist slogan, '*Nach Hitler Uns*' ('After Hitler Us'). It was the Communist International's instructions and agents who had dictated that 'suicidal idiocy' of communist persistence in its attacks on the social democrats in Germany. In 1928 it promoted the infamous 'Class against Class' strategy, which declared social democrats as 'fascists wearing a socialist mask'.[37] The likelihood of the TUC agreeing to enter a united front with the tiny CPGB in 1933, as Stafford Cripps' Socialist League and Nye Bevan advocated, was therefore nil and that message would have gone out clear from Citrine's address.

What was novel and striking about Citrine's report was that he also characterised the communist 'dictatorship of the proletariat' in the Soviet Union as a denial of democracy and liberty.[38] His claim centred on the Soviet rulers' conversion of their unions into 'transmission belts' of production since 1928. He said that, after the revolution, 'the trade unions first occupied a privileged position and were given large powers in the control of industry … [but] almost immediately the revolution was consolidated the Communist Party set out to subdue Trade Unionism to its own will, and to make it merely an instrument of the Communist dictatorship.'[39]

On his visit to the Soviet Union in 1925, Citrine had questioned their lack of independence from state control then, but his host, Mikhail Tomsky, and his colleagues in the Soviet Central Council of Trade Unions defended the system on the basis that it was their workers' state.[40] At that time, the Russian unions still had a good degree of autonomy and performed a traditional collective bargaining role, and had strikes, in the still-large private sector. In December 1928, Tomsky and his executive colleagues were removed for 'having a "British" conception of Trade Union organisation, of putting Trade Union ideals in opposition to Communism'.[41] It seems that Citrine's arguments with Tomsky and his Central Council colleagues had some effect.[42] The twenty-three unions had been broken up into 147 smaller units in 1934 and given an entirely different role. They were now focused on production questions and to promote 'socialist competition'.[43] It was considered first as 'absurd and later as a counter-revolutionary act to have recourse to a strike'.[44] So, in 1933, Citrine regarded this as similar to what was happening to the unions in Germany and Italy. He concluded that, 'under the Communist dictatorship in Russia Trade Unions have lost whatever independence they might have had. Their work is to control rigidly the Labour force of the country on the lines laid down by the Communist Party ...'[45] Nevertheless, he was at pains to stress that he did not seek to stigmatise the government of Russia as being the same as the fascists in Germany or Italy, but, rather, to highlight the dictatorial similarity of communist practices.[46]

A section of his report was also devoted to counter 'ill-instructed criticism of Parliamentary institutions' in Britain and underestimation of 'liberties of the public won over a century of struggle'.[47] Citrine said that: 'The Chairman of the Socialist League (Sir Stafford Cripps KC MP[48]) has recently written in the *Clarion* that "Free Speech", a so-called free press, are no more parts of the eternal verities than is Free Trade.'[49] Citrine went on to list those liberties which the democratic state could not take away, as was happening in Germany, Italy and the Soviet Union. On 3 July 1933, Citrine had met Cripps and key members of the Socialist League about their advocacy of taking emergency powers, if elected as a future Labour government. More than thirty of the leading lights of the League turned up at the London School of Economics to meet him, including intellectual luminaries such as G. D. H. (Douglas) Cole and Professors Harold Laski and Richard Tawney. Major Clement Attlee, the Labour deputy leader, was also there, which surprised Citrine.[50] Under the League proposals, the king would have to abolish the House of Lords immediately they took office and they would then pass an Emergency Powers Act which would enable them to nationalise the banks (including the Bank of England), by ministerial Order.[51] This was the reaction of some on the left to the 1931 Labour government experience and to events in Germany. Citrine challenged the theme expounded by Cripps, Attlee and the others that 'Parliament is

outworn, too slow, not responsive enough to the electoral will …
that the attainment of socialism through the present machinery of
Parliament is impossible'. He was concerned that such 'wild talk
is far more likely to produce an atmosphere favourable to dictatorship' (Mosley and his fascists were still a threat in 1933). He
warned that Conservative Central Office would also exploit such
'wild talk' in the next General Election, which it did.[52] Cripps had
just published a collection of essays entitled *Can Socialism Come by
Democratic Methods?*, to which his answer was a definite 'No'.[53] In
one of the essays, Attlee 'insisted that the important thing' was
'not to do things with the most scrupulous regard to theories of
democracy or exact constitutional propriety'.[54] It never got the
chance as the Conservatives won another substantial majority in
the 1935 General Election, though Labour recovered somewhat,
from the disaster of 1931. On this theme, during the Abdication crisis of 1936–37, Citrine also expounded his philosophy of
constitutional monarchy, saying, 'We were republican at heart but
we realized that the limited monarchy as it had operated in Great
Britain during the life of the late George V, was probably about
the safest system in present circumstances.'[55]

From his recent first-hand experience of events in Berlin, Citrine
was keen to remind the unions and Labour of where they were going.
At the Brighton TUC Congress that September, he articulated his
philosophy that, 'We should resist any attempt to supersede Parliament or undermine its democratic working. It still remains true that
efficient government is no substitute for self-government.'[56] Citrine's
analysis of fascism was equally penetrating.

It is not enough to regard Fascism as merely a capitalist dictatorship. … It is as much a creed as Socialism or Communism.

It … is a conception of society based upon the Corporate State in which the individual subordinates himself to the State. Its only chance of success here is that people whose faith in Parliamentary Government has been weakened by the apparent inability to restore our economic ills, particularly if unemployment becomes much worse, may in despair be ready to accept desperate remedies. Like Communism it is a disease of the stomach.[57]

Citrine saw trade unionism as an alternative model, which 'could not exist as voluntary combination of workers except by being responsive to the aspirations of its members. It cannot exist in the atmosphere of dictatorship, nor will any dictatorship allow it to exercise its functions as an independent protective organisation. Strikes are regarded as an act against the State itself.'[58]

Many speakers complimented Citrine on his powerful speech, though a few communist and other speakers were outraged that their beloved Soviet Union's treatment of unions should be likened to Nazi Germany's. Significantly, it was the recently elected young MP for Ebbw Vale, Aneurin (Nye) Bevan, who took strongest exception to the speech. He called it 'the most dangerous speech he had ever heard'. Bevan rejected Citrine's premise that capitalism could recover and saw fascism as just part of the inevitable decline and collapse of capitalism.[59] This was the Marxist line, by which Bevan was greatly influenced. Though never a communist, from his early training[60] 'he evolved a melange of democratic neo-Marxism' rhetoric.[61] Bevan had originally wanted to pursue an industrial unionist career from Tredegar by becoming chair of the powerful South Wales Miners' Federation. However, he lost out to Communist Party and Minority Movement rivals in the valleys' 'Fed' election after he failed to support Arthur Horner's efforts to continue with the strike. So, his focus switched to political action.[62] Bevan blamed the TUC and Citrine for the miners' defeat and was to remain hostile to full-time union officials throughout his life. In his TUC speech, he urged that 'Congress should get down [i.e., back] to an industrial policy, demand an increase in wages and press the attack home' instead of 'the organisation of demonstrations to expose the fallacies of Fascism'.[63] Like many on the left, he still played down the threat posed by German fascism, seeing it as just the expression of a dying capitalism. In Citrine's view, Bevan 'exercised a negligible influence on trade union policy and action'.[64] Citrine thought, 'he excelled as a critic, but, in contrast to Ernest Bevin, creative thought was not his strongest characteristic'.[65] He thought that it was typical of Bevan at that time, 'well-phrased, fluent, tricky and entirely unconvincing'.[66]

At the close of the 1933 TUC Congress debate, the delegates, including those of the Miners' Federation, approved the report 'overwhelmingly', with 'only a few hands being held up' against. Bevan had 'made little or no impression on the delegates'.[67] Citrine's statement would provide the basis for TUC and Labour Party policy for the remainder of the decade.[68] The TUC's focus became how to combat fascism wherever it appeared in different countries, as Hitler commenced his drive through Europe. Citrine was very active, both through the TUC/National Council of Labour and the IFTU/Labour and Socialist International network, assisting the trade union and Jewish victims of German fascism fleeing abroad. Bullock, and all his biographers since, gave Bevin most of the credit for these initiatives.[69] While there is no doubt about Bevin's considerable involvement and support for the anti-fascist cause on the General Council and at Labour

conferences, especially during his term as chair and president of
Congress, 1936–37, it was Citrine who was leading as general
secretary and president of IFTU.[70] Citrine and the TUC were
particularly active in Austria in 1934, where the unions did fight.
He made 'several visits to Austria' 'to see whether a bridge could
be built between the Dollfuss Government and the Socialists ... the
only hope of preventing a Nazi invasion ... but nothing tangible
resulted'.[71] All the time the TUC was pressing the Foreign Office,
'but he [Sir John Simon, the foreign secretary] wavered when it
came to doing anything about standing up to Nazi Germany'. [72]
When that failed, the TUC and IFTU raised considerable funds
and assistance for the defeated Austrian workers.[73] That same
year, his address to the Weymouth Congress on the subject of
fascism 'aroused great interest'. He moved the General Council's
resolution 'expressing abhorrence of the suppression of freedom
and democracy, the nationalist and militarist tendencies, the racial
intolerance, and the degradation of the status of women that are
characteristic of Fascism'. He emphasised the need to outlaw 'the
drilling and arming of civilian sections of the community', as this
was precisely how the operations of the fascists in Italy, Germany
and Austria developed. Bevan indulged in this type of fantasy,
leading his paramilitary-inspired Tredegar Workers' Freedom
Groups over the Welsh mountains.[74] Ultimately, as a result of
TUC and other pressure on the government, the Public Order
Act 1936 banned the wearing of uniforms.

CITRINE'S PRO-JEWISH ANTI-FASCISM

Citrine's speech impressed the editor of the New York socialist
Jewish Daily Forward so much that he reproduced it verbatim. Citrine

mused: 'This was the first time that anything I said was credited with such importance.'[75] The editor was a Mr Baruk Charney Vladeck (1886–1938) – not the Russian Jewish name under which he had emigrated – a one-time New York councillor and in 1934 City Housing Authority member. Vladeck had set up a Jewish Labor Committee of trade unionists, socialists and other anti-fascists in 1933. They greeted Citrine warmly on his visit in October 1934 and Vladeck chaperoned him and Doris around America for seven weeks. Citrine expressed glowing appreciation of his hospitality.[76]

He also received a civic reception by the noted radical mayor of New York, Fiorella La Guardia, a strong Roosevelt supporter, with a motorcycle police escort to the Town Hall, and he addressed over 2,500 people at the Mecca Temple. He then went on to the annual convention of the American Federation of Labor in San Francisco as the TUC fraternal delegate. The AFL leadership, especially William ('Bill') Green, its president and Citrine's friend, were strongly anti-fascist and facilitated these meetings.[77] Afterwards, Citrine spoke to audiences in Portland, Seattle, Los Angeles, Detroit, Pittsburgh, Chicago and other cities on the same theme: 'I tried to describe the menace which Fascism and Hitler held for the free world, and that if these dictatorships were allowed to go on unchecked, the world would most assuredly be plunged into war. By the time I had finished my audiences began to believe this.'[78]

In 1936, while in the US for another AFL convention, Citrine made contact with a number of Jewish organisations in New York and, with full TUC support, set up a non-sectarian World Anti-Nazi Council, headquartered in London, to 'arouse the public as to the dangers of the Nazi regime'.[79] It tried to promote an economic boycott of Nazi Germany, which the IFTU, L&SI,

TUC and AFL supported, through the League of Nations. It also sought to boycott international sporting events in which the Nazis were allowed to participate, such as the 1936 Olympics in Berlin, as well as the world heavyweight title boxing match between the American Joe Louis and the German Max Schmeling. Hitler saw Schmeling's first match win as a symbol of Aryan supremacy, but Joe Louis won back the title in the rematch.[80] They held large meetings in London, with prominent speakers from all parties. Churchill was the main speaker at the Albert Hall in December 1936, and Citrine again chaired the meeting.[81] A key aim of this organisation was to combat the considerable pro-German sentiment in England at the time, focused on the new king, Edward VIII (though Churchill was pro-Edward and had to be curtailed by Citrine, as chair, from championing his cause at their meeting).[82] Citrine for the TUC strongly supported Stanley Baldwin and his Cabinet's insistence on Edward's abdication over the Mrs Simpson issue. He and Doris visited Chequers on 7 November 1936 to confirm the TUC's support.[83]

So, Sir Walter Citrine (as he was from 1935) had a record as a pioneer of the anti-fascist movement globally from the early 1930s, which few can match.

THE LANSBURY HUMILIATION

Faced with the imminent threat of invasion of Abyssinia by Mussolini throughout the summer of 1935, the TUC made a major policy shift on rearmament at its Congress in Margate. On the recommendation of the National Council of Labour (NCL), it agreed 'to support for *any* action, ... to uphold the authority of the League in enforcing peace', including economic or military sanctions.[84]

On the night before the Congress, 4 September, George Lansbury, the Labour leader, met Citrine and said that 'he couldn't reconcile his personal position as a pacifist with his duties as a representative of the Labour Party'.[85] Although he 'had a strong affection for George', Citrine told him, 'You are here to convey fraternal greetings not to argue about differences in the party's international policy. Stick to the job for which you were appointed.'[86] Next day, Citrine presented the NCL resolution, in the starkest terms.

> There is only one way of dealing with a bully and that is by the use of force. Moral resolutions are no good … It may mean war, but that is the thing we have to face. There is no real alternative now left to us but the applying of sanctions involving, in all possibility, war.[87]

Lansbury kept to his word and expressed 'no word of dissent' in his speech at the TUC that day. The Congress agreed the resolution overwhelmingly.[88] Citrine regarded the NCL statement as 'far more definite than anything I had myself heard from Labour sources'.[89] Before the Labour Conference at Brighton, later in September, the week Mussolini invaded Abyssinia, Citrine called two joint meetings of the General Council, the Labour Party National Executive and the Parliamentary Labour Party Executive, to firm up some of the Labour politicians who 'searched around for loopholes'.[90] Faced with a TUC ultimatum to go public on its own, the Labour NEC did make it clear that its policy would now be to urge the League of Nations to take military action as well as economic sanctions against Italy. Lansbury was again wobbling under pressure from the other leadership figure, Sir Stafford Cripps, with the deputy Labour leader, Attlee, uncertain. But with the trade union votes 'in the bag', the NEC motion was certain to carry and Bevin, who attended both joint meetings, knew it.[91] At the Labour Conference, Bevin stole the limelight with his famous attack on Lansbury, accusing him 'of hawking his conscience around from body to body' and of being a hypocrite.[92] Citrine didn't like it at all, saying 'It was a cruel and, I thought, unnecessarily brutal assault on a man who was certainly no hypocrite and had served the Labour movement well.'[93] Even Bevin would regret his later remark that, 'he set fire to the faggots' for Lansbury's immolation.[94] But as far as the press and public were concerned – a view propagated by all his biographers since – it was Bevin's speech which made all the difference.[95] That was Bevin's style, to take the credit.

BEVIN'S POLITICAL POSITIONING

However, something that bothered Citrine more occurred after that Congress. Before he left for his 1935 visit to the Soviet Union (see Chapter 11), he was invited to Chequers by the prime minister, Stanley Baldwin, for a confidential briefing on the general rearmament issue.[96] The prime minister clearly regarded him as the key TUC figure[97] in gaining TUC support. He told Citrine 'that our armed forces had been dangerously run down and were far below the strength necessary for the defence of the country'. Citrine was already aware of the situation from other, 'fighting forces', sources.[98] So the prime minister asked Citrine to help. As Citrine was going to be away for about six weeks, he suggested that Baldwin invite a TUC deputation led by Bevin, who 'felt the same as I did', to talk about the defence situation. Citrine then spoke to Bevin about what had been said and 'impressed on him the seriousness of the situation'. Bevin agreed to lead the deputation, but while Citrine was away, changed his mind. Instead he sent Citrine a letter, 'evidently written for public consumption', expressing 'strong disagreement with my proposals' as 'going behind the backs of the leaders of the Labour Party'.[99] This was rich coming from Bevin, after his recent public humiliation of Lansbury, which had forced him to resign. Bevin had previously been critical of 'Attlee's failure to give a firm lead to the Labour Movement in international affairs',[100] but now seemed to be playing politics in support of Attlee for the Labour leadership.[101] It was a good move from Bevin's point of view, starting an alliance that would carry him into every government between 1940 and 1951. There is no reference to this important manoeuvre in any of the Bevin or Attlee biographies, the most recent of which sees Bevin's consistency as on a par with Churchill's![102] Even if Bevin felt the need to inform the Labour leadership (and Citrine did ask Baldwin to consult them), to make an issue of his change of mind in the way he did seems a devious move. Attlee, as leader, was still voting against Defence Service Estimates in the Commons in early 1936.[103] But unlike Dalton, Bevin did not tackle Attlee on this issue. Citrine, by contrast, emerges as the consistent and straight TUC and National Council of Labour leader, urging a vital change of the Labour policy on Britain's rearmament and defence. As early as March 1936, it was Citrine's proposal from the TUC which the Labour NEC discussed, 'that the Party should support rearmament ...'[104]

THE TUC AND THE SPANISH CIVIL WAR

By 1936, the Attlee leadership and the Labour Party had overcome their aversion to rearmament. This was a result of the outbreak of the Spanish Civil War, and the intervention of Nazi

Germany and Italy in support of Franco and his rebels against
the Republican Popular Front government. Citrine and the TUC
were also to play a very active role in this significant conflict,
but were attacked by Bevan and Foot for their 'failure' to shift
the British and French government policy of non-intervention,
despite their considerable effort to do so.[105] The Spanish Civil
War posed the threat of the advance of fascism all over Europe,
and the revival of communist fortunes in the unions as cham-
pions of anti-fascism. Citrine and the TUC/IFTU clearly saw
it in those terms and were active supporters of the Republican
government, working closely with the Spanish socialist prime
minister, Francisco Largo Caballero, who was also a member
of the IFTU Executive.[106] The key issue was the decision of the
French Popular Front and British Conservative governments not
to supply arms and munitions to the elected Spanish government.
That decision initially had the support of all European powers
and the Soviet Union and so the TUC and NCL accepted it, but
with considerable disquiet. Soon, the fascist German and Italian
governments brazenly flouted the international agreement and so
there was great pressure from the Labour movement in Britain
to press for the abandonment of the policy of non-intervention.
This they did readily at the Edinburgh Labour Conference of
1937, but, despite demonstrations and the lobbying of the foreign
secretary, Anthony Eden, by the TUC, 'we utterly failed to move
them'.[107] Citrine and Bevin and the Labour leadership were said
by Aneurin Bevan and his supporters to be wanting of 'fibre and
courage'.[108] Yet a definitive study of the TUC *Trabajodoras* (worker)
archives demonstrates 'just how central Citrine was to the labour
movement's debates over Spain'.[109]

TRADE UNIONISM IN THE CARIBBEAN

Citrine's major contribution towards development in the Caribbean is still remembered in the West Indies. He was the leading member of the Moyne Royal Commission (1938–40), which was sent out there to investigate the atrocious conditions West Indian workers had to endure in the British colonies. Serious riots occurred in Trinidad, Jamaica and other islands, as well as British Guiana, in 1937, with fifty-two deaths, 429 seriously injured and thousands arrested and prosecuted.[110] The TUC had set up a special Colonial Advisory Committee under the general secretary and approved his membership of the Moyne Commission in 1938, even though he would be away for about six months.[111]

Appalled by the atrocious conditions and 'apparent indifference shown by the whites', Citrine shocked the colonial authorities, planters and business elites by championing, coaching and leading the fledgling trade unions there in their evidence to the Commission.[112] Citrine established a strong rapport with one Jamaican union leader in particular, Alexander Bustamante (afterwards the first Jamaican prime minister in 1962), regarded by the authorities as a dangerous rebel whom they wanted to imprison. Citrine 'led' Bustamante skilfully through his testimony for over an hour, which made a strong impression on the other Commission members. The report was so radical that it was kept under 'lock and key' in London during the war, in case its explosive contents about conditions in the British colonies could be exploited by the Germans. When it was eventually published in 1945 (suitably moderated, of course),[113] it proved 'a turning point in colonial attitudes'.[114] It led to the introduction of trade union legislation in most of the Caribbean, with Ministry of Labour officers assisted by TUC officers to enforce it. The TUC produced an *ABC of Trade Unionism for Colonial Unions* in what became 'one of the most hopeful parts of the world for the development of trade unionism'.[115] Citrine and his wife, Doris, arrived back in Southampton on 7 April 1939.

ANTI-APPEASEMENT

The TUC/Labour leadership actively opposed the appeasement policies of Prime Minister Chamberlain's government from 1937 onwards. Their NCL deputation was pressing Chamberlain, before his second meeting with Hitler in Munich, to stand by Czechoslovakia and deter Hitler from invading, under threat of war. Chamberlain briefed them confidentially about his first meeting with Hitler at the Berchtesgaden, when the man he referred to as the 'excitable' dictator presented his demand for the incorporation of the 3 million Sudeten Germans and their territory into the Reich.[116] Chamberlain told the NCL leaders that 'it was impossible' to safeguard Czechoslovakia from German invasion as they could now do it unhindered through Austria, which they had just annexed with the Anschluss. He said that he did not believe the British people would want to go to war 'to resist the principle of self-determination' for the Sudeten Germans! (Citrine, Morrison and Dalton strongly disputed that) Chamberlain was relying on Hitler's assurance that this was the end of his demands and 'it would be possible to talk about the general situation' after they got their way in Czechoslovakia. However, at the Munich meeting Chamberlain gave Hitler all he wanted and convinced himself and the British people that he had secured 'peace in our time'.

The National Council of Labour then convened a conference of IFTU, the Labour and Socialist International and the French

CGT and Socialist Party for 21 September and called for a pact between Britain, France and Russia 'as the only hope of curbing the rapacity of Hitler'.[117] They pressed this proposal on Chamberlain at another meeting in Downing Street on 22 March 1939, but 'negotiations with Russia [which had started in April] dragged on'. By June 1939, when they again met Chamberlain, 'there was a growing feeling in the Labour movement that our Government were not anxious to conclude such a pact'.[118] And so events took their course, with the Soviets changing their foreign secretary, Litvinov, for Molotov to agree a non-aggression pact with Hitler in August, which Citrine thought 'made war inevitable'. It followed in September 1939.

What is interesting about this 'toing and froing' to Downing Street is the easy access Citrine had and 'the confidential information I received on such occasions was of the utmost value to me in trying to guide the policy of the Trades Union Congress'.[119] As we shall see in Chapter 11, it put it to good use in getting Chamberlain to instruct all departments of government to recognise and negotiate with the unions. The press didn't notice this traffic as the deputation entered from 'a corridor leading from the Treasury in Whitehall to no. 10 Downing Street'.[120] Interestingly, Citrine was one of the few prominent figures of that time who had a good word to say about Chamberlain. 'I found Neville Chamberlain different from the man my trade union friends believed him to be. His reserved nature made it impossible for him to become intimate with anyone, and undoubtedly much of his outward frigidity was due to a disturbing self-consciousness ... I can never erase from my mind the thought of his struggle, in the later days of his life, against the depression resulting from his political misfortunes and knowing that he suffered from an incurable illness.'[121] This showed how generous Citrine could be in his assessment of opponents. He also described their first meeting as 'one of the frankest interviews I had attended'.[122] Chamberlain was still the dominant figure in his government and party until he lost the confidence of the Commons and much of the Conservative Party after the disastrous early battles with Germany in Norway in April 1940. This caused the fall of the Chamberlain government and its replacement by the Churchill-led coalition of all parties.

This outline of the increasingly international focus of the unions in the course of the 1930s also highlights their growing importance in the making of the modern Labour Party. It is fair to say that the party's recovery from the nadir of its leadership's desertion in 1931 owed much to Walter Citrine and the TUC General Council for its leading domestic and international role. As a recent study concluded:

> With Labour's political leadership substantially weakened after 1931, the unions assumed a pivotal role in shaping the party's direction, to the extent by 1940, its political culture, organisation and policy had been decisively remade.[123]

Parker, who devoted his thesis 'to investigate and understand the crucial contribution of the trade unions', sees it as 'a hugely significant and underappreciated achievement in the context of the destruction of labour movements that attended the retreat of democracy across much of Europe during the 1930s'.[124] He is surely right. That contribution has been obscured by generations of commentary by historians of politics who disparagingly caricatured the Labour Party as 'the General Council Party' during this period.[125] Andrew Thorpe also concluded that 'Citrine, who had been biding his time, he struck to good effect', and 'really laid down the law', [126] and others would conclude that this influence was somehow improper. [127] But given the extraordinary circumstances of the Labour leadership's abandonment of the Party and movement which put them into office, it was surely understandable. In fact, the National Joint Council (National Council of Labour, as it became from 1934) did have a very positive influence as the liaison body on policy between the political and industrial sides of the movement. It was the answer to the poor communication record of the MacDonald governments. The highly professional and pragmatic TUC that Citrine had created and honed in relations with governments of all colours since 1927/28 greatly improved Labour's substance as a social democratic party. When some of the policies that the leading group of politicians of Lansbury, Cripps and Attlee's Socialist League would have foisted on the Labour Party are considered, the NCL proved a fount of wisdom and direction. Although Citrine never aspired to be a party politician (his lack of party political nous showed occasionally), as the creator and active participant in the National Council of Labour as joint secretary, he now became a leading figure in the politics of the Labour movement. But he relied on Bevin at the Labour conferences and the other union representatives on Labour's National Executive Council (not Bevin) to carry their agreed policy. Citrine also used to attend Labour conferences as an observer. Given the weak party leadership of the early 1930s and Citrine's TUC/IFTU international connections and perspective, the TUC side had more to offer, especially on foreign policy, which had then assumed 'a new urgency'. [128] We can assume that the leading Labour politicians (Attlee, Dalton or Morrison) were not entirely comfortable with this union 'oversight', but they came to live with the arrangement, until they acquired the status of Cabinet ministers from 1940 onwards. Yet, as we shall see, the National Council of Labour would now become the vehicle whereby the more coherent practical, but equally progressive social, programmes of the TUC would inform the policies of the Labour Party in the 1930s.[129]

CHAPTER 11

~

CITRINE'S 'SEARCH FOR
TRUTH IN RUSSIA'

Citrine's visit to the Soviet Union in 1935 is a puzzle. Why would the leading communist sceptic in the international trade union movement want to visit a country whose government he regarded as dictatorial, anti-union and in some ways akin to that of fascist Germany and Italy? He had already been there in 1925 and was initially very sympathetic to its efforts to reconstruct its backward economy and change its former tyrannical czarist society.

As we saw, relations had deteriorated dramatically since the General Strike, with the communists attacking the TUC, causing it to abandon its Anglo-Russian Joint Advisory Committee in November 1927. Since the Sixth Congress of the Communist International in 1928, there had also been a big increase in concerted attacks by the communists on what they termed the 'social fascist' trade union and socialist leaders. As Citrine remarked, 'it was only the extreme Left Wing and Communist elements who could distort their imagination sufficiently to make such an allegation'.[1] So, why had the communist leadership of the Soviet Union invited such a known critic to visit and tour, assuring him that he could go where he pleased, without restriction? The answer lay in the dramatic

change of policy announced at the Seventh World Congress of the
Communist International, held July and August 1935 in Moscow.[2]
That Congress abandoned the 'Class against Class' policy adopted
seven years earlier. The new leader of the Comintern was a Bulgar-
ian, Georgi Dimitrov (1889–1949), the communist hero who had
successfully conducted his own defence in his trial by the Nazis for
allegedly causing the Reichstag fire of 1933. He was acquitted, to
international acclaim, but was expelled to Russia. Stalin appointed
him leader of the Comintern and in 1935 he announced the very
different policy at this Congress.[3] In a Nazi prison, he had clearly
had time to review the 'suicidal idiocy' (Hobsbawm) of the previous policy. He 'laid stress on the necessity for abandoning the habit
of vilifying all the social democratic and trade union leaders ...
and he particularly blamed the stupid attempt to denounce them
as 'social fascists'. The communists also abandoned the old policy
of 'united front from below', which had meant inciting 'the masses'
to revolt against their leaders. Instead, the new policy sought a
'united front from above', to defeat fascism. This could only be
done by persuading the social democratic leaders of the 'urgent
necessity for working class organisations to survive', in the face of
the fascist German threat to their existence.[4] Soon after, Citrine
was invited to the Soviet Union, 'in all probability ... to facilitate
the United Front'.[5]

It still doesn't explain why Citrine agreed to go. The Margate
Congress had just rejected the Soviet unions' overture for a
'united front' as it thought 'no good purpose would be served'
by its meeting the Soviet 'unions'.[6] Most of his European union
IFTU colleagues didn't want to know either. On the other hand,
in France a 'Popular Front' had been established by the unions
and socialist parties. This followed the coming to power of a very

right-wing French government in 1934, which 'seriously alarmed all the working-class organisations' that France might go the way of Germany.[7] Citrine would have been briefed on the situation there by his IFTU vice-president and close colleague, Léon Jouhaux, general secretary of the Confederation of General Labour (CGT).[8] Citrine therefore had more of an open mind about who they might join with in the fight against fascism, which was now his great fear. He was conscious of the potential of the Soviet Union as a bulwark against the German fascist menace. The Soviets had just joined the League of Nations and were conducting 'a more pronounced policy of conciliation', including a pact with France, which Citrine wanted extended to Britain.[9] Like many socialists in the West, he was also very interested to learn how the first socialist experiment was developing.[10] The brutal advent of the Nazis in Germany had also changed people's perceptions of where the main threat was now coming from and, relatively speaking, the communists were less of a menace, if still not acceptable as allies on account of their known conspiratorial ways. Nevertheless, Citrine's acceptance of the invitation to go to the Soviet Union must have raised a few eyebrows in Amsterdam and at the TUC, where a strong anti-Soviet communism prevailed.[11] Citrine stressed that it was 'in a personal capacity' he would go as he and Doris set off for Russia after the TUC in late September.

Citrine's book about the visit, based on his daily diary, *I Search for Truth in Russia*, tells us much about the Soviet Union in the 1930s. It is a quite critical, but also a sympathetic and balanced, account. He insisted that he 'wanted to see the worst', as well as the best, and he acknowledged that during the subsequent weeks 'the facilities afforded us were exceptional'.[12] He was a painstaking observer, taking considerable notes in shorthand on the industrial and social state of things in the Soviet Union. No doubt much was kept from him. Nevertheless, his diary entries and rolling commentary of what he saw remain an immensely interesting historical account.

THE VISIT

The Soviet authorities, mindful of Citrine's crucial position, treated him as a special guest. By giving him the 'royal tour', the Soviet leaders clearly hoped to soften TUC and IFTU opposition to their 'united front' overture. It is an indication of their serious concern about the Nazi threat to the Soviet Union. They kept their word and didn't broach the subject formally throughout his visit, until the last meeting, as we shall see. Citrine was keen to see how things had progressed since his first visit. Since the Revolution, he had had a keen interest in the Soviet Union. The near collapse of capitalism during the 'Great Depression' then contrasted with the success of the Soviet Union's first Five-Year Plan, albeit with the transformation of the trade unions' role into 'the transmission belts' of the state. The Webbs, amazing recent converts, thought that this success would do more to spread communism than their subversive Communist Party tactics.[13] The promise of a planned economy and social advance had many attractions for socialists in the West. Citrine wrote in the preface, 'I hope the present edition will enable the reader to take a balanced view of a dramatic phase in the revolutionary history of a great country.'[14] However, he was keenly aware that though the Five-Year Plans had 'enabled the country to make giant strides towards industrial recovery', it had been at the cost of tremendous human sacrifice.[15]

The map below gives a good indication of the extent of their tour. The Citrines arrived at Leningrad on a Russian ship on

MAP OF ROUTE

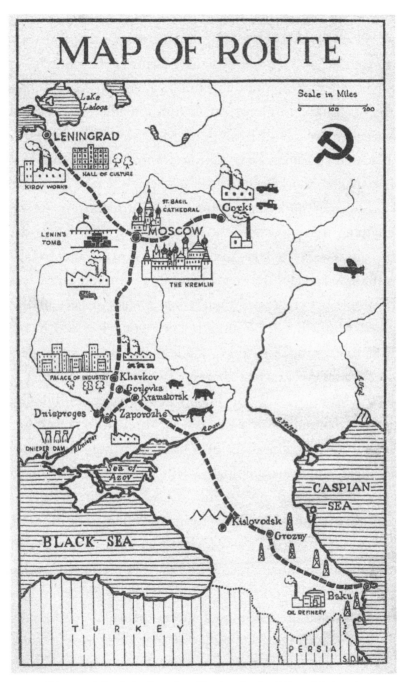

Places visited during the Citrines' trip. From his book
I Search for Truth in Russia, 1936.

Thursday, 19 September, where the president of the Leningrad
Trades Council told Citrine, 'our instructions are that you are to go
where you like, and see what you like, Comrade Citrine'.[16]

So began a most unusual 'holiday', visiting large shoemak-
ing, ball-bearing and motor car factories, textile works and other
industrial workplaces in Leningrad, Moscow, Gorki and down to
the Black and Caspian Seas. Citrine wanted to find out how they
were managed, the salaries of the workers, officials, management
and technicians and much more. The Citrines were interested
in 'anything that moved' – the overcrowded, dirty single-decker
trams, the few buses and 'practically no private motor-cars' or
even the few bicycles (too expensive) in Leningrad and Moscow.
Were people better dressed than 'when I was last here in 1925?',
he asked. Hard to say, he mused. The population had increased
considerably from 140 to 170 million in the previous decade,
causing a massive housing shortage, which the authorities were
trying to address quickly, 'shoving up' poor-quality new buildings.[17]
They were then taken on a 'sights' tour through the beautiful city
of Leningrad with its canals, iron bridges crossing the Neva and
seeing the magnificent buildings. They saw the superb architecture
of the czarist era and monuments, the famous Winter Palace and
the Hermitage. But it was the factories and other workplaces which
really interested Citrine. As a former electrical engineer, Citrine
quizzed the technical director about how they measured productiv-
ity and took copious notes on labour conditions generally. Citrine
explored in detail the earnings of pieceworkers, as compared with
time workers, and recorded tables of four categories of workers'
earnings.[18] They left a glowing testament in the visitors' book at
the Kirov Works: 'We write with a sense of pride and honour not
only for the privilege of viewing the great constructive work of the

Revolution inspired and led by Lenin', but as apparently the first Britishers to record their views in this historic book.[19]

So, we see that Citrine still had a soft spot for revolutionary Russia. In Moscow, they saw that the Volga Canal, which would link the entire region to the Baltic and Caspian seas and a huge network of rivers, was nearing completion. Citrine even got the authorities to bring Tomsky, who had been removed as leader of the Soviet unions in 1928, to meet him. Tomsky was apparently well and now in charge of the state publishing department, but they didn't discuss anything as they had in 1925.[20] The unions were now a 'pale shadow' of their former revolutionary selves with their executive councils run by a small number of state-appointed officials. These were headed by Tomsky's successor and their host, N. M. Shvernik, with whom Citrine had few dealings. Citrine recognised the many things they had achieved:[21] abolition of unemployment, a job as long as s/he liked to work, equal opportunity to rise and increased cultural and educational levels and facilities. Citrine added the abolition of literacy in a sixth of the world.[22] However, in his mind, all this was spoilt by their continuing attempt to export 'communist' revolution to the world. He thought that this weakened the Russian state's appeal for a pact with Western countries against Hitler.[23]

While they still had important functions, such as the 'protection of labour' (health and safety) and the administration of social insurance, unions had lost the core union role in the setting of wages. Their internal government was no longer democratic, being run by state appointees. The Five-Year Plan was a state-fixed affair by a Planning Commission which allotted their tasks and targets to the separate industries, which in turn were allotted to each factory by Industry Commissars. The factory administration did discuss the question of their wages with the workers through the Factory Committees, on which the trade unions sat. The central trade union council could take any dispute up with the government. A remote and long-drawn-out affair, it sounded far inferior to the immediacy of collective bargaining with local shop stewards and independent union officials at all levels, as existed in Britain and would flourish during and after the Second World War. Independent unions had no role in the 'socialist' management of the state enterprises either, to make up for their loss of collective bargaining rights. Citrine was particularly critical of the 'more intensive piece-work, bonus systems and general attempts to speed up by hard work than I had ever seen'.[24] Citrine frequently noticed that women were doing arduous and severe tasks which, in a socialist state, he thought, was quite unjustifiable. He instanced digging drains in the streets, ordinary navvy's work, pulling down houses – work 'we tried to protect them from' in Britain.[25] Yet he was told that, with equality, this was not how they saw it.

'IT IS MORE LIKE STATE CAPITALISM'

Citrine thought that 'during the period of the first Five Year Plan (1928–33), the workers' standard fell dangerously low'. The union officials replied that this was unavoidable because of the necessity for providing adequate defence against the capitalist countries, who threatened to attack Russia. Again and again, this argument was deployed to explain shortcomings in people's consumption.[26] No doubt it was a very real fear, but overused, he felt. Citrine concluded, 'they had never had Socialism ... It is more like State Capitalism.'[27] Looking around Moscow shops with Doris, he 'could not escape the feeling that something dangerously like social distinctions are arising in Russia'.[28] Nonetheless, he thought the fluidity enabling bright and able individual workers and peasants to rise to managerial and technical positions for the first time in Russia was a very good thing.

On 2 October 1935, he and Doris set off around the country, first to Gorki, some 200 miles from Moscow to the east, and then southwest down to Kharkov in Ukraine, on to the Black Sea and then over to Baku on the Caspian (see map of route above). On 8 October, they broke away from the route which was planned for them (typical Citrine) to see the real condition of the workers and peasants. They saw a far different picture – poor housing, lack of crèches, kindergartens and homes for the elderly and so on. He had a row with their guide and said, 'you give the impression to delegations of visitors that your people live in conditions far superior to other countries'.[29] Then they visited Posterchev collective farm of 3,000 acres near Zaporozhe, which had been created in 1929. It was managed by a cooperative production society. It supported 131 families with 498 children in a village with neat whitewashed thatched houses, which had a school with fifteen teachers. They were impressed.

Doris Citrine, centre, with a group of peasant women
and children at the Posterchev collective farm, 1935.

They saw many more big projects under construction near the Black Sea, such as the huge new Dnieper Dam and other hydro-electric works which generated electricity, made the river navigable and improved water supply for the whole region. Citrine, the former electrician, was in his element, inspecting the network of 'nine turbo-alternators, each of 62,000-kilowatt capacity'. These trans-mitted power to far-distant substations all around the region, as far as the Sea of Azov.[30] On 9 October they were taken round 'the great machine-building plant' at Kramatorsk by the director.[31] The largest in the world, built in 1931, it employed 28,000 and 'will have 40,000 in the production processes'. 'They are planning accommo-dation for 100,000 people, and they had already housed 28,000'.[32] It was a complex of eleven separate factories, including casting hall (the largest in Europe), tool shop, forging and stamping plants (with the largest hydraulic press in the USSR). Citrine thought, 'it is quite certain that this huge establishment has been built with an eye to military strategy as well as purely economic considerations'.[33]

On 17 October, they headed back to London via Moscow for the November 1935 General Election. On 21 October, they met a group of Russian trade unionists at a reception arranged by Shvernik. It was a question-and-answer session. Unfortunately, the issue of the 'united front' came up sharply from an interven-tion by Alexander Lozovsky, the secretary of the Red International (RILU). When Citrine realised who it was, his 'indignation soared to its heights'. He 'declined to continue the interview' as 'his organ-isation [RILU] was obnoxious to the trade unions of the West and he was believed to be the instigator of most of the intrigues and subversive actions of which they complained'.[34] Citrine left the Soviet Union in a bit of a huff. He must have been tired, in reacting to Lozovsky's challenge in that way. He was worried that being seen 'to have any dealings with Lozovsky' might be misinterpreted by his colleagues in Amsterdam and London.[35] His generous Soviet hosts must have been upset by that 'huffy' response to their hospitality, but if the invitation had been intended to 'butter up' the IFTU president for a 'united front', it was a big mistake on their part. If anything, it reinforced Citrine's hostility towards the idea and by the time of the September 1936 Congress in Plymouth, he was leading the opposition to the communist proposal.[36]

Now, on 23 October, he was back in the writing room on the ship, preparing his impressions for the press when they reached London. He would be quite positive, saying that the Soviets had only been able to get down to the 'real constructive work' in the last seven or eight years.[37] That was 'but a flash across the face of time'.[38] 'I shall have no hesitation in saying that as far as I can judge they are undoubtedly better' since he was there in 1925.[39] Another five years would give them a much higher standard of living. They were undoubtedly 'closing the gap' with Western capitalist countries and their most remarkable feat was 'to have practically abolished illiteracy', with over 24 million children now receiving regular education. This would eventually lead to freedom of thought, he believed.[40] He wondered if it would develop the individuality of the worker sufficiently and whether 'stifling of free discussion on matters concerning the body politic, will allow the development of that flexibility of mind', to produce the great artists, musicians, writers and inventors.[41]

This balanced perspective of the evolution of Soviet 'communist' society would, alas, never be realised. As they passed the Kiel Canal, Citrine saw a German steamer flying the swastika and her crew were gazing at their 'Communist sickle and hammer'. He commented, 'In a few years they may be locked together in a life-

and-death struggle. Hitler's aggressive tactics against the Soviet are unmistakeable.'[42] What prescience. He could not have imagined how the Nazi war machine would tear the guts out of all that had been achieved.

HIS BOOK *I SEARCH FOR TRUTH IN RUSSIA* – REVIEWS

The first edition of his book *I Search for Truth in Russia* appeared in 1936 and was a great success. There had been many adulatory accounts of the Soviet Union by Western visitors, notably the Webbs' tome following their 1932 trip, which was published in October 1935. It remains an interesting, if naïve, take on the Stalinist experiment by two of the outstanding Fabian socialist intellectuals of that era.[43] Citrine's slimmer volume (still over 400 pages) was a much sharper account by someone determined to probe the truth about the communist experiment and perhaps lay to rest some of his own ghosts about what he had called 'Lenin's Electric Republic'. *I Search for Truth* was reprinted twice that year and once more in 1937. Reviewed extensively in the British press, it was generally well received. E. H. Carr, the eminent sovietologist, described it as 'A fine piece of work. The most objective book yet written by a visitor …'[44] G. D. H. Cole gave it quite a positive, if critical, review for the *New Statesman and Nation*.[45] He said that those who had read the entire book (rather than newspaper articles with selective extracts from it) 'will find that there is a great deal in it that makes upon the other [Soviet] side'. Pat Sloan, a leading CPGB member who had spent five years working in the Soviet Union, also published a highly critical short pamphlet, *I Search for Truth in Citrine*, obviously with CPGB backing.[46] He had read the book, but didn't like it at all, seeing it from the perspective of a devotee of the Soviet system. Jenny Lee, a strong pro-Soviet ILPer and wife of Nye Bevan, did a 'hatchet' job for *The New Leader* of 10 July 1936. She clearly hadn't read the book.[47]

When Citrine met Stanley Baldwin in November 1936 at Chequers (to discuss the Abdication crisis), the prime minister said he had found the book interesting.[48] He talked about Stalin being at loggerheads with the Comintern over his 'pushing ahead with Russia's internal development' when they 'wanted to go for world revolution'. Baldwin said he had been advised (presumably by the security services) that there was 'a real fear that Stalin might be assassinated'. Citrine didn't 'believe much in the rumoured plot' but he 'thought the recent trials were for the purpose of giving a timely warning to any opposition'.[49] In 1937, the Moscow Trials started in earnest and an 'orgy of arrests and denunciations all-round the country started'. This caused Citrine to add a much more critical chapter attacking the trials, in a revised 1938 edition. When Zinoviev, the former Head of the Communist International and his associates, were to be tried in August 1936, Citrine sent a telegram to the Soviet government on behalf of IFTU and the Labour and Socialist International. They also met the Soviet ambassador, Ivan Maisky, to press their representation.[50] They requested that 'proper legal defence, independent of the government, should be supplied to the accused' and that they be given a right of appeal. It was met with 'a torrent of abuse' and they were 'stigmatized as the allies of the Gestapo'.[51] At the same time it was announced that Tomsky 'had shot himself rather than face arrest'. Citrine commented, 'Poor Tomsky. I knew him well … what availed him his sterling record of sacrifice and struggle against Tsarist tyranny?'[52]

The darker side of the country and the system which he had freely explored so recently and to which he had given his 'critical friend' blessing now came into sharper focus. In this revised edition he included a chilling Soviet 'Casualty List' of four pages from the *Daily Herald* of 'Death Sentences (167), Arrested, Liquidated, Denounced and executed (501)'.[53] Citrine was unsurprised that the communist hierarchy in Britain (Pollitt, Campbell and Horner included) and the 'Moscow-financed' *Daily Worker*, had 'no good word to say in defence of the accused'.[54] Instead, *The Daily Worker* published 'howls of abuse at the men whose every act it was formerly wont to extol'.[55] At the same time, he did wonder why none of the ordinary communist activists and members 'had anything to say in defence or extenuation of any one of the fallen Communist stalwarts' in its correspondence columns.[56] This experience could only reinforce the views he had expressed in 1933 about such 'democratic centralist' parties and how dictatorial they became once in power.

Little wonder, then, that Citrine and the General Council of the TUC were not interested in joining a 'united front' with communists. Bevin was equally dismissive of communist pleas for unity.[57] At Plymouth that September, Citrine, in moving the General Council Report, 'did not mince words in his attack on the Communists'. Regarding their 'united front' proposal, due to the 'pressing of a button in Moscow, Communist tactics had been changed although Communism's revolutionary aims remained unchanged'.[58] A few delegates from the body of the hall, two admitting membership of the CPGB, 'with many bitter references to Sir Walter Citrine', argued in favour of the CPGB's affiliation to the Labour Party and a united front with IFTU/LS&I. In replying to the debate, Citrine said 'that Labour would not again push into its side the thorn that it had so painfully extracted'.[59]

'SIR WALTER'

I charge thee, fling away ambition.
By that sin fell the angels.

Shakespeare, *Henry VIII.* [60]

Citrine, a great Shakespeare fan and with a full library of the Bard's works, quoted these lines on accepting his first honour, a knighthood, in 1935. He had declined a peerage in 1930 and a knighthood in 1932. Yet he denied that he had been ambitious for such recognition. 'My outlook on life was different … I certainly had no desire for a title.' He maintained that it was 'not for the purpose of reward, just self-satisfaction in the success of achievement'.[61] In May 1935, MacDonald, still prime minister, asked him, Arthur Pugh[62] and Ernest Bevin to accepted knighthoods in his retirement honours list. Citrine (and Pugh) accepted, but, after some hesitation, Bevin did not, understandably saying, 'it might create a barrier between me and the men'.[63] There is no doubt but that Citrine had earned some such recognition for his services to the trade union movement and the society generally. It was unprecedented, however, that two serving members of the TUC should be so honoured.[64] *The Times* remarked that 'the great part played in [our national affairs] by the Trade Unions is recognised by the fact that two members at the next meeting of the T.U.C. will be Sir Arthur Pugh and Sir Walter Citrine'.[65] He regarded it as an indication of how much the trade unions had become a recognised part of society. However, there was some feeling to the acceptance of such honours in the Labour movement at the time, especially as it was MacDonald's retiring gesture.[66] It was seen as separating its leaders from the ordinary trade unionist. A cartoon by Low in

the *Evening Standard* of 10 June 1935 made that point sharply. He
'depicted me entering a gilded hall with footmen on each side of
me ushering me into a group of bewildered Tolpuddle Martyrs as
"Sir Walter Citrine, K.B.E"'. Beneath was the caption: 'A hundred
years' progress in Trade Unionism.'[67] But Citrine treated it as a
sign of how much progress the union movement had made since
the days of the Tolpuddle Martyrs.[68] It was another example of his
firm character. Once he decided that a certain course of action was
right in personal matters, what others thought did not deflect him.

His neighbours in Wembley Park 'gained a good deal of
pleasure' at the news and phone calls and telegrams began 'to
arrive in plenty', including from his father and sister in Wallasey.
The Borough of Wembley held an official ceremony.[69] However,
there was also some adverse reaction. One of his officers told him
that there had been 'a good deal of tittle-tattle about my acceptance
of the honour' among a recent British union delegation to the ILO
conference in Geneva.[70] The officer reported that Ernest Bevin
had ostentatiously shown the letter offering him a knighthood to
everyone on the train to Geneva, telling 'everyone present that he
had refused'. Citrine 'was annoyed with Bevin for setting that hare
running'.[71] Bevin would milk that distinction between them for all
it was worth over the years, always calling Citrine 'Sir Walter'. The
fact that the honour came from the 'betrayer' MacDonald may
have provoked his response.

Citrine's opponents now began to exploit the issue. Was it
perhaps a mistake to give them such a stick to beat him with? At the
Trades Union Congress at Margate the following September, there
was a motion from the civil servants' union, the Women Clerks
and Secretaries, saying, 'This Congress regrets that active leaders
of the trade union movement should accept honours at the hands

of a Government which is not established in the interests of the workers.'[72] It was supported by a few speakers, all of whom stressed that it was not aimed at Citrine personally. They said that their objection to honours arose 'because it carried the assumption that the recipients had passed out of the ranks of the working class'.[73]

Citrine, clearly upset, replied to the debate himself, saying that 'he could have had a Coronet long ago if he had wanted it'. But that was hardly the point. It was a matter for each individual whether or not to accept, he claimed. That was unconvincing, as without his position in the trade unions he was hardly likely to be considered. He produced a twelve-page 'foolscap list' of individuals of the Labour movement who had previously accepted honours, without any objection from Congress. True, but as a serving officer his was a special case. He defended his record of service and asked them to allow him 'to go on serving it'. Without saying so, he clearly treated the motion as a resigning issue, feeling that his personal integrity was at stake. If it had passed, he said, 'I would feel it incumbent on me to terminate my service with the TUC'.[74] However, there was never any chance of that, as the major unions would not support (or speak for) the resolution. A procedural motion was then moved to curtail any further debate and the motion easily fell on a show of hands.[75] Nevertheless, the issue of his knighthood continued to be exploited by his enemies. A large group of delegates at the postal workers (UPW) conference at Brighton in May 1936 tried to prevent his address as a fraternal delegate because he had accepted the honour. That move was rejected but about 200 delegates were induced to walk out of the conference. Citrine told the rest of the conference, to applause, that he would not be intimidated. He knew that since August a campaign had been proceeding, but 'he … did not intend to be coerced …' or humiliated.[76]

In the prevailing climate, Citrine's book and his acceptance of a knighthood now provided a target for attack whenever his enemies could, with even Bevin in a mean-spirited way making invidious comparison. This exposed his colleague to unfair criticism in the Labour movement. In a 1936 demonstration in Hyde Park about Abyssinia: 'Uproar broke out when Sir Walter Citrine, secretary of the Trades Union Congress, tried to address the demonstration.' From the beginning he was greeted with cries of 'Get among your class Sir Walter' and 'Down with Citrine'. Clearly a Communist Party-organised affair (speeches drowned out by shouting and singing of the Internationale), and after more cries of 'We don't want Citrine' and 'traitor', he had to be escorted to the gates of the park by half a dozen policeman.[77] Considering Citrine's anti-fascist record by then, this showed the worst side of Labour movement fringes. Herbert Morrison, just re-elected as an MP, in reviewing Citrine's book for the *Daily Herald*, called him

one of the most honest analytical and objective minds in the British Labour movement. That is why he is hated by the Communists. For the man who will not cringe to them is black-listed and made the subject of abusive attack and interruption at public meetings.[78]

CHAPTER 12

⌒

AT WAR: CITRINE AND BEVIN

> At the present time he fills a position in the Labour movement
> more important to the conduct of the war than many Minis-
> terial offices.
>
> Winston Churchill to Franklin D. Roosevelt
> on Citrine, 1 November 1940[1]

The Nazis swept through Holland, Belgium, Luxembourg and
France and approached Paris from 9 May 1940.[2] Citrine, who was in
Paris for an Anglo-French Trade Union Council meeting and IFTU
executive meetings, had to leave in a hurry on the advice of the British Embassy.[3] It arranged for him to be taken to Dover on a destroyer,
an indication of his importance in its eyes. He got back in time to
attend an emergency meeting of the National Council of Labour
in Bournemouth, travelling straight from Dover that day.[4] After a
meeting of the Labour Party executive, the Labour leader, Clement Attlee, announced that Labour had agreed to enter a coalition
government with the Conservatives and Liberals.[5] Citrine insisted
that the General Council be consulted and so a joint meeting of all
three bodies ensued the following day. Although it was a formality,
Citrine's insistence that the TUC be consulted on the decision to

enter the coalition, and that one of its leading members become a minister, underlined the critical importance of the unions to Britain at that time. Having made its point, the TUC strongly supported the proposals and thereby set the scene for Labour in government again, this time as a respected partner with the total backing of the Labour movement, rather than a besieged and divided minority on sufferance as in 1924 and 1929–31.[6]

Attlee and Arthur Greenwood (the deputy prime minister) joined a War Cabinet of five and Labour got a third of all government posts outside the War Cabinet. Bevin was recommended by Attlee for one of these posts, as Churchill wanted some ministers with industrial experience. Bevin agreed to serve without hesitation as the Minister of Labour and National Service, a position then seen by some on the General Council as a lesser post, outside the inner War Cabinet. He was found a safe seat in the Central Wandsworth parliamentary constituency. However, with the approval of the T&GWU General Executive Council, he would remain general secretary, but 'on leave'. Citrine's name was also 'under consideration' for a government position, but he let them know immediately that he 'preferred to remain at my post as General Secretary of the TUC'.[7]

When Citrine met Churchill some months later, the new prime minister expressed disappointment as 'he had hoped to have me in the Government, but that he understood from Clem Attlee that I wanted to remain with the TUC'.[8] Churchill now pressed him to become a privy councillor instead, which Citrine accepted. A few days afterwards, Churchill wrote to say that the king had been 'graciously pleased to approve'. It was reported in the *Daily Mail* that he was 'the number one trades union leader and one of the most conscientious public men of today'.[9] Being a privy councillor guaranteed access to ministers and experts on a one-to-one basis, including the prime minister. Churchill (and Beaverbrook) would frequently tell important guests that it was all right to discuss sensitive war issues with Citrine present, saying, 'he is a Privy Councillor and I can talk to him frankly'.[10] Bevin once told Hugh Dalton, then a leading Labour figure in the government, that 'Citrine … was the only man he knew who thought he could walk up, without notice to No. 10 Downing Street, ring the bell and demand to see the Prime Minister straightaway and if told the P.M. was otherwise engaged, he would be most indignant and affronted'.[11] That sarcastic comment showed a certain jealousy that Citrine had more access to Churchill than Bevin at that time.

Citrine did get on extremely well with Churchill, considering their previous antagonism in the General Strike and very different political outlooks. But they had worked together from about 1936 in the Anti-Fascist Council and were both 'heart and soul' as one in fighting Hitler and fascism. Citrine was often invited to Downing Street. After they had done their business, he and Churchill often fell to regaling each other with snatches from Gilbert and Sullivan operas, reciting patriotic poetry ('Ye Mariners of England') and other poems they had learned at school. They both had phenomenal memories and 'so in this dark hour of Britain's trial, the two of us went on reciting fragments to one another of the songs and poetry of our nation'.[12] As general secretary of the TUC and president of IFTU, Citrine had an international standing and connections, which Churchill wanted to avail of. So, the war leader benefited from Citrine's enthusiasm, courage and energy as an informal diplomat to the United States and to the Soviet Union, in the critical early parts of the war – as Churchill freely acknowledged to Roosevelt.[13] In this role, Citrine would traverse the world in a form of union/national parallel diplomacy. However, he was always at pains to keep the TUC's independence from the government or Foreign Office.

The way things were looking up to September 1940, when Hitler abandoned his plans for the invasion of Britain, there was a serious risk that the country would be invaded. In preparation for this, the Gestapo compiled a list of more than 2,300 individuals who would immediately be arrested and probably executed. The list, in a booklet known as the 'Black Book', was found in the Berlin headquarters of the Reich Security Police in Berlin 1945.[14] The name of Sir Walter Citrine, general secretary of the TUC, was on the list. He was well known to the Nazis as president of IFTU from 1931 to 1933, when its headquarters was in Berlin. Also, 'Citrine was virulently attacked several days on end in the Nazi press' after his speech to the American Federation of Labor in New Orleans in 1940.[15]

It is sometimes thought that the union involvement in the war effort began with the appointment of Ernie Bevin as Minister of Labour and National Service in May 1940. In fact, the TUC was closely involved in negotiations with the Chamberlain government ministers from the declaration of war in September 1939 onwards. Citrine 'suspected they were being deliberately held at arm's length by the Government', especially by the Ministry of Supply, rather than being properly consulted. In a meeting with the prime minister in October, he pressed Chamberlain to strengthen collective bargaining with 'a list of demands' and that a joint advisory body of union and employer nominees be set up. They (Citrine and his chair, Bill Holmes) met Chamberlain again on 13 October, at which 'The PM read an instruction which he had sent around the Government Departments that prior consultation should take place with the TUC on industrial matters and that adequate representation should be asked for from the TUC on any committees which were being set up dealing with industry.'[16] This led to the establishment of a series of such joint Advisory Committees across the government, usually with five to seven union nominees from each industry. George Woodcock, the head of research (and a future general secretary), became secretary of the Ministry of Food Advisory Committee. All local food committees (about 1,500) in the country had a union representative. [17] On 18 October the National Joint Advisory Council to the Minister of Labour, with fifteen members from each side, was set up. Citrine took advantage of their strong bargaining position to get many other outstanding issues resolved. He even raised the repeal or amendment of the Trade Disputes and Trade Union Act of 1927, but though Chamberlain 'promised to think it over', he eventually declined due to 'the certainty of Conservative indignation'.[18] Although it protested after another meeting on 20 March 1940, the union's more immediate concern achieved the biggest concession from Chamberlain. This was over wages and prices during the war. In December 1939, the Chancellor of the Exchequer, Sir John Simon, stated that they would seek to restrain higher wages, which meant a decline in workers' standards of living, as they were unable to control prices. At a meeting on 3 January 1940, Citrine gave a strong reaction, arguing that workers would 'repudiate leaders who asked them to do this'. He warned that it would only play into hands of 'opposition designed to discredit the existing trade union leadership' and 'overthrow trade union authority'.[19] Even the employers' side agreed with him and soon after the Cabinet dropped the idea, saying, 'it would be unwise to attempt to secure [stabilising of prices] in return [for] an undertaking that wages would not be increased, since the trade union leaders could not guarantee fulfilment of the bargain'.[20] So it was left during the war and Bevin would build on this policy to encourage collective bargaining, though in the context of a system of compulsory arbitration of wages.

Churchill also reinforced Chamberlain's instructions that all government departments would fully consult the TUC and the unions.[21] Union collaboration became a key factor in Britain's war production drive from May 1940 onwards. However, it was not until Bevin took over at the Ministry of Labour and National Service that the unions were fully engaged.[22] The TUC was involved right across all departments. All the fifty or so Acts of Parliament that were passed in the early stages of the war with their masses of regulations had to be summarised and transmitted to the unions by the small TUC staff of sixty.[23] From his earliest days Citrine had held weekly meetings with departmental officers, encouraging a 'one TUC' approach rather than the more common departmental 'silo' one. It produced a special booklet, *The T.U.C. in Wartime*, every three months as well as a series of circulars, sometimes two a week.[24] All thirty-two General Council members were involved in the many outside bodies in their regions and industries. Churchill acknowledged their contribution fulsomely in 1945: 'We owe an immense debt to the trade unions and never can this country forget how they stood by and helped, ... willingly accepting the restraints which were necessary to win the war.'[25] It was the Citrine–Bevin 'double act', continuing their pre-war TUC partnership, which galvanised this war effort in 1940 and 1941.[26] At home, the organised Labour movement at local level gave a backbone to the national response to fascism, through the coalition government.

During the 'Phoney War' of 1939–40, Citrine was also very active on the other side of the Channel, trying to bolster French resistance through their unions. The TUC and CGT set up an Anglo-French Trade Union Council for this purpose. It met in Paris and London five times. In December 1939, 'the anti-imperialist war' *Daily Worker* ran a series of articles categorising these meetings as 'union leaders plotting with the French Citrines' to 'bring millions of trade unionists behind the war machine of British and French imperialism' in France.[27] Seven General Council members, including Citrine, took *The Daily Worker* to court for libel and won, but 'had to whistle for our damages' as usual, as the owners of *The Daily Worker* just switched ownership. Yet these ridiculous smears were still being carried in Wikipedia articles, decades afterwards (now amended)! Soon after the invasion of France in May 1940, the government and ruling elites capitulated and were allowed to set up a collaborationist regime in unoccupied France at Vichy, under Marshal Pétain. Most of the French unions collapsed and their leaders fled. After his arrival in London, the Belgian IFTU general secretary, Walther Schevenels, reported on what had happened in France. He attributed the collapse of the French ruling class to

> absence of unity in the government, Army, the masses – in fact, in the whole political and economic structure … In certain high circles of the Army, business and the middle class, there was a feeling that HITLER might as well take over to restore order and discipline – a feeling … strong enough to prevent the great majority from resisting … the inferiority [of equipment] was increased because of the lack of moral energy to fight the Germans to the limit of their resources.[28]

There were similar doubts in sections of the middle and upper classes in Britain and, had Lord Halifax become prime minister, they might well have attempted to do a deal with Hitler. Churchill and his supporters, including the Labour and union leadership, scotched any such notion and there would be no 'lack of moral energy to fight' in Britain.[29] Citrine now arranged with Schevenels to make provision for the IFTU staff, and to safeguard its funds and records.[30] On his arrival in London, the TUC provided offices for Schevenels and it also assisted many other national union officials. Though the heart of trade unionism had been torn from the European mainland, Citrine and Schevenels helped maintain the institutional framework of international trade unionism, until it was restored in 1945.[31]

BEVIN AND CITRINE

When Bevin took over the Ministry of Labour and National Service in May 1940, things 'moved up a gear or two'.[32] Within three days, Bevin and Citrine were 'closeted at the Ministry discussing how to contribute to the national production plans to repel the expected German invasion.'[33] A Joint Consultative Committee with seven employers and seven General Council members, chaired by Bevin, was set up to facilitate quick consultation. In that emergency, the Bevin–Citrine entente worked extremely well.[34] Citrine arranged a special conference of 2,000 delegates at Central Hall, Westminster, on 25 May 1940 (just days before British troops were evacuated from the Dunkirk beaches), for Bevin to make a dramatic appeal to his former union colleagues. The Minister of Labour and National Service read a letter from the prime minister 'to say that the country's needs were imperative, inescapable and imperious'.[35] Churchill sought their acceptance of the Emergency Powers Act 1940 and other Ministerial Orders banning strikes and substituting compulsory arbitration of wage claims. Bevin then made one of those powerful speeches for which he was renowned, showing his ability to bring home to ordinary workers what the war was all about.[36] He said, 'If our Movement and our class rise with all their energy now and save the people of this country from disaster, the country will always turn with confidence forever to the people who saved them.'[37] Perhaps not 'forever'! Citrine moved the Council's resolution endorsing their sacrifice of normal union rights and practices, while stressing 'their determination to preserve the powers and functions of the trade unions and to ensure the maintenance of the hard-won liberties of the workers'.[38] In response to Citrine's point about safeguards, Bevin told them that he had set up a new Labour Supply Board, over which he would preside, composed of two leading employers and two senior union leaders, 'to survey the use of labour and its transfer'. This Board would ensure 'that labour would be properly utilised', he said.[39]

Citrine had to remind Bevin of that promise a short while later. Two of the Labour Supply Board members (one union, one employer) came to him complaining that 'they and their two colleagues had been cut off, almost completely, from the Minister', and 'had to conduct all their business through the Permanent Secretary'.[40] They asked Citrine to help as 'I was the only person who could intervene with any hope of success'.[41] He reluctantly arranged to meet Bevin, who 'flared up with resentment'. Citrine told him that he was 'breaking faith with the TUC'. This 'dissertation sent up the temperature several degrees, and Bevin scowled at me with a face almost black with anger'. He rose from his desk, pulled on his raincoat and made for the door. Citrine persisted, 'in a louder voice … warning that a refusal would mean a struggle between him and the TUC. This shook him, as I could see, and,

1933 TUC Congress at Brighton with Bevin
and Alec Walkden (president).

pushing his way through the door, he growled over his shoulder: I'll see them.'[42] Bevin did see them, though the Labour Supply Board was 'quietly dropped' in March 1941.[43] This was typical Ernie, 'a man of moods', as Citrine well knew. Bullock described his 'variation of mood all the way from the sullen to the exuberant, from the truculent to the philosophical'.[44] Nonetheless, Citrine appreciated the scale of the challenge which Bevin had undertaken to build the manpower supply machine of the country in such fraught circumstances.

Despite all their personal and union difficulties over the next few years, Citrine retained a deep respect for Ernie, appreciative of his many strengths from their time together since 1926. He usually made allowance for Bevin's 'strong likes and dislikes, which coloured both his thinking and his attitude to others'.[45] The most concrete manifestation of this respect was that, soon after, Citrine helped get Bevin promoted to the War Cabinet. Arthur Greenwood, Labour's deputy prime minister, had approached the TUC leader on 17 June 1940 to discuss Bevin's unauthorised actions. Bevin had promised a delegation of agricultural and railway workers to increase their pay without the authority of, or even consultation with, the Cabinet ministers responsible (wage determination did not come within the Ministry of Labour's ambit). Only Chamberlain was there for the meeting with Citrine in Downing Street and he immediately asked Citrine, 'what are we to do with this man Bevin?'[46] Citrine 'strongly advised' him 'not to pick a quarrel with Bevin', as he would 'make an issue of the matter' and possibly resign, claiming that 'he had been victimised by the most unpopular Chamberlain while trying to serve them' (the unions and the Labour Party). 'Why not put him in the Cabinet', Citrine suggested. 'If he was a party to Cabinet decisions, he would most certainly carry them out.'[47] In a government reshuffle the following October, Bevin was promoted to the War Cabinet and Citrine believed it was on his advice, though he never claimed the credit. When revealing the episode to Churchill in 1952, Citrine added, 'I am quite sure that if Bevin had ever thought he owed his position in the Cabinet to a recommendation of mine, he would have resigned on principle. Winston laughed outright at this but did not indicate whether he was already aware

of what I had told him.' [48] Bevin thought it was Churchill's idea
and was greatly pleased (as were Citrine and the unions). Nevertheless, it was the making of Bevin's career as a government minister.

'QUISLING'

However, the next occasion on which Citrine and Bevin clashed
was far more bitter and public. This was in the autumn of 1941,
concerning the Minister of Labour's direction of skilled men from
industry to the services, under the Emergency Powers Act.[49] Under
a Restriction on Engagement Order, Bevin had taken upon himself
extreme powers over the engagement of all labour (employers could
only hire through the 1,200 local Labour Exchanges, so as to prevent
poaching). A series of Essential Work Orders gave him further
powers restricting workers from leaving a job without the employer's
'leaving certificate', but with protection against dismissal. As Ministerial Orders, Parliament could not debate or question these, almost
military, powers. But it was the system of call-up or deferment for
the forces from the skilled manpower industries that caused most
concern to the unions. In September 1941, the TUC Congress at
Edinburgh passed a resolution critical of the Ministry of Labour's
priority to call up 'all and sundry' for the armed forces. It said that
the skilled unions 'regarded the manning of industry as of equal
importance with manpower for the Fighting Services'.[50] The debate
highlighted the 'many reports' of skilled men being called up 'whose
services were being wasted in all sorts of odd jobs – peeling potatoes,
tending gardens, sweeping floors – jobs that could be done by anyone
… [while] essential war industries were being seriously depleted,
thus placing a grave handicap on the output of munitions'.[51] The
reason it had come to be articulated publicly at Edinburgh was

that Bevin had 'obstinately refused to appoint a T.U.C member to the Committee' which had been set up by his Department to examine the complaints. 'This affronted our people and criticism of the Government was stimulated.'[52] Citrine did not take part in the debate at the Congress, though he 'shared the concern of our members'.[53] Then, at a public meeting in Manchester at the end of September, he weighed in, saying, 'I view with the utmost concern, the prospect of war industry losing any more of its steadily diminishing resources of manpower. Any further rolling up of skilled men is bound to have a serious effect on production. We have not done more than scratch the surface in organising war production and the trade unions demand the right (not the privilege) to be consulted and to put our point of view.'[54] Citrine had no compunction about telling ministers, including Bevin, to respect union views. He linked the manpower issue with the deficiencies in producing arms, planes and other equipment for Russia. The TUC was about to set up a new Anglo-Soviet Trade Union Committee (see Chapter 13) and was among the first to see the importance of assisting the Soviet Union at that critical juncture in the war.[55] Citrine thought that by not including a union representative in his Departmental review, Bevin was going back on another promise. The *Daily Herald* picked up on the story and ran a number of articles critical of the government, based on the TUC complaints.[56]

At a meeting at Southampton on 27 September, Bevin reacted strongly, saying that the *Daily Herald* had been carrying on 'a nagging, miserable, "Quisling" policy now every day of our lives'.[57] He added, 'No Citrine, nobody can tell me that I shall not call upon skilled men. I mean to have sufficient of them for all Services. It shall not be on my conscience that I risked a single airman's life.'[58] He believed that Citrine, vice-chair of the *Daily Herald* board,[59] was behind the articles (giving some basis to Bevin's suspicion, though Citrine firmly denied it) and the *Herald* made a 'spirited reply … against this most unjust accusation'.[60] That it should be the *Daily Herald*, 'a paper that I helped to build', taking this line, made Bevin too angry to contain himself'.[61] But to use such terms as 'Quisling' or 'traitor', the greatest insult imaginable at that time, and to personalise it with Citrine so insultingly, jeopardised their entire relationship. Bevin later denied using the word 'Quisling', but two other papers, the *Daily Express* and London *Evening Standard*, also reported his words.[62] Citrine's response was remarkably calm, writing a very conciliatory letter to Bevin the same day, giving him a graceful way out, saying, 'we were all suffering from war strain and we must allow for Ministers becoming hyper-sensitive of criticism'.[63] He also said that he regarded Bevin as the 'most outstanding personality in the labour movement'.[64] However, Citrine still pursued the issue that Bevin had not allowed a TUC nominee on his 'inquiry' committee. Citrine told him straight that 'there was a genuine difference of opinion on the issue of manpower and this should not be distorted into a personal quarrel'.[65] Soon, all the other newspapers picked up on the row; '*Bevin v Citrine, Open if undeclared war is now raging between them*', declared the *Evening Standard*.[66] Churchill instructed Attlee to write to both, urging them to calm down, which they did, at least in public.[67] Citrine told Attlee, 'Bevin went out of his way to attack me and when I tried to patch the matter up I received no reply.'[68] Bevin did reply after Attlee contacted him, though his letter to Citrine was not at all conciliatory.[69] He denied that he had used the word 'Quisling' and gave no apology. Graciously, Citrine accepted that it may not have been aimed at him personally: 'I knew his habit of not properly preparing his speeches, and his tendency to fly off the handle.'[70] But there was no attempt at reconciliation from Bevin. Stiffly he said, 'With regard to my reference to you, if the policy of the Government is attacked, Ministers must answer ...'[71] There was no meeting between them to clear the air and the whole incident could only have soured their relationship. Citrine later recalled that well-known trait of Bevin's character, that 'he was a man who could not brook opposition ... That was one of his outstanding weaknesses. He always person-alised opposition.'[72] Another sympathetic biographer, Lord Jenkins, acknowledged this trait: 'He never accepted opposition easily or tolerantly. He personalized it, quickly imported a deep note of bitterness into most disputes and used phrases like "the stab in the back" more freely than reasoned argument.'[73]

The Ministry of Labour inquiry committee under William (later Lord) Beveridge 'confirmed many of the [TUC's] criti-cisms'.[74] As a result, 'the Cabinet cut the Service demands for skilled men in the period up to March 1942 from 26,000 to 8,600'.[75] However, Beveridge, who did so much sterling work in the department as an under secretary, was transferred out. He went on to greater things with his landmark report on social insurance of 1942.[76] In directing manpower supply, Bevin and the Ministry of Labour and National Service were exercising nigh-on dictatorial powers. In his defence, it could be said that the exigen-cies of the war, which Britain was losing in 1941, justified extreme measures. A junior department before the war, dealing mainly with matters such as unemployment insurance, it had been built up under Bevin and it had grown in staff from just under 30,000 in 1939 to 44,500 at its peak in 1943.[77] Citrine saw their role at the TUC as upholding the safeguards against bureaucracy and authoritarianism (natural in times of war), though he never got in the way of Bevin's genuine manpower mobilisation drives (including the conscription of women). Speaking at the 1941 TUC Congress, Citrine explained, 'that he had been determined from the outbreak of the war to ensure that the TUC acted "to restrain the inevitable development of bureaucracy"'.[78] Bullock, and all Bevin biographers since, present this massive mobilisation achievement – 'twenty-two-and-three-quarters men and women out of a population of thirty-three million between the ages of 14 and 64' – as having been achieved 'on the basis of consent, with the minimum of coercion'.[79] Undoubtedly, they were 'working with the grain' of popular consent to win that war of survival. But to leave out the enormous trade union assistance in every factory, workshop and office, and the unpopularity they often encountered from their own members, is to take away their share of the credit. On behalf of the General Council, Citrine was also determined to ensure they 'were going to retain trade union independence, to retain the maximum of our liberties irrespective from what quarter the encroachments came'.[80] The usual criticism of the TUC leadership (by Nye Bevan and his small band of supporters in the House of Commons) was that they were blind lackeys of the government throughout the war years. As we can see, this was far from the case. Bevan, as a leading backbench MP, did not have any responsibility during the war, or any liaison with the more representative union officials, his old friends in the South Wales Miners' Federation perhaps excepted. He didn't see much of them either, as his visits to his Ebbw Vale constituency were most infrequent from the early 1930s.[81] But, as self-appointed champion of the individual worker against the organised ones, i.e., the union officials (dismissed as proponents of the 'corporate state'), the 'part proletarian, part intellectual' (Morrison's description) Bevan was able to carve out a niche for himself in Parliament as a formidable critic of the government, especially of Bevin.[82]

The disparity in power between Bevin and Citrine was also growing. Bevin was resourced by a very large Ministry of Labour, with very able and determined senior civil servants in charge, particularly Frederick Leggett[83] and Godfrey Ince,[84] the two extremely competent deputy permanent secretaries, responsible for industrial relations and manpower matters respectively. Bevin relied on their advice and briefings more and more, rather than on what the unions or Citrine might say. However much he protested that he was still just a 'union man', the reality had to be different as he was then a powerful Cabinet minister in charge of one of the major war departments; Bevin 'in practice was continually pressing the unions to make concessions and accept responsibilities in the national interest, which cut across their original function of defending the particular interests of their members.'[85] Bullock recognised there had to be 'some degree of compulsion to labour' (especially with the vast numbers of new female labour being conscripted). Under Citrine, the TUC was doing all it could to get unions to accept those responsibilities. But to retain its credibility, it also had to defend its members' occupational interests, where their complaints were reasonable. However, a 'testy' Bevin increasingly saw Citrine's insistence that the unions were consulted properly and their point of view respected as hostile criticism. As the war wore on to its third, fourth and fifth years, fatigue and friction would grow, and the strain would begin to show. A more careful assessment of the balanced role Citrine had undertaken shows the tensions, misunderstandings and unfair attacks the people he spoke for were subjected to, by one side or the other across the political spectrum.

BEVIN THE POLITICIAN

There was another factor at play: Bevin had become a leading politician. Citrine was always conscious of that dual aspect of Bevin's
character. The T&GWU leader had kept out of Parliament until
late in life, but here he was aged fifty-nine, ambitious for the extra
power it would give him, as well as taking on such a challenging
role at that age. In the past, Citrine said that Bevin 'had sought my
advice on more than one occasion'.[86] Citrine had always advised
him that he should 'stick to the trades union movement', but, 'he
never seemed reassured by my advice, and deep down in him there
must have been some hankering after political power. I thought
he had plenty of it, as I had, without crossing the threshold of St
Stephen's.'[87] Bevin had tried to get into Parliament in 1931 when
he was very popular in the party for his stance against MacDonald
and Snowden. However, he suffered a heavy defeat in a previously
rock-solid Newcastle Labour seat, due to the scale of MacDonald's 'National government' victory. He also had a brief association
with G. D. H. Cole's left-wing Society for Socialist Information and
Propaganda (SSIP), which he chaired.[88] However, when it merged
with the former ILP Labour Party left-wing 'remainers' to form the
Socialist League in 1932, their intrigue lost him the chair, leaving
him with a grudge against 'intellectuals' for the rest of his career.
So, he 'took his bat away' from Labour Party matters for a time.[89]
Bevin finally made it to the Labour front bench in 1940, without
having to go through the usual parliamentary candidate selection
and election process because of the war. With his top-level union
experience, once in the inner Cabinet, Bevin was in his element in
the committees (his forte), which did most of the business under
a key Cabinet figure, Sir John Anderson, the Lord President of

the Council.[90] Though Bevin still believed himself to be a union man and used his considerable union credentials and language to present himself as 'the Churchill of the proletariat in the Workers' War',[91] Bevin's actions were increasingly those of a Minister of the Crown, like all the other Cabinet members. From his days on the Bristol docks and creation of the T&G to his ministerial career, Bevin developed all the ruthlessness, wiles and penchant for intrigue characteristic of success in top-level politics. They would be deployed even in his relations with Citrine and the TUC. His biographers have not given serious attention to this powerful dimension of their subject's character.

BEAVERBROOK AND BEVIN

Bevin's 'turf wars' with Lord Beaverbrook in late 1941/early 1942 illustrate this dimension.[92] Beaverbrook, as Minister of Aircraft Production (1940–41) and then Minister of Supply (tanks) for the rest of 1941, got most of the credit for the much greater numbers of planes, tanks and guns his ministries now produced.[93] His reputation was high as 'someone who got things done', if somewhat high-handedly.[94] Bevin undoubtedly also made a big difference in expanding the Ministry of Labour and National Service's remit, making it the dominant department supplying the manpower for all the services.[95] However, the two 'larger than life' beasts of the wartime Cabinet (sometimes more like 'bulls in a china-shop') continuously locked horns over manpower issues which overlapped between their departments. This was much to the exasperation of their more experienced and calm colleagues, especially when the war was going badly. A. J. P. Taylor called these manpower tussles 'the great undisclosed theme of British government throughout 1941'.[96]

'The Beaver' was a close personal and political ally of Churchill's and it was he who was sent to Moscow in October 1941
on the joint US/UK mission about the military supplies requirements of the new Soviet ally. He also accompanied Churchill to
Washington later in December and impressed Roosevelt, when
they agreed to combine US and UK production for the war. So,
on his return in January 1942, Churchill announced the setting up
of a new Ministry of Production to oversee all UK war production services, with Beaverbrook as the minister. The proverbial hit
the fan. Bevin, understandably, reacted explosively, especially at the
prospect of having to report to Beaverbrook on manpower issues.
He threatened to resign and make a public stink.[97] But it seems that
Clem Attlee's intervention 'swung it' for Bevin as the Labour leader
threatened to bring down the coalition over that and other issues.
This was at a time when there was much criticism of Churchill as
the war was going badly (the loss of Singapore and Tobruk were
huge blows to national confidence). The Commons were becoming
increasingly restive, and many MPs expressed a lack of confidence
in Churchill's leadership.[98] As often in such cases, a reshuffle was
the answer. As part of it, Churchill climbed down in his plan for
the Ministry of Production and left manpower supply to Bevin.
This precipitated Beaverbrook's resignation, a month after he had
become the new minister, partly due to ill health (severe asthma),
but the main reason seems to have been his failure to get the extra
powers.[99] The much-criticised and underrated Attlee had shown
his teeth on Bevin's behalf, in his quieter but more ruthless way,
hence Bevin's legendary loyalty to him.[100] Attlee had also wanted
to curtail Beaverbrook's powers ('whose hostility to Attlee knew no
bounds'[101]). The new deputy prime minister's victory in the resul-
tant reshuffle (if, at the cost of his deputy Arthur Greenwood's

displacement from the Cabinet and Cripps' joining it) signified 'a deliberate elevation of the Labour Party's standing in the coalition with Attlee and Cripps acting as general coordinators'.[102] From here on Bevin would become a leading figure in the wartime coalition.

Citrine favoured a single Ministry of Production with full powers over all aspects, including manpower, to avoid the 'silo' departmental mentality which was affecting wartime production. Originally, Beaverbrook agreed with Citrine that Bevin 'would be the most suitable person to be appointed Minister'.[103] However, Citrine now believed that, 'in the present circumstances',[104] 'it would be said that Bevin had beaten the Prime Minister once and there would be no holding him. He might even provoke a political crisis at a later date as he was so intent on securing power.'[105] As a result of Beaverbrook's heavy lobbying, Citrine seemed to accept that 'all he [Bevin] thinks about is getting power'.[106] Citrine's advice to Beaverbrook, therefore, was that he should 'take the post', but only if he were to change his attitude. Citrine, who was always on very friendly terms with Beaverbrook, was quite direct with him: 'You make up your mind too quickly and you are impulsive. You ride roughshod over opposition, and you have caused a good deal of resentment.'[107] Amazingly, a contrite Beaverbrook accepted Citrine's advice and invited him to chair an Advisory Committee of employers and union representatives in the new ministry, as a token of his good intentions to change. Citrine accepted.[108]

After Beaverbrook's sudden resignation, Citrine stayed on as chair of the joint Advisory Committee, publishing a report on the powers of the Ministry of Production's Regional Boards.[109] However, he would have burned his boats with Bevin (and with Attlee, too, probably), as they would have seen his closeness to Beaverbrook, and acceptance of that position, as a betrayal. In

April 1942, Citrine stood down to go to America (see Chapter 13),
to get the unions there onto the proposed Anglo-Soviet-American
Trade Union Committee, and so there would be no opportunity
to discuss their differences.[110] Citrine concluded that the antipa-
thy between Beaverbrook and Bevin 'blurred their appreciation of
one another's qualities. Both had creative minds and great driving
force and were equally intolerant of opposition.'[111] But Bevin
would not have forgotten Citrine's 'betrayal'. So, the outcome to
the Cabinet power struggle of 1942 undoubtedly marked the start
of the Attlee–Bevin ascent to power and the beginning of Citrine's
decline in influence.

BEVAN, BEVIN AND CITRINE

Our exploration of these wartime tensions would not be complete
without reference to Bevin's handling of the major industrial
disputes of the war – especially in the coal mines during the winter
of 1943–44. At the start of the war, Bevin had encouraged miners
to leave the industry for the forces. His later Bevin Boys scheme
was one attempt to recover that situation. By 1941, there was an
acute shortage of mining manpower at a time of high and growing
production demand. Now they were having to consider releasing
about 7,000 former miners from the armed forces.[112] The miners'
union (MFGB), now back in a strong bargaining position and with
growing communist influence, sought to extract the maximum in
pay concessions. The very able communist Arthur Horner was
president of the South Wales Miners and the leading figure on the
MFGB National Executive. It was involved 'in endless rounds of
negotiation' with the Mines Department and Bevin's Ministry of
Labour. In May 1942, 'a series of disruptive strikes occurred in

the coal fields over wages and conditions, involving 58,000 men'.[113] Citrine and the TUC came under pressure to 'provide unqualified support' to the union. But Citrine was said to be 'concerned to moderate what he regarded as the MFGB Executive's implacable determination to use the war as a means to redress the balance of class power in coalmining.'[114] So, they gave Horner 'qualified acceptance' as a national union leader, bringing him onto one of the General Council's committees (on workmen's compensation), and not opposing his election as a TUC delegate to the American Federation of Labor Convention in September 1943.[115] They also supported MFGB president Ebby Edwards for chair of the General Council and Citrine worked closely with him afterwards. In this way, Citrine helped moderate the miners' threat to the coal production drives and to achieve settlements with the union and progress towards the goal of coal industry nationalisation.

Reverting to the rhetoric of his earlier extreme left-wing socialist days, Aneurin Bevan as an MP now latched on to growing miners' and other workers' discontent over pay and wartime conditions after three years of carnage, stress and strain. A rash of unofficial strikes also took place all over the coalfields in the winter of 1943. For weeks in early 1944, they involved over 100,000 miners in South Wales and 120,000 in Yorkshire alone, the centres of the action. This was at the time when preparations for the D-Day landings in Normandy were intensifying and so Churchill and the Cabinet looked to Bevin to get the situation under control quickly.[116] The crisis plunged him into the thick of political controversy, spearheaded by Aneurin Bevan in the Commons.[117] Bevin attended the TUC General Council personally at Transport House on 5 April 1944 to appeal for it 'to issue as strong a statement as possible condemning the strikers'. It did so after much debate, and Citrine and his chair, Ebby Edwards, issued a statement which 'gave Bevin the full backing of the trade-union movement'.[118] As a result, a delegate conference of the Miners' Federation accepted the wage proposals on 20 April.

But Bevin and his officials were not satisfied with that, alarmed that the unofficial actions might be spreading to other industries. He therefore instructed his officials to amend the Defence Regulations by Ministerial Order, penalising anyone 'who attempted to foment or exploit a strike in an essential service'.[119] This was his infamous Regulation 1AA, which threatened anyone inciting an unofficial strike with a maximum of five years' penal servitude or £500 fine (or both). Again, the TUC accepted the change as a temporary measure – an Order in Council rather than legislation. Prosecutions against a tiny Trotskyist sect under the 1927 Act were also used, as Bevin tried to argue that there were real anti-war forces at work, but this was not taken seriously. This use of the law showed how authoritarian he could be, but with TUC and union backing, it had the desired effect and the Regulations never had to be invoked against anybody.[120] But Regulation 1AA enabled Aneurin Bevan to launch a bitter attack on the minister of labour *and* the trade union leadership. Accusing the minister of bypassing Parliament, Bevan skilfully fastened on the extreme terms of the regulations, rather than on the settlement of the disputes, which were a major improvement for the miners. Even Bullock acknowledged that 'Bevin failed to make the best of his own case'.[121] Turning to the unions, Bevan made the most extraordinary attack on the TUC and the official leadership of the unions. He denounced them as being 'out of touch with rank-and-file opinion in the unions' and that 'it [the TUC] represented only the trade union officials', whose 'only way he can keep them in order is to threaten them with five years in gaol'.[122] He even broadened the attack on union rights generally, suggesting that Parliament should scrutinise their rules and break up their 'monopoly' privileges in representing workers.[123] This was all done from a 'defence of Parliament' and of 'the individual worker' stance, alleging 'that it is the enfranchisement of the corporate society and the disenfranchisement of the individual'.[124] But to malign union officials generally, as he did in his Commons speech over Regulation 1AA in 1944, at a time when they were doing so much to help the government to organise war production and mobilise the country's manpower, and get away with it, seems incredible, even today. Arthur Greenwood, the former Cabinet minister and deputy Labour leader told him that his speech was 'of an anti-trade-union character the like of which I have never heard from the most die-hard Tory in this House or outside'.[125] Yet because Aneurin Bevan's target was Ernest Bevin's draconian Regulation 1AA, only 56 out of 165 Labour MPs voted in support of that measure. Aneurin Bevan narrowly escaped expulsion from the Labour Party (again) over this attack on Bevin and the unions.[126] He escaped a vote for him to be disciplined on the Parliamentary Labour Committee narrowly, because Shinwell (with a soft spot for Bevan, as he himself was once a militant rebel), got support for his amendment only requiring Bevan to sign an undertaking to behave in the future.[127]

Bevan (and his wife Jenny Lee), definitely 'had it in' for Citrine.[128] Apart from his jibe about Citrine's 'card-index mind' and 'poor fellow, he suffers from files', which we have already noted[129] Bevan once said,

Sir Walter should be repudiated by the General Council. When he speaks for himself he is not dangerous. His drab and colourless personality, without the fortification of his position, raises not a flicker of interest in anybody. Divested of authority his opinions are those of a political illiterate. He should confine himself to his filing system. I am told he is quite good at that.[130]

A famous *Tribune* cartoon of April 1939, 'Blimp's Purge', was another example of Bevan targeting Citrine. This time it was over Bevan's expulsion from the Labour Party with Sir Stafford Cripps. This was for Bevan's refusal to drop their campaign to link up with the Communist Party in a 'united front', despite Conference support for the NEC's decision. Although Citrine and the TUC had nothing to do with that Labour Party decision, *Tribune*, under Bevan's editorship, published a cartoon with the caption 'Citrine is right. The Labour Party is quite right to expel all but sound Conservatives', which showed its determination to focus on 'the apparatchik' and 'the bureaucrat'.[131]

Citrine's criticisms of Michael Foot's *Tribune* book, *Guilty Men*, as 'as a thinly veiled attempt to go back on Labour's entry into the coalition government' in 1940, would not have endeared him to them either.[132]

But as Bevan acquired a considerable left following from his wartime opposition to the government role, Attlee brought him into the Labour government and Cabinet in 1945, channelling his talent into constructive health and housing reforms. There is little justice in politics!

CITRINE AND ATTLEE

The key figure influencing the course of the Citrine–Bevin partnership was Clement Attlee, now deputy prime minister. As we saw above, but for Attlee, Bevin might not have survived in the Cabinet over his depressed reaction to the Beaverbrook promotion as minister of production in January 1942. Citrine and Attlee were never close, possibly because of Attlee's flirtation with Cripps' Socialist League. He expressed 'surprise' about Attlee's presence at his LSE meeting with Cripps and fellow League luminaries in July 1933. He thought the League 'never really understood the trade union movement' and he included Attlee in that.[133] Initially, Bevin was equally unimpressed by Attlee, only supporting him for leader in 1935 to block Herbert Morrison. They were not hugely impressed initially with Attlee's performance as leader.[134] Citrine was mainly sceptical on account of Attlee's weakness on the key rearmament issue, though he gave him full credit for taking on the deputy leadership role.[135] Attlee, as acting leader, had led the Labour Opposition in the Commons' debates on foreign policy in 1934 when they voted strongly against the Defence estimates. At a time when Churchill was calling for a quadrupling of the RAF's capability, Attlee, as Leader of the Opposition in Parliament in the Commons debate of 13 July 1934, opposed the government's move for some increase. Attlee minimised the threat from Hitler, saying, 'I think the whole movement towards dictatorships in Europe has reached its highest point and that there is a decline in the movement towards dictatorships owing to the failure of the dictators. I think that Hitler and his movement is the last move ... I think we can generally say to-day that this dictatorship is falling down.'[136] One of his biographers, Robert Pearce, has acknowledged this stance 'as verging on the ridiculous'.[137] It certainly would have seemed so to Citrine after his IFTU experience in Berlin in 1933. Nevertheless, in 1935, Attlee, with his 'reputation for hard work, reliability and trustworthiness', just won the Labour MPs' vote from the recently re-elected

Morrison and Arthur Greenwood MP.[138] Citrine, of course, took
no part in that Parliamentary Party contest, but, if he had had a
vote, it would probably have gone to Morrison.

Eventually, after the Brighton Conference decision in 1935 where
the TUC and National Council of Labour view had prevailed, Attlee
and his team accepted the 'new realism of Labour's foreign policy'
which 'had been achieved against his considered judgement'.[139] There
was, however, no close liaison between Citrine and Attlee. On the
National Council of Labour, Attlee was deeply uncommunicative,
being known as 'Clam Attlee' by the General Council members. His
habit of 'expressing himself in a few sentences, or just sit doodling'
annoyed Citrine. 'We had a right to expect Attlee to give us guidance,
but he told us very little.'[140] Attlee's views about the TUC input at
that time are not explored at all by his biographers but he must have
resented its outspoken criticisms of the PLP's voting conduct in the
Commons on the defence estimates and of his leadership. Bew just
says that he relied on Bevin 'to marshal the unions', which confirms a
weak liaison with the other key union leader, Citrine.[141] As the Parliamentary Labour Party recovered from the 1931 catastrophe (in 1935
it improved the position from 46 to 154 seats), the 'Citrine doctrine',
as Attlee's biographer Francis Beckett called it, must have irked
Attlee, which may also explain his taciturnity with the union leaders.
This 'doctrine' was that, 'The general council should be regarded
as having an integral right to initiate and participate in any political
matter which it deems to be of direct concern to its constituents.'[142]
This led to the setting up of the liaison committee (the NJC, later the
NCL) on Citrine's initiative when Henderson was leader in 1931/32,
as we saw in Chapter 9.[143] Thereafter, as joint secretary, Citrine's
input on the NCL was always constructive, if firm, on TUC policy
about dictatorship and democracy, and the need for rearmament

and, if necessary, war, to combat Hitler's Nazi dictatorship. Bevin also came to play a major role on the NCL as as TUC member and at Labour Conferences with his TGWU votes and speeches. So, it was the union influence that secured the policies which served the national interest, rather than any narrow union (or party/personal) one. The TUC loyally supported Attlee throughout the war, and he proved a very able leader, once in office, as deputy prime minister, from 1942 onwards.[144]

It is a mistake to think that the unions always got their way. In fact, as we have seen above, they were very much junior partners, especially after the threat of invasion passed in 1940. This was vividly shown in the case of the TUC lobby which failed to persuade Churchill or Attlee even to amend the 1927 Trade Disputes and Trade Union Act. Attlee was not prepared to tackle Churchill (nor were Bevin or Morrison) by making this an issue in the coalition government. It would not even champion the civil servants' case for reaffiliation to the TUC and Attlee made that clear to Citrine in a one-to-one interview in August 1943.[145] Citrine then had to persuade the postal workers, who were gearing up to defy the law by affiliating anyway, not to do so in case their members were penalised with the loss of their civil service status and pension rights, which Labour ministers would enforce. So, the underlying relationship remained uneasy, with the Labour ministers clearly having the upper hand the longer they were in government. By contrast, 'Herbert Morrison, never hesitated to give me the low-down on any matter of general policy' and so he was the Minister with whom Citrine had most contact.[146] However, though Citrine felt that 'he understood our movement a good deal better than most of his colleagues, past and present', not much detail is provided of their relationship. It seems likely that Citrine favoured him for the leadership in 1935. This may also explain Attlee's reticence.[147]

This exploration of wartime relations between Citrine and the Labour ministers of the coalition government highlights the major role which the unions played under Citrine/TUC direction. In tracing the individual ministers' relationships, we do not seek to detract from their overall courage, commitment and record in their collective Cabinet achievement in conducting the anti-fascist war effort, which has been fully documented by others. While it is the case that Bevin had the more public role in raising the labour supply, it was Citrine's work behind the scenes which was pivotal in the complex and delicate task of persuading unions to suspend hard-won rights. They worked together, despite Bevin's increasing hostility, for the common aim of victory in the war. But ultimately it was Citrine and his General Council's persuasion, as much as Bevin's orders, which helped achieve such high levels of mobilisation and defused incipient disputes and strikes. Here we shed new light on their occasional frailties under severe pressure and this needs to be factored into any overall assessment and history of the times. It also points up the limitations of union power faced with the growing power of the coalition government and Cabinet in wartime, an imbalance which continued into the post-war Labour government.

CHAPTER 13

~

THE DREAM OF INTERNATIONAL WORKERS' UNITY

We saw how Citrine's tour of the United States and Canada in late 1940 helped to combat American isolationism, as 'the American public as a whole were not then disposed to come into the war'.[1] It was that mood which President Roosevelt had combatted successfully to secure an unprecedented third term in office in November 1940. Although he knew that, as a wily politician, Roosevelt was no saint, Citrine had been an admirer since he first came to office in 1932. As well as giving America hope for recovery from the Great Depression, Roosevelt's administration provided union rights and a very different global vision than was evident in Britain or Europe.[2] Citrine's invitation from Bill Green, its president, to address the American Federation of Labor (AFL) Convention in New Orleans was part of that union's anti-isolationism. The AFL leadership were strong Roosevelt supporters, unlike the leader of their rivals, John L. Lewis, president of the Congress of Industrial Organisations (CIO).[3] So, Citrine's speech on Monday 25 November was carried widely on US news networks and warmly welcomed by the US president and Cabinet.[4] Citrine brought home to the American people the spirit of resistance to fascism developing in Britain.

Churchill was very pleased when they discussed the trip.[5] The prime minister had then arranged for him to have 'a Diplomatic Status' and a letter to President Roosevelt, which said: 'This is to introduce you to my friend, Sir Walter Citrine. He worked with me three years before the war in our effort to arouse all parties in the country to the need of rearmament against Germany.'[6]

Citrine, therefore, was fulfilling a diplomatic role for Britain and the unions at a critical time. With great enthusiasm the AFL arranged his itinerary and he addressed more than fifty trade union and other meetings, some involving thousands. He also spoke at smaller gatherings with opinion formers in Rotary Clubs, Chambers of Commerce, university faculties and so on, and made numerous broadcasts. His extended tour 'from the South, by stages, back to Washington and from thence across to San Francisco' can best be seen from the map in *My American Diary*, which he published at the time.[7]

Not content with touring America, and despite his poor health, Citrine recrossed the continent again to Canada – to Vancouver,

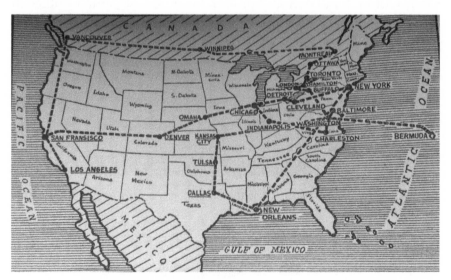

Map of Citrine's US and Canadian tour, 1940.

Winnipeg, Montreal and Toronto – and met union and other audiences and leaders. Mackenzie King, the Canadian prime minister
and a close friend of Roosevelt, told him his speech was the finest

> which had ever been delivered to the [Canadian] Club ... You
> are doing a magnificent job over here. Have you noticed how
> American public opinion has moved since you came over?
> Why, the President himself is using the same sentiments as you
> did to the American Federation of Labour.[8]

Back in the USA, Citrine addressed 'a large and representative luncheon conference' convened in New York by the AFL
Executive organisation (The League for Human Rights, Peace
and Democracy) on 26 December. Its president, Matthew Woll,
cabled Churchill 'in response to a moving and eloquent plea by Sir
Walter Citrine for stepping up production of war planes and war
supplies' for Britain. He said that 'it was the sense of our meeting
that this should be done without delay to insure [sic] perpetuation
of democracy and freedom in the world also be advised American
labour under auspices of the League of Human Rights, Freedom
and Democracy plan a nationwide campaign to support British
labour in meeting their needs for relief and other aid'.[9] Citrine
then returned to Washington where he met President Roosevelt at
the White House in January 1941.[10] They talked about his visits to
many munitions and aircraft factories (to which he had been given
special access[11]), so that he could report back about the supply
situation to Britain. The president told him how American unions
(AFL and CIO) were now cooperating to boost the production
of war materials. Citrine found him very engaging and interesting to talk to. Churchill had previously told Roosevelt that, as a

privy councillor, Citrine could be trusted to discuss matters confidentially and so they ranged over many international issues, not least Citrine's visits to the Soviet Union. The success of this tour in 1940–41 would have boosted the British TUC leader's standing with the American unions.

TO RUSSIA, BOLSTERING
THE ANGLO-SOVIET ALLIANCE

Effective resistance to the Nazi invasion by the Soviet Union in 1941 changed attitudes to the communist regime there. In Citrine's opinion, this was the 'dramatic turn which was destined to affect the whole future of the war'.[12] Relief in Britain was particularly intense and the public 'transformed themselves into a high state of almost unreasoning admiration' of the Soviet Union.[13] Assisting Stalin to resist the German invasion became an important part of British and later American war strategy.[14] On Citrine's initiative, the TUC decided to revive the Anglo-Soviet Trades Union Committee (ASTUC) in October 1941.[15] He now sought to outflank those communists (and former Socialist Leaguers like Cripps) riding on the backs of popular pro-Soviet sentiment, with the TUC taking the lead. He worked with Anthony Eden, the foreign secretary, and the prime minister for this purpose, but was not part of the state's diplomacy, as some on the pro-communist left claimed, which doesn't explain his acceptability to the Soviet leaders.[16] But this was more than just a manoeuvre to sideline the British communists, as some have cynically portrayed it.[17] It was a brave mission to assist the development of a crucial alliance. Citrine himself led the British delegation to Moscow at the time Hitler was closing in on the Soviet capital. They set off for Moscow on 5 October, and Churchill sent 'his best wishes for a prosperous voyage and a successful outcome to your important work'.[18] They travelled by destroyer via Iceland, to avoid the U-boats, but the sea was as much of a challenge. 'There was a really heavy swell, some of the waves rising … at least thirty feet above the deck.'[19] As they headed towards the North Pole, one night he was 'hurled right across the cabin onto the floor'.[20] After five days of this daunting sea passage, the TUC delegation disembarked at Archangel and was greeted by the leader of the Soviet trade unions, Nicolai Shvernik, who Citrine had met in 1935.[21] They flew down to Moscow to be met by the British ambassador, none other than Citrine's old Socialist League adversary, Sir Stafford Cripps,[22] one of the strongest advocates of British assistance to the Soviet Union. The Germans were then 'a tram-ride from Moscow' and all embassies were evacuating to Kuibyshev, about 500 miles to the south-east.[23] The TUC delegation went by train (another five and a half days) and set up the Anglo-Soviet TUC. It quickly agreed all eight points, summarising 'the (non-interfering) duties of the Committee', without difficulty.[24] Significantly, Vyacheslav Molotov (1890–1986), the Soviet foreign secretary and close colleague of Stalin's, asked to meet them and Ambassador Cripps asked to accompany them. Molotov wanted to convey Stalin's displeasure over Churchill's refusal to open a second front in Western Europe or send troops elsewhere. Stalin had asked for Britain to send 'twenty-five to thirty divisions via Archangel or Iran' but Molotov claimed they had not even received an answer.[25] Cripps said that Churchill *had* responded, via the Soviet ambassador in London, Ivan Maisky, but that the answer had been that it was impossible to send troops, only war materials. Citrine agreed to relay Stalin's concerns to Churchill personally on his return.[26] Cripps later explained to Citrine that the 'Russians did not trust us' and had not provided him with any information or allowed embassy people 'anywhere near the fighting line'.[27]

It seems that Molotov trusted the TUC more. 'He shook hands with me warmly' and 'conveyed his good wishes to me personally and for the work of the Anglo-Soviet Trades Union Committee'.[28] Shvernik asked for the ASTUC to be extended to the American unions and Citrine undertook to try for this as part of their new alliance. Ironically, here he was agreeing to use his influence as president of IFTU to bring the Soviet unions, which he knew 'had no independent existence', into the ranks of the international union fraternity.[29] War makes for strange bedfellows. This was something he had been averse to since their bitter experience of the previous attempt in the 1920s. His realisation about the repressive nature of the Soviet dictatorship which had developed there in the 1930s (as we saw in Chapters 6 and 11) reinforced that aversion. Citrine had also recently visited Finland and strongly supported the resistance to Soviet incursions in the winter war of 1939–40 there.[30] But he was now able to put aside those deep reservations. In the dire circumstance facing Britain, Citrine had no hesitation in supporting the Anglo-Soviet alliance. Trade unions were something the two nations had in common and the presence of the British union leader was important psychologically in cementing the alliance, until more serious military assistance could be arranged. Molotov asked him whether he thought the Americans would enter the war; he was uncertain. Hence the Soviet concern to win over the American unions through the Anglo-Soviet-American Trade Union Committee. Pearl Harbor settled any doubts the following December.[31] Despite having just been to the United States the previous February, Citrine now felt that he had to go again in person, to honour his promise to Shvernik and Molotov, and to get the American union colleagues to extend the ASTUC. This was his contribution to reducing the deep distrust of their putative allies by the Soviet leadership.[32] So, despite having so much to do at home, he arranged to travel to the US again, after he had hosted a return visit by the Soviet unions to Britain.

Citrine and the TUC delegation arrived home from Russia on 29 December 1941, after another arduous and dangerous journey. The winter of 1941–42 'was a grim period for the Allies' as the Germans 'were sweeping across the Russian plains' and 'submarines were inflicting dreadfully heavy losses on British shipping'.[33] Citrine briefed the foreign secretary, Anthony Eden, and gave Churchill a copy of his notes of the meeting with Molotov, which they discussed.[34] His General Council approved the extension of the ASTUC to the American unions. Eden would soon be in Moscow for talks also, returning to London with the Soviet ambassador, Ivan Maisky, and the Russian union delegation. Citrine also compared notes with Beaverbrook, who had been to Moscow not long before, 'about the supply of acutely needed equipment'.[35] Even after his resignation from the Cabinet later on, Beaverbrook continued to campaign as a newspaper magnate and influential Tory politician for 'the Second Front'. It was a very popular cause at the time.[36] Citrine accepted Churchill's judgement and the military advice that Britain was not up to an invasion of the European mainland at that time and so his emphasis was on the supply of tanks, planes and munitions to the Soviets.

So, here was the TUC general secretary in the thick of the war effort and at the pinnacle of his influence. He gave a broadcast and wrote some articles about his impressions of Russia.[37] He led the TUC in hosting the return visit of the Soviet trade union delegation led by Shvernik to Britain from 29 December to February 1941.

This was to bring some of the Russian 'heroes' to encourage British workers to greater effort in producing the necessary war equipment for Britain and the Soviet Union. Citrine took them personally all over Britain on a major tour of munitions factories, shipyards and other places engaged in war work. They were warmly greeted with many demonstrations, culminating in a meeting with Churchill at Downing Street (see photograph below).[38]

Citrine's remarkable stamina in undertaking such globe-trotting journeys in indifferent health underlines his commitment to winning the war against fascism.

Citrine would return to Moscow in June 1943 for the third meeting of the Anglo-Soviet Trade Union Council, with three General Council members and Victor Feather 'of the TUC staff' (a future TUC general secretary).[39] They flew via Gibraltar, Cairo and Tehran to Moscow, 'where the people seemed far more buoyant

The Soviet union delegation on its return visit to Britain, being received by Churchill at 10 Downing Street, late 1941–January 1942.

and cheerful than when I was last in Moscow' and 'the danger of attack was imminent'.[40] This time they were greeted warmly, with the entire audience of the theatre they visited rising to applaud for a long time. Much time was taken up with explanations of 'our attempts to induce the American Federation of Labour to join a tri-partite committee' (see below). They went on to explain the considerable British aid to the Soviet forces – aeroplanes, tanks, munitions and transport, as well as funds raised by the National Council of Labour and others. The Russians were puzzled 'that strikes could still occur in Britain during this life and death struggle with fascism'. Everywhere they went, they were pressed as to when a Second Front would be opened by the Allies. Citrine loyally tried to explain the difficulties of a 'small country' like Britain (population 45 million) putting an army on the Continent which would match the Germans. In any case, it was for the leaders – Churchill, Stalin and Roosevelt – to decide such matters. They then toured the Soviet factories (some of 26–27,000 workers, mostly women making shells), hospitals and union rest homes extending to the Ural Mountains and Siberia and as far as Stalinsk in the Kuzbas mining district near Mongolia. The British ambassador, Sir Archibald Clark-Kerr, found it amazing 'the intimate manner in which our delegation had been treated', as he couldn't get to go anywhere, and the Soviets were even holding up an agreement to fly directly from London to Moscow.[41] This was all part of their pressure on Churchill to open 'the Second Front'. In October 1944, at the final meeting of this Anglo-Soviet committee in London, the Soviet side picked up on a 1943 TUC Congress resolution that not just the Nazis, but the German people as a whole, 'could not be absolved from all responsibility for the inhuman crimes against the people in all Occupied Countries and against the Jewish people in particular'.[42] This had been softened to just 'the Nazis' by a TUC amendment, but the Soviet side wanted 'the German people's' responsibility restored (the distinction had the important implication of reparations owing, which would loom large as an issue between the former Allies after the war). The whole Anglo-Soviet committee passed a resolution restoring the wider responsibility of the German people and Citrine included it in his report to the September 1944 Congress, as he felt it keenly. When some at the TUC tried to refer back this section of his report, Citrine made 'a robust defence' of his attitude, insisting that the entire German people could not be acquitted of all responsibility and should make reparations. The reference back was defeated by four to one.[43] This was before the full scale of Nazi atrocities was revealed, when the concentration camps were opened, which Citrine would himself see later that month, at the Breendonk concentration camp near Antwerp (see below). The Americans were equally intent initially on making all Germans know that they were a defeated nation this time, by a policy of 'demilitarization, denazification, deindustrialization'. However, after some initial steps they changed 'largely due to the darkening prospect for U.S.-Soviet relations' and instead sought to enlist the Germans in feeding their own people and rebuilding the country.[44]

GOVERNMENT INTERFERENCE

By contrast to the warm reception in the Soviet Union, Citrine would experience a very different reception in the United States as he sought to extend the Anglo-Soviet Committee to the American unions. At the Blackpool Congress in September 1942, he commented sourly on the failure of this mission. He told the Congress that the General Council had just been 'persuaded' by

the government to call off a meeting with the American Federation
of Labor (AFL). Citrine did not mince his words.

> The General Council did not feel disposed to accept the
> untested word of the British Government or its estimate of
> the situation, because – he had never said it before but he was
> going to say it now with plainness – he had no more confidence
> in the capacity of the people who were advising the British
> Government from Washington on these matters ... [45]

As general secretary, Citrine said that he was expressing 'the
natural resentment which every member of the General Council
felt, to a purely trade union matter being lifted into a complex,
controversial, political sphere'.[46] The notion that the TUC under
Citrine simply did the government's bidding during the war is shown
by this episode to be another total misreading of their relationship.

What had so upset Citrine and the TUC? Its efforts to bring
the American unions into an Anglo-Soviet-American Trade Union
Committee had run into trouble when he approached the American
Federation of Labor, its long-standing fraternal American union.
Dominated by an anti-communist group, the AFL executive
council would not join any body with the Soviet unions, in any
circumstances.[47] It suggested, instead, just an Anglo-American
Committee, leaving the TUC to liaise with the Soviet unions. But
it was its insistence on having a veto on what other 'bona fide'
American unions could join (meaning its bitter rival, the CIO,
and the Railway Brotherhoods), which it regarded as communist-
dominated, that the AFL mainly objected to. Citrine dismissed this
claim, while accepting that there was some 'strength of communist influence lower down in the C.I.O.'.[48] But the AFL said that it

would treat any invitation from Citrine to the CIO as an 'unfriendly act', which would lead to the breaking off of AFL relations with the TUC. Naturally, the CIO leaders were outraged that Citrine seemed to be accepting the AFL veto and its Anglo-American committee proposal.

Citrine therefore found himself in an unenviable situation. He tried to overcome it by enlisting the support of President Roosevelt, who had 'expressed a desire to see me …'.[49] Citrine first saw Harry Hopkins,[50] who was known as Roosevelt's 'deputy president', in the White House on 7 May. Hopkins declared 'that the President himself must take a hand in the business, as it was a matter of high policy'.[51] Hopkins saw the importance of the proposed Anglo-Soviet-American Committee, to gain Soviet trust for the wider alliance between them. He told Citrine, 'we must consider how the news will be received in Moscow'.[52] After a full discussion with the president, the next day, 8 May, Roosevelt decided to take up the matter with both the AFL and CIO leaderships, with whom he was well acquainted, saying, 'leave it with me'. As he left Citrine for another engagement, he shouted, 'I'll get them on a committee with you'.[53] But even the US president's pressure on the AFL failed to shift the AFL anti-communists. The hard-line group that controlled its Executive Council was determined to oppose the creation of any international union body with the Soviet state-controlled unions and to prevent the CIO getting on to such a body with international recognition.[54]

Perhaps Citrine should have left the whole thing alone, as he was being drawn into the mire of American union/national politics? The CIO had separated from the AFL in 1938, ostensibly because of a difference in philosophy about the best methods concerning methods of union organisation, craft or industrial. But there was much more to it. Occupational power struggles and personality clashes were also at work. Citrine's visit in 1942 coincided with one of the most bitter ones. A profound quarrel developed between 'the strongest personality of the American Trade Union Movement', John L. Lewis,[55] and his successor as CIO president, Philip Murray. Lewis, the leader of the mineworkers since 1920, resigned as president of the wider federation, when his fight with Roosevelt backfired.[56] But he had planned to continue calling the shots through his deputy, Phillip Murray. But Murray, a tough ex-Scottish miner and steelworkers' organiser, proved 'his own man' and changed the CIO policy to one of cooperation in the war industries. Their struggle became so bitter that Lewis had Murray unceremoniously removed as vice-president of their UMWA at about the time Citrine arrived in 1942. So, when the AFL reignited their battle with the CIO by vetoing its membership of the international committee proposal, it was a perfect opportunity for Murray to prove himself as the new CIO leader.

All these currents were in full flow when Citrine arrived in New York in April 1942. Press sentiment towards his project had changed and 'a barrage of hostility' greeted him.[57] A *Boston American* editorial declared 'the arrival in this country of Sir Walter Citrine, General Secretary of the British T.U.C., a noted extreme left-winger', as 'a bid to embroil American unions in an international Labour movement'.[58] That would later draw loud laughter from the TUC delegates in Blackpool, but it showed the vigour of the isolationist strand in America still.[59] Although he was fairly well informed about American unions after his three previous visits (1934, 1936 and 1940), Citrine was clearly not up to speed on Lewis and his maverick behaviour.[60]

The problem was that Citrine could not deal with the CIO formally. It was a matter of TUC protocol that required him to deal only with the AFL as its American union contact and he couldn't invite it onto his Anglo-Soviet-American Committee, as the CIO leadership wanted. The AFL was the TUC's long-term (nearly fifty years) American fraternal body, which Citrine had just persuaded to rejoin IFTU in 1936. They were the ones who had provided the platforms for Citrine to 'beat the drum' for the British war aid in 1940, while Lewis, as CIO leader, made hostile representations to the White House against assisting. The AFL leaders now reminded Citrine of this.[61] Citrine's General Council, with whom he was in close contact by cable, did not want to sever relations with the AFL over this issue.[62] So Citrine decided to go along with the 'half-a-loaf' Anglo-American Committee arrangement for the present, perhaps expecting that Roosevelt could overcome AFL opposition.

The British Embassy officials were no help in navigating these rapids. They had little interest in or knowledge of US industrial relations or union affairs, normally relying on the Ministry of Labour in London for advice. In mid-1941, the Foreign Office/Ministry of Labour had sent over an English academic, Professor Richard Tawney (on Clem Attlee and Ernie Bevin's recommendation[63]), to advise the ambassador, Viscount Halifax, on 'labour' affairs. Tawney, though an eminent left-wing historian, educationalist and Labour (Socialist League) activist, had no experience of American unions and made little contact with them for much of his time in the US.[64] Following complaints by Citrine, Halifax reported to Anthony Eden, the foreign secretary, who consulted Bevin and they pressed Tawney for a report.[65] Stung by this, the elderly Tawney hastily produced one, blaming Citrine's 'clumsy' diplomacy and saying that he should instead formally include the CIO in the Anglo-Soviet-American Committee. Citrine should be 'warned' of the damage he was causing. He should be told to 'desist'[66] and face down the AFL's 'bluff'.[67] Tawney's advice now became the basis for official embassy and Foreign Office responses. Their near panic is reflected in the high levels of abuse of Citrine contained in the exchanges between Washington and London. A sample will suffice: 'Sir Walter Citrine is a conceited, flabby-minded man'[68] and 'Sir W. Citrine by his impetuosity and unwillingness either to consult or to take advice, is a threat to our vital interests.'[69] Tawney claimed that Citrine's activities had damaged Anglo-American relations generally (he clearly had no knowledge of Citrine's friendly dealings with Roosevelt and Hopkins). Citrine wasn't even given a copy of Tawney's report. Rather than sitting down with him and trying to inform themselves on this complex Anglo-American union mess, the Foreign Office and Ministry of Labour's focus convinced them of Citrine's 'pig-headedness'.[70] They believed Tawney when he wrote that 'The British T.U.C. has, in fact, unintentionally dealt a gratuitous blow to Anglo-American relations as a whole.'[71]

Had Citrine fully appreciated the tensions in the CIO, especially between Murray and Lewis, from Halifax, Tawney and his senior embassy officials, he might have abandoned the effort to set up an Anglo-Soviet-American Committee and simply reported back to the Anglo-Soviet body. He clearly underestimated the ferocity of the new CIO president's reaction. He would live to regret it, as Murray, like Lewis, both 'rugged characters, moulded by the hardship and strife of their early life as miners',[72] proved most persuasive with the gentle Eton-Harrow-educated souls of the Washington embassy and Foreign Office. Halifax complained that Murray had berated him on the phone for over an hour without let-up on one occasion![73] So, instead of the considerable diplomatic expertise of the British Embassy and the Foreign Office being deployed to support the TUC initiative (a failing for which Halifax,

Eden and Bevin were responsible), they bent under the influence
of their 'expert' Tawney and forceful pressure from Murray, whose
CIO they 'trembled' before. In fact, they were most interested in
not upsetting the CIO. A senior Foreign Office official put it this
way to Attlee, which was copied to Bevin and Eden: 'From the F.O.
point of view we are merely concerned because the good will of
the C.I.O. whose membership is drawn largely from the vital war
industries, is more important to our cause than that of the A.F.L.'[74]
Citrine claimed that 'the Embassy had all been nobbled by the
C.I.O.' and that no such serious fall-out was likely. But no serious
attempt was made by either Eden, Bevin or Attlee to discuss the
matter with the TUC general secretary. It seems that Eden wanted
to meet Citrine, but he put it off as he couldn't enlist the obvious
person for the task, Bevin, because 'his relations with Sir W.C. are
bad'.[75] Attlee also wanted it handled at non-ministerial level. Eventually, Eden had a report drafted for Churchill's attention and the
issue seems to have been raised in a meeting with Citrine by an
official, Harold Butler, but not directly between the prime minister
and Citrine. Citrine would certainly have acceded to Churchill's
wishes if he had had a face-to-face discussion and felt that the
Foreign Office case had substance.[76] But despatches from political masters and their servants disclose a hostile and disparaging
attitude to the TUC general secretary.

Philip Murray's campaign revived after a notice appeared
in *The Times* on 7 August 1942, announcing the meeting of the
Anglo-American Committee on 23 September in Washington. He
threatened to denounce the Anglo-American Committee publicly
at the upcoming CIO Convention and did so at the United
Autoworkers Convention (part of the CIO federation). Notes
and telegrams about the proposed Anglo-American Committee

meeting show the atmosphere of alarm and panic generated.[77] With the revival of the row, Eden and the Foreign Office/Ministry of Labour/Washington embassy went into overdrive, behind Citrine's back, to get the Anglo-American Committee meeting on 23 September 1942 'postponed'. Sneakily, they used their considerable contacts on both sides of the Atlantic. That was why Citrine was furious at Blackpool that month and all the TUC delegates strongly backed him.

This extraordinary interference in union affairs by the British government had its effect. In the end, the AFL was persuaded by the White House to ask for a postponement. Citrine accepted it, in view of all the fuss. In agreeing, he told Eden that he had done so 'with considerable reluctance' and that the government was 'unduly influenced by representatives in Washington', 'in whose competence ... they [the General Council] have little confidence.'[78] He was confident that 'means would have been found to bring about closer relationship among the parties ... But this would have been done personally and not by correspondence.'[79] Citrine also advised that the General Council was in the mood 'to have nothing to do with the British Embassy' concerning its affairs in the future.[80] The issue was raised in Parliament by Manny Shinwell on 11 September, who questioned whether Tawney 'was the proper person to decide on matters affecting trade union organisations.'[81] Eden responded, saying he had relied on Tawney's credentials in accepting 'the soundness of his advice', but hardly in glowing terms.[82] After they got their way, Eden told his officials 'after consulting Mr Ernest Bevin', that 'that it is probably better to "lay off" Citrine for the present'.[83]

The postponed Anglo-American Committee meeting was rescheduled for January 1943 and then came and went without 'the roof falling in' on the war production industries. Citrine led the TUC delegation to Florida for the meeting and there pressed the AFL harder to include the CIO on the Anglo-Soviet-American Committee. It still refused, and his old friend William Green, the AFL president, 'publicly called him a traitor'.[84] Citrine then insisted that they change the name to the 'AFL/TUC Committee', which then faded away.[85] The TUC delegation also met the CIO leaders in Miami but it was in 'an atmosphere of unfriendliness bordering on hostility'.[86] So, in his efforts to coordinate international union energies, Citrine found that the Anglo-Soviet-American Committee vehicle was no longer serviceable. He was 'bitterly disappointed at the outcome of our mission'.[87]

Opening meeting of the World Trade Union Conference in
Paris in 1945, which Citrine chaired, with General de Gaulle
and the Soviet leader, V. Kuznetsov.

However, he didn't give up on the project of international workers' unity. In September 1943, the TUC agreed to organise a World Trade Union Conference (WTUC), as the successor to IFTU, to which the Soviet unions and all the American unions were invited. A new World Federation of Trade Unions (WFTU), which Citrine chaired, met in Moscow in October 1945 and initially went well. Even the Soviet union leader, V. Kutnezov, 'deferred to British demands' for a non-political approach.[88] The Soviet unions actually wanted Citrine to continue as chair after 1946, worrying that his replacement, Arthur Deakin of the T&GWU, would follow Foreign Secretary Bevin's anti-Soviet policy.[89] In his opening address in October 1945 in Paris, Citrine warned that if the WFTU departed from the common ground of trade union issues, it would divide and weaken its influence. But this advice from the elder statesman of the IFTU fell on deaf ears (it also downgraded Schevenels to assistant secretary). Citrine now believed that 'influences were already making themselves felt to develop the enlarged Federation as a political force with a predominantly communist outlook, rather than as the trade union organisation which the British TUC had originally conceived'.[90] Citrine chaired it for the last time in Moscow in June 1946, and he was replaced as president by Arthur Deakin, who would be decidedly under the Foreign Secretary Bevin's influence.[91] From 1946 to 1947, tensions and distrust were growing between the great powers, with Bevin to the fore. He was now pursuing an active British anti-Soviet policy over issues about the future of Germany and threats to oil interests in the Middle East. Soon, Truman's new advisers would change their earlier Rooseveltian leaning towards a deal with Stalin and the Soviet Union.[92] In 1948, the Cold War divisions over the Marshall Plan (European Recovery Program funding by the US) caused a terminal dispute and the

TUC severed its connection with WFTU, ironically to join with the AFL in a new International Confederation of Free Trade Unions (ICFTU).[93] But Citrine 'had no hand in the events which led to the break-up of the WFTU'. The dream of international workers' unity would now founder on the rocks of the Cold War.[94]

It was a remarkable episode, the complexity and many-sidedness of which needs some elaboration. We need to explore Citrine's side of things in view of the doubts raised about his role by British diplomats, politicians and some historians. Undoubtedly, Citrine's reputation in Labour Party leadership circles and at the highest level of British government, including Churchill, suffered from official hostility to this international union initiative.[95] When we ask how this could come about, how such an admirable purpose provoked such a storm, obscuring Citrine's contribution to wartime diplomacy since 1940, it is plain that someone had it in for him. The evidence points to Ernest Bevin.

BEVIN'S FURTIVE ROLE

Smarting from Citrine's criticisms about the competence of the Washington embassy on union affairs, in May 1942, the foreign secretary, Anthony Eden, consulted Bevin about getting someone more practical to advise and assist them in such matters. He told Bevin, 'I cannot truthfully say that Tawney has furnished us with much information on the complicated but highly important Labour situation in the US. The supply of this is really the crux of the business.'[96] So, Halifax drew up 'terms of reference' for a replacement and naturally consulted with the Foreign Office and Ministry of Labour. It is their discussion around the status and terms of reference of this adviser which is so revealing. Bevin recommended one of the Ministry of Labour officials he had come to rate, Archibald Gordon. However, he didn't want him to be described as being responsible for advising on labour relations involving the British and American unions! The officials were puzzled by this insistence, wondering why they needed a Labour attaché in Washington if he wasn't to perform such duties. Bevin's concerns are made clear in another exchange, as an objection to Gordon's explicit responsibilities (not that he shouldn't perform the role). Gordon was sent to Washington in September 1942 as the Labour attaché in all but name. His terms of reference were in effect written with Bevin's sensitivities in mind,[97] so as not to appear to be a replacement for Tawney in advising on labour affairs. It was made clear by his department that he (Bevin) 'does not wish to be explicitly stated doing so'[98] and that he (Bevin), 'objects to these things being put down in black and white'.[99] Eden, who was then very close to Bevin, agreed to this furtive procedure, overruling his own officials, saying, 'Mr Bevin knows his men'.[100] Despite this attempt not to be seen publicly to be behind the embassy appointment, in case of union criticism, he clearly was. The Foreign Office official said, 'Mr Bevin may well be fearing a repetition of the recent incident when publicity was given to a conflict of views between the Embassy and Sir Walter Citrine, and Professor Tawney was mentioned by name as one of Lord Halifax's advisers. The new Labour Attaché is a Ministry of Labour man, and Mr Bevin is probably anxious not to get involved through him, in possible fresh trouble with the T.U.C.'[101] Bevin's key industrial relations official, Frederick Leggett, was said to have been 'very helpful during the Citrine incident'.[102]

This is firm evidence that Bevin was now actively involving himself in British/American trade union matters, without discussing them with Citrine and the TUC. At no time did he try to speak to or correspond with the TUC leader, or anybody else at their shared offices in Transport House (which he still visited frequently). Bevin's biographers are strangely silent on this whole episode. Yet he seemed to have been interfering actively from 'behind the scenes', via Lord Halifax, the British ambassador in Washington, and John Winant, [103] the American ambassador in London. Bevin's network was extensive both as Minister of Labour and through his still strong senior T&GWU/TUC British union contacts. (He was only 'on leave' from his position as general secretary and his replacement, Arthur Deakin, was very much his protégé.) He also had important CIO/AFL associates in America and globally. These he had developed since his visits to the US in 1915 and 1926, and later involvement on the International Transport Workers Federation (ITF), IFTU and the ILO, in the 1930s.[104] In 1942, he lent another Ministry of Labour official, Myrddin Evans, to assist the CIO deputy leader, Sydney Hillman, as chair of the US War Production Board.[105] As a key Cabinet minister in London, he had only to pick up the phone to speak with key players.

With Archibald Gordon as his 'eyes and ears' (as much as for the embassy and Foreign Office), he was in a position to intervene and he seemed particularly keen to throw spanners in Citrine's operations in the US. Two left-wing General Council members, Bryn Roberts, general secretary of the public services union, NUPE,[106] and Jack Tanner,[107] president of the AEU, became involved. They were concerned by the General Council's failure to bring the CIO onto the Anglo-Soviet Committee,[108] and that the Soviet unions were being excluded from the Anglo-American Committee.[109] Roberts and Tanner went to Canada that year as fraternal TUC delegates to the AFL Convention and, while there, 'just happened' to be invited by the CIO to its Convention in the US. They also addressed many joint meetings of both unions locally, being chaperoned by Gordon, who 'accompanied them to Detroit, Chicago, Cleveland and Pittsburgh'.[110] This, of course, undermined the General Council majority and its general secretary's stance, as it was meant to. In another letter, Philip Murray thanked Bevin for his help – 'your good friend and representative, Mr A. A. Gordon called on me the other day. I had a very interesting chat with him …' Murray expressed his appreciation 'for the information which he has and is supplying us. It is of tremendous educational value to our people …'[111] Indeed! This is often how things are done at general secretary level in unions, but it was a clear breach of faith with the TUC general secretary. Yet none of them challenged Citrine's report in Blackpool in September 1942, not even the T&GWU delegation. So, the Congress overwhelmingly backed Citrine's account.[112] Nonetheless, this deep division between the two former leading union leaders, who could not even sit down to discuss their differences, could only have weakened the TUC general secretary's authority on domestic as well as foreign union issues. With Bevin's growing influence in the Cabinet and with the prime minister, it would weaken TUC influence considerably, as Citrine's international diplomacy became the butt of Washington embassy, Foreign Office and Ministry of Labour hostility.

HOSTILITIES RESUMED

By April 1944, uncharacteristically Citrine was clashing openly with Bevin's officials at the International Labour Organisation conference in Philadelphia. At the end of the First World War, a Labour Charter had been agreed by the victors as part of the Versailles Peace Treaty and the ILO was shaped by the key union

leaders of Britain, France and the US (Samuel Gompers), but
the influence of its Conventions diminished in the 1930s.[113] This
ILO conference was regarded by Citrine as an opportunity to do
better this time and the ILO officials put forward an ambitious
programme. Bevin sent a team of senior officials led by his Parliamentary secretary, George Tomlinson MP, who made it clear that
Britain was opposed to the ILO officers' proposals. Bevin instead
favoured 'a general statement of principles' from the ILO to the
founding United Nations conference in 1945.[114] Ironically, it used
to be Bevin who had majored for the TUC at the ILO in Geneva
throughout the 1930s, when the Conservative-dominated Ministry
of Labour was obstructing ratification of the ILO Conventions.[115]
In Philadelphia in 1944, the minister of Labour's representatives
were still doing so, only now 'the poacher had turned gamekeeper'
for the imperial government.[116] In a letter to Churchill afterwards,
Bevin complained about Citrine, claiming that the TUC leader
had alleged that 'the British government delegates were sent over
with instructions to agree to nothing at this conference and that if
he [Citrine] were challenged he could prove it up to the hilt'.[117] So
Bevin said, 'I think it is a matter for regret that a man in his position
should attribute such an unfair statement to the British government. ... I think you ought to know of his action over there.'[118]
Instead of having it out with Citrine, Bevin wrote this sneaky letter
to Churchill, denying that he had given instructions 'to agree to
nothing' and instead trying to undermine Citrine in the eyes of
the prime minister. Churchill may not have appreciated the importance of the ILO for the forthcoming United Nations founding
conference, or, if he did, from a British Empire perspective, would
not have been sympathetic to a greater ILO role raising standards
in many of the colonies. Bevin's representatives (Tomlinson and

Leggett) resisted all specific roles for the ILO, and it was afterwards excluded from the UN Charter by the American government. Professor Van Goethem, an expert on these international agencies and the UNO, recently explained this: 'The [US] State Department set up a "special division" to study the establishment of a new "World Organisation" after Pearl Harbor [December 1941]. They worked in secrecy because the subject was highly controversial in the States. But in this process "Labor" was pushed to the side-line. One of the reasons was that an extension of the mandate of the ILO to other policy domains would have resulted in trade unions having a say in these domains. The New Deal supporters in the States (Lubin, Perkins, Goodrich ...), the ILO itself and the TUC was in favour, but the State Department and the American industrial lobbied against. They wanted an "open trade economy" without too much interference of the trade unions. But the British government too, although initially pro, turned against the idea in the run-up to Philadelphia. It did not want to give the ILO a real mandate to intervene on a global scale in order to protect their interests as an imperial power.'[119]

Citrine was angry that on Bevin's instructions his officials were 'discarding from forty to sixty per cent of the [ILO officials'] text'.[120] Citrine afterwards conceded that he had spoken 'more harshly than the circumstances warranted' ('a weakness of mine to think only about the subject').[121] Bevin would not forget that one either, when it came to the UN conference in San Francisco in 1945.

Despite these tensions, as we have seen, Citrine and the TUC still supported Bevin's highly controversial Regulation 1AA later that year, which made it a criminal offence to incite unofficial action.[122] In June 1944, Churchill upheld Bevin's decision not to consult the Joint Consultative Committee on his ministry's demobilisation plans. Nor would Bevin be required to circulate other ministry proposals to the TUC before they were laid before Parliament.[123] From early 1942, Citrine had been on a Joint Advisory Committee with the then minister Arthur Greenwood MP, the Labour deputy leader, which began consideration of peacetime reconstruction, including demobilisation. The TUC head of economics and research, George Woodcock, was secretary of that committee. However, with Greenwood's removal from the Cabinet in the reshuffle, that committee lost momentum.[124] It was then that William Beveridge was also considering radical proposals for social insurance. The TUC was the first organisation to submit detailed evidence and to strongly support the ultimate Beveridge Report of December 1942. This initially encountered strong resistance within the coalition Cabinet, including from Bevin, 'who did not really approve of Beveridge's attitude'.[125] Bevin issued his White Paper on Employment in early 1944, with its attempt to continue 'a much more interventionist role for the state' post-war, including a 'new code of conduct for industry'. Citrine was minded to consider it, but in October his General Council demanded the restoration of freedom from legal restraints over wage bargaining, as had been promised in 1940.[126] Had there been the old rapport and partnership between Bevin and Citrine, the TUC might well have engaged in devising a post-war national economic strategy covering employment, incomes and prices with the government.[127]

On 28 March 1944, Bevin wrote to Washington ambassador Halifax about the World Trade Union Conference which Citrine was again trying to hold. In a very cloak-and-dagger letter, dated 28 March 1944 (marked 'Private and Extremely Confidential'), he told Halifax that he thought the TUC was having difficulties organising the conference and said it should be left to 'prove its own weakness and the ill-considered basis upon which it is being organised'. He adds:

> With regard to the difficulties over there, I agree with you that the steps that have been taken have widened the breach, as you and I agreed that it would when his previous visit was made. But if the Embassy again steps into this business … it will, I am sure, produce the very situation that he wants.[128]

That 'he' was undoubtedly Citrine and it was clearly about the difficulties with the AFL and CIO, for which he blamed Citrine. Soon after, the government got the TUC to postpone that World Trade Union Conference, because of the expected D-Day landings of May 1944. Citrine, who was already in the US for the ILO Conference at Philadelphia on 17 April, took the opportunity to meet the Soviet ambassador, Andrei Gromyko (1910–89), later foreign secretary, to brief him about the postponement. He also met President Roosevelt for over an hour, who this time 'looked weary and haggard'. Roosevelt just asked how he was getting on with the AFL, and Citrine simply said, 'not very well'. However, they didn't get into the reasons why the president had been unable to get the American unions onto the Anglo-Soviet-American Committee. They had another long discussion about the future, centring on how relations with Stalin and the Soviet Union would develop after the Allies' decisive military victories and the Tehran Conference of December 1943. Roosevelt said, 'Stalin is a great fellow. He is a realist. He knows that Russia is at the crossroads.'[129] Roosevelt thought Stalin was mellowing, though Citrine doubted whether the Soviet regime could so easily change. Roosevelt believed that after the carnage of war, the Soviet leadership were now searching for a way to a post-war accommodation with their allies. That said, Roosevelt remarked, 'I watch them all the time and I let them know I am watching them. But we must try to be friendly with them. It's the only way.'[130] Had he lived, would Roosevelt have encouraged a very different US–USSR evolution which would possibly have helped avert the Cold War? In that environment, could Citrine and the TUC's global unity policies have borne fruit? A British Empire greatly weakened by the war effort, even with a Labour government, would not be disposed to such idealistic possibilities. One cannot but admire the grand vision and idealism underpinning Citrine's 'international workers' unity' initiative, so far from the 'bureaucratic, apparatchik' image he is often saddled with.

Citrine returned to running the TUC and the annual Congress at Blackpool in September 1944. Yet he would soon again have to travel abroad on international union and national business. He went first to Belgium where IFTU was called upon to help restore the unions in their devastated cities and sort out problems between three rival union tendencies contending for representation. Although victory in the war was in sight, minds were now turning to what countries like Britain and America, which had escaped Nazi occupation, could do to help the overrun peoples of Europe. He visited the Breendonk prison camp near Antwerp, which had been used by the Nazis to hold and torture trade unionists, resistance fighters, Jews and other political prisoners, perpetrating horrific atrocities on them.[131] Scenes like that had an effect on feelings about retribution against the Germans, including Citrine's, as the Allies closed in on the Third Reich.

In January 1945, Churchill prevailed on Citrine to lead a TUC delegation to Greece to help sort out the complex union situation which had arisen there on liberation from the Nazis. This was part of a wider crisis after liberation. Though he was 'tired of charging about the world and leaving my wife to shift for herself', Citrine agreed to lead the delegation.[132] Between them, Stalin and Churchill had agreed that Greece would be the British responsibility, while Romania would be the concern of the Soviets. However, local republican/communist-dominated partisans (EAM-ELAS) were attempting to take over in Athens.[133] Churchill initially wanted to restore the Greek monarchy, but after the fatal shooting of demonstrators by the Papandreou government, the British Army sent there to prevent an EAM takeover became associated with that repression. After stormy debates in the Commons and the Labour Conference at Westminster in December threatening the coalition, Churchill was forced to drop the king and seek an alternative 'regency' arrangement. The TUC delegation (which included union representatives of both sides of the Labour Conference divide) was part of that new approach.[134] When they arrived, the TUC delegation of five, led by Citrine, 'found ourselves caught up in a jigsaw puzzle of tension, suspicion, recrimination and fear'.[135] So, they conducted detailed investigations trying 'to pronounce a definite opinion'.[136] In the brutal civil war that followed liberation, it was estimated that 'at least ten thousand' people had been murdered by rival groups.[137] The TUC delegation interrogated the British soldiers (who had been accused of serving 'reactionaries against a democratic people') for two hours, in five groups without their officers. They unanimously concluded in separate written reports that the 'grotesque stories' put around by the communist-led partisans were unfounded and accepted the British troops' version. The troops said that ELAS were 'the dirtiest lot of fighters our chaps had ever encountered', responsible for 'cold-blooded murder of citizens'. The British troops felt that if they were recalled 'there would be a wholesale massacre'.[138] The return journey from Athens was also a nightmare, and they almost didn't make it in the derelict York aircraft which had been sent to fetch them (two exhausted engines packed up over the Mediterranean).[139] Another eventful year for the TUC general secretary. When he met Churchill after the war at Buckingham Palace, Churchill, who had had a minor stroke, didn't immediately recognise him, but when told it was 'Citrine', he responded, 'Yes, and you made that most convincing report on the occurrences in Greece which enabled us to convince the Americans of the rightness of our policy.'[140]

It seems there was an element of jealousy on Bevin's part towards Citrine. Even as a Cabinet member, Bevin seems to have resented Citrine's greater access to Churchill and all senior ministers as a privy councillor. In September 1944, we find him telling a government Labour colleague, Hugh Dalton:

> Bevin then speaks disparagingly of Citrine and the General Council. Citrine, he says, is always trying to be a super Foreign Secretary and is always flying about, to Washington, Moscow etc. But he doesn't run his office nearly as well as old Charlie Bowerman and doesn't really get as much out of the Government. The General Council, Bevin thinks are a hopeless lot.[141]

This was so far from the truth in Citrine's case (except, perhaps, that Citrine would have made a very good foreign secretary from 1945), but shows Bevin's style in dealing with rivals. Citrine's work rate and performance were notoriously phenomenal, and, when away, he regularly communicated by cable with General Council members as well as sending his shorthand reports to be typed up and circulated. The team he had built under his able lieutenant, Vincent Tewson, covered well for him. Bevin's crack about the General Council merely confirms that his intrigues didn't move it against Citrine. However, the importance of the TUC general secretary's international role was not apparent to everybody and so such snide remarks from Bevin may have had effect on some union or Labour leaders who did not appreciate the importance of the TUC's international role in the extraordinary circumstances of that life-and-death struggle.

REBUFF IN SAN FRANCISCO

President Roosevelt died on 12 April 1945; Citrine felt as if 'a disaster had overtaken mankind', saying that the 'great influence of the President at a most critical moment had been lost to the world'.[142] His 'other half', Harry Hopkins, would die of cancer soon after, at the age of forty. The loss of such key American leaders changed the dynamic of global progress, as the New Dealers were ousted by the Cold Warriors in the State Department.[143] Although the new president, Harry Truman, continued with Roosevelt's policies for a time, he 'had none of Roosevelt's vision as an international leader'. Without Roosevelt's relationship with Stalin, events in Europe polarised Western opinion behind Churchill and Bevin's hostile 'containment' strategy.[144]

Now fifty-eight, Citrine must have been worn out by his endless travelling and the strain of all the manoeuvring by politicians and government officials. A final blow to his confidence occurred later that month when he led a TUC delegation to the founding United Nations Conference in San Francisco, expecting to get it to adopt the ILO recommendations. After journeying across the continent, Clement Attlee, who was there for the British government with Anthony Eden, the foreign secretary, informed the TUC delegation that the coalition Cabinet in London had decided (on hostile Foreign Office advice) not to include the TUC in the British delegation, even as advisers. This was an extraordinary snub to Citrine and the TUC. Citrine was angrier than he had ever been, as many of the other countries were including their unions as advisers or delegates. He rounded on Attlee: 'I told him plainly, that I couldn't remember a single occasion when he had ever helped us since he had taken office.'[145] He and miners' leader Ebby Edwards, then chair of the General Council, threatened that the TUC would fall out with Labour over it. They asked whether this was 'a portent for the future and that the government were going to keep the T.U.C. out of any participation in the making of the peace?'[146] Attlee refused to budge, saying the decision had been fully discussed by the Cabinet in London. [147] Only one of Bevin's biographers, Trevor Evans, drew attention to this shameful episode, aptly describing it as 'When Leaders Were Scorned', in a headline of his book, followed by: 'Yet in the same city of San Francisco … Bevin's great rival, Sir Walter Citrine, was kicking his heels and bruising his knuckles knocking on the doors of diplomats who paid no attention to the attempt of organised labour to have a say in leaving "Labour's impress" on the newer peace of a more shattered world.'[148]

Evans confirmed that 'Bevin was one of the most influential members of a Government which spurned Citrine's efforts'.[149] Hugh Dalton's diary entry for 23 February 1945 recalled that: 'Citrine was complaining that, though the Big Six of the Trade Union Conference had today met Eden, Gusev and Winant [US and USSR ambassadors to London] at a specially arranged lunch to discuss trade union participation at San Francisco, they had got nowhere. Eden had told him that members of our own Government as well had objected 'on principle to trade union participation. Citrine added that "of course it was Bevin"; neither could speak long without an ill word for the other.'[150] Long after, according to Citrine's memoir, it still rankled. 'I blamed both Attlee and Bevin for our exclusion from the Conference.'[151] It seems that Bevin was prepared to exclude the TUC to get back at Citrine. Such behaviour diminishes his reputation considerably. It wasn't just a question of his 'many mean qualities' and 'petty spite when dealing with people he did not like or trust'.[152] The cumulative list of moves to undermine Citrine, culminating in his exclusion from the UN conference at San Francisco in 1945, shows a ruthless, devious character, which in others would be condemned, not praised. He ended the 'partnership' and what had been a powerful complementarity which swept all before them, damaging the unions' efforts to influence global peace. In post-war trade union movement affairs, the loss of the Citrine–Bevin partnership undoubtedly created an immense vacuum. Certainly, Ernest Bevin's reputation as the 'Churchill of the proletariat of the Workers War', which was widely touted in the British press, and is widely believed to this day, is seriously in question.[153]

The TUC delegation set off home 'fully determined to expose the attitude that Attlee and his colleagues in the government had taken'.[154] The General Council shared his intention 'to have a showdown'. However, it was overtaken by bigger events – Hitler's suicide and the end of the war, with victory in Europe and the tussles about the life of the coalition and timing of the 1945 General Election.[155] When it was held in July, with strong TUC backing, against all expectations Labour was elected in its biggest ever landslide victory. [156] Labour polled just under 12 million votes to the Tories, 8.66 million and won 393 seats, with an overall majority of 158.[157] Bevin persuaded Attlee to go to the Palace and become prime minister, rather than wait a day for a leadership challenge by Herbert Morrison.[158] This gave Attlee the 'inside track' to lead the first majority Labour government in history. As prime minister, Attlee told the TUC Congress at Blackpool later that year that 'this Trades Union Congress of 1945 takes its place among the victory parades of the forces of the United Nations'![159] In the euphoria of having a Labour government able to carry through a radical social democratic programme, such rhetoric went unchallenged, though Citrine must have been reminded of his exchanges with Attlee in San Francisco. Citrine was satisfied that the Labour government's substantial and radical programme owed much to them at the TUC and in the unions.

This extraordinary odyssey of Citrine on his union diplomacy for the war effort during the Second World War has barely been glimpsed before now. His globe-trotting alone since 1939 at age fifty-two deserves credit. As we saw, he went first to France and had to be evacuated by destroyer as Hitler approached Paris. He then addressed the AFL Convention in New Orleans to counter isolationism and toured all over the USA and Canada taking the message that Britain was fighting the Nazis, but needed help. Then back across the Atlantic in a flying boat during the most unimaginable storm (twenty-six hours in the air). Next, he was off to Moscow in winter, facing a North Sea and Arctic swell thirty feet above the ice-covered ship, at a time when Hitler was 'within a tram ride' of the Russian capital. This was to set up an Anglo-Soviet committee, to help the new Anglo-Soviet alliance. Hardly back home, he was off again, back to the US, to persuade the American unions to join, only to encounter strong hostility from both the AFL and CIO and with little understanding and no assistance from the

British embassy or Foreign Office/Ministry of Labour. While he was doing all this, as we have seen, under his direction and close involvement, the TUC and the unions were deeply involved in the war production industries, having suspended all rights to strike and restrictive practices. With access to all ministers and departments, and working closely with the prime minister, Sir Walter Citrine was, as Churchill told President Roosevelt, more important to the war effort than most politicians and many ministers. And yet the toll began to tell on him as jealous politicians conspired to undermine his standing. It is a sad story that needs telling to remind us that Walter Citrine was one of the finest products of the British working-class and Labour movements.

CHAPTER 14

~

CITRINE AND PUBLIC OWNERSHIP
– COAL AND ELECTRICITY

I parted with the T.U.C. with deep regret. It had been my life's work.[1]

Disillusioned by the Labour leadership's treatment at San Francisco in April 1945, Citrine's 'energies seemed drained away' and 'for a time [he] experienced some restlessness of mind'.[2] He got over it and immersed himself in the work of the TUC with the new Labour government, although he hadn't played much part in the election campaign in July.[3] He wasn't interested in becoming a minister in the new government (not that Attlee was offering) or in using his vast experience commercially in business. As we saw, the TUC was a major influence on that government's programme with the implementation of the land-breaking Beveridge Report of 1942, the Education Act of 1944, on reconstruction, on the vast nationalisation programme of key industries and on the restoration of collective wage bargaining in a full-employment economy.[4] Citrine studied with keen attention the nationalisation programme of the government, and 'derived immense satisfaction in seeing that the general lines of the proposed legislation followed quite closely the views we had put forward in documentary form in 1944 and 1945. But I had not thought of taking an active part in the industries and services which were looming up for prospective national ownership and operation.'[5] Many union officials were being recruited at national, regional and district levels on government panels and for permanent positions after the war. Some of the best brains and most effective administrators/negotiators were drained from the trade unions.

Then in November, Citrine was approached by the minister of fuel and power, Emmanuel Shinwell MP, who pressed him to take a post on the new National Coal Board (NCB), as the director of welfare and training for the miners. Although important enough, this was hardly a fitting recognition of someone of his standing. Something like the directorship of the International Labour Organisation (then vacant) would have been more appropriate. However, being part of the exciting new nationalised industry programme appealed to Citrine, especially in the coal industry with the miners, who had so many historic associations with the Labour movement. Citrine also knew the industry well, since his early days as an electrician in the South Lancashire coalfield and the General Strike.

However, he was reluctant to leave his post at the TUC, 'as it would mean stepping down from the position of influence and power that I enjoyed as Secretary of the TUC' for a far lesser post. Even to think of leaving such a high-profile position was an indication of his deep disenchantment with the Labour leadership. Though the NCB job was much better paid – £5,000 per annum, as opposed to his TUC salary of £1,600 – that was not a major consideration for Citrine. He feared that 'his identity, and possibly a large part of my individuality, would be submerged'.[6] Most of the members of the General Council were, to put it mildly, 'taken aback at the

prospect' of losing their longstanding and esteemed general secretary. Citrine did not wish to be 'stigmatised as a job hunter', and
so it took two meetings, with the minister in attendance at one, to
settle the matter. Shinwell persuaded them that Citrine was vital to
their nationalisation plans, which 'were on trial and must not fail'.
In the end they gave him 'leave of absence' with the assurance that,
if it didn't work out for him, he would be guaranteed a position on
the TUC 'equal in status to the one I had vacated'.[7] So, with their
blessing, if not any enthusiasm, the TUC General Council and the
trade union and Labour movement lost their unique, outstanding leader of the previous decades. For Citrine, 'being cut off for
all time from the movement that for thirty-one years had been so
big a part of my existence', felt 'like a monk quitting his cloister'.[8]
Fulsome tributes were paid to him at the Congress in October 1946
at Brighton and his fellow members of the General Council 'placed
on record their high appreciation of the services he has rendered
to the Trades Union Movement during his long tenure of office
in a momentous and difficult period'.[9] In his farewell address, he
recalled with satisfaction how far they had come, saying, 'We have
passed from the era of propaganda to one of responsibility...'[10]
He, of course, received the gold medal of Congress.[11]

BARON CITRINE OF WEMBLEY

In July 1946, he became the 1st Baron Citrine of Wembley. Prime
Minister Clement Attlee said it was because 'they needed some-
body with trades union experience to serve in the House of Lords'.
In fact, Citrine did not attend that House in case it conflicted with
his non-political role at the NCB. He would continue that practice
at the British Electricity Authority (BEA, later renamed Central

Electricity Authority) until the late 1950s, as we shall see. He made up for it from the early 1960s, with many appearances in the Lords, when he finally 'retired', as we shall see in the next chapter.[12]

The title was a belated recognition of his wartime services by the government. This time there was no hostile reaction in the Labour movement. The title he chose was a tribute to his home in Wembley Park since 1926. His coat of arms symbolised his Wallasey origins (the three ships); the Middlesex county axes and their beloved Alsatian Rex, whom he had regularly walked around the nearby King Edward VII Park, until he died in an air raid in 1941; his global role – the globe on Rex's shoulder 'charged with

Lord Citrine of Wembley's coat of arms.

a human heart'; and his trade union work – the pick and spade on the lion's shoulder. His chosen motto, *Pro Recto Labora*, 'Strive for Right', reflected his philosophy on life.[13]

AT THE COAL BOARD

From April 1946 until May 1947, Citrine made the most of his stint at the NCB, improving pit-head conditions and welfare quite markedly. Arthur Horner, his old communist adversary, now secretary of the National Union of Mineworkers (as the MFGB had become), remembered Citrine's period at the NCB very favourably, saying, 'we owe a lot to his early work' as welfare director. He also said 'that the men from the trade union movement who went on the Board, men like Ebby Edwards, Citrine and Jim Bowman, in particular, did an amazingly good job'.[14] The extension of the pit-head baths scheme to all collieries, old and new, and getting the NCB to pay for it entirely, was a major achievement of Citrine's. Another improvement he oversaw was to the bad lighting in mines and 'cumbersome equipment'. 'I visited many collieries, and always made a point of going underground to see the men at work.'[15] He also initiated the system of summer schools for employees and the establishment of machinery for joint consultation. Horner also gave him full credit for his pioneering work on training, which 'had never been taken seriously under the old coal owners'.[16] 'We (the NUM) were thinking of getting quite a limited expenditure for training but Citrine had his own ideas, and we got more than we expected.'[17] He also instituted some of the administrative systems which he had introduced at the TUC, such as regular departmental conferences. Citrine adopted the same method to engage with the new NCB officials, at which he 'expounded' his ideas and got much feedback. He also participated fully on the Board concerning the industry as a whole, submitting many suggestions in the form of his now famous 'Memoranda'. It was clearly a very intense, if short, period with the new public-sector body. One mustn't be surprised by all this, as Citrine was no careerist passing through. He had deep sympathy with the miners' lot, from the days he lived with a miner's family in a collier's cottage. 'I admired their sturdy independence and resourcefulness.'[18] He had tried his best to help the MFGB leaders before and during the General Strike (which Arthur Cook and Herbert Smith appreciated). So, he now took the opportunity of his influence in the publicly owned NCB to do something tangible to help the mining community.

He was clearly effective in his new Board role, but had hardly got going with the NCB when, later that year, an opening arose for a role he could not refuse. The prime minister summoned him out of his Miners' Welfare Commission meeting one day and asked him to be chair of the recently nationalised British Electricity Authority (BEA) board. Ironically, it was Clement Attlee who was now offering him this plum job. Could it be that he wanted to make amends for the treatment Citrine had received at San Francisco, which had caused him to leave the TUC? Hardly. The suggestion had again come from Manny Shinwell (still minister of fuel and power and chair of the Labour Party), on Attlee's authority.[19] It has been suggested that the promise of the BEA position was an inducement from Attlee and Shinwell to get him out of the TUC in 1946.[20] One of Gaitskell's diary entries seemed to lend credence to such guesswork by Clegg – 'I could not help feeling that it was perhaps a mistake to have taken him out of the T.U.C. … he will not get used to running such a vast organisation compared with the T.U.C.'[21] Citrine gives no inkling of such a motive and his dedication to the NCB role suggests he thought he would be there for some time. Citrine was very keen to take the job at the BEA, but he was anxious lest the miners should feel let down. He needn't have worried, as he had performed creditably for them; although sorry to see him go, they wished him well with his new challenge.[22] His experience at the NCB was a useful preparation for being chair of the BEA and it was fortuitous that electricity nationalisation was delayed until 1947.

CITRINE'S 'ROMANCE' WITH THE ELECTRICITY AUTHORITY

'It's just like a romance, Shinwell said. "Here is a boy who goes into the electrical trade and rises to be Chairman of the Electricity Authority."'

It was certainly a love affair for Citrine, whose 'life was so wrapped up in my electrical activities that it didn't seem like work'.[23] If Doris and his grown-up sons (Norman[24] and Ronnie, a doctor) were perhaps looking forward to seeing more of their famous spouse and dad, it was not to be. Citrine became 'wrapped up' in another job with equally heavy, if very different, responsibilities. He would take bulky memoranda home with him 'which I diligently read, always marking in black-lead the passages which seemed to me to contain the heart of the subject'.[25] He even dreamed about the job and, perhaps 'tongue in cheek', regarded himself as 'a study for "psycho-analysts"'![26] Citrine would spend the next fifteen years in what he called his 'second career' in the electricity supply industry. It 'proved to be the happiest period of my whole life'.[27] It gave him the same 'thrill' in a new venture as when he joined the TUC in 1924, he said. Now 'he would be able to do something creative,

Cover of book by Leslie Hannah showing Citrine with the king and Gaitskell at the opening of a new power station at Kingston. From one of the posters Citrine commissioned.

something in which I believed', rather than just operate 'in the realm of ideas of the social, economic and industrial sphere', as he had been doing for the unions. He still regarded the TUC as 'his life's work' and would retain his interest in and sympathy for the fortunes of the unions throughout his life, as we shall see.[28] Citrine would also take with him the outlook his union involvement had created. There would be lots of scope to contribute his experience to running one of the largest publicly owned utilities for such a long period in his later career.

Characteristically, Citrine set about creating a team of senior executives to handle the immense post-war challenge of generating and distributing the nation's burgeoning electricity needs throughout the country. They had to create one organisation with fourteen area boards from 553 electricity undertakings (200 private companies and 369 local authorities), in England, Wales and Northern Ireland (Scotland had its own Hydro-Electric Board).[29] It was 'by any standards an industrial giant'.[30] They were helped by the fact that many of the power stations and other generating plant were already in public (local authority) ownership and 'most homes in Britain were connected to a public electricity supply during the 1930s'.[31] Most of the other senior managers and engineers joined the new nationalised authority, though issues of pay arose. The Board was restricted by public-sector limits as to what level of salary it could offer the very capable and experienced senior engineers and managers, many of whom had options of higher salaries in the private sector. But the BEA avoided the problems of coal nationalisation 'where politics had long bedevilled management relations with both government and workers and nationalisation led to the departure of senior managers in large numbers'.[32]

One of his vice-chairs, recruited with Shinwell's help, was Sir Henry Self,[33] then permanent secretary in the Air Ministry. He once remarked that Citrine was the only chap where the civil service tactic to bury an inquisitive minister in documents until he got sick of them failed to work, as he (Citrine) insisted on having 'more than a nodding acquaintance with what was going on'.[34] The other key appointment Citrine made was to keep the popular chief engineer of the ex-Central Electricity Board, John Hacking, who 'faced less initial distrust than … Citrine and Self'. He and his colleagues had run nearly 300 power stations for 130 generating authorities and so Hacking commanded the professional engineers' and managers' trust. This formidable trio became 'the central triumvirate' which ran the BEA.[35] Self would go on to chair the successor Electricity Council in 1958, when Citrine stepped down to become a part-time member of the Board, until 1962.[36]

The winter of 1946–47 was the worst the twentieth century had yet experienced, when energy demands were highest and the old industry plant showed many deficiencies, leading to many lengthy power cuts. The British economy was still largely coal-based. So desperate were the politicians responsible (Shinwell and his junior ministers, Hugh Gaitskell and the young Harold Wilson) that they turned to Arthur Horner, the communist secretary of the NUM, to help persuade the watermen and tugmen unions in London to cooperate in delivering enough coal from Durham to the power stations then dotted along the Thames. Horner, now a much more moderate union leader, helped and they averted a complete break-down of electricity generation in the capital.[37] The following winter, 1947–48, was milder but there were still frequent power cuts.

The BEA officially came into being on 1 April 1948. So anxious were Citrine and his chief administrator, Henry Self, that they slept in the office the night before, 'in order to be in hand in case anything went wrong'.[38] It didn't. As at the TUC, Citrine appreciated the importance of PR and he regularly met the editors of the industries' technical journals for off-the-record briefings. He also commissioned a series of illustrated publicity leaflets and poster hoardings 'showing what was involved in building a power station' (as seen above).[39] He thought that this kept down the level of complaints, though 'industrialists and the public growled loudly'. The Opposition made much of this and other gripes about his often over-consultative style, in the debate on the first detailed BEA Annual Report of July 1950.[40] However, the report, presented by the then minister, Philip Noel-Baker, and replied to by his very able parliamentary secretary, Alf (later Lord) Robens, had a relatively easy passage through the Commons. Robens reminded the Opposition that, before nationalisation, 150 electricity undertakings had made losses of £7 million, which would have led to much higher prices.[41]

Sir Arthur Gridley, Conservative MP for Southport South, and a respected former senior CEB engineer, called for a review of the limitations of capital expenditure by the chancellor (Gaitskell), because of the danger of overload and overheating of transformers likely to cause explosions. The 'insatiable' post-war demand for electricity also required a massive programme of expansion with new and bigger power stations, and as fast as possible. However, as a hugely capital-intensive business, this meant borrowing heavily. The post-war Treasury and government resisted BEA demands for more capital grants because of other priority social demands – the Welfare State and the NHS. Gaitskell was the minister and later (1950–51) Chancellor of the Exchequer 'with whom I had a few trenchant arguments' about financing their capital programmes.[42]

Gaitskell had 'a terrible row', 'my first public squabble with Citrine' in 1948.[43] This was about his policy of getting the BEA to operate a 'differential tariff, higher in winter and lower in summer' for domestic consumers. At first Citrine went along with this, but then, as all his experts were violently opposed to it, he supported them. When his Area Board chair weighed in, there was uproar at a meeting Gaitskell attended. 'Citrine virtually, pretty well, losing his temper and accusing the Ministry of trying to dominate the Board and so on.'[44] Citrine 'forgot' what he had agreed with Gaitskell, but 'got them to accept the principle' as a compromise (though at a very small differential). After a long, friendly talk with Citrine, Gaitskell appreciated his difficulty that the Area Board chairs regarded him as a politician and confidence in him would only come in time. So, he had to speak up for them. His old union skills in play!

Gridley, probably primed by his former colleagues in the Area Boards, also questioned the BEA Boards' 'top heavy' structure as centralised 'bureaucracy gone mad', and argued for 'greater responsibility for the Area Boards' and 'a reduction in the number of committees sitting in London and the mass of paperwork'.[45] However, Robens capably batted these interventions away in a very low-key debate, most 'civilised' by Commons standards, on nationalisations. There were no personal criticisms of Citrine, who seems to have commanded respect across the Commons. Citrine was also keen to switch some sources from coal and oil to nuclear, as being cheaper. However, 'the advent of nuclear power gave further emphasis to our need for increased capacity investment' and, with Conservative government support (Minister Geoffrey Lloyd), they embarked on a major programme of building nuclear power stations, starting with the first one in the world at Calder Hall (later Sellafield, Cumbria) in 1955. In his autobiography, Citrine included a photograph of himself in a huge bulldozer cutting the first sod for the next station at Bradwell, Essex, in 1957.[46] These were followed by many more 'of considerably greater capacity' in his last years as chair. Citrine became a part-time member of the BEA and UK Atomic Energy Authority when he stood down as chair of the BEA in 1958.[47]

Nationalisation had long featured in the programme of the Labour movement, 'but the methods by which the industries would be acquired had not been thought out with any real precision'.[48] Citrine first set about closely studying the quite detailed Electricity Act 1947 to enable his Board, chief officers and Area Boards to shape its policies. He committed to memory and notes every clause of the Act, interleaved copies of which he had prepared for the Board and Area Board members. He told Gaitskell that this was to impress his Board members, who he felt didn't initially respect him.[49] He would also use this mastery of the Act in his addresses to many gatherings at which he explained the purposes of nationalisation and his Board's functions. He disarmingly acknowledged his limitations and imperfections for this role as he had 'never been afraid of exposing my ignorance'. He began his many visits to electrical power stations where he insisted on climbing ladders to see boilers and turbines over ninety feet off the ground! Word got around, so a visit from the chair was a nervous time. One divisional controller later told him he 'always ordered all ladders to be locked away whenever I visited his division'!

In the image below he is seen opening the headquarters of the Yorkshire Electricity Board.

The Labour government's nationalisation programme created public corporations for all the utilities and other nationalised industries, such as the railways.[50] This was a policy which had been debated keenly in the 1930s in the Labour movement, around the rhetoric of 'workers' control' in transport and electricity. Ernest Bevin and the T&GWU argued fiercely with Herbert Morrison[51] over his championing of the London Transport model.[52] The TUC came to accept the Morrisonian concept. This meant there would be 'consultation' with the workers, but not the right of unions to appoint workers to the Board. This was implemented successfully in London Transport and the Central Electricity Board (forerunner of the BEA) in the 1930s and so became the model for post-war nationalisation. So, in theory, the public corporations were to have substantial operational autonomy from political interference. Of course, they were answerable to Parliament through the Secretary

Lord Citrine, chair of the British Electricity Authority,
opens a new headquarters near Leeds, 1950.

of State for Fuel and Power. He was appointed the boards and had ultimate power to determine their policies. With experienced, independent-minded chairs like Citrine, particularly with his senior Labour movement leadership background, asserting ministerial authority would not always be easy.[53] These tensions would emerge more after the young, ambitious Hugh Gaitskell took over as the minister from October 1947 to 1950.[54]

As the historian of the industry Leslie Hannah noted, 'The rhetoric of participation was to achieve its concrete expression principally through the appointment of Lord Citrine as chairman. Citrine was a powerful symbol of the elevation of workers to a new role in the industry.' The romance of the boy apprentice electrician who had become chair of the Board was part of that symbolism. Even better, Citrine's acknowledged credentials as 'an administrator and committeeman of high repute with members of all political parties' crowned his appointment.[55] Another able union official, Ernest Bussey, president of the Electrical Trade Union, well known to Citrine from his old union, also joined the BEA Board as director of labour relations and welfare. Despite pressure from the Area Boards to devolve labour relations to them, Citrine insisted on retaining that role as a central one.[56] Together, he and Bussey developed 'an unrivalled record of good labour relations' in an industry then employing about 140,000 workers and with the unions on the National Joint Industrial and Advisory Committees.[57] In this, he sought to 'broaden the understanding of the work-people, and create in them the feeling that a great human change must accompany nationalisation if it is ever to obtain the maximum of success'. As well as 'the vital consideration of the balance sheet', Citrine sought 'the development of a spirit of public service'. So, they sought 'to create machinery for the ventilation of grievances and their speedy elimination and the removal of their causes.'[58]

Again, as in the NCB, Citrine was keen to improve training, education and welfare. He and Bussey 'brought growls' from area managers and engineers when they sent out questionnaires to all staff seeking their comments about conditions. These 'forms' high-lighted many inadequate welfare conditions of the old separate undertakings and led, with the collaboration of the unions, to major revisions to things like washing and bathing accommodation at the power stations, medical attention, accident prevention and so on.[59] As a result, he thought that 'the electricity supply industry today will bear comparison with the general welfare conditions of any public or private undertakings in the world'.[60] Citrine's belief in 'consultation' – getting the views and arguments of those being affected – found greatest expression in the BEA. It introduced an elaborate 'consultative system' at every level and all divisions for the staff, with over 500 committees. It also devised other consulta-tive committees for consumers. All of these he described in detail, but they drew some criticism from avowed opponents of nation-alisation, as well as resentment from some managers unused to sharing information with their 'subordinates'.[61] In the Commons' debate on the First Annual Report of July 1950, Sir A. Gridley described it as 'the Socialist method; no individual to take respon-sibility. It is all settled by Committees.'[62] But Citrine ensured that all managers were trained in human relations and expected to treat 'those working under them' with respect. Under him, the British Electricity Authority was a pioneer in organising induction courses, spring and summer schools (five a year for 600 employees, most of which Citrine addressed), producing monthly newspapers, illustrated booklets and pamphlets, with visits to power stations for other staff and much else. He concluded, '[I] know of no organisation which carried out these methods more extensively or thoroughly than we did.'[63]

Nevertheless, it faced unofficial strike action in 1949 by 300 power workers at the South Wales stations and a more serious one by 1,600 workers in three London stations. Although he was not directly involved, Citrine regarded them as 'an ugly blot on my escutcheon'.[64] He discovered evidence that his old adversary, the Communist Party, was behind these 'spontaneous outbreaks' and that an unofficial union organisation had emerged with 'the inevitable nucleus of active communists, inspiring, organising and stimulating its activities'.[65] Citrine's immediate response was to contact the ETU president, Frank Foulkes,[66] chair of the Workers' Side of their National Joint Industrial Council. Foulkes was 'an avowed communist' but an 'excellent negotiator' and, for Citrine, a man of his word. As a result, he 'disavowed the strike' and advised a return to work, which was achieved.[67] Nonetheless, Citrine was disappointed that the workers in the power stations, on the transmission system and on the distribution network, felt that the new public organisation seemed to be 'very much the same as before'. They saw the same people, who had given the orders prior to nationalisation, doing so again.[68]

In July 1950, they had a far more serious unofficial electricity strike in London. Citrine had warned Gaitskell 'over a year ago of the possibility' that there 'might be trouble at some of the Power Stations'.[69] Gaitskell got Cabinet Emergency Committee approval to put in troops in the event of a threat of their closure. Negotiations with the unions endeavoured to get the men back to work, but communist control of the ETU made this difficult. Even though the union denounced the strikers officially, Gaitskell was 'perfectly certain the unofficial elements are largely guided and controlled by the communists as well'. Interestingly, 'Citrine was not so sure'.[70] However, Gaitskell 'saw a great deal of Citrine during the strike and was much impressed by his determination and firmness'.

At sixty, was Citrine too old to take on this mammoth task of directing such a massive organisation? Gaitskell initially thought so, though it proved otherwise. Citrine was blessed with robust good health and all his faculties into his sixties and seventies (though Gaitskell complained of his 'forgetfulness'). Obviously to the bright new Gaitskell, from a quite narrow middle-class background (public school, Oxford, economics lecturer, wartime civil servant), Citrine, 'the union bureaucrat', in his eyes, might have seemed past it, though he changed that opinion during their industrial actions in 1949–50.[71] Apparently, at the beginning, he appeared to the industry's senior managers and engineers 'as a strong-willed, humourless, puritanical idealist' and so 'the early steps in their relationship were not easy'. However, they soon recognised that he 'was acquiring a strong sense of identity with the industry's interests', the challenge enabling him to show his 'creativity and other faculties'.[72] Dealings between Gaitskell and Citrine, with the latter as chair of the BEA, were sometimes difficult.[73] By standing up to the minister, Citrine was showing the BEA Area Board directors, who were initially sceptical of him as being a political appointment, that he would be a strong and independent chair.

Hannah dubbed the BEA centralised policymaking and coordination model of nationalisation 'Citrine's Way'. 'Collective decision-making, the sharing of responsibility, and solidarity in a common task had been Citrine's way of life in the Labour movement; and the new organisation should be formed in that image.'[74] This was at variance with liberal individualist doctrines, 'the cornerstone of British management ideology', a culture which he had inherited. Hannah thought that 'Japanese businessmen would probably find them [referring to Citrine's approach] more intelligible'. Nevertheless, 'Managers and engineers could not help but admire the assiduity with which he could wear down its opponents in discussion'.[75] Nonetheless, against the fourteen Area Board chairs, who had considerable seniority and experience, the Central Authority had to give ground to their 'statutorily entrenched independence'. Citrine did so (much to the annoyance of the minister, Hugh Gaitskell) and so a compromise with a policy of decentralisation of certain roles was arrived at. Four Area Board members were brought onto the main Board and frequent conferences and periodic meetings became the way policies were decided. Though criticised as taking area directors away from their area work to attend frequent meetings in London, it worked and in time Citrine's Way 'produced formidable business success'.

Hannah's overall assessment of Citrine's approach is worth recalling.

> Trained in the hard school of the Labour movement to win legitimacy for their political aspirations toward higher living standards and greater popular participation, he also had a realistic appreciation of the benefits of the economic organisation already achieved by capitalism ... He relished the thought of showing that he could create a viable large-scale industrial organisation in the public sector, as they had in private industry. His mission was to show that socialism was not only politically possible but could work well in practice, a natural extension and not (as it was sometimes portrayed by the left) a betrayal of his previous commitment.[76]

Not a bad testament to Citrine's contribution to the development of publicly owned industry, which lasted over fifty years. When he finally left the Board in 1962, aged seventy-five (the last five years as a part-timer and infrequent attender), this fitting assessment and tribute appeared in the final report of the Central Electricity Authority (soon to become the Electricity Council). It called him 'The father of our industry in its present form'.[77]

> The outstanding and nationally acknowledged abilities and gifts of leadership – developed over the years in trades union and public affairs, notably as General Secretary of the T.U.C. from 1926 to 1946, and first brought to bear on a great National industry when he was appointed to the new National Coal Board – have made an unrivalled contribution to the successful integration of the electricity supply industry and to its vigorous and efficient growth.[78]

He must have grieved when the forces of privatisation and liberalisation in government came to break up 'his' electricity authority.

CHAPTER 15

~

IN THE HOUSE OF LORDS

Though he finally 'retired' from the electricity industry in about 1962, at the age of seventy-five, Walter Citrine was determined not to vegetate, as he put it, 'to keep my mind active and to retain and *widen* my interests'! So, he turned to politics (not party politics, 'although I never weakened in my allegiance to the Labour Party'). Although he had been a member of the House of Lords since 1946, he made just a few 'sporadic appearances', deliberately staying out of it, while he became 'engaged in electricity supply'. It was thirteen years before he made his maiden speech, in what Lord Mancroft (a *Punch* contributor) humourlessly described as 'one of the few Houses where a maiden can become a teenager before uttering a single word'.[1]

Now freed from the electrical industry, he 'felt at home' in that House, with its gentler 'pulse' and absence of 'acerbity' in speeches. However, he thought it a 'curious anachronism', composed then, as it was, mainly of hereditary peers until the Life Peerages Act of 1958. He was opposed to the principle which permits a son to succeed his father as a matter of right, but clearly this didn't influence both his sons, when it was their turn to become the 2nd and 3rd Baron Citrine.[2]

Walter's first recorded contribution in the Lords was on 29 October 1959, when he was still a part-time Board member of the BEA. It was just after the General Election that month, with the Conservatives back in power for the third consecutive term, though Labour, under Gaitskell since 1955, had been expected to win. With the economy prospering, the wily Tory leader, Harold Macmillan (1894–1986), waged a far more effective campaign, saying that 'most of our people have never had it so good'. He won an even bigger majority (345 seats to Labour's 277). After his defeat, Gaitskell tried to abandon or revise key planks of Labour's traditional policies, on nationalisation (Clause IV) and unilateral disarmament. He failed, due to strong union opposition, though Citrine would have been uneasy about Gaitskell's abandonment of nationalisation policy. His experience at the NCB and BEA could have informed the future development of improved Labour public-sector policies, but there is no evidence that Gaitskell's leadership team consulted him. He would have preferred Herbert Morrison as leader, instead of Gaitskell in 1955, as 'he [Morrison] understood our movement a good deal better than most of his colleagues, past and present'.[3] Citrine thought that, 'he [Morrison] was one of those who gave Labour's policy on nationalisation a practical turn and transformed it from little more than a slogan to a workable economic system of great potentiality'.[4]

In a low-key maiden speech, Citrine contrasted the serenity of that Chamber with 'the environment in which I functioned in the trade union movement'. Macmillan, a 'one-nation' Tory, was still notionally committed to the 'full employment' policies of the post-war Labour governments. So, Citrine accepted that there was no fundamental difference between the parties on this issue. He saw the fears of unemployment as 'at the root of so much of our industrial trouble', particularly 'vexatious demarcation questions' (then common). These, in his view, 'make the trade union movement look ridiculous in the eyes of the public and which are the bugbear of all balanced trade union officials'. He was consistent in this, and had been since his earliest days on Liverpool as the District ETU official and secretary/president of the Federation of Engineering and Shipbuilding Trades (FEST), thirty or more years earlier.

He also talked about the Index of the cost of living, on which wage movements were based, which, he said, had been 'under scrutiny of the trade unions for years' by TUC researchers. TUC officials remained sceptical about the 'weightings' by government committees dealing with the Index, but, as it had been 'relatively stable over the last eighteen months or two years', he concluded that Macmillan had been 'lucky' with the economy. He recalled also having 'the honour of helping to initiate' the National Joint Advisory Council of the Ministry of Labour in the early part of the war, aimed at keeping down prices and noted their current efforts. He expressed concern about a trend whereby employers were bargaining directly with local unions and shop stewards, rather than through employer associations on the National Joint Industrial Councils. This move away from national bargaining would accelerate in the early 1960s with plant and enterprise bargaining 'leapfrogging' wage and price increases.[5] He questioned the minister whether it was now government policy to favour this trend 'even if those wages increases are above the increase in the national production?'[6] He recalled his eighteen years as president of IFTU and WFTU, promoting collective bargaining internationally. He hoped 'that nothing will be done to fetter the freedom of collective bargaining between employers and trade unions in industry'.

UNOFFICIAL STRIKES

Lord Citrine then turned to the increasingly topical subject of unofficial strikes referred to in the minister's opening statement. Industrial relations were then a lead news item, with every paper having its own specialist industrial correspondent. The one common theme was that the unions were to blame for not being able to control their local members or shop stewards. Citrine said that 'no one is more troubled about the epidemic of unofficial strikes than the ordinary trade union officer. They are vexatious; they are irritating; they discredit the trade unions, and they endanger the agreements upon which collective bargaining rests.' At the same time, 'we have got to keep things in perspective. The numbers affected are small' and, by comparison with big strikes in the US (such as one in the steel industry then, which had lasted fourteen weeks), minor. However, he thought they reflected a weakness in the structure of national negotiations which 'takes (i.e., needs) time' and often mature consideration, to consider issues affecting what could be a million or more men and women in a dispute. He thought the nature of national bargaining 'poses a very real problem of internal government in the trade union movement, because of inability always to communicate accurately and speedily with the individual men and women in the workshops'. Some unofficial actions he saw as just 'a stimulus to speed up negotiations'. National agreements were increasingly ignored by shop stewards and managements in favour of direct negotiations and local agreements between them. But the press tended to focus on the more sensational aspects of work and production stoppages. He acknowledged that, 'Undoubtedly there is a measure of Communist exploitation behind these strikes. It is not always very obvious. But one can always be certain that somewhere in the heart of the shop stewards' committees, or whatever bodies there may be, there will be some nucleus of communists.' This was Citrine's old theme as general secretary in the 1920s (see Chapter 6), when he led the TUC's counterattack on the CPGB and Communist International's attempt to take over leadership of the British unions. Now, thirty years on, he seems to have had a milder perspective on their renewed activities.

> Your Lordships should remember that these people genuinely believe that employers and workers are in two hostile camps – as it were, two armies prepared to do battle on the first opportunity. Do not dismiss this as some kind of malicious thinking, because this thought is present in the minds of many good and competent workmen who have been misguided enough to find their way into the Communist Party or under their influence. They do not want industrial peace. Why should they? They believe that the capitalist system is collapsing. I myself have been looking rather keenly over a period of some fifty years or so for signs of the collapse, but I am very sorry to say that my perception is inadequate and I cannot see them clearly. ... But the Communist sees things tottering ... a crisis of unemployment ... and the class war ... I myself think that it is a fantastic interpretation of history, but there are thousands who believe it.[7]

He went on to answer the question on the minds of some Lords, 'why does not the union discipline their members?' His answer was that as voluntary organisations with only moral authority over their members, unions do not usually have the powers to do so, even if they wished. He also scotched the idea that the union should exclude such men from the workplace, as they are usually those who keep the union going in that workplace. Similarly, employers didn't usually enforce breaches of contract law to recover damages from their workers after strikes. It was because they wanted good relations after the strike, seeing this as the best means of increasing output. He seems to have softened his attitude towards the revived communist influence in the unions since the wartime.[8] Instead, Citrine looked to the 'very serious inquiry' by the TUC, to address the problem.

He popped up again in November 1960, when the Earl of Craven drew attention to an article by William Carron,[9] president of the AEU, in *The Sunday Times*. This was headlined 'Strikes, the Unions and Society' and Craven thought it 'shows up a deplorable and dangerous state of affairs', and what was the government going to do about it? Citrine drew Craven's attention to a paragraph of the article saying, 'It is foolish to expect trade-union officials to persuade their members that social morality applies only to them. The State will need to exert more control on some people at high levels if those at other levels are to act with greater social consciousness.'[10]

In October 1960, Lord Citrine had spoken at length on a topic close to his heart, 'the responsibilities of management'. He was supporting the motion of a former Labour minister and fellow Labour peer, Lord Shackleton.[11] Citrine entered the debate 'as one who has seen this problem from the standpoint of the workman, a trade union official, and, more latterly, as the chairman of a nationalised industry', and he was keenly listened to.[12] His argument was that with the extension of the publicly owned industry and private-sector mergers/takeover bids creating massive private corporations, managers should learn more 'public accountability'. He stressed the need for more training for managers, especially in larger companies. This had become a wider topic as *The Times* (his paper for years) reported that 'out of some 11,000 public and 310,000 private companies in the United Kingdom, only 400 have some kind of management training'. Lord Citrine said that from his wide travels around the world he found 'a greater reluctance on the part of British people to adopt new ideas'. He spoke of the 'inexorably intertwined qualities' of leadership and management to get the best out of the people they employed. 'Leadership is an elusive quality and many people search for it', though many seek to avoid its responsibilities. In his time he had 'seen a complete change in the attitude of mind in regard to the rights of work-people and their representatives, the trade unions'. He posed the question, 'can industrial autocracy go side by side with political democracy?'. In the nationalised industries, 'the employee's status is legally recognised in a different way from private industry'. They had the right 'conferred by Statute, to engage in discussions which are of mutual interest to the boards'. He then talked about the electricity supply industry, which, as we saw in Chapter 14, had 500 local consultative committees. He stressed the need for better communication from the top and to 'personalise your manage-ment'. His contribution was warmly greeted and generally agreed by the peers present.

On 8 November 1961, Lord Citrine intervened again in a very different mood, this time seconding a Labour amendment to the Queen's Speech. This opposed Chancellor of the Exchequer Selwyn Lloyd's 'wage pause' policy. Citrine was opposed to such wage restraint as there had been no warning or consultation with the unions. In his time, this wouldn't have happened! Even during the wars, the unions had opposed any formal agreement on pay restraint. He called Selwyn Lloyd's action 'precipitate and provoc-ative'. It is likely that Citrine had been briefed by his successor at the TUC, Vincent Tewson,[13] and so his unusually hard-hitting speech may have been for that audience also. He still attended the TUC Congress annually as an observer. Now he conveyed the full strength of feeling there as 'we will resist and we will fight this measure of dictation'. He warned of 'the most serious industrial disturbance since 1926' unless Prime Minister Harold Macmillan thought again. They could otherwise expect 'a bitter autumn'.

Citrine argued that he was not 'attacking the policy of wage-restraint. I have long supported that policy and have advocated it in public and in private, because I believe that it is necessary not only in the interests of the nation as a whole, but in the interests of trade unionists themselves. But always the base of that belief is that there should be equitable and similar treatment in broad character in regard to the incomes of other sections of the community.'[14] Towards the end of the war, they had engaged with Sir William Beveridge on the implications of the government's policy of 'full employment' (a maximum level of 2.5 per cent, that 'every man whose present job comes to an end for any reason can find fresh employment without delay').[15] Beveridge had posed the dilemma that the policy could lead to 'a rising spiral of wages and prices leading to inflation' and Citrine had acknowledged this. He said that if the Labour government could assure the unions that it would 'take all necessary steps to control prices', they would not object to the continuing wartime system of compulsory arbitration of wages (it lasted until 1951, when industrial action by strongly organised groups, like the dockers, ended it). He admitted that the whole issue of prices and incomes policy, which would come to dominate union–Labour government relations in the 1960s and 1970s, 'has never been treated in the Congress discussions with the precision it deserved'.[16]

The Selwyn Lloyd contractionary policy was scrapped in March 1962 and he was removed as chancellor by Macmillan, following the heavy defeat of the Conservatives in a famous Orpington, Kent, by-election by the Liberals. The irony was that Selwyn Lloyd had just invited the union leaders and employers onto a National Economic Development Council (it became known as NEDDY) of permanent consultation. This conformed with Citrine's ideas (though he was never a corporatist) and would shape corporate employer–union–government relations for decades after. In his speech, he welcomed this and urged the unions not to be put off joining by the mishandling of the 'pay pause'. Again, another weighty intervention. Citrine was enjoying himself at seventy-five, wearing both his old TUC and more recent NCB/BEA employers' hats! He also made a number of minor interventions with questions to ministers, for example, sparring with the Leader of the Lords, the 5th Marquess of Salisbury, about their meetings during the Spanish Civil War over the Conservative government policy of non-intervention, which entrenched Franco in Spain (see Chapter 10).

In May 1962, Lord Citrine made a significant intervention during the debate on a transport bill to reform British Railways. He welcomed it as an 'important and comprehensive Bill', but regretted that it would abolish the only coordinating body BR had had and would 'dispense with the services of some 150,000 people'. This happened a couple of years later, following the Beeching 'Axe' Report, which listed 2,363 stations and 5,000 miles (8,000 km) of railway line for closure, 55 per cent of stations and 30 per cent of route miles. Citrine's interest in this bill was as a 'believer in nationalisation as a system of economic organisation' with his fifteen years' experience with the NCB and BEA. He had also been involved at the TUC in the formulation of the principles which resulted in

Labour's legislation nationalising the transport system (in part) in 1948, as British Railways. He acknowledged that there 'has been a measure of disappointment' even to supporters of nationalisation, 'who perhaps, expected too much from a change from private ownership to nationalisation'.[17] However, 'the searchlight of public criticism' was focused on these public corporations, while 'great aggregations like I.C.I., Courtauld's, Lever's, Dunlop's and other private large companies, with their "assumed efficiency", escaped examination'. Citrine instanced the case of the Electricity Boards, which in 1953 were made to operate rural electrical services, which would never be economical without government subsidy.

But Citrine's main concern was to highlight the degree of ministerial interference in the decisions of the nationalised boards. 'Can we be absolutely certain that ... there will be found men of such independence of mind that they could stand up to the systematic and continued pressure of a Minister who, in turn, is reflecting the view of the Government of the day?' He said that in light of his own experience with Labour and Conservative ministers since 1947. The minister would appoint everybody on the Advisory Council and so they would not be representative of separate organisations. Also, he complained that 'no one is to be drawn from the ranks of the workers; nobody'. This informed criticism made little difference to the Conservative government's plans.

At that time, May 1962, negotiations were proceeding in regard to Britain's application to join the European Common Market, and Citrine drew attention to the possibility of 'very material changes in the Bill as a consequence of what may eventuate'! In August, he returned to that theme in a debate on 'Britain and the Common Market'.[18] Citrine, a staunch internationalist, having 'spent a good many years of my life trying to spread that unity over as wide a field as possible', wanted 'to endow the United Nations with a good deal more power than up to this stage'. So, he was strongly in favour of the British application to join what he preferred to call 'the European Economic Community' with its wider social connotation than the 'Common Market'. He dwelt on 'this miracle' of the successful bringing together of the Six in the Treaty of Rome since 1957. Yet, the Labour movement in Britain was 'now assailed by doubts and hesitations' about joining. The Labour Conference agenda had fifty-eight resolutions on it, all but three being against joining. At the TUC, only one out of ten resolutions 'is for entry to the Common Market'. Citrine attributed this reluctance to hostility to and mistrust of the government, over their policies in labour relations – the 'wages pause' policy. He recognised, though, that 'the real root fear, of course, is of loss of control over our own affairs'. From a union point of view, he felt that the key fear was the loss of British full employment and what they considered to be their superior labour conditions. He argued that both fears were exaggerated as the EEC would, if anything, strengthen the economy and full employment. He thought there had been 'a great levelling up in their labour conditions in the last few years', as to be on a par with Britain. Another big concern was labour mobility. 'I have heard it said by sensible people in the trade union movement that they are afraid of a flood of foreign labour coming into this country.' He thought it was not a real danger, as there were safeguards in the Treaty of Rome and there was 'a shortage of labour in practically every one of those countries'. So he had no doubts about the advantages of joining. Ironically, the decision was postponed as the French president, de Gaulle, vetoed British membership with a 'Non' that time, but the same lines of opposition would take place in the Labour movement of the 1970s. Far-sighted leaders like Citrine would be ignored.

And so he went on for another ten years in the Lords, with interventions on a variety of issues (271 in all from 1959 to 1973), a number of speeches each year, the highlights being: industrial training (1963); electricity, gas and atomic energy industries (1964); the trade disputes bill restoring union immunities after a (then) notorious *Rookes v Barnard* court case infringed the 1906 Act and another on industrial disputes (1965); the seamen's strike of 1966; an electricity bill (1967); fuel policy (1968); release of Mr Gerald Brooke, a British spy in the Soviet Union, in return for one of theirs (1969); the equal pay bill (1970); the Post Office workers' dispute (1971); the European Communities bill (1972); and, finally, the insurance companies bill (1973). He generally defended Labour government measures but, on the European Communities bill, he was firmly pro-entry.

Of particular interest was his intervention in 1971, pressing the minister, Lord Drumalbyn, on behalf of the postal workers (UCW) to resolve their long-running (eleven-week) dispute with the Post Office. Citrine, who hadn't lost any of his sharp forensic skill, wanted a full Court of Inquiry, saying, 'it looks very much as if what the government are aiming at is to starve these people into some kind of settlement'.[19] Citrine was supported by many other peers, including Lord Delacourt-Smith, the former general secretary of the Post Office Engineering Workers (POEU). A clearly embarrassed minister agreed to take the issue to the main minister in the government with a view to arranging arbitration of the issues. The postal workers had to go back defeated.

On 10 August 1972, Lord Citrine excused his absences from the House's debates 'mainly because of a physical disability'. This was during an intervention he made on the European Communities bill – again supporting entry, even though Labour opposed the bill. His contribution was clear but at the end he pleaded, 'my inadequacy

Addressing the TUC in 1975, aged eighty-eight, with Marie Patterson, chair of the General Council, and Len Murray, general secretary.

… has prevented me from developing this case in the way that I should have liked'.[20]

This brief summary of Lord Citrine's activities in the House of Lords from 1959 to 1973 sheds new light on the vigour of his 'declining' years, until physical disability weakened him. He had moved to Brixham in 1973 after his wife, Doris, died. For a time, he still travelled to the Lords and other (mainly union) events, until the journey became too much for him (at eighty-six!). He lived with his son Norman in Brixham, but in 1978 it was reported that he had moved out to a nearby cottage (perhaps a family falling-out?[21]). He lived on for another nine years in Devon and died in January 1983, when he was interred with Doris in Harrow Weald Cemetery.

A truly remarkable man.

~

HIS PLACE IN HISTORY

How do we place Walter Citrine's undoubtedly brilliant contributions to the making of the Labour movement and the country in the wider frame of history? Born into the squalor of Liverpool's dockland at the end of the nineteenth century, he suffered a life-threatening lung and kidney infection from his first job in a dusty flour mill at the age of twelve and almost died. The 'curse of the Citrines' – tuberculosis – would later carry off his mother, a sister and a brother – hence his rigorous health regime all his life.[1] To rise from these humble origins and lead the largest trade union centre of the world for two decades (1926–46), would itself be noteworthy. However, as he left the TUC for an equally responsible role on both the newly nationalised industries, National Coal Board and British Electricity Authority, which he chaired from 1947 to 1957, his achievements as trade union leader faded from the public eye. The comparable union and statesman-like figure Ernest Bevin (1881–1951), who became foreign secretary after the war, had also left him in the shade, on account of his great office and newsworthy prominence. Meanwhile, Citrine fiddled at the TUC, away from the main government and Cabinet action, particularly after having fallen out with both Attlee and Bevin. Soon, Bevin's fame as the 'proletarian Churchill' would be written up, before and after his death in 1951.[2] The first volume of Lord Bullock's monumental three-volume biography, which would copper-fasten his reputation, would follow in 1960. It was left to Lord Citrine to write his own autobiography in two volumes – *Men and Work* and *Two Careers* – in the 1960s. The eminent biographer of Churchill and of many other leading politicians, Lord Roy Jenkins, described Citrine's first volume as 'the most informative volume of memoirs to come out of the Labour movement since Lord Dalton's three-tier autobiography'. The respected biographer of Ramsay MacDonald, Professor David Marquand, also wrote of Citrine, 'he has now contributed as much to the writing of twentieth-century Labour history as he previously did to its making'.[3]

Accordingly, it is a puzzle why no other academics of standing embarked on a full biography of Lord Citrine at that time or since.[4] It isn't as if there was any shortage of material, as he left a voluminous legacy of contemporary reports, diaries, letters and notes from his time at the TUC and after, which his autobiography was based on. These are mainly collected in the LSE Library Archive and the TUC Library Collections at the London Metropolitan University or Warwick University Modern Records Centre and have formed the basis of this study, centred as it is on a critical examination of Citrine's own accounts.[5] One reason for that academic reticence could be that his autobiography is so vivid, with, as Lord Jenkins elegantly called it, 'a sense of "actuality" and pace which is rarely found in the evening reflections of elderly statesmen'. Could it also be that Citrine wanted to control what was written about him, as he was always sensitive about the distortions and libels he had suffered since the 1930s from his adversaries in the communist movement?

Citrine's reputation as 'the Witch-finder General of the left',[6] especially in some far-left-leaning union and academic circles, certainly discouraged more nuanced judgements on the Citrine–Bevin era. It is now generally agreed by most historians that Citrine made a major contribution to the trade union movement (whether they liked it or not) in his leadership of the TUC since the General Strike.[7] Lord Bullock frequently acknowledged Citrine's contribution. Although too accepting of his own subject's tendency to claim the credit for other people's ideas, Bullock very fairly attributed the TUC's success to their 'involuntary partnership' and complementary skills.[8]

In choosing a union career, Citrine expected neither fame nor fortune. Considering his brilliant intellect, imaginative administrative flair and highly effective forensic skills, he could have risen to the top in most professions, even in those class-restrictive days. In choosing a union career, which he did very consciously as we saw, he could not have foreseen the distance it would take him from his beloved Merseyside. But like many other bright working-class youngsters, his development as a union leader was also a factor of being drawn into 'this great movement of ours' (as some have described it). His very left-wing youthful socialism and industrial unionist ideology could be seen as a response to that class-conscious Edwardian society as well as to his personal attraction to severe social remedies then. Channelling his militancy through the Electrical Trades Union and the Independent Labour Party on Merseyside (though Liverpool was then a hotbed of syndicalist and communist propaganda) was a good move, as it enabled him to settle with a calm and discerning judgement.

Undoubtedly, Citrine's pioneering contribution to the creation of the modern Trades Union Congress ranks as his greatest achievement. He took over responsibility for the administration of a ramshackle lobby, with illusions (including his own) that it would become the 'general staff' of a Labour movement which could overthrow and replace the capitalist system. He was disabused of that illusion by the bitter experience of the General Strike. Yet, it was Citrine and Bevin who best articulated the lessons learned, especially the limitations of the aggressive deployment of union power.

Another of Citrine's distinctive contributions was his insistence on keeping the British TUC independent of party politics, able to deal with all governments through a highly trained and motivated staff team. This was an outstanding contribution to establishing a strong and independent union centre which commanded the respect of employers and government. It brought the trade union movement 'into the counsels of the nation' through the Labour Party policies during the 1930s and in the wartime coalition.[9] Although he remained a strong Labour supporter all his life, for him the trade unions were the core of that Labour movement. Hence, he decided early on to concentrate on a union role. At the same time, the unions' umbilical link with the Labour Party and governments was preserved. It proved quite a challenge, particularly during the first periods of Labour governments in 1924 and in 1929–31. This was largely on account of Labour politicians' unwillingness to consult properly or deal openly with the unions in case they be seen as being 'in the pockets of Transport House'. Their 'contentious alliance' (Lewis Minkin's term[10]) would continue through the Second World War and into the third, this time majority, Labour government, as we saw in Chapters 12 and 13.

Maintaining a single centre of the trade unions, despite the divisions created by the General Strike, was vital to the unique British movement's unity and strength. Citrine's cool advice and leadership of the General Council were key to this. In most European socialist and trade union movements, deep divisions had resulted in many centres since the First World War. But the Citrine–Bevin team led the retreat from the debacle of the General Strike and regrouped for a more cooperative stance with large employers in the Mond-Turner talks. This also helped Labour's claim to govern again in 1929. What started as a more hopeful relationship (see Chapter 9) fell foul of the Great Depression and mass unemployment as well as weak and divided political leadership. Citrine's serious illness prevented him having a more restraining influence on the more assertive General Council, commanded by Bevin. Their anger was perhaps understandable on account of the government's failures to repeal or even amend the anti-union law of 1927 and its adoption of severe austerity measures with hardly any consultation. However, it gave rise to such unforeseen adverse circumstances and blame as to provoke great heart-searching for generations, too easily focused on MacDonald's betrayal. More positively, Citrine characteristically provided a practical solution with his proposal for structured liaison and consultation between the two sides of the Labour movement. He made sure that the arrangement worked as joint secretary of the new policy-making National Council of Labour (NCL). This body now ensured full coordination between all sections of the Labour movement. This made it the substantial social-democratic policy-making force which enabled the Labour leadership to join in the government of the country from 1940. The National Council of Labour gave the lead in combating fascism and in changing Labour's pacifist policies on rearmament to fight it. By ensuring a coherent and effective working-class party, the unions provided that organised class with a leadership which helped marginalise the appeal of Hitler and Mosley-led fascist movement to people of all classes in Britain. Citrine was to the fore in this regard and Anti-Nazi Council/Focus Group extended its influence to all other classes. The National Council of Labour also helped shape the radical programme which the Labour government of 1945–51 would implement, the TUC providing many of the concrete ideas as well as the union vote 'ballast' to carry them. When the Labour leadership became a governing party again with the coalition government of 1940, it was the TUC leadership which helped give it strength and courage to face the threat of invasion and a minister of labour and national service in Bevin, who could rally the country with Churchill. As a Privy Council member, Sir Walter Citrine was the effective liaison from outside the government on behalf of the unions. He was a supreme 'behind the scenes' player who, by involving the TUC at every level, greatly facilitated the country's productive effort in support of the government (see Chapter 12).

As president of IFTU at Amsterdam, Citrine's international role brought involvement with the continental union and political leaders. It also brought a wider perspective and experience in the fraught European scene of the 1930s, which few others enjoyed. Inspired by his early sympathy for the Russian Revolution, Citrine was pleased to visit when he joined the TUC, when its left leadership was trying to help the Soviet Union in 1925. However, the divisive and hostile reaction of the Soviet leaders to the TUC over the decision to call off the General Strike a year later finished all Anglo-Soviet Union cooperation for more than a decade. As president of IFTU he would become openly hostile to the communist interference in European trade union affairs. However, he would become one of the first to appreciate the strategic significance of the Soviet Union for the war with Germany and quickly restored those Anglo-Soviet Union links in 1941, as we saw in Chapter 13.

These wartime engagements – he met Molotov on that visit and would work with the Soviet Union leaders during the war – showed a willingness to rethink and reform difficult relationships. He used these links and his close relationship with Roosevelt to establish a global trade union presence which sought to influence the ILO and United Nations Organisation (UNO), as we saw in Chapters 11 and 13. Unfortunately, for reasons outside his control with the US unions and lack of British government support, his union diplomacy was not successful.

Citrine was one of the first senior union leaders to highlight the menace of Hitlerian fascism, with his 1933 reports to the General Council and Congress from Berlin. Entitled *Dictatorships, and the Trade Union Movement*, it became a hugely influential document – see Chapter 10. TUC assistance to German and Austrian trade unions and Jewish refugees was a notable feature of their operations as well as campaigns to assist the Spanish Republicans and high-level lobbies of the British and French governments – Vincent Tewson, the assistant general secretary, and his wife majored on a project to take more than 4,000 Basque children to Britain after the bombing of Guernica.[11] Noteworthy also was the TUC's contribution to the development of trade unionism in the Empire, particularly in the West Indies, where Citrine personally helped shape the radical Moyne Commission of 1938–39.[12] He also promoted a prominent role for women in the TUC, as the female membership grew to over half a million by 1938.[13] He had been a strong supporter of women's equality and opponent of sex discrimination in the unions since he stood as a Labour candidate for Parliament for Wallasey in 1918.

Citrine's deep commitment to the fight against fascism again brought him into a leading role with the coalition government during the Second World War. Churchill, with whom he had worked closely in the Anti-Fascist Council since 1936, gave him direct access to all ministers as a privy councillor from 1940 and they developed a close personal rapport. Together with the appointment of a senior union leader, Ernest Bevin of the T&GWU as minister of labour and national service, the TUC helped mobilise the country's manpower at every level. Citrine was deeply involved in various joint employer/union production committees, notably with the Ministry of Aircraft Production with Lord Beaverbrook, during the Battle of Britain. Though the unions willingly agreed to suspend the right to strike and other restrictive practices, Citrine, always in contact with the war leaders, stood up to ministers and senior civil servants when required and justified, Bevin in particular.

He also undertook a number of important international diplomatic missions on behalf of the government, notably to America and the Soviet Union, where he met President Roosevelt and Foreign Secretary Molotov as president of IFTU as well as TUC general secretary. As a result, the TUC set up global union structures to cement the Anglo-Soviet-American alliance. His global travels in an era of doubtful and dangerous airpower are a remarkable feature of his bravery and commitment. Always looking ahead, in performing this important diplomatic role Citrine was not only helping to defeat fascism, but also seeking to secure the unions' place at the international table. His strategy was to influence post-war reconstruction and employment standards globally, through the International Labour Organisation and a more powerful United Nations. Citrine's use of his personal rapport with both Churchill and Roosevelt to facilitate such global initiatives for a time was imaginative. However, it also stoked jealousies in the coalition government which proved more than his lone abilities could overcome.

Sadly, the war effort strained Citrine's unique partnership with Ernest Bevin to breaking point. Although never close personally, before Bevin became a minister they had enjoyed an amazingly effective interdependent relationship in union and Labour affairs. Together they were seen as 'a force of nature'.[14] But after an initial period of close cooperation during the Second World War, the tensions of the war and Bevin's pursuit of personal power drove them apart (see Chapters 12 and 13). Citrine's insistence on standing up to the minister on issues brought to him by the unions (and employers) was seen as opposition and created hostility. Citrine's informal diplomatic role internationally also created jealousies and led to friction between the erstwhile partners, leading to open clashes which fractured their relationship. It culminated in the exclusion of the TUC from the British delegation at the founding conference of the United Nations by Attlee, Bevin and the coalition government. This caused Citrine to leave the TUC prematurely, weakening the union leadership considerably.

As we saw in Chapter 14, in 1946 Citrine left the TUC for an entirely different role in the newly nationalised industries, ultimately chairing the important British Electricity Authority. This was 'the happiest period' of Citrine's life, giving free rein to his creative and constructive abilities. Here he changed the individualistic culture of managerial practice, infusing it with a more collective, committee method of decision-making, without becoming bureaucratic. It also provided a much-expanded service of electricity supply. It built a strong culture of partnership which avoided strikes and built respect for workers. The electricity industry became a model of what a good public service should look like.

The loss of these two giants, Citrine and Bevin, from the post-war TUC left a serious leadership gap at a time when the

Labour movement needed its best counsel and leadership. With the death of Roosevelt in 1945, the global environment in which Citrine had operated was transformed. The Anglo-Soviet-American alliance ended, and Britain's empire faced its sunset relying on the new US dominance to help sustain British interests worldwide. The Cold War with the Soviet Union replaced their wartime alliance, which statesmen like Citrine had helped cement. But there was no call for his more judicious counsel in the subsequent atmosphere. Perhaps he was better off to depart.

CITRINE'S PLACE IN HISTORY

Broadening our conclusion about Citrine's influence on the fortunes of the British and global scene, we can now say that Walter Citrine was probably the most powerful figure to have graced the Labour movement in the twentieth century. Like many of his eminent colleagues, he was a product of the British trade unions which were emerging as a considerable social and political force towards the end of the nineteenth century, on the basis of their organised and growing industrial strength. That collective force, working closely with sympathetic, if ambitious, social democratic Labour leaders, created a new political party, which became the major Opposition in Parliament and by degrees the government party. For his part, Citrine made the profound decision not to become an MP but to develop the TUC as an independent body. It would have considerable influence with all parties of government, while staying close to Labour, a unique relationship of British society. However, when the need arose, as in 1931, he brought the unions back into a close liaison with Labour, helped revive the organisation, parliamentary representation and to shape its key policies, foreign as well as domestic. It was the resulting deepening of Labour's social democracy which enabled it to join the coalition government which withstood the threat of invasion and fascist dominance. This, in turn, prepared the Labour leadership for sole government in 1945, and Citrine reverted to his role as TUC general secretary outside the government. Though he did many other things, such as running one of the new nationalised industries and attending the House of Lords, Citrine remained a union man and his longevity can also be attributed to his mental strain for a better society. He has not had his due from that society or trade union movement, but this account of his life and achievements will hopefully go towards correcting that deficiency.

NOTES

Foreword

1 Robert Taylor, *The TUC From the General Strike to New Unionism* (Palgrave, 2000), p. 20.
2 *Ibid.*

Introduction

1 Citrine, *Two Careers* (Hutchinson, 1967), vol. 2 of his autobiography, p. 64.
2 *Ibid.*, pp. 67–8.
3 *Ibid.*, p. 78.
4 *Ibid.*, p. 69.
5 Citrine, *My American Diary* (1942), appendix, p. 352 reproduced his speech in full, pp. 327–53 at p. 352. University of Cambridge, 539.1.d.775.1. Also, Churchill Archives, CHAR 20/4B/148.
6 Citrine, *Two Careers*, p. 78.
7 *Ibid.*, pp. 97–9.
8 *Ibid.*, pp. 116–24 describes it, as we will see.
9 It follows my earlier contribution, *Walter Citrine: A Union Pioneer of Industrial Cooperation*, in *Alternatives to State-Socialism in Britain: Other Worlds of Labour in the Twentieth Century* (eds Peter Ackers & Alastair J. Reid, Palgrave, 2016), pp. 179–209.
10 *Men and Work* (Hutchinson, 1964), vol. 1 of his biography, p. 70.
11 *Ernest Bevin, Labour's Churchill* (Biteback Publishing, 2020).
12 Citrine, *Two Careers*, pp. 257–66. See Chapter 14.
13 Michael Foot, *Aneurin Bevan* (Reader's Union, 1962), vol. 1, pp. 177–8. Foot's biographer, Professor Kenneth Morgan, carried on that tradition, referring to Citrine as 'the supreme apparatchik'; *A Life of Michael Foot* (Harper Press, 2007), p. 254.
14 For the early ETU Citrine, John Lloyd's history of the EETPU, *Light and Liberty* (Weidenfeld & Nicolson, 1990), cannot be surpassed. Other key influences are: Robert Taylor's two chapters in his *TUC: From the General Strike to New Unionism* (Palgrave, 2000); Neil Riddell's *History* article, 'Walter Citrine and the British Labour Movement 1925-1935' (2000), vol. 85, pp. 285–306; Jonathan Davis, 'An Outsider Looks In: Walter Citrine's First Visit to the Soviet Union, 1925' (2013), vol. 26, issue 2. (*Revolutionary Journal*, vol. 26, no. 2, 2013). We should also notice Tom Buchanan's excellent 2004 entry in the Oxford Dictionary of National Biography, *Walter McLennan, First Baron Citrine* (1887–1983).

Chapter 1

1 Lord Citrine, *Men and Work* (Hutchinson, 1964), vol. 1, p. 19. In later years, he was a regular visitor and often gave talks at his old Poulton Road Board school (Liverpool City Council archive press cuttings, *Daily Post*, 1940).
2 Baptism Certificate from St Timothy's Church, Everton, Parish of Walton-on-the-Hill, County of Lancaster, 1887.
3 Courtesy of Liverpool National Museums.

4   Olivier Sykes, Jonathan Brown,
    Matthew Cocks, David Shaw
    and Chris Couch, 'A City Profile
    of Liverpool', Cities (2013), p.
    1. http://dx.doi.org/10.1016/j.
    cities.2013.03.013.
5   Ibid., p. 2. The slave trade was
    a central part of Liverpool's
    prosperity.
6   https://www.liverpoolcitypolice.
    co.uk/home, A History of Liverpool
    City Police. Shaun R. Rothwell,
    retired police officer, 1919.
7   Citrine, Men and Work, p. 12.
8   Ibid., p. 15.
9   Ibid.
10 Citrine, Men and Work, p. 18.
11 UK Census, Seacombe, Wallasey,
    the Wirral, Cheshire, 1901.
12 Ibid., p. 24.
13 Ibid., p. 27.
14 Ibid., p. 12.
15 LSE Library, Citrine 1/6, More
    Lessons, 12 February 1926, 'Some
    principles which I should observe at
    meetings'.
16 Ibid., pp. 12–13.
17 Ibid., p. 13.
18 Ibid., pp. 23–4.
19 Liverpool Echo, 13 December 1918,
    p. 5.
20 Citrine, Men and Work, p. 15.
21 Ibid., p. 17.
22 Citrine, Two Careers, pp. 363–4.
23 Citrine, Men and Work, p. 17.
24 Ibid., p. 27.
25 Ibid., p. 25.
26 Ibid., p. 19.
27 Ibid., p. 40.
28 Ibid., pp. 71–2.
29 Ibid., pp. 98–9.
30 Ibid., p. 27.
31 Ibid. This suggests that he wasn't an
    indentured apprentice, an important
    distinction then in that craft-based
    trade.
32 Ibid., pp. 27–9.
33 Ibid., p. 30.
34 Ibid., pp. 30 and 61.
35 Ibid., p. 30.
36 Ibid.
37 Ibid., p. 62.
38 Wikipedia, 'The Clarion'. https://
    en.wikipedia.org/wiki/The_
    Clarion; Working Class Movement
    Library, Manchester. WCML.org.
    uk.
39 Citrine, Men and Work, p. 75.
40 Ibid., p. 62.
41 Ibid., p. 63.
42 Ibid., p. 62.
43 Ibid.
44 Ibid., p. 63.
45 Ibid., p. 31.
46 Ibid., pp. 31 and 33.
47 Ibid., p. 31.
48 Ibid.
49 Ibid., pp. 31–2.
50 Ibid., p. 32.
51 Ibid.
52 Ibid.
53 Ibid., p. 33.
54 Ibid.
55 Ibid. Sadly, these notebooks do
    not appear to have survived as
    Citrine was not prepared to hand
    them over to the LSE staff when
    collecting his materials for their
    archive. Lord Norman Citrine,
    the 2nd Baron's response to John
    Lloyd's inquiry of 21.9.87. Ibid.,
    p. 35.
56 Ibid.
57 Ibid., p. 40.
58 Ibid.
59 Ibid., p. 33.
60 Ibid., p. 15. 'The Picton Library'.
    Liverpool Central Library booklet
    – 'Archive, Discover, Enquire,
    Imagine, Read', 2019, p. 18.
61 Citrine, Men and Work, pp. 32–3.
62 Ibid., p. 46.

63 Citrine, *Men and Work*, p. 34. A remarkable instance of the intelligence and union-inspired education among Britain's coalminers.

64 *Ibid.*, p. 34.

65 John Lloyd, *Light and Liberty: One Hundred Years of the Electrical, Electronic, Telecommunications and Plumbing Union* (Weidenfeld & Nicolson, 1990), p. 75.

66 *Ibid.*, p. 34.

67 *Ibid.*, p. 36.

68 *Electrical Trades Journal (ETJ)*, August 1918, p. 39. The ETU records are in the Warwick Modern Records Centre, University of Warwick, vols 5, 6, 7 and 8 (1911 onwards), Shelfmark 053.

69 His nine books and pamphlets are listed in volume 1 of his autobiography, *Men and Work – ABC of Chairmanship* (1939); *The Trade Union Movement of Great Britain*; *Labour and the Community*; *I Search for Truth in Russia* (1936); *My Finnish Diary* (1940); *My American Diary* (1942); *In Russia Now* (1943); and *British Trade Unions* (1942). The titles give a flavour of his wide range of activities and interests.

70 Citrine, *Men and Work*, p. 24.

71 *Ibid.*, p. 34.

72 *Ibid.*, pp. 75–6.

Chapter 2

1 Citrine, *Men and Work*, p. 51.

2 *The Times*, 15–22 August 1911, covered that unrest extensively.

3 The LSE Library, Citrine Archive 4/2, p. 5, from his talk to TUC summer school students at Ruskin College, Oxford, in July 1931.

4 *The Times*, 16 August 1911.

5 *Ibid.*, 15–21 August 1911.

6 *Ibid.*, 18 August 1911.

7 In 1987, Dr John Lloyd was told by the archivists at the London School of Economics that Lord Citrine 'was not prepared to hand them over' (his pre-1924 notebooks and other materials). John Lloyd, National Officer, EETPU 21.9.1987 to Lord Ronald Citrine and his reply, 5.x.87.

8 Neil Riddell, 'Walter Citrine and the British Labour Movement, 1925–1935', *History* (April 2000), vol. 85, no. 278, p. 288.

9 Walter M. Citrine, *Trade Unionism – Its Rise, Development and Future*, a five-part series in the ETU *Electrical Trades Journal*, December 1912–May 1913. LSE Library, Citrine 4/1.

10 *Ibid.*, December 1912, p. 1.

11 *Ibid.*, April 1913, p. 1.

12 *Ibid.*, p. 3.

13 *ETJ*, May 1913, p. 2.

14 Lloyd, *Light and Liberty*, pp. 94–5.

15 Citrine, *Men and Work*, p. 47.

16 *Ibid.*; the Webbs' *Industrial Democracy* appeared in 1897, second edition, 1920.

17 *Ibid.*, p. 47.

18 Clegg, *A History*, vol. II, p. 15.

19 *Ibid.*

20 Citrine, *Men and Work*, p. 38.

21 Clegg, *A History*, vol. II, p. 19.

22 Citrine, *Men and Work*, p. 38.

23 Clegg, *A History*, vol. II, pp. 1–23, has a useful description of the unions in 1910 and an overview of their functions in 1910.

24 Citrine, *Men and Work*, p. 38.

25 *Ibid.*; Lloyd, *Light and Liberty*, p. 72 put the figure at 1,871 in 1910.

26 Citrine, *Men and Work*, pp. 39–40 and 53–4.

27 *Ibid.*, p. 39.

28 Lloyd, *Light and Liberty*, p. 116.

29 *Ibid.*, p. 39.

30 *Ibid.*

31 *Ibid.*, pp. 39–40.
32 *Ibid.*, p. 40.
33 *Ibid.*
34 *Liverpool Echo*, 1 July 1914,
      p. 8, 'Happy Strikers. Liverpool
      Electricians as Contractors.'
35 *Ibid.*
36 *The Challenge of Socialism*, ed. Henry
      Pelling (Adam & Charles Black,
      1954), p. 247 – articles on Guild
      Socialism by A. J. Penty and G. D.
      H. Cole and R. H. Tawney, pp.
      217–31.
37 Citrine, *Men and Work*, p. 57.
38 Lloyd, *Light and Liberty*, pp. 94–5.
39 *Ibid.*
40 *Ibid.*
41 *Ibid.*, p. 96.
42 *Ibid.*, p. 98. Also, Citrine, *Men and
      Work*, p. 41.
43 They moved to the Arcade, Lord
      Street, Liverpool, by 1918. Citrine,
      Men and Work, p. 64.
44 *Ibid.*, p. 44.
45 *Ibid.*, p. 43.
46 *ETJ*, May 1917, pp. 30–31.
47 Citrine, *Men and Work*, p. 51.
48 *Ibid.*
49 *Ibid.*
50 Citrine, *Men and Work*, pp. 54–60.
51 *Ibid.*, p. 56.
52 *Ibid.*, p. 60.
53 LSE Library, Citrine 4/2, 'More
      Lessons', 18 February 1926.
54 The general issue of conscription
      and the electricians is discussed
      in detail by John Lloyd, *Light and
      Liberty*, at pp. 110–16.
55 Citrine's report from the Labour
      Party Conference at Southport,
      ETJ, July 1919, p. 24 is clearly anti-
      war.
56 Lloyd, *Light and Liberty*, p. 99.
57 *Ibid.*, p. 102. This was an agreement
      of all the wartime industry unions,
      which suspended the right to strike

and other restrictive practices for
the duration of the war. It was
reinforced by the Munitions of War
Act 1915.
58 *Ibid.*, pp. 104–10.
59 See *ETJ*, Mersey District Reports,
      April–October 1917.
60 *ETJ*, August 1917, p. 69. For
      Rowan's view, Lloyd, *Light and
      Liberty*, p. 81.
61 *ETJ* (March 1915–April 1917), vol.
      7, no. 12. Warwick Modern Records
      Centre, Shelfmark 053.
62 Lloyd, *Light and Liberty*, p. 77.
63 *Ibid.*, pp. 274–5.
64 *ETJ*, August 1917, pp. 68–9.
65 Riddell, 'Walter Citrine', p. 288.
66 Lloyd, *Light and Liberty*, p. 112.
67 *Ibid.*, p. 78.
68 *Ibid.*, p. 104.
69 *Ibid.*, p. 104.
70 At an ETU Conference in Central
      Hall, Westminster, September 1924.
71 Clegg, *A History*, vol. II, pp. 204–5.
72 *Ibid.*, p. 248.
73 Citrine's Letter in the *ETJ*, June
      1919, pp. 3–4.
74 Minutes of the First Meeting of the
      National Joint Industrial Council for
      the Electrical Contracting Industry,
      Leeds, 22 and 23 January 1919,
      pp. 1, 5–6.
75 J. T. Murphy, *Labour's Big Three*
      (Bodley Head, 1948), p. 166.
76 Citrine, *Men and Work*, pp. 44–5.
77 *Liverpool Echo*, 18 October 1918.
78 *ETJ*, January 1919, p. 142.
79 Citrine, *Men and Work*, p. 65.
80 *Ibid.*, p. 65.
81 *ETJ*, September 1919, p. 83.
82 Clegg, *A History*, vol. II, p. 286.
83 *Liverpool Daily Post*, 4 August 1919.
84 *The Times*, 6 August 1919, p. 12.
85 *Ibid.*, 6 August 1919, p. 12.
86 A. V. Sellwood, *Police Strike* (W. H.
      Allen, 1978), p. 51.

87 *The Times*, 8 August 1919, p. 16.
88 *ETJ*, September 1919, p. 84.
89 Citrine, *Men and Work*, pp. 67–8.
90 Sellwood, *Police Strike*, p. 51.
91 Lloyd, *Light and Liberty*, p. 146.
92 *ETJ*, 21 April 1920, p. 13.

Chapter 3

1 Citrine, *Men and Work*, p. 65.
2 He received 4,865 votes in the first round and 6,239 (to his nearest opponent's 3,282 votes) in the run-off. Lloyd, *Light and Liberty*, p. 146.
3 Citrine, *Men and Work*, p. 68.
4 *Ibid.*
5 *Ibid.*
6 *Ibid.*
7 Lloyd, *Light and Liberty*, pp. 70–2.
8 *Ibid.*, pp. 72–3.
9 *ETJ*, March 1921, p. 332.
10 *Ibid.*, January 1921, p. 257.
11 Citrine, *Men and Work*, p. 66.
12 Lloyd, *Light and Liberty*, pp. 147.
13 *Ibid.*
14 *ETJ*, April 1921, p. 364.
15 Citrine, *Men and Work*, p. 68.
16 *ETJ*, May 1921, p. 406.
17 Citrine, *Men and Work*, p. 68.
18 See Alastair J. Reid, *The Tide of Democracy: Shipyard Workers and Social Relations in Britain, 1870–1950* (Manchester University Press, 2010), in a similar-sized Boilermakers' union, pp. 140–4.
19 *Ibid.*, p. 69.
20 *ETJ*, July 1922, p. 123; January 1923, pp. 243–4; February 1923, pp. 259–60.
21 Robert Currie, *Industrial Politics* (Oxford University Press, 1979), pp. 35, 61.
22 Citrine, *Men and Work*, p. 69.
23 *Ibid.*, p. 68.
24 Lloyd, *Light and Liberty*, p. 151.
25 *Ibid.*, p. 69.
26 *Ibid.*, p. 151.
27 Citrine, *Men and Work*, p. 69.
28 Lloyd, *Light and Liberty*, pp. 72–3.
29 *The Labour Chairman and Speaker's Companion, Guide to the Conduct of Trades Union and Labour Meetings*, March 1921. Foreword by J. H. Thomas, NUR.
30 *ETJ*, May 1921, pp. 414–15.
31 Alan Johnson, *The Long and Winding Road* (Bantam Press, 2016), pp. 193–4. General secretary of the Communication Workers Union, 1992–7.
32 Lloyd, *Light and Liberty*, pp. 157–8.
33 *ETJ*, March 1922, p. 50.
34 *Ibid.*, June 1922, p. 83.
35 Citrine, *Men and Work*, pp. 69–70.
36 *Ibid.*
37 ETU Executive Council Minutes, March 1922 to July 1923. Warwick Modern Records Centre, Shelfmark 053.
38 Labour Conference at Scarborough, August 1920, *ETJ*, pp. 75–6; TUC and Labour joint conference on unemployment, London, *ETJ*, March 1921 and many others.
39 *ETJ*, March 1921, p. 352.
40 *Ibid.*, February 1918, p. 245.
41 Citrine, *Men and Work*, p. 67.
42 *Ibid.*
43 *Ibid.*, p. 42. He had a typist from the Gregg School at the TUC to transcribe his many reports on his travels.
44 *Ibid.*
45 *Ibid.*
46 Lloyd, *Light and Liberty*, pp. 90–5.
47 *Ibid.*, p. 97.
48 *Ibid.*, pp. 104–8.
49 Electrons are negatively charged subatomic particles. The term was being used by the left-wing electrical engineers as a revolutionary metaphor.

50 H. A. Clegg, *A History of British Trade Unions since 1899*, vol. II, *1911–1933* (Clarendon Press, 1988), p. 274.

51 Lloyd, *Light and Liberty*, pp. 84–6.

52 An annotated copy is with Citrine's papers, LSE Library, Citrine 11/9.

53 Lloyd, *Light and Liberty*, pp. 132–3, 154.

54 *Ibid.*, p. 132.

55 *Ibid.*, p. 133.

56 *Ibid.*, p. 134.

57 *Ibid.*

58 *Ibid.*, pp. 84–6.

59 *Ibid.*, p. 136.

60 *Ibid.*, p. 135. The *ETJ* (January 1918) printed a long article of his on 'Industry v Craft'.

61 *Ibid.*, p. 139. By the end of 1923, membership had fallen to 26,165, forty-six per cent of its 1920 record level of 57,292 (ibid., p. 145).

62 *Beatrice Webb's Diaries*, 1924–1932, ed. Margaret Cole (Longman, Green & Co., 1956), pp. 210–11.

63 Lloyd, *Light and Liberty*, p. 146.

64 *Ibid.*, pp. 147–8.

65 *Ibid.*

66 *Ibid.*, p. 150.

67 *Ibid.*

68 *Ibid.*

69 *Ibid.*, pp. 149–50.

70 *Ibid.*, pp. 164–9.

71 *ETJ*, July 1922, p. 30.

72 Lloyd, *Light and Liberty*, p. 152.

73 Citrine, *Men and Work*, p. 72.

74 *Ibid.* This was one of Citrine's idiosyncrasies.

75 *Ibid.*, pp. 72–3.

Chapter 4

1 Clegg, *A History*, vol. II, pp. 568–9.

2 Alan Bullock, *The Life and Times of Ernest Bevin*, vol. I, *Trade Union Leader* (Heinemann, 1960), pp. 287–9.

3 Clegg, *A History*, vol. II, pp. 308–10; Ross M. Martin, *The TUC: The Growth of a Pressure Group 1868–1976* (Clarendon Press, 1980), pp. 181–2.

4 G. A. Phillips, *The General Strike: The Politics of Industrial Conflict* (Weidenfeld & Nicolson, 1976), pp. 14–15.

5 Clegg, *A History*, vol. II, p. 573, and Robert Taylor, *The TUC*, pp. 8–9.

6 ILO Convention agreed at Washington 1919, but which successive British governments failed to ratify. As late as 1929–31 Citrine was lobbying the Labour government to ratify. An hours of work bill fell with the government. Clegg, *A History*, vol. II, p. 282.

7 *Forty-Five Years, International Federation of Trade Unions* by Walther Schevenels (general secretary 1931–1945), Brussels, 1956, pp. 91–7.

8 G. A. Phillips, *The General Strike*, pp. 2–14. See below at Chapter 5.

9 Bullock, *Bevin*, vol. I, *Trade Union Leader*, pp. 287–8; Clegg, *A History*, vol. II, pp. 390–1.

10 Phillips, *The General Strike*, pp. 54–8.

11 *Beatrice Webb's Diaries*, p. 75.

12 Clegg, *A History*, vol. II, p. 390.

13 James Ramsay MacDonald (JRM, as he was known), 1866–1937; David Marquand, *Ramsay MacDonald* (Jonathan Cape, 1977), pp. 297–309.

14 One of his works, a two-volume *Socialism and Government*, MacDonald produced in 1909 for the ILP. *The Socialist Library*, VIII, gave him a high standing in the Labour Party and the Second International of socialist parties.

15 Arthur Henderson (1863–1935) is one of the most underrated early Labour figures. From a nonconformist Scottish and Newcastle union (ironfounders) and Liberal background, he helped

create the Labour Party as an organised electoral force, stepped in as leader of the Parliamentary Party when required and willingly relinquished it when someone with more flair, like MacDonald, wanted it. As a former union (ironfounders) official, he was much more union-sensitive than MacDonald, but his advice was not always treated with respect by the leader.

16 Stanley Baldwin (1867–1947). He came from an industrial (iron and steel) employer background in a family firm at Bewdley, Worcestershire (his earldom) and so was a less narrow party leader than most Tories. He became prime minister first in 1923 in a power struggle and fought the election on tariffs. Losing their majority, he sat back to let MacDonald 'learn the ropes', sure of picking up the reins of government again for the Conservatives before long, which proved to be the case.

17 The following profiles are sketched from Clegg's biographies of leading trade unionists in his *A History of British Trade Unions Since 1889*, vol. II, pp. 572–81.

18 James Henry ('Jimmy') Thomas MP (1874–1950) had risen to become general secretary of the NUR/ASRS in 1916 as a left-winger in its syndicalist or very left-dominated executive council. He led the successful national rail strike of 1919. However, now much changed in outlook and also a Labour politician, he was the leading right-winger on the General Council.

19 Harry Gosling (1861–1930), secretary of the Amalgamated Society of Watermen and Lightermen (1893–1921), then

president of the T&GWU until 1930. TUC Parliamentary Committee, 1908–23; MP, 1923–30; and minister of transport and Paymaster General, 1924.

20 Margaret Bondfield (1873–1953), a shop assistant union activist in the late 1890s and early 1900s. On the TUC Parliamentary Committee and General Council (1917–24), she became chief women's officer of the municipal general workers' union (NUGMW) (1921–38) and an MP (1923–24) under secretary at the Ministry of Labour; again 1926–31 and minister of labour. She chaired the General Council which appointed Citrine in 1923. Citrine, *Men and Work*, pp. 72 and 91.

21 Frank Hodges (1887–1947), though a very able young miners' leader, lost the confidence of his union executive over a compromising speech he made as secretary of the MFGB in 1921 during the Black Friday strike defeat. A few years later, he switched to becoming a Labour MP and left politics for a business career (Central Electricity Board, 1927–47).

22 Thomas Shaw (1872–1938), a miner's son, who was active in the Northern Counties Textile Trades Federation and became a Preston MP from 1918 to 1931. He became minister of labour, though not in the Cabinet, in 1924 and secretary of state for war in the 1929–31 Labour government.

23 Albert Arthur (A. A.) Purcell (1872–1935), a London-born French polisher whose tiny union merged with the Furnishing Trades Union (NAFTA) in which he became a national organiser from 1910 to 1928. Before joining the TUC

Parliamentary Council in 1919, filling the vacancy left by Bramley's promotion to assistant secretary, he was mainly active as chair of the powerful Manchester and Salford Trades Council. K. Morgan, *Bolshevism, Syndicalism and the General Strike: The Lost World of A. A. Purcell* (Lawrence & Wishart, 2013), pp. 10–20 and 42.

24 Bramley had been an ILP activist and chair of the very left-wing London Labour Party and a parliamentary candidate, which he had to give up on becoming the full-time general secretary of the TUC in 1923. Barbara Nield and John Saville, *Dictionary of Labour Biography*, vol. IX (Palgrave MacMillan, 1993), pp. 16–20.

25 Morgan, *Bolshevism, Syndicalism and the General Strike*, pp. 10–20 and 42.

26 George Hicks (1879–1954), a bricklayer. General secretary AUBTW to 1940 and General Council member, 1921–40. A close friend of Citrine's who went to Russia with him in 1925. Also an MP, 1921–50, and a minister, 1940–45.

27 NAFTA had only 21,000 members, but the Woodworking and Furnishing Group was dominated by Hicks' large AUBTW membership. TUC Annual Reports 1923–28, Trade Group elections.

28 ISEL was the main British syndicalist organisation, founded in Manchester in 1910. It was modelled on the French General Confederation of Labour (CGT), by Tom Mann. It sought to disseminate syndicalist ideas within the Labour movement and had links with like-minded syndicalists in the ILP, Social Democratic Federation and the Clarion Movement, but it collapsed in 1913.

29 Citrine, *Men and Work*, p. 80.

30 *Ibid.*, p. 77.

31 *Ibid.*, pp. 80–85. He recalled at length their social call on the famous late- nineteenth-century union leader (engineer and dockers leader) and Liberal Cabinet minister (1905–14; he resigned in protest over their entry into the war) John Burns (1858–1943), who was still spritely and combative.

32 See Chapter 6. Also, Geert Van Goethem, *The Amsterdam International: The World of the International Federation of Trade Unions (IFTU), 1913–1945* (Ashgate Publishing, 2006), pp. 37–43, 90–96.

33 *Ibid.*

34 Alonso Beaumont Swales, known as 'AB' (1870–1952), was national organiser and senior executive council member of the left-wing Amalgamated Society of Engineers (ASE), 1912–35. It became the Amalgamated Engineering Union (AEU) in 1920 – Tom Mann (1856–1941), the legendary syndicalist, was president. Clegg, *A History*, vol. II, pp. 577 and 579.

35 Arthur J. Cook (1883–1931), a Somerset militant who moved to South Wales and was deeply influenced by the Plebs League syndicalism. He became a miners' agent for the Rhondda, South Wales colliers, 1912–24. Executive Committee, MFGB, 1921–22. A former communist and still a militant Marxist, he would dominate the miners' struggles from there on. Clegg, *A History*, vol. II, p. 574. See Chapter 5 below on the General Strike.

36 Robert Taylor, *The TUC*, pp. 20–22.

37 This was established c. 1906 under Henderson's leadership and the Bowerman-led TUC Parliamentary Committee had accepted this generally.

38 John R. Clynes (1869–1949), a former NUGMW gas workers' leader. He majored on politics as Labour MP from 1906 and briefly became leader (1921–22). Served in the wartime coalition government and with MacDonald as Leader of the Parliamentary Party in 1924. Home secretary from 1929 to 1931.

39 Sidney Webb (1850–1947), Fabian Society founder and eminent trade union writer. Labour MP, 1918–31, and Board of Trade minister, 1924. See Chapter 5.

40 Marquand, *Ramsay MacDonald*, p. 298. MacDonald had to persuade the National Executive and the TUC General Council at a joint meeting.

41 *Beatrice Webb's Diaries, 1912–1924*, p. 259.

42 Sir Allan Smith (1871–1941) was a former Glasgow solicitor and the hard-line secretary of the EEF, part of the National Confederation of Employers' Organisations (NCEO). He was a founder member of the anti-union Economic League, which sought to root out union militants. See Chapter 8 for their clashes over the years after. Clegg, *A History*, vol. II, p. 339.

43 Citrine, *Men and Work*, p. 70. See also pp. 54 and 247 for other brushes they had to 1928/29. See below Chapter 8.

44 Ernie (1881–1951), as he was known, remains the most remembered trade union leader of this era, due to the eminent positions in British governments he came to hold. Also, he has had so many biographers. His reputation rests on the monumental but rather uncritical three-volume *Life and Times* series by Lord Alan Bullock – vol. I, *Trade Union Leader 1881–1940* (Heinemann, 1960); vol. II, *Minister of Labour 1940–1945* (Heinemann, 1967); and vol. III, *Foreign Secretary 1945–1951* (Heinemann, 1980).

45 Bullock, *Bevin*, vol. I, *Trade Union Leader*, pp. 251 and 236–47.

46 Samuel Gompers (1850–1924), president of the American Federation of Labour for more than forty years and architect of 'business unionism'. Bevin had admired his organisation and his style of running the AFL since his first visit to that union's convention in 1916. Bullock, *Bevin*, vol. 1, *Trade Union Leader*, pp. 51–4.

47 Andrew Adonis, *Ernest Bevin, Labour's Churchill* (Biteback Publishing, 2020), p. 57. Compared him also to John L. Lewis, the legendary American miners' leader (see Chapter 13).

48 Bullock, *Bevin*, vol. I, *Trade Union Leader*, pp. 287–8.

49 Marquand, *Ramsay MacDonald*, p. 328.

50 Trevor Evans, *Bevin* (Allen & Unwin, 1946), p. 96.

51 *Ibid.*

52 Emmanuel Shinwell MP (1884–1986) had quite an industrial militant pedigree from Glasgow; as a leader of the wartime Shop Stewards Movement he was once jailed over the militants' 'robust' reception of Lloyd George there. Bullock, *Bevin*, vol. I, *Trade Union Leader*, pp. 245–6. His vivid memoir of those times, *The Labour Story, Being a History of the Labour Party* (Macdonald, 1963), gives a flavour.

53 Shinwell, *The Labour Story*, p. 123.

54 Bullock, *Bevin*, vol. I, *Trade Union Leader*, pp. 258–60.

55 *Ibid.*, pp. 364–5.

56 *Ibid.*, p. 365.

57 *Ibid.*, pp. 244–6; Adonis, *Ernest Bevin, Labour's Churchill*, pp. 59–60.

58 Bullock, Bevin, vol. I, *Trade Union Leader*, p. 236.

59 Francis Williams, *Ernest Bevin: Portrait of a Great Englishman* (Hutchinson, 1952), p. 119.

60 *Ibid.*

61 Bullock, *Bevin*, vol. I, *Trade Union Leader*, pp. 236–43.

62 Citrine, *Men and Work*, p. 78.

63 They were right that Purcell and other pro-Soviet union leaders were involved, though not about the extent of their influence with MacDonald and his chief negotiator, Arthur Ponsonby MP, his parliamentary secretary. Daniel F. Calhoun, *The United Front, The TUC and the Russians 1923–1928* (Cambridge University Press, 1976), pp. 52 and 59.

64 Marquand, *Ramsay MacDonald*, p. 362.

65 Citrine, *Men and Work*, p. 88.

66 Calhoun, *The United Front*, p. 143.

67 *Ibid.*, pp. 159, 163, 165.

68 Marquand, *Ramsay MacDonald*, pp. 361–4.

69 Citrine, *Men and Work*, pp. 79–80. He referred in 1931 to 'when the Government was brought down because of friction with the Trades Union Congress over the Russian Treaty'. LSE Library, Citrine 4/2, 'Points to be Considered', 2 November 1931.

70 *Ibid.*, pp. 74–7.

71 Clegg, *A History*, vol. II, p. 390. See Chapter 5.

72 *Beatrice Webb's Diaries, 1924–1932*, p. 75.

73 Marquand, *Ramsay MacDonald*, pp. 381–8.

74 Citrine, *Men and Work*, pp. 117–18. This was a forged letter by White Russian opponents of the Bolsheviks, purporting to instruct the British Communist Party to prepare for revolution in Britain by agitating in the armed services. It was used for the Tory opposition in the October 1924 election by the *Daily Mail*, which MacDonald failed to respond to effectively while electioneering. In fact, the impact of that affair was far less than other factors and the result for Labour was by no means a disaster like 1931.

75 Citrine, *Men and Work*, p. 63.

76 *Ibid.*, pp. 78–80.

77 *Ibid.*, p. 79.

78 V. L. Allen, 'The Reorganization of the Trades Union Congress, 1918–1927', *British Journal of Sociology* (1960), vol XI, p. 36.

79 *Ibid.*, p. 80.

80 Martin, *The TUC*, pp. 188–91.

81 Marquand, *Ramsay MacDonald*, p. 387.

82 Citrine, *Men and Work*, p. 86.

83 *Ibid.*, pp. 86–7.

84 TUC Annual Report, Resolutions Passed, pp. 503–4 (TUC Library Collections, London Metropolitan University, HD6475).

85 Clegg, *A History*, vol. II, pp. 551 and 563–4.

86 Henry Pelling, *A History of British Trade Unionism* (Pelican Books, 1963), p. 262.

87 Phillips, *The General Strike*, pp. 17–18.

88 The Industrial Workers' Charter motion called for wholesale nationalisation, workers' control,

minimum wage, maximum hours (forty-four per week), state pensions at sixty and so on. Martin, *The TUC*, p. 188.

89 TUC Annual Report 1924, p. 503.

90 Clegg, *A History*, vol. II, pp. 455–6.

Chapter 5

1   Citrine, *Men and Work*, p. 189.

2   LSE Library, Citrine Archive 2/2.

3   *Ibid.*, lecture in the campaign against the trades union and trade disputes bill, 11 May 1927.

4   A select bibliography runs to over twenty pages in the spring 2006 issue of *Historical Studies in Industrial Relations (HSIR)*, no. 21, pp. 183–206.

5   Citrine, *Men and Work*, pp. 129–219. Typed up in 1957.

6   Martin, *The TUC*, p. 171.

7   Clegg, *A History*, vol. II, table 1, p. 26.

8   *Ibid.*, pp. 136–8.

9   *Ibid.*, p. 137.

10 *Ibid.*, pp. 10–11, 24–31, 43–52.

11 Phillips, *The General Strike*, pp. 39–42; 'the most authoritative account', Clegg, *A History*, vol. II, p. 424.

12 Citrine revised his views somewhat later, 'from what I was told by Ernest Bevin and Jimmy Thomas, both of whom took an active part'. This was because of the miners' leaders 'keeping them out of the negotiations' etc. (*Men and Work*, p. 131).

13 *Beatrice Webb's Diaries, 1912–1924*, p. 208.

14 Frank Hodges, the secretary of the MFGB, made a speech in the Commons which 'suggested willingness to compromise.' The MFGB Executive repudiated Hodges' 'offer', but the NUR and TWA leaders 'called off their strike

by telegraph' (ibid., p. 207, note 1).

15 Citrine, *Men and Work*, p. 167.

16 Bullock, *Bevin*, vol. I, *Trade Union Leader*, pp. 286–7.

17 Phillips, *The General Strike*, pp. 54–8.

18 Citrine, *Men and Work*, p. 133.

19 Bullock, *Bevin*, vol. I, *Trade Union Leader*, p. 281. Citrine noted that 'Bevin's part in 1925 was inconspicuous'. Notes for a review of Francis Williams' *Ernest Bevin* British Book Centre, 1952, LSE Library, Citrine 10/5.

20 *Ibid.*, pp. 135–6. Tracey (1884–1955) had been a member of the headquarters' staff of the Labour Party and TUC since 1917 and directed the TUC's separate Publicity Department from 1926 to 1949. He edited the TUC's *British Worker* during the General Strike and was closely associated with *The Labour Magazine* in which many of Citrine's reports appeared. From Cardiff and largely self-educated, he had held the pastorate of two Methodist chapels in the mining valleys of South Wales.

21 *Ibid.*, pp. 133–4.

22 *Ibid.*, p. 136.

23 *Ibid.*, p. 138.

24 *Ibid.*, p. 141.

25 Phillips, *The General Strike*, pp. 60–1.

26 Citrine, *Men and Work*, p. 142.

27 Phillips, *The General Strike*, pp. 72–9.

28 *Ibid.*

29 Martin, *The TUC*, p. 175.

30 Clegg, *A History*, vol. II, p. 403.

31 Citrine, *Men and Work*, p. 135.

32 Citrine, *Two Careers*, p. 12.

33 *Ibid.*, p. 143.

34 *Ibid.*, pp. 129–42.

35 Riddell, 'Walter Citrine', p. 292. Also Taylor, *The TUC*, p. 27.

36 Phillips, *The General Strike*, pp. 84–7.

37 *Ibid.*

38 Clegg, *A History*, vol. II, p. 574.

39 *Ibid.*, pp. 22–3.

40 *Ibid.*

41 Phillips, *The General Strike*, pp. 95–8.

42 *Ibid.*, pp. 70–71.

43 Walter M. Citrine, 'Lessons of the Mining Dispute' in *The Labour Magazine* (September 1925), pp. 198–200. A summary is in *Men and Work* at p. 143. Herbert Tracey commissioned most of its copy.

44 A. Steele-Maitland to W. Churchill, Chancellor of the Exchequer, covering note 2 October 1925. The Churchill Archives, CHAR 18/23.

45 Citrine, *Men and Work*, p. 142.

46 As far back as 1911, during the big transport and other mining strikes, Churchill had considered the 'General Strike' as a 'deliberate political project' and 'the supreme weapon of labour' of the unions, to be countered. The Churchill Archives, CHAR 12/6/40-49.

47 Citrine, 'Lessons of the Mining Dispute', p. 198.

48 *Ibid.*

49 *Ibid.*, p. 200.

50 *Ibid.*

51 *Ibid.*

52 Phillips, *The General Strike*, p. 125.

53 Taylor, *The TUC*, p. 31.

54 Citrine, 'Lessons of the Mining Dispute' in *The Labour Magazine*, p. 199; Taylor, *The TUC*, p. 28.

55 *Ibid.*, p. 200.

56 *Ibid.*, p. 199.

57 Phillips, *The General Strike*, p. 68.

58 *Ibid.*, p. 69.

59 Bullock, *Bevin*, vol. I, *Trade Union Leader*, p. 271.

60 *Ibid.*, p. 68.

61 Citrine, 'Lessons of the Mining Dispute' in *The Labour Magazine*, pp. 199.

62 Citrine, *Men and Work*, p. 161. He reverted to calling it the *Diary of the General Strike* towards the end. Ibid., p. 177, and following.

63 Bullock, *Bevin*, vol. I, *Trade Union Leader*, p. 321.

64 *Ibid.*, p. 283.

65 *Ibid.*, p. 284.

66 Citrine, *Men and Work*, p. 144.

67 Alonso Beaumont Swales (1870–1952), known as 'AB', was a towering engineer and AEU national organiser from Middlesbrough, who had 'chaired' the Scarborough Congress in a distinctly left direction as regards debates and decisions driven by the Minority Movement/CPGB delegates. (Clegg called him 'the most incompetent president of the Congress of the twentieth century so far'! *A History*, vol. II, p. 395).

68 Pugh (afterwards Sir Arthur, 1870–1955), steel smelter and general secretary of the important Iron & Steel Trades Confederation, 1917–37. He had been on the Parliamentary Committee/General Council from 1920 to 1935. No 'right-winger', he became a member of the very left-wing Socialist League in the 1930s. Clegg, *A History*, vol. II, p. 578.

69 *Ibid.*, p. 580. Thomas (1874–1950), a one-time left-wing general secretary of the ASRS/NUR and MP for 'railway city', Derby, in succession to Richard Bell MP. He led the NUR national railway strike of 1919 successfully and also chaired the IFTU (1920–24) on behalf of the General Council. Close to Ramsay MacDonald, he had been a Cabinet minister in the first Labour government of 1924.

70 Citrine, *Men and Work*, pp. 184–5.
In all, there were forty-seven diary
references to their driving around
London to meetings together, for
example, to see Herbert Samuel
seeking his mediation (p. 190);
'Thomas and I went to Downing
Street in his car' (p. 201).

71 Phillips, *The General Strike*, pp. 87–90.

72 *Ibid.*, p. 284.

73 Bullock, *Bevin*, vol. I, *Trade Union
Leader*, p. 283.

74 Citrine, *Men and Work*, pp. 88–128
contains his account of that trip.
See Davis, 'An Outsider Looks In:
Walter Citrine's First Visit to the
Soviet Union, 1925. Moher, 'The
Visit of Walter Citrine in 1925',
Labour Affairs (January–March 2018)
(http://labouraffairsmagazine.com).

75 Citrine, *Men and Work*, p. 145.

76 *Ibid.*, pp. 145–54; LSE Library,
Citrine 1/2, pp. 26–8.

77 *Ibid.*, p. 31.

78 *Ibid.*, p. 133.

79 *Ibid.*, pp. 146–53. Bullock called it
'a characteristically clear-headed
memorandum in which he asked
a number of pointed questions on
policy and preparation.' Bullock,
Bevin, vol. I, *Trade Union Leader*,
p. 290.

80 *Ibid.*

81 *Ibid.*, p. 150.

82 Phillips, *The General Strike*, pp. 86–7.

83 *Ibid.*, p. 88.

84 Smith, then in his sixties, was
president of the Yorkshire miners
and of the Miners' Federation. He
withdrew from the General Council
to focus on the coal dispute and was
a leading figure in all discussions
with the mine owners, TUC and
government. Highly respected by
Citrine: 'straight as a die. I liked his
calm way of looking at difficulties.

Always cool and steady, he never
got flustered.' There were hints that
he sought a way out early on, but
Cook negated his, at times, softer
approach (*Men and Work*, pp. 133–4
and 166). This, and other comments
on other General Council members,
belies Beatrice Webb's caricature
(below and no. 148).

85 Citrine, *Men and Work*, p. 86.

86 *Ibid.*, p. 154.

87 Bullock, *Bevin*, vol. I, *Trade Union
Leader*, p. 286.

88 Royal Commission on the Coal
Industry, Report, Cmnd. 2600,
1926.

89 Phillips, *The General Strike*, pp. 77–9
and 105.

90 *Ibid.*, pp. 105–6. The 'dour and
unimaginative Pugh' is blamed in
the most recent (Adonis, *Ernest Bevin,
Labour's Churchill*, pp. 68–9) account,
but this seems unfair as the TUC
had no ability to speed up the coal
owners' or government responses.
Phillips, *General Strike*, pp. 100–105,
gives the background.

91 *Ibid.*, p. 104.

92 Citrine, *Men and Work*, p. 155.

93 *Ibid.*, p. 163.

94 Bullock, *Bevin*, vol. I, *Trade Union
Leader*, pp. 305–6.

95 Citrine, *Men and Work*, p. 162. He
would later resile from that offer.

96 Bullock, *Bevin*, vol. I, *Trade Union
Leader*, pp. 305–6.

97 Citrine, *Men and Work*, p. 163.
Citrine gave his account, pp.
162–70.

98 Bullock, *Bevin*, vol. I, *Trade Union
Leader*, pp. 305–6.

99 Citrine, *Men and Work*, p. 171.

100 Adonis is scathing about the
TUC leadership's handling of the
negotiations/ strike, suggesting
that, had Bevin been in charge,

a deal would have been reached or the strike made more effective. *Ernest Bevin, Labour's Churchill*, pp. 68–80. But Bevin opposed the involvement of the Trades Councils, who effectively came to run the strike locally. Citrine, *Men and Work*, pp. 177–8.

101 Phillips, *The General Strike*, pp. 127–33. Phillips discusses whether a strike was avoidable.

102 *Ibid.*, pp. 177–207.

103 *Ibid.*, pp. 178 and 190.

104 Lord Citrine's notes on Bullock's *Bevin*, vol. I, *Trade Union Leader*, 8.3.1960, LSE Library, Citrine 10/5.

105 Adonis, *Ernest Bevin, Labour's Churchill*, p. 80.

106 Citrine, *Men and Work*, p. 83.

107 *Ibid.*, p. 180.

108 Martin, *The TUC*, pp. 218–19.

109 Citrine, *Men and Work*, p. 191.

110 *Ibid.*, p. 190.

111 *Ibid.*, p. 180.

112 *Ibid.*

113 Phillips, *The General Strike*, p. 150.

114 Citrine, *Men and Work*, p. 196.

115 *Ibid.*

116 *Ibid.*, p. 195.

117 *Ibid.*, p. 213.

118 *Ibid.*, p. 212.

119 *Ibid.*, p. 189.

120 Phillips, *The General Strike*, pp. 225–33.

121 Citrine, *Men and Work*, p. 204.

122 The extremely one-sided Arthur J. Cook's *The Nine Days: The Story of the General Strike Told by the Miners' Secretary*, was rushed out on 1 January 1927, financed, Citrine suspected, by the Minority Movement/CPGB.

123 Citrine, *Men and Work*, pp. 209 and 214.

124 *Ibid.*, p. 216.

125 Citrine, *Men and Work*, p. 204.

126 *Ibid.*, p. 211.

127 Robert Taylor, 'Citrine's Unexpurgated Diaries, 1925–26: The Mining Crisis and the National Strike', *Historical Studies in Industrial Relations* (2005), vol. 20, no. 1, pp. 67–102..

128 Citrine, *Men and Work*, p. 234.

129 *Ibid.*, p. 209.

130 *Ibid.*, p. 210.

131 *Ibid.*, p. 155.

132 *Ibid.*, p. 210.

133 Citrine toned down his harsher judgements on Cook (see Robert Taylor, 'Citrine's Unexpurgated Diaries', pp. 98–9), probably in light of his premature and sad end.

134 *Ibid.*, p. 210.

135 Bullock, *Bevin*, vol. I, *Trade Union Leader*, p. 346.

136 Citrine, *Men and Work*, p. 189.

137 Clegg, *A History*, vol. II, p. 423.

138 *Ibid.*, p. 455.

139 Martin, *The TUC*, pp. 202–3.

140 Citrine, *Men and Work*, p. 189.

141 Riddell, 'Walter Citrine', p. 293.

142 Citrine, *Men and Work*, pp. 37 and 47.

143 *Beatrice Webb's Diaries, 1912–1924*, p. 90.

144 MacDonald, as we saw, even made 'a glorious speech' in support at the conference of union executives who authorised the TUC to call the strike (Citrine, *Men and Work*, p. 163). At the miners' insistence, and due to the TUC's desire for the strike not to be seen to be political, MacDonald and Henderson were not enlisted to intervene, though they were 'around'.

145 Marquand, *Ramsay MacDonald*, pp. 423–4.

146 *Ibid.*, pp. 439 and 434–5.

147 *Beatrice Webb's Diaries, 1924–1932*, pp. 93 and 95.

148 *Ibid.*, p. 91.

149 *Ibid.*, p. 75 (2 October 1926).

150 *Ibid.*, pp. 146–9.

151 *Ibid.*, p. 147.

152 *Beatrice Webb's Diaries, 1924–1932*, p. 147.

153 *Ibid.*

154 Citrine, *Men and Work*, p. 272.

155 *Beatrice Webb's Diaries, 1924–1932*, p. 149.

156 Ramsay MacDonald's biographer, David Marquand, whose subject received far more of Webb's caustic treatment, said, 'Beatrice Webb had sharp eyes as well as a vivid pen, and her picture undoubtedly bore some resemblance to the original. But it was a hostile caricature not a rounded portrait.' Marquand, *Ramsay MacDonald*, p. 404.

157 Citrine, *Men and Work*, pp. 272–4.

158 *Beatrice Webb's Diaries, 1912–1924*, where her editor, Margaret Cole, winces about 'the many savage things' she had to say about trade union officials (xiii).

Chapter 6

1 Citrine, *Men and Work*, p. 88.

2 *ETJ*, May 1921, pp. 398–9.

3 Citrine, *Men and Work*, p. 88.

4 *Ibid.*

5 Calhoun, *The United Front*, p. 106.

6 'Russia: The Official Report of the British Trades Union Delegation to Russia and Caucasia', November and December 1924. TUC General Council 1925.

7 *Ibid.*, p. 145.

8 *Ibid.*, pp. 100–102. Mikhail Tomsky (1880–1936), chair of the All-Russian Central Council of Trade Unions. CPSU Politburo member. Calhoun, *The United Front*, pp. 120–21.

9 *Ibid.*, pp. 49–50.

10 *Ibid.*, p. 184.

11 *Ibid.*, p. 116. LSE Library, Citrine 1/6 – an eleven-page note entitled, 'A Preliminary Trial', 12 August 1925, documents Bramley's mental illness and irrational behaviour.

12 *Ibid.*, pp. 165–6.

13 Martin, *The TUC*, pp. 199–200.

14 Citrine, *Men and Work*, pp. 74–7.

15 *Ibid.*, p. 95. See also Davis, 'An Outsider Looks In'.

16 Calhoun, *The United Front*, p. 143.

17 *Ibid.*, pp. 49–50.

18 Citrine, *Men and Work*, pp. 101–3.

19 *Ibid.*, pp. 100–102; Simon Sebag Montefiore, *Stalin: The Court of the Red Tsar* (Weidenfeld & Nicolson, 2003), p. 30.

20 Citrine, *Men and Work*, p. 97.

21 *Ibid.*

22 See below, Chapter 10.

23 *Ibid.*, p. 118.

24 *Ibid.*, p. 108.

25 *Ibid.*, pp. 92–3. Citrine added 'to which we were becoming inured'.

26 The earlier TUC decline of a £26,000 gift from the Russian miners (equivalent to about £1 million today) to fund the General Strike also caused upset. It was afraid it would be used by the press and government to accuse it of being dependent on 'Russian gold' and so undermine public support.

27 *Ibid.*, p. 92.

28 Calhoun, *The United Front*, p. 238.

29 *Ibid.*, pp. 320–6. Jim Moher, 'British Trade Unionists and the Soviet Union, Part 3,', *Labour Affairs* (April 2018), pp. 18–19 (http://labouraffairsmagazine.com).

30 *Ibid.*, p. 337.

31 *Ibid.*, pp. 340–1.

32 *Ibid.*, p. 342.

33 *Ibid.*, pp. 342–3.

34 *Ibid.*, p. 343.

35 Joseph Stalin, *On the Opposition*
   (Foreign Languages Press, 1974)
   (1974 compilation of his speeches
   by Chinese Communist Party),
   pp. 765–6, 797–802.

36 *Ibid.*, p. 800.

37 Calhoun, *The United Front*, p. 23.

38 *Ibid.*, pp. 10–20.

39 Roderick Martin, *Communism and the
   British Trade Unions, 1924–1933:
   A Study of the National Minority
   Movement* (Clarendon Press, 1969),
   pp. 37–54.

40 *Ibid.*, pp. 10, 45–6 and 67–8.

41 Citrine said he was 'an inherently
   decent fellow', despite their deep
   political differences. Similarly with
   Arthur Horner. *Men and Work*,
   p. 257.

42 Martin, *Communism and the British
   Trade Unions*, pp. 35–6.

43 *Ibid.*

44 Phillips, *The General Strike*, p. 85.

45 *Ibid.*, and Citrine, *Men and Work*,
   pp. 177–8.

46 Martin, *Communism and the British
   Trade Unions*, pp. 55–77.

47 *Ibid.*, p. 82. Quote by George
   Hardy, secretary of the Minority
   Movement.

48 Bullock, *Bevin*, vol. I, *Trade Union
   Leader*, p. 217.

49 Citrine, *Men and Work*, pp. 254–5.

50 Walter M. Citrine, TUC Library
   Collections, HD 6661.

51 Citrine, *Men and Work*, p. 254.

52 TUC Annual Report (Swansea)
   1928, pp. 354–5.

53 *Ibid.*, pp. 255–6.

54 Bullock, *Bevin*, vol. I, *Trade Union
   Leader*, pp. 385–6.

55 Martin, *Communism and the British
   Trade Unions*, p. 73.

56 Citrine, *Democracy or Disruption? – An
   Examination of Communist Influences in
   the Trade Unions* (CPS for the TUC.
   1928), p. 6.

57 Arthur Horner, *Incorrigible Rebel*
   (MacGibbon & Kee, 1960), p. 67.

58 *Ibid.*, p. 84. Raymond Postgate,
   assistant editor of the very left-wing
   Lansbury's Weekly, had confirmed
   this.

59 Martin, *Communism and the British
   Trade Unions*, p. 1.

60 Subsequent research in the former
   Soviet archives and of the CPGB's
   papers have not disturbed Citrine's
   conclusions. Andrew Thorpe,
   'Comintern "Control" of the CPGB
   1920–43', *Economic History Review*
   (June 1998), pp. 637–62.

61 Horner, *Incorrigible Rebel*, p. 66.

62 Martin put the figures even higher,
   but regarded them as 'probably
   grossly exaggerated', by double- and
   triple-counting of some delegates in
   different positions. *Communism and the
   British Trade Unions*, pp. 56–7.

63 Horner, *Incorrigible Rebel*, p. 68.

64 Twelve CPGB leaders, including
   Pollitt and Gallagher, were jailed for
   six to twelve months on seditious
   conspiracy charges. Martin,
   *Communism and the British Trade
   Unions*, pp. 69–71.

65 Arthur Horner, *Incorrigible Rebel*,
   p. 71; Nick Thomas-Symonds, *Nye:
   The Political Life of Aneurin Bevan* (I.B.
   Tauris, 2015), pp. 50–1.

66 *Ibid.*, p. 81.

67 *Ibid.*, pp. 74–90. Horner changed
   considerably after a spell in prison
   in 1932.

68 Citrine, *Democracy or Disruption?*,
   p. 13.

69 *Ibid.*, pp. 14–15.

70 *Ibid.*

71 *Ibid.*, pp. 15–16, and Citrine, *Men
   and Work*, p. 255.

72 *Ibid.*, pp. 15–16.

73 *Ibid.*, p. 16.
74 Horner, *Incorrigible Rebel*, pp. 72 and 94.
75 Martin, *Communism and the British Trade Unions*, pp. 90–3.
76 Citrine, *Democracy or Disruption?*, p. 21.
77 *Ibid.*
78 Citrine, *Men and Work*, pp. 253–4.
79 Bullock, *Bevin*, vol. I, *Trade Union Leader*, pp. 217, 285, 417–18.
80 Martin, *Communism and the British Trade Unions*, pp. 93–4.
81 *Ibid.*, p. 101.
82 Thorpe, 'Comintern "Control" of the CPGB', p. 655.
83 Gidon Cohen and Kevin Morgan, 'Stalin's Sausage Machine. British Students at the International Lenin School 1926–1937', Twentieth Century British History (2002), vol. 13, no. 4, pp. 327–55.
84 Report of the Activities of the Executive Committee of the Communist International (ECCI), 26 July 1935 to the Seventh World Congress, Moscow, July–August 1935 (Modern Books Ltd), pp. 13–14.
85 *Ibid.*
86 *The Manchester Guardian*, 13 August 1938. See also Andrew Thorpe, 'The Membership of the CPGB 1920–1945', *Historical Journal*, vol. 43, no. 3, pp. 787–8.
87 Citrine, *Men and Work*, p. 118.
88 *Ibid.*, p. 254.
89 *Ibid.*, p. 257.
90 The Home Office publication *Communist Papers, 'Documents Selected from those Obtained on the Arrest of the Communist Leaders on the 14th and 21st October 1926'*, showed that £4,000 was contributed to *The Sunday Worker.* Ibid., p. 257. Harriette Flory, 'The Arcos Raid and the Rupture of Anglo-Soviet Relations 1927', *Journal of Contemporary History* (October 1977), vol. 12, no. 4, n. 4, p. 721.
91 Citrine, *Men and Work*, p. 258.
92 *Ibid.*, p. 257.

Chapter 7

1 Citrine, *Men and Work*, p. 47.
2 *Ibid.*, p. 37.
3 Talk to a summer school of union students about the bill on 11 May 1927, as part of the TUC Trade Union Defence Campaign. LSE Library, Citrine 2/2, p. 72.
4 LSE Library, Citrine 2/2, pp. 72–3.
5 Sir Walter M. Citrine, *British Trade Unions* (William Collins, 1942), p. 2.
6 Sidney and Beatrice Webb, *The History of Trades Unionism, 1666–1920* (self-published by the authors 'for the trade unionists of the UK', first edition, 1894), 1920 edition, pp. 264–5.
7 Alastair J. Reid, *United We Stand: A History of Britain's Trade Unions* (Penguin Books, 2004), pp. 149–55, has an excellent summary.
8 Norman A. Citrine, *Trade Union Law* (Stevens & Sons Ltd, 1960), pp. 3–28, has a very clear history of unions and the law. The author was Walter's eldest son, who became legal adviser to the TUC after he left (1946–51). He lived in Brixham, Devon, to where his father retired in 1975 after Doris Citrine's death.
9 John Saville, 'The Trade Disputes Act 1906', *Historical Studies in Industrial Relations* (March 1996), no. 1, pp. 11–45.
10 Citrine, *Men and Work*, p. 37.
11 *Taff Vale Railway Co. v Amalgamated Society of Railway Servants* (1901), A.C. 426. H. A. Clegg, Alan Fox

and A. F. Thompson, *The History of British Trade Unions from 1889 to 1910*, vol. I (Clarendon Press, 1962), pp. 313–14.

12 Philip S. Bagwell, *The Railwaymen: History of the National Union of Railwaymen* (Allen & Unwin, 1963), pp. 202–15.

13 G. W. Alcock, *Fifty Years of Trade Unionism* (Co-operative Printing Society, 1922), p. 311. Alcock was a union trustee.

14 Saville, 'The Trade Disputes Act 1906', p. 15. James G. Moher, 'The Osborne Judgement of 1909: Trade Union Funding of Political Parties in Historical Perspective', History & Policy, Trade Union Forum paper, 2009.

15 The chair was David Shackleton MP (1863–1938), a weavers' union official and one of the first Labour MPs (1902). He became parliamentary secretary of the Ministry of Labour, 1916–21.

16 Saville, 'The Trade Disputes Act 1906', pp. 15–16.

17 *Ibid.*, p. 15.

18 *Ibid.*, clause iv.

19 Walter Milne-Bailey, *Trade Unions and the State* (George Allen & Unwin, 1934), pp. 54–9, has the full Act.

20 LSE Library, Citrine 4/2, 23.8.1928.

21 Clegg, *A History*, vol. II, pp. 36–9; 71–2.

22 House of Commons debate on the amendment bill of 1931; Sir William Jowitt KC recalled these powers, 22 January 1931, Hansard, vol. 247, p. 392.

23 Keith Middlemas, *Politics in Industrial Society: The Experience of the British System since 1977* (André Deutsch, 1979), p. 196.

24 Citrine, *Men and Work*, p. 159.

25 Sir John Simon KC, a Liberal Party former attorney general and home secretary, argued strongly that the strike was illegal. A Justice Astbury described it as 'the so- called general strike ... is illegal ... [as] no trade dispute does or can exist between the Trades Union Congress ... and the Government and the nation ...' This was not in the judgement, however. Adrian Williamson QC, 'The Trade Disputes and Trade Unions Act 1927 Reconsidered', *Historical Studies of Industrial Relations* (2016), no. 37, p. 43.

26 Trade Disputes and Trade Unions Act 1927, Section 1. *Ibid.*, pp. 34–82.

27 *Ibid.*, pp. 52–3.

28 *Ibid.*, p. 46.

29 *Ibid.*, pp. 46–7 and 49.

30 Middlemas, *Politics in Industrial Society*, p. 204.

31 Williamson, 'The 1927 Act Reconsidered', saw the Act as, 'going to the heart of the instrument by which [workers] can make their force felt, which is the strike: sympathetic action and peaceful picketing, rights to strike, take sympathetic action and peaceful picketing' (ibid., p. 60). Clegg thought it 'a relatively light curb on their activities' (*A History*, vol. II, p. 558).

32 Citrine, *Two Careers*, p. 241.

33 Speech to Ruskin College union students of 9 April 1927 (LSE Library, Citrine 1/6, 4/2 and 5/6). Citrine and his staff generated a large number of files.

34 Hansard (HC), 205, 3 May 1927, col. 1477.

35 LSE Library, Citrine 2/2.

36 James Michael Trevor Parker, 'Trade Unions and the Political

Culture of the British Labour Party, 1931–1940' PhD thesis, University of Exeter, 2017 (online), pp. 68–9.

37 LSE Library, Citrine 2/2; TUC leaflet, 'Labour Opens its Attack – Shattering Exposure of the Government's Sinister Proposals' (TUC Publications, HD6661); speeches of Hicks, Citrine, Henderson, Bevin and Clynes at the National Conference of Trade Union Executive Representatives, pp. 7–9.

38 TUC Annual Report September 1927, pp. 248–9. TUC Library Collections at London Metropolitan University HD6661.

39 Walter Milne-Bailey, ed., *Trade Union Documents* (G. Bell & Sons, 1929), in *Organisation of Trade Union Campaign*, pp. 402–5.

40 Williamson, 'The 1927 Act Reconsidered', p. 59.

41 LSE Library, Citrine 1/6. Also, on 11 May 1927, Citrine 2/2.

42 Marquand, *Ramsay MacDonald*, p. 448.

43 Williamson, 'The 1927 Act Reconsidered', p. 63.

44 *Ibid.*, p. 71.

45 LSE Library, Citrine 4/2, Report of discussion on Mr. Citrine's Lecture at TUC summer school 1931. Question and answer session, p. 2.

46 *Ibid.*, p. 3.

47 Citrine, *Two Careers*, p. 242.

48 Churchill to Citrine, 22 September 1941, The Churchill Archives, CHAR 20/22B/126 and 145.

49 Citrine, *Two Careers*, pp. 241–2.

50 Churchill to Citrine, 2 September 1942, The Churchill Archives, CHAR 20/54A/70

51 Memorandum of Interview, 9 August 1943, Rt Hon. C. R. Attlee and Sir Walter Citrine on Trade Disputes and Trade Unions Act 1927. LSE Library, Citrine 5/6.

52 Citrine, *Two Careers*, devoted four pages to the issue after the war, pp. 241–4. The TUC had to persuade the UPW not to defy the law by affiliating to the TUC, in case of its members losing their pension rights.

53 *Ibid.*, p. 244. The author has been a keen student of these laws since his time as the national legal secretary of the National Communications Union and has written a number of papers and booklets over the years, starting with *Trade Unions and the Law: The Politics of Change'* for the Institute of Employment Rights in 1995, culminating in a seminar he organised with the Trade Union Employment Forum in 2017 entitled 'The Future of Trade Union Law' (2017).'

Chapter 8

1 Bullock, *Bevin*, vol. I, *Trade Union Leader*, p. 399. TUC Industrial Committee Report, 17.2.1927, pp. 7–8.

2 *Ibid.*, p. 399.

3 Bevin was invited by the Ministry of Labour to tour American manufacturing cities in 1926, which made a big impression on him. Bullock, *Bevin*, vol. I, *Trade Union Leader*, pp. 357–63. The minister, Steele-Maitland, also met other members of the General Council, including Citrine.

4 *The Manchester Guardian* supplement, 30 November 1927, p. 8. It was republished in Milne-Bailey, ed., *Trade Union Documents*, pp. 431–8.

5 Citrine, *Men and Work*, pp. 243–4.

6 Citrine, 'The Next Step in Industrial Relations', *The Manchester Guardian*, p. 8.

7 *Ibid.*

8 *Ibid.*

9 *Ibid.*

10 *Ibid.*

11 Riddell, 'Walter Citrine', p. 293.

12 Named after the Speaker of the House of Commons, J. H. Whitley, his Committee recommended industry-wide regulation of industrial relations where none existed, leading to a large number of joint industrial negotiating committees. Clegg, *A History*, vol. II, pp. 204–7; Milne-Bailey, ed., *Trade Union Documents*, pp. 32, 70 and 487.

13 Sir Alfred Mond MP (1868–1930), later Lord Melchett. Of German Jewish extraction and a prominent Zionist in the inter-war years.

14 Milne-Bailey, ed., *Trade Union Documents*, pp. 253–4.

15 TUC Annual Report 1928, p. 408, TUC Publications HD6661 and online.

16 *Ibid.*

17 *The Times*, 6 January 1928, noticed this.

18 Citrine, *Men and Work*, p. 247.

19 Middlemas, *Politics in Industrial Society*, pp. 205 and 207.

20 *Ibid.*, p. 206; Bullock, *Bevin*, vol. I, *Trade Union Leader*, p. 395.

21 Middlemas, *Politics in Industrial Society*, p. 206.

22 Citrine, *Men and Work*, p. 245.

23 Middlemas, *Politics in Industrial Society*, p. 208.

24 *The Times*, 21 July 1928, p. 17, and 6 September 1928, p. 7.

25 TUC Annual Report 1928 (Swansea), p. 97, TUC Library Collections HD6661.

26 Citrine, *Men and Work*, pp. 244–5.

27 *The Times* report on the Trades Union Congress, 1928, 27 August 1928, p. 7.

28 *Ibid.*

29 Citrine, *Men and Work*, p. 245 for the full list.

30 Bullock, *Bevin*, vol. I, *Trade Union Leader*, p. 399.

31 *The Times* report, 7 September 1928, p. 7.

32 Milne-Bailey, ed., *Trade Union Documents*, p. 427.

33 Citrine's account is at pp. 247–8 of *Men and Work*.

34 TUC Annual Report 1928, pp. 408–9.

35 Bullock, *Bevin*, vol. I, *Trade Union Leader*, pp. 397 and 399.

36 *Ibid.*, p. 446.

37 *Ibid.*, p. 337.

38 *Ibid.*, p. 448. Not as elegant in his speech construction as Citrine, but the substance was there also.

39 TUC Annual Report 1928. For the amendment ... 768,000 Against ... 2,921,000, p.451. *The Times*, 7 September 1928, p. 12.

40 Bullock, *Bevin*, vol. I, *Trade Union Leader*, p. 402.

41 Citrine, *Men and Work*, pp. 249–50; Middlemas, *Politics in Industrial Society*, p. 209.

42 Bullock, *Bevin*, vol. I, *Trade Union Leader*, p. 591.

43 Citrine, *Men and Work*, p. 67.

44 *Ibid.*, p. 235. Citrine gave this incident as the beginning of their poor relationship in notes he drew up for a review of Francis Williams' biography, *Ernest Bevin* (Hutchinson, 1952). LSE Library, Citrine 10/5.

45 *Ibid.*

46 *Ibid.*, pp. 234–5.

47 Notes for a review of Williams' *Ernest Bevin*. LSE Library, Citrine 10/5, pp. 2–3. Bullock acknowledged 'his habit of appropriating other people's ideas', *Bevin*, vol. 1, *Trade Union Leader*, p. 369.

48 LSE Library, Citrine 10/5, p. 2 of a note he made on 14 January 1957.
49 Review of Bullock, *The Life and Times of Ernest Bevin*, vol. I, for the Iron & Steel union journal *Man and Metal*, April 1960, p. 70.
50 Bullock, *Bevin*, vol. I, *Trade Union Leader*, pp. 590–1; Riddell, 'Walter Citrine', pp. 293–4.
51 Bevin offered to take the ETU into the T&GWU in 1925 (Bullock, *Bevin*, vol. I, *Trade Union Leader*), but the electricians did not support that merger either (p. 414).
52 *Ibid.*, pp. 238–9. Bullock called it a 'powerful natural intelligence'; *Bevin*, vol. I, *Trade Union Leader*, p. 368.
53 Adonis, *Ernest Bevin, Labour's Churchill*, pp. 145–9.
54 Bullock, *Bevin*, vol. I, *Trade Union Leader*, p. 591.
55 Citrine, *Men and Work*, p. 239.
56 Riddell, 'Walter Citrine', pp. 286–7.
57 Bullock, *Bevin*, vol. I, *Trade Union Leader*, p. 564.
58 *Ibid.*, pp. 405–7.
59 Citrine, *Men and Work*, p. 239.
60 *Ibid.*, p. 240.
61 Citrine, *Men and Work*, p. 239.
62 *Ibid.*
63 *Ibid.*, p. 78.
64 LSE Library, Citrine 10/4.
65 Of course, Bevin also had his own excellent T&GWU staff, who interfaced with Citrine's team continuously, being in the same building. He only ever had two personal secretaries, an indication of the loyalty he inspired.
66 Williams, *Ernest Bevin*. Williams was one of the few close to Bevin.
67 Adonis, *Ernest Bevin, Labour's Churchill* – 'Bevin the big man of the strike' (p. 78); the Mond-Turner talks – 'their genesis was an approach directly to Bevin by Lord Weir' (p. 83); the war, Bevin was more strong-minded and consistent even than Churchill' (p. 123), and so on.

Chapter 9

1 At the General Election of 30 May 1929, Labour polled 8,389,512 votes (287 seats) to the Conservatives, 8,664,000 (261 seats) and Liberals' 5,300,000 (59 seats). Marquand, *Ramsay MacDonald*, p. 488.
2 Riddell, *Labour in Crisis*, p. 221; Martin, *The TUC*, p. 224.
3 Bullock, *Bevin*, vol. I, *Trade Union Leader*, p. 448.
4 Riddell, *Labour in Crisis*, p. 61. 'Only one of the union priorities – on housing and slum clearance – had been met by July 1931' (ibid., p. 89).
5 Marquand, *Ramsay MacDonald*, pp. 501–6.
6 *Ibid.*, pp. 499–501.
7 *Ibid.*, pp. 566–7 and 593. An electoral reform bill with the 'alternative vote' system even got a Second Reading in February 1931, but fell with the government. Marquand, *Ramsay MacDonald*, pp. 584–5.
8 LSE Library, Citrine 4/2. Citrine at a summer school on the bill at Ruskin College, Oxford, July 1931.
9 *Ibid.*, p. 11.
10 Proceedings on the 'Amending' bill in the House of Commons, Parliamentary Papers Online. Report & Special Report from Standing Committee C, 3 March 1931, pp. 871–83.
11 On 28 February 1931, Citrine had an altercation with two of the Scottish Labour MPs, who resented his (overheard) criticisms of their voting. LSE Library, Citrine 1/1. Also Riddell, *Labour in Crisis*, p. 74.

12 *Ibid.* This showed the very different intake of Labour MPs after the 1929 election.

13 LSE Library, Citrine 10/8, paper, 'The Prime Minister', 29 January 1931.

14 *Ibid.*, his meeting with MacDonald in the prime minister's rooms in the Commons, 29 January 1931.

15 *Ibid.*

16 *Ibid.*, pp. 5–6.

17 *Ibid.*, Citrine 4/2.

18 Marquand, *Ramsay MacDonald*, p. 489.

19 LSE Library, Citrine 10/8, 10 June 1929 paper, 'Cabinet Making', p. 5.

20 *Ibid.*, 4/2, 'Points to be considered in relation to the forthcoming meeting with the Labour Party executive', 2 November 1931. Also *Men and Work*, p. 281.

21 LSE Library, Citrine 10/8, point 3.

22 Riddell, *Labour in Crisis*, pp. 56 and 89; Martin, *The TUC*, p. 225.

23 An example was the *Daily Mail*'s lurid front-page headlines of 29 January 1931, which ran 'THE UNION BOSSES, ORDERS TO THE CABINET. PREMIER TRYING TO OBEY.' LSE Library, Citrine 5/13.

24 LSE Library, Citrine 10/8, 10 June 1929, 'Cabinet Making', p. 5.

25 Beatrice Webb, whose husband Sidney was in his Cabinet, thought MacDonald 'indifferent to home affairs …' and 'completely absorbed in foreign affairs and India …' *Beatrice Webb's Diaries, 1924–1932*, p. 277.

26 Marquand, *Ramsay MacDonald*, pp. 501–6.

27 *Ibid.*

28 *Ibid.*, pp. 499–501, p. 276,

29 *Ibid.*, pp. 523–4.

30 *Ibid.*, p. 240.

31 Bullock, *Bevin*, vol. I, *Trade Union Leader*, p. 436.

32 An influential and respected academic socialist economist and theoretician and copious writer on Labour policies. He had just set up a Socialist Society for Information and Propaganda (SSIP), with Bevin as chair to bring the unions into support for socialist policies. He would regret joining with the confrontational Socialist League and did not play much part in it. G. D. H. Cole, *A History of the Labour Party since 1914* (Routledge, 1948), p. 282. See Chapter 12.

33 An economic historian and educationalist close to Clement Attlee since their Workers' Educational Association days. He helped produce the Labour Manifesto for the 1929 election. See Chapter 13.

34 Robert Skidelsky, *Politicians and the Slump: The Labour Government of 1929–1931* (Macmillan, 1967), p. 136.

35 Riddell, *Labour in Crisis*, p. 84.

36 *Ibid.*

37 Bullock, *Bevin*, vol. I, *Trade Union Leader*, p. 438.

38 Marquand, *Ramsay MacDonald*, pp. 524–5; Citrine, *Men and Work*, pp. 280–1.

39 Riddell, *Labour in* Crisis, p. 88.

40 *Beatrice Webb's Diaries, 1924–1932*, MacDonald to Sidney Webb (Lord Passfield), 14 July 1931, 'I am in a most awful difficulty about the House of Lords', p. 276.

41 Citrine, *Men and Work*, pp. 312–13. He had probably taken 'soundings' from his senior T&G executive members, who would have advised him against.

42 *Ibid.*

43 Skidelsky, *Politicians and the Slump*, pp. 205, 210–13.
44 Keynes initially advised Lloyd George on their 1929 election manifesto, 'We Can Conquer Unemployment'. Robert Skidelsky, *John Maynard Keynes: The Economist as Saviour 1927–1937* (Macmillan, 1992), pp. 343–5.
45 Citrine, *Men and Work*, pp. 136–7 and 240–1.
46 Adonis, *Ernest Bevin, Labour's Churchill*, pp. 96–8.
47 *Ibid.*, Skidelsky, *John Maynard Keynes*, p. 345.
48 Citrine, *Men and Work*, p. 240.
49 *Ibid.*; p. 274. Fred Bramley had also been sent on one before he died – not a good omen. Citrine was later reminded by W. J. Bolton, Head of the International Department since 1903, that 'out of four secretaries in his time three died of the effects of the work and the fourth had a breakdown'! Ibid., p. 339.
50 Set up in 1929 by Citrine at Milne-Bailey's urging, to provide the TUC with the machinery to intervene effectively in international conferences, such as the Imperial Conference of 1930 in London, with the distinctive union outlook. Bullock, *Bevin*, vol. I, *Trade Union Leader*, pp. 439–40.
51 *Ibid.*, pp. 439 and 509. Riddell, *Walter Citrine*, p. 296.
52 *Ibid.*, p. 440.
53 *Ibid.*, pp. 126–38. He was the first full-time union researcher (for the postal workers) and then for the Labour Party/TUC. A Guild Socialist, he became Head of the TUC Research Department in 1926. He died in December 1935. Dave Lyddon, 'Walter Milne-Bailey, the TUC Research Department, and the 1926 General Strike: The Background to 'A Nation on Strike', *Historical Studies in Industrial Relations* (2010), no. 29/20, pp. 123–51 at 123–5; 133 and 138–9.
54 Harold Laski (1893–1950) had been asked to draw up Labour's 1931 election manifesto and became active in the Socialist League. He was a regular contributor to *The New Clarion*, a weekly which Bevin promoted from 1932. (Bullock, *Bevin*, vol. I, *Trade Union Leader*, p. 505, n. 2.) Laski chaired the Labour Party's NEC in 1944 and the Annual Conference in 1944–5, urging Bevin to challenge Attlee for the leadership.
55 Lyddon, *Walter Milne-Bailey*, pp. 138–9.
56 Citrine, *Two Careers*, p. 26.
57 Citrine, *Men and Work*, pp. 241 and 135.
58 Cole figures throughout Beatrice Webb's diaries, first as the young left-wing Fabian/Guild Socialist, and later as a significant influence with Labour Party leaders (Henderson especially) and governments. He was noticed so much perhaps because his wife Margaret edited the diaries! *Beatrice Webb's Diaries, 1912–1924* (1952), p. 266 (index of his many entries).
59 Skidelsky, *Politicians and the Slump*, p. 271.
60 Bullock, *Bevin*, vol. I, *Trade Union Leader*, p. 502.
61 Cole, *A History of the Labour Party since 1914*, p. 282. Cole saw that as a great mistake by the League. He left it after a time.
62 *Ibid.*, Economic Committee Report, pp. 257, 264 and 282. (The vote figures at p. 287.) For his Trade Disputes and Trade Unions

Act repeal report, p. 375. His 'Rationalisation and Reorganisation' motion is at pp. 336–7.

63 TUC Annual Report 1930, p. 375.

64 Shinwell, *The Labour Story*, p. 123. One of the most remarkable characters of that century, whose great age and extraordinarily long Labour movement contribution spanned the century. The son of Polish Jewish emigrants (one of thirteen), born in Spitalfields, London, in 1884. They had moved to Glasgow by the turn of the century, where he became a tailor and soon active in the union. He soon developed a wider union role in the pre-war Glasgow area militancy to organise the seamen. In 1911–12 he became a full-time organiser. Jailed in 1919 along with other Red Clydesiders for 'incitement to riot' in clashes with the police during the '40 hours per week' movement. ILP activist and a Labour MP in 1922 and minister in 1924 and 1929–31 governments.

65 Bullock, *Bevin*, vol. I, *Trade Union Leader*, pp. 476–503 and p. 491.

66 Beatrice Webb, though hardly an unbiased observer, was expecting the government to fall as early as 1930. *Diaries, 1924–1932*, 28 July 1929, 'after the fall of the Labour Government some 18 months hence', p. 213; 4 February 1931, pp. 264–5; 31 May, pp. 271–2; 4 August, when she said, 'The best thing that can happen to the Labour Government is that it should be defeated in its refusal to carry out the [May] report', p. 277.

67 Citrine's estimation of Keynes as 'Britain's foremost economist' was tempered by the qualification, 'It is true that he was apt to change

his mind, but Keynes had courage, knowledge and insight.' *Men and Work*, p. 240.

68 Martin, *The TUC*, p. 225.

69 Skidelsky, *Politicians and the Slump*, p. 262.

70 *Ibid.*, p. 263.

71 *Ibid.*

72 *Ibid.*, p. 268. Bondfield was close to MacDonald and his wife, but did not defect with him.

73 *Ibid.*, p. 269.

74 *Ibid.*, pp. 300–2.

75 Marquand, *Ramsay MacDonald*, p. 589. Today's equivalent (2018), c. £84 billion. In fact, the deficit turned out nearer to £200 million (= £140 billion).

76 The very experienced former president, Arthur Pugh of the Iron and Steel Workers, wrote the minority report, with Charles Latham of the Automobile Trades Association.

77 Juliet Gardiner, *The Thirties: An Intimate History* (Harper Press, 2010), p. 112; Marquand, *Ramsay MacDonald*, p. 609.

78 Skidelsky, *Politicians and the Slump*, pp. 352–4. Henderson was suspected by MacDonald of using the crisis to unseat him. Chris Wrigley, *Arthur Henderson* (University of Wales Press, 1992), p. 174.

79 Riddell, 'Walter Citrine', p. 297; F. M. Leventhal, *Arthur Henderson* (Manchester University Press, 1989), p. 185.

80 Citrine, *Men and Work*, p. 281.

81 *Ibid.*, pp. 281–2.

82 Bullock, *Bevin*, vol. I, *Trade Union Leader*, p. 482.

83 Citrine, *Men and Work*, p. 284.

84 Bullock, *Bevin*, vol. I, *Trade Union Leader*, p. 482.

85 Citrine, *Men and Work*, p. 284.

86 *Ibid.*, pp. 284–5.

87 *Ibid.*, p. 285.

88 Shinwell, *The Labour Story*, p. 142, 'Henderson, seeking a new master, seems to have already believed that he had found one in Bevin and had suggested that Bevin should oppose MacDonald at Seaham when the election came.'

89 *Ibid.*, p. 281.

90 Bullock, *Bevin*, vol. I, *Trade Union Leader*, p. 490.

91 *Ibid.*, p. 489.

92 See Chris Wrigley's chapter, 'Labour Dealing with Labour: Aspects of Economic Policy' in John Shepherd, Jonathan Davis and Chris Wrigley, eds, *The Second Labour Government: A Reappraisal* (Manchester University Press, 2012).

93 *Beatrice Webb's Diaries, 1924–1932*, p. 281. Webb, a Cabinet minister, was still respected as a founder of the Fabians and the Labour Party.

94 Citrine, *Men and Work*, p. 286.

95 *Ibid.*, p. 63.

96 *Ibid.*, p. 281. See also Robert Taylor's excellent section in chapter 1 of his *The TUC*, pp. 52–9.

97 Colin Cross, *Philip Snowden* (Barrie & Jenkins, 1966), pp. 54–6; Skidelsky, *Politicians and the Slump*, p. 288.

98 *Ibid.*; see also Keith Laybourn's *Philip Snowden: A Biography* (Dartmouth Publishing, 1988). Snowden died in 1937, after resigning from the 'National' government, 'hating MacDonald'.

99 Skidelsky, *Politicians and the Slump*, pp. 326–7.

100 Skidelsky, *John Maynard Keynes*, p. 345.

101 Bullock, *Bevin*, vol. I, *Trade Union Leader*, p. 427.

102 Skidelsky, *Politicians and the Slump*, p. 369.

103 *Ibid.*, pp. 370–1, citing Bullock, *Bevin*, vol. I, *Trade Union Leader*, p. 441.

104 *Ibid.*, pp. 370 and 165.

105 Adonis, *Ernest Bevin, Labour's Churchill*, p. 102.

106 Robert Taylor, *The TUC*, pp. 54–5.

107 Skidelsky, *Politicians and the Slump*, pp. 369–70; Adonis, *Ernest Bevin, Labour's Churchill*, pp. 106–7.

108 Bullock, *Bevin*, vol. I, *Trade Union Leader*, pp. 492–3.

109 Shinwell, *The Labour Story*, pp. 142–3.

110 Adonis, *Ernest Bevin, Labour's Churchill*, pp. 110–11. The seat had a Labour majority of 16,700 in 1929, but he lost it to a National Government candidate by the margin of 12,938 in 1931.

111 Shinwell, *The Labour Story*, p. 143.

112 *Ibid.*, p. 142 for his use of the *Herald* against the National Government.

113 Skidelsky, *Politicians and the Slump*, pp. 368–9.

114 *Ibid.*, p. 369.

115 *Ibid.*, p. 375.

116 Citrine put it in those terms in his second volume of autobiography, *Two Careers*, in 1967, p. 241.

117 Robert Skidelsky's, *Politicians and the Slump: The Labour Government of 1929–1931* remains the most detailed study. But there are other interpretations. See Ross McKibbin's article, 'The Economic Policy of the Second Labour Government, 1929–1931' in his *The Ideologies of Class* (Oxford University Press, 1987), pp. 197–227. More recently, Riddell, *Labour in Crisis*, and Chris Wrigley and Jonathan Davis' articles in *The Second Labour*

Government: A Reappraisal (Oxford University Press, 2012), have shed further light on a still unsettled controversy.

118 Riddell, 'Walter Citrine', p. 299.

119 This was the arrangement which Citrine had tried to set up with MacDonald. See n. 12 above. It became the National Council of Labour from July 1934.

120 Bullock, *Bevin*, vol. I, *Trade Union Leader*, p. 512.

121 *Ibid.*, p. 512.

Chapter 10

1 Clegg, *A History*, vol. III, p. 93.

2 Parker, 'Trade unions and the political culture of the British Labour Party'. This superb recent study by a young scholar is available online under that title.

3 Professor Geert Van Goethem, *The Amsterdam International: The World of the International Federation of Trade Unions (IFTU), 1913–1945*, remains the classic Study (Ashgate Publishing, 2006), p. 6.

4 Reiner Tosstorff, *The Red International of Labour Unions (RILU) 1920–1937* (Brill, 2004); 916 pages, English translation 2016 by Professor Ben Fowkes).

5 Moher, *Walter Citrine: A Union Pioneer of Industrial Cooperation*, pp. 197–9.

6 Citrine, *Men and Work*, p. 338.

7 Walther Shevenels, IFTU secretary, *Forty-Five Years – IFTU – A Historical Precis, 1956*, pp. 195–218 and 202–4. TUC Publications, HD6475.

8 TUC Annual Report 1933, p. 318. TUC Publications, HD6661 and online.

9 Citrine's TUC Report from the IFTU Executive Meeting, 16–18 February 1933. Churchill Archive Centre, Cambridge, G.C.7/3a/1932-33. TUC Library Collections at the London Metropolitan University, HD6661.

10 *Ibid.*, para. 7, p. 2.

11 *Ibid.*, para. 17, p. 5.

12 Citrine's TUC Report from the IFTU Executive Meeting, ibid., paras 12 and 13, p. 2.

13 *Ibid.*, para 14, pp. 2–3.

14 Citrine, *Men and Work*, p. 343.

15 *Ibid.*, pp. 343–4. Report 23.5.1933, para. 19.

16 Van Goethem, *The Amsterdam International*, p. 48.

17 Citrine, *Men and Power*, pp. 343–4.

18 Citrine's TUC Report from the IFTU Executive Meeting, paras 17 and 18, p. 3.

19 *Ibid.*, para. 18, p. 3.

20 *Ibid.*

21 Richard J. Evans, *The Third Reich in Power 1933–1939: How the Nazis Won Over the Hearts and Minds of a Nation* (Penguin Books, 2006), pp. 455–65.

22 Citrine's TUC Report from IFTU Executive, para. 18, p. 3.

23 *Ibid.*, paras 26–7, p. 4.

24 TUC General Council Report, *Dictatorships, and the Trade Union Movement*, memorandum by W. M. Citrine, 23.5.1933, Churchill Archive Centre, Cambridge, G.C.10/4/1932–33. TUC Publications, HD6661. Sixty-six paragraphs. Citrine's *Men and Work*, pp. 344–5, provides a synopsis of it.

25 Richard J. Evans, *The Third Reich in Power*, prologue, pp. 1–17, gives a good flavour.

26 *Ibid.*, p. 2.

27 *Ibid.*, paras 2 to 4.

28 Berlin exhibition, 2016. *Berlin 1933–1945: Between Propaganda and Terror*, exhibition catalogue by the Topography of Terror Foundation, Berlin, p. 18.

29 Citrine, *Men and Work*, p. 343.
30 Eric Hobsbawm, *Interesting Times: A Twentieth-Century Life* (The New Press, 2002), pp. 67–8. The KPD was the Communist Party, formed in opposition to the SPD by Rosa Luxemburg and Karl Liebknecht.
31 *Ibid.*
32 Richard J. Evans, *Eric Hobsbawm: A Life in History* (Little, Brown, 2019), p. 31.
33 *Ibid.*, pp. 31–2: 'In the central district of Berlin … 60 per cent of members were under thirty with the under twenty-fives predominant.'
34 *Ibid.*, p. 32.
35 Hobsbawm, *Interesting Times*, p. 68.
36 *Ibid.*
37 Calhoun, *The United Front*, p. 10.
38 TUC Annual Report 1933, pp. 325–40, including Citrine's responses.
39 Citrine's General Council Memorandum, *Dictatorships, and the Trade Union Movement*, para. 23, p. 8.
40 Citrine, *Men and Work*, pp. 96–8. See Chapter 6.
41 Moher, 'British Trade Unionists and the Soviet Union', pp. 13–15.
42 Citrine, *Men and Work*, pp. 96–8.
43 John Russell, 'The Role of Socialist Competition in Establishing Labour Discipline in the Soviet Working Class, 1928–1934'. PhD thesis, University of Birmingham, 1987, pp. 70–71 and 121–2.
44 Citrine's General Council Memorandum, *Dictatorships, and the Trade Union Movement*, quoting Alexander Lozovsky, the head of RILU, para. 28.
45 Citrine's General Council Memorandum, 1933, para. 34, p. 10.
46 TUC Annual Report, 1933, p. 337. TUC Publications HD 6661.
47 Citrine's General Council Memorandum, para. 60. Also *Men and Work*, pp. 293–301.
48 Cripps (1889–1952), a wealthy lawyer who had recently joined the Labour Party and become an MP and minister (solicitor general) in the 1929 Labour government. He funded the Socialist League and was taking it in a very leftward direction. Expelled from the Labour Party for defying its policy on the 'united front', he reinvented himself during the war as champion of the popular pro-Soviet alliance (ambassador to Moscow, 1940–42, and Cabinet minister, 1942–45). He would become a very orthodox austerity-minded Chancellor of the Exchequer, 1947–50.
49 Citrine's General Council Memorandum, para. 63.
50 Citrine, *Men and Work*, p. 294. Nicklaus Thomas-Symonds' *Nye* noticed the significance of this intervention by Citrine, pp. 71–2.
51 Ben Pimlott, *Labour and the Left in the 1930s* (Cambridge University Press, 1977), p. 52.
52 *Ibid.*, p. 298.
53 John Bew, *Citizen Clem: A Biography of Attlee* (Riverrun, 2016), pp. 173 and 584.
54 *Ibid.*, p. 174. Bew excused Attlee of being 'slightly dazzled by Cripps and the gatherings at Goodfellows' (Cripps mansion in the country where 'the great and the good of socialist society' gathered).
55 Citrine, *Men and Work*, p. 327.
56 Citrine's TUC General Council Memorandum, para. 60.
57 *Ibid.*, paras 61–2.
58 *Ibid.*, para. 63.
59 TUC Annual Report 1933, p. 326. TUC Publications, HD6661 and

online. *The Times*, 8 September 1933. John Campbell, *Nye Bevan: A Biography* (Metro Books, 1987), p. 58.

60 Bevan (1897–1960). As a young militant miner, like many other leading South Wales Miners' Federation activists such as Noah Ablett, Arthur Cook and Arthur Horner, he was trained in the syndicalist 'Ruskin College/Central London College' Plebs League group, 1919–21. Thomas-Symonds, *Nye*, pp. 33–4.

61 Campbell, *Nye Bevan: A Biography*, introduction, p. xiii; Thomas-Symonds, *Nye*, pp. 21–7 and 46.

62 Thomas-Symonds, *Nye*, pp. 43–7.

63 Citrine, *Men and Work*, p. 346. Bevan soon departed from local politics and rarely visited his Ebbw Vale constituency, except at election times, thereafter. His 'agent'/fellow soul, Archie Lush, helped him keep control of the constituency party. Thomas-Symonds, *Nye*, pp. 46–7, 67 and 82.

64 Citrine, *Men and Work*, p. 346. Bevan was, for a time, in Mosley's 'inner circle', before Mosley left the Labour Party to form the British Union of Fascists. Thomas-Symonds, *Nye*, pp. 60–2.

65 Citrine, *Men and Work*, p. 345. Thomas-Symonds, *Nye*, noted this comment but argued that Bevan later developed the self-confidence he was to display as minister of health and housing from 1945 to 1951, pp. 71–2.

66 *Ibid.*, p. 346.

67 *Ibid.*

68 Ben Pimlott, ed., *The Political Diary of Hugh Dalton, 1918–40, 1945–60* (Jonathan Cape, 1987), p. 182.

69 Bullock, *Bevin*, vol. I, *Trade Union Leader*, pp. 546–51, 561–4; vol. III, *Foreign Secretary*, p. 63.

70 The diaries of key players such as Hugh Dalton, chair of the Labour NEC, confirm this. See his *The Fateful Years. Memoirs 1931–1945* (Frederick Muller, 1957), pp. 65, 89, 176, 188–91, 293 and 314.

71 Citrine, *Men and Work*, p. 347.

72 *Ibid.*

73 The TUC Annual Report for 1934 documents these considerable efforts and preparations for an Austrian workers' general strike, pp. 249–55. TUC Library Collections, HD6661 and online http://unionhistory. info/reports/index.php.

74 Thomas-Symonds, *Nye*, p. 67. The *Western Mail* described him jokingly as 'Cymric Hitler'! This marked a final note in Bevan's involvement in local politics as he became 'permanently based in London'.

75 Citrine, *Men and Work*, pp. 305–6.

76 LSE Library, Citrine Archive 6/1. 'Together we sped across the Continent. Through thousands of miles of mountains and deserts, with orange groves, canyons and dried river beds … We traversed the Western coast to Portland, Seattle, then down to Los Angeles.'

77 The AFL, one of the founder members of IFTU, had dropped out in 1920. Citrine finally got it to rejoin in 1934. Van Goethem, *The Amsterdam International*, p. 6.

78 Citrine, *Men and Work*, pp. 308–9.

79 Roy (Lord) Jenkins regarded this body (originally called the 'Focus Group') of the great and the good non-Jewish supporters as significant. Among its members were prominent Labour MPs – Herbert Morrison, Hugh Dalton, Philip Noel-Baker; Winston Churchill and

other Conservative MPs; the Liberal leader Archibald Sinclair and the Liberal Lady Violet Bonham Carter; Sylvia Pankhurst, still a communist, and the prominent independent MP Eleanor Rathbone and many other prominent people. The fact that Sir Walter had agreed to chair their meetings with official TUC approval was regarded as important by Churchill. Lord Roy Jenkins, *Churchill* (Pan Books, 2002), pp. 494–5 and 498.

80 Fortunately, Louis recovered the title he had lost to Schmeling in 1936, with a trouncing and early knockout of the Aryan idol in their 1938 rematch at Yankee Stadium, New York.

81 Citrine, *Men and Work*, p. 328.

82 *Ibid.*

83 Citrine, *Men and Work*, pp. 323–8.

84 *Ibid.*, pp. 350–1 (Citrine's emphasis).

85 *Ibid.*, p. 350

86 *Ibid.*

87 TUC Report, 1935, p. 349. Bullock, *Bevin*, vol. I, *Trade Union Leader*, pp. 562–3.

88 Citrine, *Men and Work*, p. 352. The vote was 2,962,000 to 177,000.

89 *Ibid.*

90 *Ibid.*, p. 350.

91 Bullock, *Bevin*, vol. I, *Trade Union Leader*, pp. 565–6.

92 Citrine, *Men and Work*, p. 352.

93 *Ibid.*

94 Bullock, *Bevin*, vol. I, *Trade Union Leader*, pp. 568–70.

95 Adonis, *Ernest Bevin, Labour's Churchill*, pp. 125–35.

96 Citrine, *Men and Work*, p. 353.

97 *Ibid.*, pp. 323–8.

98 *Ibid.* This was from RAF officers at their staff college at Andover, where he lectured on trade unionism.

99 *Ibid.*, pp. 353–4.

100 Williams, *Ernest Bevin*, pp. 230–31.

101 Bew, *Citizen Clem*, p. 198; Adonis, *Ernest Bevin, Labour's Churchill*, p. 131.

102 Adonis, *Ernest Bevin, Labour's Churchill*, pp. 115–41 at p. 120.

103 A. J. P. Taylor, *English History 1914–1945* (Oxford University Press, 1965), p. 382.

104 Bernard Donoghue and G. W. Jones, *Herbert Morrison: Portrait of a Politician* (Littlehampton Book Services, 1973), p. 262. NEC Minutes, vol. 70, 4 March 1936.

105 *Ibid.*, pp. 221–31. Citrine's account of their efforts, *Men and Work*, pp. 357–60, has since been confirmed by Tom Buchanan's study of the TUC *Trabajodoras* archives, *The Impact of the Spanish Civil War on Britain: War, Loss and Memory* (Sussex Academic Press, 2007), Wikipedia article 29.10.2015.

106 Citrine, *Men and Work*, p. 358.

107 *Ibid.*, p. 359.

108 Michael Foot, *Aneurin Bevan* (two volumes), vol. I (MacGibbon & Kee, 1962), p. 226.

109 Tom Buchanan, 'The Trades Union Congress and the Spanish Civil War', University of Warwick, University Library, Modern Records Centre.

110 Sahadeo Basdeo, *Colonial Policy and Labour Organisation in the British Caribbean 1937–1939: An Issue in Political Sovereignty* (Centre for Latin American Research and Documentation, 1981), p. 6.

111 *The Times*, 14 October 1938; Citrine, *Men and Work*, pp. 329–37, where he devotes a chapter to it.

112 Sahadeo Basdeo, 'Walter Citrine and the British Caribbean Workers' Movement during the

Commission Hearing', *Journal of Caribbean History* (1983), vol. 18, no. 2, p. 48. Weiler's *British Labour and the Cold War*'s entire chapter 1 (pp. 28–52), manages to ignore this authoritative account altogether! Perhaps it didn't fit in with his theme of Citrine and the TUC's 'collaboration' with the imperial and colonial authorities? Legalisation of trade unions and the outspoken criticism and assistance of the TUC to West Indian trade unionists is just seen as managing discontent to avoid it becoming communist-led. He does, however, acknowledge Citrine's union diplomacy and shocked reaction to conditions there ('I am ashamed to be British'). *Ibid.,* p. 38.

113 Wikipedia, 'The Moyne Commission', https://en.wikipedia.org/wiki/Report of West_India_Royal_Commission_ (Moyne_Report).

114 Basdeo, *Colonial Policy and Labour Organisation in the British Caribbean,* p. 46.

115 *Ibid.*, pp. 10–11.

116 Although a very 'cold fish', Citrine was really impressed with how frank and open Chamberlain was with them, contrasting this with Attlee's reticence ('I never had a really intimate talk with him'). *Men and Work*, pp. 366–8.

117 *Ibid.*, p. 368.

118 *Ibid.*, p. 369.

119 *Ibid.*, p. 367.

120 *Ibid.*

121 *Ibid.*, p. 368.

122 *Ibid.*, p. 366.

123 Parker, 'Trade Unions and the Political Culture of the British Labour Party', pp. 31–46.

124 *Ibid.*

125 Henry Pelling, *A Short History of the Labour Party* (Macmillan & Co, 1961, 1968), chapter v, pp. 71–87.

126 Andrew Thorpe, *The British General Election of 1931* (Clarendon Press, 1991), p. 261.

127 Ross McKibbin, *The Economic Policy of the Second Labour Government* (Clarendon Press, 1990), pp. 64–5, saw Citrine 'lecturing Henderson on the primary purpose of the creation of the Labour Party'. Minutes of the Joint Meeting of the General Council of the TUC and the National Executive of the Labour Party, 10 November 1931.

128 Pelling's elegant chapter 'Convalescence: The General Council's Party (1931–40), in *A Short History of the Labour Party* (Macmillan & Co, 1961, 1968), pp. 77–8, acknowledged as much.

129 Bullock, *Bevin*, vol. I, *Trade Union Leader*, p. 512; McKibbin, *The Economic Policy of the Second Labour Government*, pp. 64–5.

Chapter 11

1   Citrine, *Men and Work*, pp. 317–18.

2   Sidney and Beatrice Webb, who had visited in 1932, attributed it to this change in their *Soviet Communism: A New Civilisation?* (Longman, Green & Co., 1935), pp. 1107–10.

3   Georgi Dimitrov, *The Working Class Against Fascism*, (Speech before the Seventh World Congress of the Communist International Executive, 2 August 1935) (Modern Books, 1936).

4   Webb and Webb, *Soviet Communism*, pp. 1107–10.

5   Citrine, *Men and Work*, p. 122.

6   TUC Annual Report 1935, pp. 320–30. Also *The Times*, 5 September 1935, p. 9.

7 Webb and Webb, *Soviet Communism*, p. 1112.

8 Léon Jouhaux (1870–1954), a veteran of the French anarcho-syndicalist movement and general secretary of CGT since 1909. A key figure in European unionism of the inter-war years.

9 Citrine, *Men and Work*, p. 368.

10 Jonathan Davis, 'Labour and the Kremlin' in Shepherd, Davis and Wrigley, eds, *The Second Labour Government: A Reappraisal*, pp. 150–65.

11 Bevin, in particular, was having a lot of trouble from nests of communists in 'rank-and-file' committees, for example, in London bus garages. Bullock, *Bevin*, vol. I, *Trade Union Leader*, pp. 522–3.

12 *Ibid.*, p. 122.

13 Webb and Webb, *Soviet Communism*, pp. 1104–10.

14 Citrine, *I Search for Truth in Russia* (George Routledge & Sons Ltd, 1938 edition), preface, p. vi.

15 *Ibid.*, preface, p. vii.

16 *Ibid.*, pp. 28–9. Citrine was always wary of their interpreters, suspecting them of being security officials.

17 *Ibid.*, pp. 144–5.

18 *Ibid.*, pp. 49–51.

19 *Ibid.*, p. 43 dated 22 September 1935.

20 *Ibid.*, p. 354. Tomsky gave Citrine a beautifully illustrated *Saga of Igor*.

21 *Ibid.*, pp. 87–8.

22 *Ibid.*, p. 121.

23 *Ibid.*, p. 117.

24 *Ibid.*, p. 129. He returned to this theme frequently.

25 *Ibid.*, p. 130.

26 *Ibid.*, p. 166.

27 *Ibid.*, p. 131. Was Citrine a pioneer of this view? Tony Cliff, Marxist/Trotskyist theoretician, wrote his

State Capitalism in Russia in 1948 as an internal Revolutionary Communist Party document. It was later published in 1955 and 1974 by Bookmark Publications. Trotskyists of various hues have adopted varieties of their masters' categorisation. Although entirely different in outlook from Trotsky the revolutionist, Citrine had admired his role in the Bolshevik Revolution and thought Trotsky would be Lenin's natural successor when he visited in 1925. See Chapter 6 above. *Men and Work*, p. 98.

28 *Ibid.*, p. 299.

29 *Ibid.*, pp. 205–6.

30 *Ibid.*, pp. 192–3.

31 *Ibid.*, pp. 221–32.

32 *Ibid.*, p. 221.

33 *Ibid.*, p. 226.

34 Citrine, *Men and Work*, p. 127.

35 *Ibid.*, p. 127.

36 TUC Annual Report, pp. 423–9, 435–7. TUC Library Collections at London Metropolitan University, HD6661 and online.

37 Citrine, *I Search for Truth in Russia*, p. 311.

38 *Ibid.*, p. 314.

39 *Ibid.*, p. 311.

40 *Ibid.*, p. 312.

41 *Ibid.*, p. 314.

42 *Ibid.*, p. 318.

43 Webb and Webb, *Soviet Communism* (October 1935 edition). They removed the question mark in their 1937 edition!

44 *Sunday Times*, 10 July 1936, p. 21.

45 *New Statesman and Nation*, press cutting July 1936 in Citrine's Archive 5/2 (LSE Library).

46 Pat Sloan, *I Search for Truth in Citrine* (Lawrence & Wishart, 1936).

47 LSE Library, Citrine Archive 5/2.

48 Citrine, *Men and Work*, p. 323.

49 *Ibid.*

50 Gabriel Gorodetsky, ed., *The Maisky Diaries 1932–1943* (Yale University Press, 2015), p. 25, n. 64.

51 Citrine, *I Search for Truth in Russia*, p. 354.

52 *Ibid.*

53 *Ibid.*, pp. 361–4. The *Herald* coverage was strongly critical of the Soviet trials.

54 *Ibid.*, p. 369.

55 *Ibid.*

56 *Ibid.*

57 Bullock, *Bevin*, vol. I, *Trade Union Leader*, pp. 522–8.

58 TUC Annual Report 1936 (Edinburgh), pp. 423–8; *The Times*, 12 September 1936, p. 12.

59 *Ibid.*, 1936, pp. 434–7.

60 Shakespeare, *Henry VIII*, quoted in *Men and Work*, p. 310.

61 *Ibid.*

62 Pugh (1870–1955), steel smelter and founder, general secretary of the iron and steel union (BISKRA). TUC's Parliamentary Committee, then General Council member, 1920–36. He was chair during the General Strike and is pictured with Citrine leaving Downing Street during the negotiations (see Chapter 5).

63 Citrine, *Men and Work*, p. 313.

64 Previous knighthoods to Ben Turner (textile workers), James Sexton (dockers) and Robert Young (engineers), in 1931, were to retiring union leaders in their political capacity. V. L. Allen, *Trade Union Leadership* (Longmans, Green & Co., 1957), p. 32, n. 3.

65 Clegg, *A History*, vol. III, p. 112. *The Times*, 3 June 1935.

66 Citrine had led the campaign to prevent MacDonald returning to the Labour Party in 1932, but he would afterwards feel sorry for the isolated and declining figure. *Men and Work*, pp. 287–9. Along with Attlee, Citrine would be one of the pallbearers at MacDonald's funeral in 1937. He would also deliver the main speech at a Ceremony of Unveiling Memorial to James Ramsay MacDonald, Westminister Abbey, 12 March 1968. His son, Malcolm, who had joined his father in the National government, was abroad and couldn't attend, but he wrote to Citrine expressing his appreciation, saying, 'Your long association with father in many great affairs, and your close personal friendship with him through good times and bad, and through agreements and disagreements, were always treasured by him' (Occasional Paper No. 20, December 1968, p. 12). The fact that he offered knighthoods to Bevin, Citrine and Pugh suggested that MacDonald regretted the great error he made in 1931. Ironically, his memorial lies beside a tablet to Ernest Bevin, but Citrine doesn't even have a gravestone in Harrow.

67 Sadly, it could not be found in the Low Collection, the Beinecke Library, Yale University.

68 This Low cartoon would have hurt, as Citrine held the persecution of the Tolpuddle Martyrs close to his heart as symbolising the trade union struggle historically. In 1934, he produced a beautifully illustrated 100th anniversary TUC book in which Low did some of the cartoons. Citrine contributed a very heartfelt vivid and very detailed 100-page account. 'The Martyrs of Tolpuddle' the lead article,

written by Citrine, in the book
he commissioned for the TUC:
*The Book of the Martyrs of Tolpuddle
1834-1934* (TUC: London, 1934),
pp.1–103.

69 *Ibid.*, pp. 313–14.

70 *Ibid.*, p. 315.

71 *Ibid.*

72 *Ibid.*, p. 318.

73 *Ibid.*, p. 319. *The Times*, 7 September
1935, p. 12.

74 *Ibid.*

75 The debate was recorded in the
TUC Annual Report for 1935,
pp. 426–32. TUC Library
Collections, HD 6661.

76 *The Times*, 6 May 1936.

77 TUC Annual Report, 29 June 1936,
p. 8. TUC Library Collection.

78 *Daily Herald*, 6 July 1936.

Chapter 12

1 *The Churchill Documents*, ed. Sir
Martin Gilbert, vol. 15, *Never
Surrender, May 1940–Dec 1940*
(Blackwell, 2011), p. 1018.

2 Van Goethem, *The Amsterdam
International*, pp. 229–33.

3 Citrine, *Two Careers*, pp. 37–8.

4 *Ibid.*, pp. 38–9.

5 *Ibid.*, p. 40.

6 *Ibid.*

7 *Ibid.*, p. 41.

8 *Ibid.*, p. 53.

9 *Ibid.*, p. 54.

10 *Ibid.*, p. 130.

11 *The Second World War Diary of Hugh
Dalton*, ed. Ben Pimlott (Jonathan
Cape 1986), p. 798.

12 Citrine, *Two Careers*, pp. 198–9.

13 *The Churchill Documents*, p. 1018.

14 Guardian Century, *Nazi's death
blacklist discovered in Berlin* 1940–
1949, https://www.theguardian.
com/century/1940-1949/
Story/0,,127730,00.html.

15 Walther Schevenels, *Forty-Five Years:
International Federation of Trade Unions
1901–1945* The Board of Trustees,
IFTU, Brussels, (1976), p. 290.
Schevenels, the general secretary,
was with Citrine on that tour.

16 Clegg, *A History*, vol. III, p. 166.

17 Citrine, *Men and Work*, pp. 25–31.

18 Clegg, *A History*, vol. III, p. 167.

19 *Ibid.*, pp. 168–9.

20 *Ibid.*, p. 169.

21 Taylor, *The TUC*, pp. 78–81.

22 Bullock, *Bevin*, vol. II, *Minister of
Labour*, pp. 11–14.

23 Citrine, *Two Careers*, p. 28.

24 Robert Taylor, *The TUC*, p. 90.

25 *Ibid.*, p. 77. Hansard Parliamentary
Debates, vol. 410, 2 May 1945, c
1405.

26 Taylor has a detailed account in *The
TUC*, pp. 81–91.

27 Citrine, *Men and Work*, pp. 260–1,
and *Two Careers*, pp. 37–8.

28 *Statement by W. Schevenels to the
TUC International Committee*, 5
December 1940, p. 1 (TUC
Library Collections at the London
Metropolitan University, HD 6661).

29 A. J. P. Taylor, *English History
1914–1945*, p. 489.

30 *Ibid.*, p. 53. Most of IFTU's records
were later captured by the Gestapo
and taken to Berlin, where it is
believed they were later destroyed in
Allied bombing. Ibid., p. 53.

31 Citrine, *Two Careers*, p. 53. Citrine
wrote a warm foreword to Schevenels'
history of IFTU, *Forty-Five Years:
International Federation of Trade Unions
1901–1945* in 1956. TUC Library
Collections HD6475.A25ch.

32 See Robert Taylor's chapter 2,
'Bevin, Citrine and the TUC's War'
in *The TUC* for the initial period of
close consultation with the TUC,
pp. 81–91.

33 *Ibid.*, pp. 45–6.

34 Taylor, *The TUC*, pp. 81–9.

35 Citrine, *Two Careers*, p. 48.

36 *Ibid.*

37 *Ibid.*, p. 26. Bevin also made a number of broadcasts to North America in 1940 and 1941. See his *The Job to Be Done* in September 1941 (Heinemann, 1941), pp. 1–112. As did Citrine, *Two Careers*, p. 203.

38 Robert Taylor, *The TUC*, pp. 84; Citrine, *Two Careers*, p. 48.

39 *Ibid.*

40 Thomas Phillips was permanent secretary, with Frederick Leggett (industrial relations) and Godfrey Ince (manpower), his deputies. Ibid., p. 49. Bullock, *Bevin*, vol. II, *Minister of Labour*, pp. 118–20.

41 Citrine, *Two Careers*, p. 48.

42 *Ibid.*

43 *Ibid.*, p. 50; Bullock, *Bevin*, vol. II, *Minister of Labour*, p. 119.

44 Bullock, *Bevin*, vol. II, *Minister of Labour*, p. 101.

45 LSE Library, Citrine 10/3. Bullock, *Bevin*, vol. I, *Trade Union Leader*, pp. 100– 102, describes Bevin's various characteristics at age forty-five quite well.

46 Citrine, *Two Careers*, p. 50.

47 *Ibid.*, p. 51.

48 LSE Library, Citrine 10/6, 18 November 1952 paper, pp. 10–11, where Citrine gave his full version of this incident from a discussion he had with Churchill and others at 10 Downing Street.

49 Citrine, *Two Careers*, p. 93.

50 *Ibid.*, p. 94.

51 *Ibid.*

52 *Ibid.*

53 *Ibid.*

54 *The Manchester Guardian*, 29 September 1941 (e.a.).

55 *Ibid.*, see Jonathan Schneer, *Ministers at War: Winston Churchill and his Cabinet* (Oneworld, 2015), pp. 159–66, for a full account of this Soviet supply problem. Bevin does not appear to have been very interested, being absorbed in the domestic labour supply issues. Bullock, *Bevin*, vol. II, *Minister of Labour*, p. 68 just says, 'it was hard to grasp this [its significance] at the time'.

56 *Ibid.*, pp. 94–5.

57 *Ibid.*, p. 133.

58 *Ibid.*

59 Citrine had been a director of the TUC-owned *Daily Herald* since 1926 and became vice-chair in 1940 after Bevin became a minister. They had both been active in extending the influence of a more popular daily paper in promotional tours from 1928. Odhams Press had taken over the business and financial aspects in 1928 and boosted its circulation from 250,000 to over 2 million, an achievement that Bevin was particularly proud of. Citrine, *Two Careers*, pp. 348–9.

60 *Ibid.*, p. 94.

61 Bullock, *Bevin*, vol. II, *Minister of Labour*, p. 133.

62 *Evening Standard*, 29 September 1941, and *Daily Express*, 30 September 1941.

63 Citrine, *Two Careers*, p. 95. Bullock acknowledged Citrine's point about the strain Bevin was under. For their exchange of letters, see *Bevin*, vol. II, *Minister of Labour*, at pp. 134–5.

64 Citrine, *Two Careers*, p. 95

65 *Ibid.*

66 *Evening Standard*, 29 September 1941.

67 Bullock, *Bevin*, vol. II, *Minister of Labour*, p. 134.

68 *Ibid.*, p. 96.

69 *Ibid.*, pp. 135–6. His most recent biographer, Lord Andrew Adonis, *Ernest Bevin, Labour's Churchill*, seeks to justify Bevin's behavior, saying it was really 'an argument about respect' (p. 205).

70 Citrine, *Two Careers*, p. 95.

71 Bullock, *Bevin*, vol. II, *Minister of Labour*, p. 135.

72 *Ernest Bevin, A Radio Portrait* introduced by Christopher Mayhew, West of England Home Service, 23 April 1957, p. 8. LSE Library, Citrine 10/3.

73 *Ernest Bevin: A Contemporary Biography*, by Lord Roy Jenkins, serialised in *The Times*, 7–9 June 1971, at 8 June, p. 12. LSE Libraries, Citrine 10/5. This did not become a book.

74 Bullock, *Bevin*, vol. I, *Trade Union Leader*, p. 132.

75 *Ibid.*, p. 134.

76 *Ibid.*, pp. 46–8, 119.

77 Bullock, *Bevin*, vol. II, *Minister of War*, pp. 120–1.

78 TUC Annual Report 1941, pp. 364–5.

79 Bullock, *Bevin*, vol. III, *Foreign Secretary*, p. 854.

80 Taylor, *The TUC*, pp. 90–1.

81 Thomas-Symmonds, *Nye*, pp. 52–3, 67.

82 Michael Foot's biography of *Aneurin Bevan*, vol. I, pp. 440–63, has been described as 'so slanted, that his portrait, though wonderfully vivid, frequently tips over into hagiography'. Campbell, *Nye Bevan*, introduction, p. xi.

83 Sir Frederick Leggett (1884–1983), the Department's industrial relations' officer, had known Bevin since 1916. In 1926, he recommended Bevin for inclusion on the Ministry of Labour industrial mission to the USA. They were both involved at the ILO as government and TUC representatives in the 1930s (Bullock, *Bevin*, vol. II, *Minister of Labour*, p. 120). In a *Radio Portrait*, 'Ernest Bevin', in 1957 (West of England Home Service, 24 April 1957), Leggett confirmed Citrine's experience of one of Bevin's traits: 'Sometimes we would put to him an idea and he would not take much notice of it; perhaps in two- or three-days' time he would refer to this idea as his own and we would have to appear not to have heard it before.' LSE Library, Citrine 10/3, p. 12. See also Rodney Lowe's entry about Leggett in the *Oxford Dictionary of National Biography*, 2004.

84 Sir Godfrey H. Ince (1891–1960) knew Bevin first as joint secretary of the Shaw Inquiry 1920, where Bevin made a name as 'the Dockers' KC'. Ince specialised in unemployment insurance in the 1930s and became under secretary of national service in 1939, and permanent secretary in 1944–1956. Bullock, *Bevin*, vol. II, *Minister of Labour*, pp. 120–1. See also Rodney Rowe's revealing entry about Ince in the ODNB 2004. Lowe says he was 'convinced of the soundness of his own judgements he was not an easy person with whom to negotiate. He was at times unwilling, or perhaps unable, to admit the honesty of opinions running counter to his own …' Citrine experienced that over the skilled-manpower issue.

85 *Ibid.*, p. 131.

86 Martin, *The TUC*, p. 281.

87 *Ibid.*

88 Douglas Cole, a leading left-winger who was close to Bevin on the Macmillan Committee (see Chapter 9), invited him to chair the SSIP in

1931. G. D. H. Cole, *A History of the Labour Party from 1914* (Routledge and Kegan Paul, London, 1948), p. 282, and A. J. P. Taylor, *English History 1914–1945*, p. 349n.

89 Richard Crossman MP's review of Bullock's first volume, *Bevin, Trade Union Leader*, in *The Guardian*, 14 March 1960. Also A. J. P. Taylor in his *English History 1914–1945*, p. 382.

90 Bullock, *Bevin*, vol. II, *Minister of War*, pp. 110–11. Anderson, a former senior civil servant, he had organised the government's strike-breaking Organisation for the Maintenance of Supplies in 1926. Anderson entered the 'National' government with Chamberlain in 1938 as a non-party MP (Scottish Universities) and held most of the key posts during the coalition, including Chancellor of the Exchequer. He seems to have had a strong influence on Bevin (they would have had much to talk about from the General Strike!). He was known as Churchill's 'Prime Minister of the Domestic Front'.

91 Taylor, *The TUC*, p. 273. This description has now been adopted by Lord Adonis in his *Ernest Bevin, Labour's Churchill*, perhaps uncritically, like all his other biographers.

92 *Ibid.*, pp. 148–51 gives Bevin's side of things.

93 Max Aitken, Lord Beaverbrook (1879–1964), was a Canadian of Scottish Presbyterian stock who entered politics as a British Tory MP in 1910 and government office from 1918. He built a newspaper empire in London after the war, including the *Daily Express* and *Evening Standard*. A press baron, he

interfered frequently in Tory Party and political affairs, generally at the highest levels. Citrine devoted an entire chapter to 'Beaverbrook and Bevin', *Two Careers*, pp. 125–39.

94 Bullock, *Bevin*, vol. II, *Minister of War*, p. 46.

95 *Ibid.*, pp. 36–9.

96 A. J. P. Taylor, *English History 1914–1945*, p. 509.

97 Bullock, *Bevin*, vol. II, *Minister of Labour*, p. 149.

98 Bew, *Citizen Clem*, pp. 280–2, captures the atmosphere of the resulting Cabinet reshuffle quite vividly; F. Beckett, *Clem Attlee* (Politico's, 2000), p. 174.

99 Citrine, *Two Careers*, p. 137.

100 Robert Pearce, *Attlee* (Addison Wesley Longman, 1997) – 'Attlee threw his weight behind Ernie', p. 105.

101 Bew, *Citizen Clem*, p. 293.

102 *Ibid.*, p. 282.

103 bid., p. 127.

104 Citrine was told by one of the union Labour advisers to the Ministry of Aircraft Production and Ministry of Supply's Jack Stephenson that Bevin was 'in a desperate state', drinking heavily (in the office) and 'muddled in conversation'. He said Bevin was 'the main cause of the trouble' between him and Beaverbrook. Stephenson was secretary of the Plumbers' and Domestic Engineers' Union, whom Citrine regarded highly. Citrine, *Two Careers*, pp. 125–6.

105 *Ibid.*, p. 127. This suggests that Citrine was worried as to what Bevin wanted more (state) power for. It certainly didn't seem to him to be about enhancing union power anymore, though Bevin

would have dressed it up as that. As his career unfolded to being number three or four in the Cabinet and foreign secretary, it became clear that it was national/imperial power that he was aiming for.

106 *Ibid.*

107 *Ibid.*, p. 128.

108 *Ibid.* A full account of his extraordinary interview with the 'chastened' Beaverbrook at 11 Downing Street in early February 1942 is at pp. 126–33. He went to Beaverbrook's Cherkley Court, near Leatherhead, on a number of occasions. Bevan and Foot were also beneficiaries of the Beaverbrook charm offensives. Thomas-Symonds, *Nye*, pp. 72–5.

109 *Ibid.*, p. 133.

110 *Ibid.*, pp. 357–8, where he explained why he was closer to Beaverbrook personally; 'I never recall spending a weekend with either Attlee or Bevin', while he 'saw much of Beaverbrook socially at his home and elsewhere.'

111 *Ibid.*, p. 137.

112 *The Second World War Diaries of Hugh Dalton*, ed. Pimlott, p. 354.

113 *Ibid.*, p. 355.

114 Nina Fishman, *Arthur Horner: A Political Biography* (Lawrence & Wishart, 2010), p. 476.

115 *Ibid.*, p. 475. Fishman reckoned that 'his overwhelming victory … would have been impossible without Citrine's & Deakin's (T&GWU) tacit support'.

116 Citrine, *Two Careers*, p. 194.

117 *Ibid.*, pp. 298–303.

118 *Ibid.*, pp. 301–2.

119 *Ibid.*, p. 302.

120 The General Council only just prevented that year's Congress from rejecting Regulation 1AA, after they had modified Bevin's original draft to narrow its target to unofficial strike action. The TUC vote went 3,686,000 to 2,802 against. Citrine, *Two Careers*, p. 193.

121 Bullock, *Bevin*, vol. II, *Minister of Labour*, p. 304.

122 *Ibid.*, pp. 305–6.

123 *Ibid.*, p. 306.

124 *Ibid.*, p. 305.

125 *Ibid.*, p. 308.

126 Brendan Bracken MP, the Tory minister of information, once called Bevan, 'You Bollinger Bolshevik, you ritzy Robespierre, you lounge-lizard Lenin. Look at you swilling Max's [Beaverbrook] champagne and calling yourself a socialist.' Thomas-Symonds, *Nye*, p. 73.

127 Foot, *Aneurin Bevan*, vol. I, p. 458.

128 Michael Foot, 'The Fight with Bevin', in *Aneurin Bevan: A Biography, vol. I: 1897–1945*, pp. 415–19 and 440–463.

129 *Ibid.*, p. 178.

130 *Ibid.*, pp. 319–20.

131 *Tribune*, 6 April 1939. See Campbell, *Nye Bevan*, p. 83.

132 Robert Crowcroft, *Attlee's War* (I.B. Tauris, 2011), p. 67.

133 Citrine, *Men and Work*, pp. 300–1. See Chapter 9.

134 Pearce, *Attlee*, p. 76, 'Bevin, Citrine and Francis Williams, editor of the *Daily Herald* had been saying that Attlee should go.' Also Crowcroft, *Attlee's War*, p. 31. 'Dalton likened the leader to a rabbit or a mouse' (ibid., p. 77).

135 Citrine, *Men and Work*, p. 351.

136 Hansard Parliamentary (Commons) Debate 13 July 1934, vol. 292, column 689. Cited by Martin Gilbert, *Winston S. Churchill,*

vol. 5, '*The Prophet of Truth*', *1922–1939* (Hillsdale College Press, 2015), p. 553.

137 Pearce, *Attlee*, p. 86.

138 Bew, *Citizen Clem*, p. 198.

139 *Ibid.*

140 *Ibid.*, p. 367. Also Pearce, *Attlee*, p. 86. Some of this is explained by Attlee's 'ingrained shyness' (ibid., p. 104), but that was hardly an adequate excuse at that level.

141 Bew, *Citizen Clem*, p. 516.

142 Beckett, *Clement Attlee*, pp. 106–7. Bew, *Citizen Clem*, has little to say about his relationship with any of the TUC leaders other than Bevin.

143 Minutes of the Joint TUC General Council and Labour Party NEC, 10 November 1931, Citrine's speech, pp. 2–4. Bevin Papers 1/8, Churchill Archives Centre. Bevin didn't attend.

144 Crowcroft, *Attlee's War*. His 'uniquely powerful [behind-the-scenes] position', pp. 64–5 and the following chapters. Beckett's *Clement Attlee* and Bew's *Citizen Clem* have since developed that case for Attlee.

145 *Memorandum of Interview*, 9 August 1943, Rt Hon. C. R. Attlee and Sir Walter Citrine re Trade Disputes and Trade Unions Act 1927. LSE Library, Citrine 10/5.

146 Citrine, *Two Careers*, pp. 356–7.

147 *Ibid.*, p. 357. Citrine thought Morrison should have succeeded Attlee as Labour leader, but he was again passed over for Gaitskell.

Chapter 13

1 Citrine, *Two Careers*, p. 72.

2 *Ibid.*, pp. 77–81.

3 John L. Lewis (1880–1969), president of the United Mine Workers of America (UMWA), the largest (c. 600,000) union, and creator of the CIO federation which separated very acrimoniously from the AFL in 1938. They became bitter rivals, with the CIO making great inroads in the automobile, steel and other booming war industries (each having over 5 million members). Lewis was originally a strong supporter of Roosevelt for his second re-election. In 1936, he fell out bitterly with him, causing convulsions on 2 October 1940 by urging 30 million Americans on radio not to vote for Roosevelt on anti-war grounds. Conrad Black, *Franklin Delano Roosevelt: Champion of Freedom* (Weidenfeld & Nicolson, 2003), pp. 588–9.

4 See Introduction. It was reproduced in Britain (The Churchill Archives, CHAR 20/4B/148) and as an Appendix to Citrine's *My American Diary* (Routledge, 1941), University of Cambridge Library, 539.1.d.775.1.

5 Churchill to Citrine, 6 September 1940. The Churchill Archives, CHAR 20/4B/134.

6 *Ibid.*, CHAR 20/4B/144–146.

7 Citrine, *My American Diary*, picture facing p. 1 (see Introduction).

8 Citrine, *Two Careers*, pp. 73–4.

9 Woll's message arrived in London on 28.12.1940 and Churchill's Foreign Office response was dated 4 January 1941. The Churchill Archives, CHAR 20/4B/150.

10 *Ibid.*, pp. 77–80, 'At the White House'.

11 *Ibid.*, pp. 81–2. He had 'warm credentials' from Churchill and Lord Beaverbrook, minister of aircraft production, for access to war factories and Henry Self, the

director general of the British Air Commission, facilitated them. They would again team up on the Board of the British Electrical Authority from 1947, when Citrine recruited Self from the permanent secretaryship of the Ministry of Aircraft Production (see Chapter 14).

12 Citrine, *Two Careers*, p. 97.

13 Van Goethem, *The Amsterdam International*, p. 238.

14 Taylor, *English History 1914–1945*, pp. 542–3.

15 Citrine, *Two Careers*, p. 98.

16 Geert Van Goethem thought he was 'sent' on missions' of this nature, 'Bevin's Boys Abroad: British Labor Diplomacy in the Cold War Era', *New Global Studies* (2017), vol. 2, no. 2, p. 2., p. 2. It was still a bold undertaking in October 1941, just when the Nazi invasion had reached 'within a tram-ride of Moscow'.

17 Peter Weiler, *British Labour and the Cold War* (Stanford University Press, 1988), pp. 55–7. This extremely anti-Citrine and pro-communist interpretation by an American academic naively saw Citrine's initiative entirely as his 'attempt to head off the growth of unofficial [pro-Soviet] committees' in Britain. In this vein, his judgements were extremely biased. See also pp. 17–18, re. Citrine.

18 Citrine, *Two Careers*, p. 99.

19 *Ibid.*, pp. 99–101, describes their horrendous North Sea winter passage.

20 *Ibid.*, p. 100.

21 N. M. Shvernik (1889–1952) replaced Tomsky as secretary of the Soviet TUC in 1928, a position he held until 1944. He was also responsible for the evacuation of Soviet industry and became chair of the Supreme Soviet from 1946 to 1953.

22 *Ibid.*, p. 102. Sir Stafford Cripps (1889–1952). Though expelled from the Labour Party in 1939, as an independent pro-Soviet left-wing MP he became ambassador to the Soviet Union, 1940–42. In 1942, he became Lord Privy Seal in the Cabinet. He rejoined the Labour Party and became Chancellor of the Exchequer from 1947 to 1950.

23 Citrine, *Two Careers*, p. 117.

24 His full report is in the TUC Annual Report (Blackpool), 1942–43, pp. 58–61.

25 Citrine, *Two Careers*, p. 112.

26 *Ibid.*, p. 113.

27 *Ibid.*, pp. 113–14.

28 *Ibid.*, p. 110.

29 *Ibid.*, p. 103.

30 He produced a booklet urging British assistance for the Finns. Sir W. Citrine, *My Finnish Diary* (Penguin Books, 1940).

31 Citrine, *Two Careers*, p. 111.

32 Tony Judt, in his excellent *Postwar: A History of Europe since 1945* (Vintage, 2010), highlights this important factor of mistrust to be overcome (short of opening a Second Front if the alliance was to hold) (pp. 103–4).

33 *Ibid.*, p. 117. The surrender of Singapore in January 1942 signified the loss of British influence throughout South East Asia.

34 *Ibid.*, p. 116.

35 *Ibid.*, p. 117

36 Schneer, *Ministers at War*, pp. 166–78. In Birmingham, Beaverbrook addressed a crowd of over 50,000, and 10,000 workers and Home Guarders with clenched fists marched past the Anglo-Soviet Unity platform, ibid., p. 173. He took his campaign to America,

where they wanted Britain to open the 'Second Front' also.

37 Citrine, *Two Careers*, p. 116.

38 *Ibid.*, pp. 118–24.

39 *Ibid.*, p. 154.

40 *Ibid.*, p. 158.

41 *Ibid.*, p. 164.

42 Clegg, *A History*, vol. III, p. 285, citing Citrine's report to the TUC in 1943, Annual Report, pp. 329–33.

43 *Ibid.*, p. 286. TUC Annual Report 1944, Appx C, pp. 253–68.

44 Judt, *Postwar*, pp. 105–6.

45 TUC Annual Report, Blackpool, 1942. General secretary's statement on the General Council's report, p. 244. TUC Publications, HD 6661 and online.

46 *Ibid.*

47 'Labour's Second Front: The Foreign Policy of the American and British Trade Union Movements during the Second World War', Geert Van Goethem, in *Diplomatic History* (OUP, 2010), pp. 673–5. From a pro-communist left perspective, Peter Weiler adopted the Foreign Office/Professsor Tawney criticisms of Citrine's 'obstinacy and perversity and clumsiness', *British Labour and the Cold War*, pp. 59–62 but especially n. 43, pp. 304–5. See below.

48 Citrine, *Two Careers*, p. 71.

49 *Ibid.*, p. 143.

50 Harry Hopkins (1890–1946), a strong 'New Dealer' and close confidant of President Roosevelt in the White House, became his envoy to Churchill in 1941 when they extended aid to Britain ('Lend-Lease').

51 Citrine, *Two Careers*, p. 143.

52 *Ibid.*, pp. 143–4.

53 *Ibid.*, p. 146.

54 *Ibid.*, p. 144.

55 John L. Lewis (1880–1969). In 1940, Lewis resigned as president of the CIO after his members voted for Roosevelt, though he had strongly recommended the Republican candidate, Wendell Willkie, on isolationist grounds. Lewis remained leader of his 600,000 mineworkers' union (UMWA), which he had built since the 1920s and achieved great things for. He was succeeded by his deputy, Philip Murray (1886–1952), a Roosevelt supporter, who soon changed the CIO approach dramatically by adopting a 'no strike' policy in the war industries where the CIO was by far now the largest union. Lewis was regarded by Roosevelt as the 'really dangerous' man in American politics as he was suspected of encouraging miners' strikes and CIO militancy in the war industries in a continuation of his opposition to Roosevelt (Foreign Office correspondence F.O.371.30700. A8035). He took the UMWA out of the CIO in 1942. Wikipedia, 'John L. Lewis'. Citrine, *Two Careers*, pp. 71, 141, 147–9.

56 Citrine, *Two Careers*, p. 71. Lewis fell out with Roosevelt for not backing him in his often violent battles with employers. He broadcast against the president during the presidential elections in 1940. Black, *Roosevelt: Champion of Liberty* traces his tempestuous career and clashes with Roosevelt since 1937, pp. 321, 393, 417–18 and 588–9.

57 *Ibid.*, p. 141.

58 *Ibid.*

59 TUC Annual Report, 1942, p. 241.

60 Citrine, *Two Careers*. 'Lewis, I regarded as the most dynamic person in the American labour movement.' Because of his

'resolution and skill he had worked miracles for the standard of life of the miners'. Citrine did add that 'Lewis was looked upon as unsociable to the point of belligerency ... self- centred and somewhat contemptuous of the opinions of others', p. 147.

61 Citrine, *Two Careers*, p. 224. They called the CIO 'scallywags and splitters who paraded at the White House to prevent America giving help to Britain in the early stages of the war'.

62 *Ibid.*, p. 144. Weiler said Citrine later 'deceived' the General Council into accepting the AFL proposal, *British Labour and the Cold War*, pp. 61–2 and n. 41, p. 304. His anti-Citrine animus was evident throughout this section of his book – Citrine was 'rigid and somewhat narrow-minded' (p. 59); 'His bungling trade union diplomacy' (pp. 61–2); 'the whole affair reveals a vain and duplicitous streak in him' (p. 305, n. 45), and so on.

63 J. M. Winter, introduction to R. H. Tawney's book of his report, *The American Labour Movement* (St Martin's Press, 1979, English edition), pp. xiii–xiv. Tawney and Attlee went back a long time to the Workers' Educational Association and Tawney was often called upon to assist with Labour manifestos. He may have prejudiced Attlee's view of Citrine's exploits.

64 *Ibid.*, pp. xvii–xviii. All the following references have been checked at the National Archives in the Foreign Office files and many others added. They are published here in accordance with the Open Government Licence of Crown Copyright material.

65 Winter, introduction to *The American Labour Movement*, p. xvii, described it as 'a highly critical report' by Halifax.

66 His full report is in F.O.371.30701. A9103, *The American Labour Movement*. See also F.O.371.30676. A7044.

67 F.O.37000.A5826, Neville Butler from the Washington embassy, 9.8.42.

68 F.O.371. 30701.A9091, Harold Butler, Foreign Office, 1.10.1942.

69 F.O. 371.30700. A7518, Sir Ronnie Campbell, Head of the Washington embassy to the foreign secretary, 12.8.1942 (copied to Bevin and Attlee).

70 A Mr McDonnell from the embassy on 22.9.42 wrote that 'a pig-headed man like Citrine can be in a position to do such harm', whereas 'old man Tawney' was a 'dear old boy'. F.O.371.30701. A9072.

71 Tawney, *The American Labour Movement*, p. 84.

72 Citrine, *Two Careers*, p. 147.

73 Another official said, 'Murray spoke for nearly an hour without stopping', F.O. 371.30701.A8866.

74 Harold Butler, Foreign Office to Major Attlee, 19.8.42. F.O. 371.30700. A7352.

75 F.O.371.37000.A7378, Eden note, 13.8.42.

76 F.O. 371.30700.A8044, 31.8.42. Winter, introduction to *The American Labour Movement*, p. xxi.

77 Foreign Office Correspondence Index 1942, vol. 93, 1, pp. 612 onwards. F.O371/34097–8; 371/30652-4; F.O371/30676 and F.O371/30700-2.

78 Winter, introduction to *The American Labour Movement*, p. xx.

79 Citrine to Grant MacKenzie at the embassy, 24.9.42. F.O.371.30701. A9091. MacKenzie had been Attlee's personal secretary from 1940, and was then in the British Information Service in Washington.

80 *Ibid.*

81 F.O.371.30701.A524, 11.9.42

82 Winter, introduction to *The American Labour Movement*, p. xxi.

83 Eden's officials to Halifax, 22.10.42. F.O.371.30702.A9525.

84 Van Goethem, 'Labor's Second Front', p. 677.

85 Citrine, *Two Careers*, p. 153.

86 *Ibid.*, p. 152.

87 *Ibid.*, p. 153.

88 Weiler, *British Labour and the Cold War*, pp. 77–8.

89 Citrine, *Two Careers*, p. 237. See Adonis, *Ernest Bevin, Labour's Churchill*, chapter 9, 'Stalin', pp. 233–92.

90 *Ibid.*, pp. 231–2.

91 Citrine, *Men and Work*, p. 237.

92 Adonis, *Ernest Bevin, Labour's Churchill*, pp. 250–60.

93 *Ibid.*, pp. 237–8.

94 *Ibid.*, p. 231.

95 Van Goethem, 'Labor's Second Front', p. 673.

96 F.O.371. 30700.A4657. Eden to Bevin, 27 May 1942. Eden said that he had first raised the matter of Tawney's ineffectiveness with him on 3 October.

97 Van Goethem thought it was Eden who drafted them. 'Bevin's Boys Abroad', p. 4.

98 F.O.371. 30701.A8502, 14 September 1942.

99 F.O.371. 30702.A9249, Ministry of Labour to the Foreign Office, 7.10.42.

100 F.O.371.30701.A8828, 1.9.42.

101 F.O. 371.30700 point 3. Foreign Office, 28.9.1942, CS King 'to Private Secretary for Mr Bevin, after Cabinet meets'. King discusses the wording entirely having regard to Bevin's sensitivities.

102 F.O.371.30702.A11825, Harold Butler F.O. to Sir Ronnie Campbell (Embassy Head).

103 A former ILO director general, well known to Bevin from his days there, he was sent to London by Roosevelt in 1941, and in 1942 took the Foreign Office's side and disparaged Citrine as an 'overzealous obstetrician' (F.O.371.30700.A7518).

104 Bullock, *Bevin*, vol. I, *Trade Union Leader*, pp. 407–10, 557–8 and others.

105 SFO.371.37000.A4137.

106 Bryn Roberts (1897–1964) had been one of the South Wales Miners' Federation/Plebs League syndicalists. Thomas-Symonds, *Nye*, pp. 33 and 51.

107 Frederick John Tanner (1889–1965), a former leading syndicalist and communist.

108 TUC Annual Report, 1943, p. 288.

109 Roberts' article for *The Daily Telegraph*, 'British Unions and America's Labour Rivalries', 19 December 1942.

110 F.O. 371.30702.A9525. Viscount Halifax to the Foreign Office, 6 November 1942, all under the auspices of the embassy and Ministry of Labour attaché (Gordon remained on the latter's establishment).

111 *Ibid.*, Murray to Bevin, 19 October 1942.

112 Citrine's Report to Congress, TUC Annual Report, pp. 239–45, at p. 244.

113 Schevenels, *Forty-Five Years: International Federation of Trade Unions 1901–1945*, by the former general secretary with foreword by Lord Citrine (Brussels, 1956), pp. 91–8.

114 Minister's (Nine Point) Statement made to the British delegation to the ILO Conference 31 March 1944. Churchill Centre Archive, Bevin papers 3/2; Citrine, *Two Careers*, p. 183.

115 Bullock, *Bevin*, vol. I, *Trade Union Leader*, pp. 506–8. It was there that Bevin strengthened his relationship with Frederick Leggett, who would become one of his key officers in the Ministry of Labour during the war.

116 Citrine, *Two Careers*, p. 182.

117 Bevin to Churchill, 16 May 1944. Churchill Archive Centre, Bevin papers 3/1.

118 *Ibid.*

119 Professor Van Goethem to the author, 9 November 2020, commenting on this chapter.

120 Citrine, *Two Careers*, p. 183.

121 *Ibid.*

122 See Chapter 12, and Thomas-Symonds, *Nye*, pp. 115–17.

123 Bevin Papers, The Churchill Archive, CHAR 20/137C/273–5.

124 Taylor, *The TUC*, pp. 92–3. Attlee sacrificed Greenwood but enhanced his own status as deputy prime minister. Bew, *Citizen Clem*, pp. 280–1.

125 *Ibid.*, pp. 93–4 and 97. After receiving his report on skilled manpower in 1941, which he didn't like (see Chapter 12), Bevin had Beveridge shifted.

126 *Ibid.*, pp. 97–8.

127 Citrine, *Two Careers*, pp. 241–2. Citrine would keep a keen interest in the unions' influence on government 'full employment' and relations with Labour governments as late as 1966, as we shall see.

128 Bevin Papers 3/2, The Churchill Archives, Bevin to Lord Halifax, 28 March 1944. Presumably he meant the breach between the AFL and the CIO.

129 Citrine, *Two Careers*, pp. 187–8. Churchill had expressed similar sentiments.

130 *Ibid.*, pp. 186–90.

131 Wikipedia. Of the 3,590 prisoners known to have been imprisoned at Breendonk, 303 died or were executed within the fort itself but as many as 1,741 died subsequently in other camps before the end of the war.

132 Citrine, *Two Careers*, pp. 210–18.

133 Michael Foot's *Aneurin Bevan*, vol. I, p. 480, confirms this.

134 This was the conference where Bevin was put up (not Attlee) to face the strong left opposition to the takeover. With the aid of the unions, he saw off Nye Bevan's attack. Lord Adonis, rehashing Bullock's account (*Bevin, Minister of Labour*, pp. 341–7) in his *Ernest Bevin, Labour's Churchill*, pp. 211–14, gives Bevin all the credit for a speech, 'though not directly involved in these events', as Citrine was.

135 *Ibid.*, p. 210.

136 Citrine, *Two Careers*, p. 211.

137 *Ibid.*, p. 213.

138 *Ibid.*, p. 214. Even Foot acknowledged the 'undoubtedly ruthless methods of E.L.A.S.' *Aneurin Bevan*, p. 483.

139 *Ibid.*, pp. 215–18. Beaverbrook urged Citrine to complain, but he wouldn't.

140 *Ibid.*, p. 353.
141 *The Second World War Diary of Hugh Dalton*, entry for 1 September 1944, p. 783. Bowerman (a Labour MP as well as secretary of the TUC, 1911–23), was the last part-timer! His successor, as we saw in Chapter 4, Fred Bramley (the first full-time secretary, 1923–5), spent much of his time on international business even without a war.
142 *Ibid.*, p. 224.
143 Van Goethem, 'Labor's Second Front', pp. 678–80.
144 Adonis, *Ernest Bevin, Labour's Churchill*, pp. 233–40.
145 Citrine, *Two Careers*, pp. 226–7.
146 *Ibid.*
147 Attlee reported the row to Eden on 27 April 1945, The Churchill Papers, CHAR 20/216/73.
148 Evans, *Bevin*, p. 65.
149 *Ibid.*
150 *The Second World War Diary of Hugh Dalton*, p. 838.
151 Citrine, *Two Careers*, p. 227.
152 Donoghue and Jones, *Herbert Morrison*, p. 345. They included Morrison and Beaverbrook and 'many lesser trade unionists who had crossed his path'.
153 Taylor, *The TUC*, p. 273. The title of Lord Adonis' book, *Ernest Bevin, Labour's Churchill*, recalls this description.
154 *Ibid.*, p. 228.
155 Bullock, *Bevin*, vol. II, *Minister of Labour*, pp. 372–4.
156 Taylor, *The TUC*, p. 100.
157 *Ibid.*, p. 390.
158 Beckett, *Clem Attlee*, p. 198.
159 Trades Union Congress Annual Report 1945, po. 263. Taylor, *The TUC*, p. 77.

Chapter 14
1 Citrine, *Two Careers*, p. 250.
2 *Ibid.*, p. 245.
3 *Ibid.*
4 *Ibid.*, pp. 92–5.
5 *Ibid.*, p. 245.
6 *Ibid.*, p. 247. Arthur Horner, his old communist adversary, now secretary of the renamed National Union of Mineworkers, confirmed that 'he [Citrine] also had to undergo many heart-searchings before he agreed, but took the view that the trade union movement must play its part [in the nationalisation programme]', Horner, *Incorrigible Rebel*, p. 180.
7 *Ibid.*, p. 248.
8 *Ibid.*
9 *Ibid.*, p. 250.
10 TUC Congress Report, 1946, p. 269.
11 *Ibid.*
12 Citrine, *Two Careers*, p. 252. See Chapter 15.
13 'The Arms of Lord Citrine', courtesy of the College of Arms. My thanks to their archivists.
14 Horner, *Incorrigible Rebel*, pp. 182–3 and 195–6.
15 Citrine, *Two Careers*, pp. 251–2.
16 Horner, *Incorrigible Rebel*, p. 202.
17 *Ibid.*
18 Citrine, *Men and Work*, p. 133.
19 Shinwell was moved from the Ministry of Fuel and Power in October 1947, to be replaced by his PPS, Hugh Gaitskell MP (1906–63), a career politician who had less affinity with Citrine. Gaitskell stayed in that ministerial position for over two years, lunching regularly with Citrine. Although initially dubious about Citrine's fitness for the job, he came to be 'much impressed by his determination and firmness' during the big electricity strike of 1950.

Gaitskell was Chancellor of the Exchequer in 1950–51, and later leader of the Labour Party until his untimely death in 1963. *The Diary of Hugh Gaitskell 1945–1956*, ed. Philip Williams (Jonathan Cape, 1983), p. 159.

20 It was the historian Hugh Clegg who surmised that in 1946, Shinwell, on Attlee's authority, 'assured him that provided he joined the Coal Board, he could rely on being appointed chairman of British Electricity Authority, when electricity was nationalized – as in fact, he was'. Clegg, *A History*, vol. III, *1934–1951*, p. 318. But that was conjecture on Clegg's part, perhaps from Gaitskell's ambiguous diary entry (n. 21).

21 Gaitskell wrote, 'I could not help feeling that it was perhaps a mistake to have taken him out of the T.U.C. … he will not get used to running such a vast organisation compared with the T.U.C.' That is open to different interpretation, and in any case, Gaitskell added, 'I think he will do well.' *The Diary of Hugh Gaitskell*, p. 50.

22 Citrine, *Two Careers*, p. 255.

23 *Ibid.*, p. 254.

24 Citrine, *Trade Union Law*. TUC legal adviser, 1946–51.

25 *Ibid.*, p. 255.

26 *Ibid.*

27 *Ibid.*, p. 262.

28 *Ibid.*, pp. 348 and 250.

29 Leslie Hannah, *Engineers, Managers and Politicians: The First Fifteen Years of Nationalised Electricity Supply in Britain* (The Electricity Council, 1982), p. 7.

30 *Ibid.*, p. 3.

31 *Ibid.*, p. 1. About a third still lacked a supply at the outbreak of the war and the new BEA under Citrine prioritised extending its supply to rural parts.

32 *Ibid.*, p. 10.

33 Citrine, *Two Careers*, p. 266. Sir Henry Self (1890–1975) first impressed Citrine in 1940, when he was visiting US war factories making planes and munitions for the British war effort. Self was in America as director general of the British Air Commission, there to procure the best aircraft and munitions for the RAF. Back in Britain, they bumped into each other when Citrine chaired the Advisory Committee of the Ministry of Aircraft Production (see Chapter 12). Securing Self's services for BEA was one of Citrine's strategic successes. Citrine, *Two Careers*, p. 268.

34 *Ibid.*, p. 266.

35 Hannah, *Engineers, Managers and Politicians*, p. 21.

36 The BEA was first absorbed by the Central Electricity Authority in 1955 and then by the Electricity Council Central Electricity Generating Board in 1958. The industry was split in three and privatised in the 1980s.

37 Horner, *Incorrigible Rebel*, pp. 179–80.

38 Citrine, *Two Careers*, p. 268.

39 *Ibid.*, pp. 273–4.

40 First Electricity Industry Annual Report 1950, Hansard, 25 July 1950, vol. 478, pp. 329–68.

41 *Ibid.*, p. 365.

42 Citrine, *Two Careers*, pp. 296–7. He recalled an interview with Prime Minister Clement Attlee, having impressed on him 'how desperately short of plant capacity we were to carry on essential work'.

However, Attlee 'seemed to me to be terribly tired, almost to the point of exhaustion', and so, 'I made no impression upon him whatever.' Citrine, *Two Careers*, p. 297. Attlee supported Gaitskell in that tussle.

43 *The Diary of Hugh Gaitskell*, pp. 78–9.

44 *Ibid.*

45 Citrine, *Two Careers*, pp. 359–61.

46 *Ibid.*, opposite p. 241 and pp. 302–3.

47 *Ibid.*, p. 347.

48 *Ibid.*, p. 263.

49 *The Diary of Hugh Gaitskell*, ed., Williams, p. 50.

50 For the full list in date order, see Wikipedia, 'Attlee Ministry'.

51 Baron Herbert Morrison (1888–1965), Labour MP and minister of transport, 1929–31. Then leader of the London County Council in the 1930s and MP again from 1935. Home secretary, 1940–45, and responsible for Labour's 1945 election campaign victory. Lost a challenge to Attlee for leader but became deputy prime minister, responsible for Labour's nationalisation programme, 1946–51. Friendly with Citrine throughout, who favoured him for leader.

52 Bullock, *Bevin*, vol. I, *Trade Union Leader*, pp. 514–15.

53 Hannah, *Engineers, Managers and Politicians*, pp. 262–4.

54 Hugh Gaitskell (1906–1963). Ironically, his first experience of a wider Labour movement involvement was in 1934, when, at Citrine's TUC/IFTU request, he supervised the administration of relief funds for the Viennese workers. Citrine, *Men and Work*, p. 347.

55 Hannah, *Engineers, Managers and Politicians*, pp. 10–11.

56 *Ibid.*, p. 19.

57 Citrine, *Two Careers*, pp. 259 and 266. By 1967, the number of employees had grown to 228,000 (ibid., p. 290); Hannah, *Engineers, Managers and Politicians*, pp. 13 and 15.

58 *Ibid.*, pp. 281–2.

59 *Ibid.*, p. 282.

60 *Ibid.*, p. 283. The writer, as a young T&GWU pensions officer, who negotiated many occupational pension schemes for manual workers in the 1970s, was particularly impressed by the Electricity Council's schemes for all its workers.

61 Citrine, *Two Careers*, pp. 289–90.

62 Hansard, House of Commons, vol. 478, p. 357.

63 Citrine, *Two Careers*, p. 293.

64 *Ibid.*, p. 283.

65 *Ibid.*, p. 284.

66 Frank Foulkes (1899–?), president of the ETU until 1961, when he was forced out of office by a court judgement which found widespread ballot-rigging for the general secretary's post in 1959. A rare occasion when the TUC acted to discipline an affiliate. Lloyd, *Light and Liberty*, gives the background in chapters 18 to 21.

67 *Ibid.*

68 *Ibid.*, p. 285.

69 *The Diary of Hugh Gaitskell*, pp. 158–9.

70 *Ibid.*, editorial note, p. 159. Citrine would have known the power station scene well from his early days on Merseyside and in London as the ETU executive 'trouble-shooter' in 1921 (see Chapter 3). He probably also had inside information at that time from Foulkes and power station representatives.

71 Gaitskell became Chancellor of the Exchequer in 1950–51 and leader of the Labour Party after Attlee in 1955. Tragically, he died in 1963 before realising his full potential.

72 Hannah, *Engineers, Managers and Politicians*, p. 11.

73 *The Diary of Hugh Gaitskell*, p. 50.

74 Hannah, *Engineers, Managers and Politicians*, p. 16.

75 *Ibid.*

76 *Ibid.*, pp. 12 and 15.

77 Citrine, *Two Careers*, p. 373.

78 *Ibid.*, p. 372.

Chapter 15

1 Citrine, *Two Careers*, pp. 359–60; Hansard 1803–2005, 29 October 1959, House of Lords debate, vol. 219, cc 137–238.

2 Norman (1913–1997), a practising solicitor at the TUC and in Brixham, Devon, took the title on his father's death in 1983. His other son, Ronald (1919– 2011), became the 3rd Baron in 1997, but he emigrated to New Zealand and didn't use the title. As neither had heirs, the title then died. Because of his long absences from home (Harrow and Wembley) as they were growing up, relations with their father seemed strained.

3 Citrine, *Two Careers*, p. 357. Morrison joined Citrine in the Lords. Seated in front of Citrine, his eyesight was so poor that Citrine had to tell him the time on the Lords clock. Ibid., p. 356.

4 Citrine's generous appraisal of Morrison, *Two Careers*, pp. 356–7.

5 Peter Ackers, 'Saving Social Democracy? Hugh Clegg and the Post-War Programme to Reform British Workplace Industrial Relations: Too Little, Too Late?',

in *Social Movements and the Change of Economic Elites in Europe after 1945*, Palgrave Studies in the History of Social Movements, eds Stefan Berger and Marcel Boldorf (Palgrave Macmillan, 2018), pp. 257–77.

6 Hansard, 29 October 1959, vol. 219, cc 164–9.

7 *Ibid.*

8 This was at the time when the issue of communist control of the ETU was being litigated in the courts, with much press attention, over the exposure of ballot-rigging. Citrine doesn't mention it in his autobiography, though he probably watched it with interest, knowing many of those concerned, like Frank Foulkes (see Chapter 14).

9 Bill Carron (1902–1969), Baron Carron of Hull, a leading right-wing post-war union leader – AEU (1956–67) and TUC General Council (1954–68). Although he served the TUC after Citrine's departure, they probably knew each other from the UKAEA, on whose board they both served.

10 Hansard, House of Lords sitting, 9 November 1960, vol. 226, cc 397–8.

11 *Ibid.*, 25 October 1960, House of Lords debate 25, vol. 225, cc 1001–85.

12 *Ibid.*, cc 1025–8.

13 Sir Harold Vincent Tewson (1898– 1981), a life-long union staffer since leaving school in Bradford (Dyers' and Bleachers' Amalgamated Society and a member of the ILP). He was award the Military Cross as a lieutenant in the West Yorkshire Regiment for 'gallantry and devotion to duty' during one attack. He rejoined the Dyers and Bleachers after the war and was

appointed as organisation secretary at TUC in 1925. This started a long association with Citrine, Tewson becoming assistant general secretary in 1931. They worked closely throughout Citrine's rise to fame and authority, with Tewson ably deputising for the general secretary on his many absences on national and international business until 1946, when Tewson became general secretary. He was not so successful in stepping up to that role, perhaps due to changes in the governing General Council relationships – perhaps due to the large unions' (e.g., Arthur Deakin of the T&GWU) greater assertiveness and his more low-profile character. He retired in 1960.

14 *Ibid.*
15 Citrine, *Men and Work*, p. 238.
16 *Ibid.*, p. 241.
17 Hansard, House of Lords sitting, 8 May 1962, vol. 240, cc 103–214.
18 *Ibid.*, 1 August 1962, vol. 243, cc 292–338.
19 *Ibid.*, 11 February 1971, vol. 315, cc 262–8.
20 *Ibid.*, 10 August 1972, vol. 334, at cc 1297–8 to 1300.
21 The *Herald Express*, Torbay, carried an item on 20 January 1978, 'New Life in Brixham at 90 for ex-TUC Giant', saying that he 'had moved out of his son's plush Brixham home to a small cottage with a family to live'.

Epilogue

1 Citrine, *Two Careers*, p. 363, and see Chapter 1.
2 Trevor Evans' *Bevin* appeared in 1948 and Francis Williams' *Portrait of a Great Englishman* in 1952. Williams was the pre-war *Daily*

Herald editor and Attlee's wartime public relations man.
3 Both comments appeared on the flyleaf of *Two Careers* in 1967.
4 As we have already noted, the late Robert Taylor did a couple of chapters in his *The TUC* in 2000, and Neil Riddell also wrote a learned article in *History* that same year.
5 The writer is most grateful to the staff of all these archives for their assistance and permission to reference Citrine's material and photos.
6 Fishman, *Arthur Horner*, vol. I, p. 38.
7 The late Robert Taylor (who sadly died in August 2020) started the processwith his study of the TUC, and at the same time (2000), Dr Neil Riddell's *Walter Citrine 1925–1945* reinforced it. Dr Jonathan Davis' article on Citrine's first visit to the Soviet Union (see Introduction, n. 14, for full details of their work) also helped.
8 See Chapter 8.
9 Cover sleeve of *Two Careers*.
10 Lewis Minkin, *The Contentious Alliance: Trade Unions and the Labour Party* (Edinburgh University Press, 1991).
11 Wikipedia, 'Sir Vincent Tewson'. He and his wife also organised a committee in Barnet that involved forty organisations, including 'three churches, each political party, the Odd Fellows, the British Legion and several others', all of which agreed to support individual Basque children financially. The Tewsons helped to run the Barnet home until 1946. Sir Vincent was made an OBE in 1942.
12 Citrine, *Men and Work*, pp. 329–37.
13 In an anniversary of the founding

of the TUC commemorative
book in 1938, *Seventy Years of
Trade Unionism, 1868–1938* (TUC
Publications, HD6661), he
devoted an entire section on his
meeting with a number of the
key women trade union leaders
which highlighted their immense
contribution.

14 Bullock, *Bevin*, vol. I, *Trade Union
Leader*, p. 401.

INDEX

Page numbers in *italic* refer to illustrations. A topic reference in **bold** refer to the corresponding topic heading within the main entry for Walter Citrine ('Citrine, Walter McLennan'), who is referred to elsewhere in the index by the abbreviation 'WMC'. Publications (shown in *italic*) by Walter Citrine are listed in his main entry under **Writings**. Publications not by Walter Citrine are listed under their own main entries by title, followed by the author(s) name(s) in brackets.

ABC of Chairmanship (1939). *See* writings
ABC of Trade Unionism for Colonial
    Unions (TUC) 178
Abdication of Edward VIII (1936-37)
    167, 172
Abyssinia. *See* Ethiopia
activism. *See* Electrical Trades Union;
    strikes
Adonis, Andrew Adonis, Baron 4, 60,
    83, 134, 154
Albert Hall (London) 45, 172
All-Union Central Council of Trade
    Unions. *See* USSR
Allgemeiner Deutscher
    Gewerkschaftsbund 158, 160–161
Amalgamated Engineering Union 77
American Federation of Labor 1, 171,
    172, 204, 206, 223, 231, 233, 239,
    241–248, 252, 257
Anderson, Sir John 218–219
Anglo-Russian Joint Advisory
    Committee. *See* TUC
Anglo-Soviet Trade Union Committee
    (ASTUC) 234, 236–238, 240–242
Anti-Cigarette League 9
appeasement, WMC opposes 178–182
Atomic Energy Authority, WMC part-
    time Board member (1958) 278
Attlee, Clement 120, 157, 166, 167,
    173, 175, 181, 201, 202, 214,
    220–221, 221, 226–230, 244, 246,
    262, 263, 266, 268, 271, 299, 307

autobiography. *See* writings

Baldwin, Stanley 54, 70, 74, 85, 88,
    115–116, 154, 172, 174, 175, 195
Ball, Jack 29, 37
BEA. *See* British Electricity Authority
Beard, John 138
Beaverbrook, Max Aitken, 1st Baron
    154, 219–222, 227, 237, 306
Beckett, Francis 228
Beeching Report (1962) 294
Bell, Richard 112
Berlin Olympic Games (1936) 172
Bevan, Aneurin (Nye) 4, 104, 164,
    168–170, 176, 195, 216, 222–226
Beveridge Report (1942) 256, 266
Beveridge, William Beveridge, Lord
    215, 256, 293
Bevin, Ernest: actions under
    Emergency Powers Act 1940 212;
    admires Samuel Gompers 58; anti-
    fascism 170; anti-Soviet policy 249;
    attacks Lansbury's 'hypocrisy' (1936)
    174; attends Economic Advisory
    Council 142; believes in industrial
    action for political ends 80; Bevan
    criticises 217; against Beveridge
    Report 256; Bevin Boys (1944) 222;
    biographies 4, 61, 83, 215, 262,
    300; at Brighton TUC Congress
    (1933) *210*; changeable moods
    210–211; Christian influence 131;

'Churchill of the proletariat' 219, 263, 300; Churchill's closeness to 253; complains to Churchill about WMC 254; complementarity with WMC 132; compliments WMC's speeches 32; 'containment' strategy towards USSR 261; creation of TUC General Council 58; *Daily Herald* vice-chair 155; Deakins's closeness to 252; death (1951) 300; demobilisation plans 255–256; derides Trade Disputes and Trade Union Act 1927 118; dislikes MacDonald 59–60, 146, 150, 153; dislikes Snowden 152–153; dispute with WMC over skilled labour conscription policy (1941) 212–216; economic policy ideas 154; Eden's closeness to 251; encourage wartime collective bargaining 206; encourages Attlee to become Prime Minister 264; establishes Labour Supply Board (1940) 209; Foreign Secretary (1945) 226; forms Transport and General Workers' Union (1922) 58; friendships 133; General Strike (1926) 76, 82, 83–85, 87, 302, 303; handling of wartime industrial disputes (1942-44) 222–225; 'involuntary partnership' with WMC described 128–135; involvement in wartime UK/ US trade union matters 250–265; jealous of WMC's Privy Councillor status 203; joins TUC General Council 61, 78; Keynes's influence on 143–144, 153; libel award against Workers Press (1927) 109; loyalty to Attlee 220, 227, 228, 229; Macmillan Committee 143–145; on mass use of union power 60–61; meets WMC (1919) 128; militancy 58–59; and Walter Milne-Bailey 144–145; Minister of Labour and National Service (1940) 202, 204, 208, 304, 306; Mond-Turner Talks

(1927-29) 121, 126–127; MP for Central Wandsworth (1940) 202; 'Napoleon' Bevin 61; National Joint Council member (1932) 157, 228; and nationalisation programme 279–280; *New Clarion* chair 155; opposes Ministry of Production (1942) 220; opposes Trades Councils 100; overshadows WMC in labour movement history 4, 299; physique 128; political positioning on rearmament (1935-36) 174–176; political role during World War 2 218–219; possibly appropriates WMC's ideas for TUC reform 43; 'Quisling' incident and WMC 213–215; recommends Archibald Gordon as labour relations adviser in US (1942) 251; recommends Richard Tawney as Lord Halifax's labour affairs adviser 244, 246, 247; refuses MacDonald's offer of knighthood (1935) 197; refuses MacDonald's offer of peerage 142–143; Regulation 1AA (1944) 224–225, 255; resents WMC's access to Churchill 260; and second Labour government (1929-31) 141–147, 150–156; 'Sir Walter' jibe at WMC 198, 200; Skidelsky's assessment of 155; Society for Socialist Inquiry and Propaganda chair (1931) 145–146, 155, 218; Spanish Civil War 177; stands for Parliament for Gateshead (1931) 155, 218; start of Attlee-Bevin ascendence (1942) 222; supports Attlee as Labour Leader 175; supports Attlee on trade union law reform (1943) 120; supports WMC against National Minority Movement 101, 106; syndicalism 58; takes credit for others' work 130; takes credit for repeal of 1927 Act 120; Trade Disputes and Trade Union Act 1927 120; Trade Disputes and Trade Union (Amendment)

Bill 1930 138–139; TUC Economic Committee member (1930) 144–145; War Cabinet (1940) 211–212, 218; wartime disputes with Lord Beaverbrook (1941-42) 219–222; WMC's respect 61, 211; works with WMC on Mond-Turner Talks 121, 127; World War 2 relationship with WMC 208–230, 307

Bevin, Florence 128

Bew, J. 228

Birkenhead Borough Brass Band 16–17

'Black Book' 204

Blatchford, Robert 11

Bolshevik Revolution (1917). See USSR

Bolton, W. J. 66

Bondfield, Margaret 40, 54, 55, 141, 147–148

Bowerman, Charles 260

Bowman, Jim 270

Bradwell nuclear power station 278

Bramley, Fred 11, 17, 48, 51, 52–53, 55–56, 57, 61, 62, 63, 64, 72, 78, 93–94, 99

brass bands 16–17

Brett, Tom 11

British Electricity Authority, WMC's career: accepts Chair from Attlee (1946) 271; achievements 274–285; achievements assessed 307; approach to nationalisation 284–285; 'consultation' approach 281–282; establishment of BEA (1948) 276; first Annual Report (1950) 276, 282; hailed as 'father of our industry in its present form' 285; loves job 272–273; nationalisation programme 278–280; nuclear power station programme 278; opens Yorkshire Electricity Board HQ (1950) 279; organisational reform 274–275; part-time Board member (1958) 275, 285; relationship with Gaitskell 277, 283–284; retirement (1962) 285; Shinwell recommends

for chair 272; unofficial strikes (1949-50) 282–283; winter of 1946-47 275–276

Brixham (Devon), WMC moves to (1973) 298

Bromley, John 76, 85

Brown Free Library (Liverpool) 14

Brownlie, J. T. 126, 127

Bullock, Alan Bullock, Baron 60, 76, 78, 83, 87, 130, 132, 134, 146, 155, 156, 169, 210, 217, 224, 300, 301

Bussey, Ernest 280–281

Bustamante, Alexander 178

Butler, Harold 246

Caballero, Francisco Largo 176

Calder Hall nuclear power station 278

Cammell Laird shipbuilders 21, 22

Campbell, John 100, 196

Campbell-Bannerman, Sir Henry 112

Can Socialism Come by Democratic Methods? (Cripps) 167

Canada, WMC tours (1940) 1–2, 231–234

Caribbean colonies, working conditions in. See Moyne Commission

Carr, E. H. 194

Carron, William 291

Carter, Sir George 21

Chamberlain, Neville 178–180, 204–205, 211

Christianity. See Bevin, Ernest;
Character and Attributes

Churchill, Winston: agrees with Stalin on Greece 259; Beaverbrook and 220; Bevin resents WMC's access to 260; Bevin complains about WMC 254; Bevin's influence on 253; biographies 300; 'containment' strategy towards USSR 261; delays Second Front 235, 237, 239; Eden briefs on relations with US trade unions (1942) 246; establishes Ministry of Production (1942) 220–221; General Strike (1926) 71, 74, 82; good relationship with

WMC 203; introduces WMC to Roosevelt 1–2, 134, 232, 233–234, 265; invites WMC to be Privy Councillor 202–203, 306; Matthew Woll cables after speech by WMC 233; meets Soviet trade union delegation (1941-42) 238; memory 203; persuades WMC to lead TUC delegation to Greece 258–260; rallies the country during World War 2 304; return to Gold Standard (1925) 69, 143; supports Bevin on demobilisation plans 255–256; supports Edward VIII 172; supports RAF expansion 227; supports wartime consultation with TUC 206; Trade Disputes and Trade Union Act 1927 116, 119–120, 229; War Cabinet 202; warns against Nazism 4, 172; WMC briefs on 1941 Moscow visit 237; WMC discloses role in Bevin's War Cabinet appointment (1952) 211–212; WMC discusses reform of 1927 Act 119–120; WMC's consistency compared with 175; and WMC's wartime reputation 250

cigarettes 9

CIO. *See* Congress of Industrial Organisations

Cirtini, Francisco (WMC's grandfather) 8

Cirtini family (WMC's Italian ancestors) 8

Citrine, Alfred (WMC's father) 8

Citrine, Doris (WMC's wife) 2, 8, 10, 13–14, 44, 89, 171, 172, 178, 185, 190, 191, 259, 272–273

Citrine, Isabella (née McLellan) (WMC's mother) 9

Citrine, Norman, 2nd Baron Citrine (WMC's elder son) 3, 8, 10, 44, 272–273, 286, 298

Citrine, Ronnie, 3rd Baron Citrine, (WMC's younger son) 3, 272–273, 286

Citrine, Walter McLennan (Sir Walter Citrine from 1935; 1st Baron Citrine of Wembley from 1946)

— **Importance, Achievements and Legacy**: assessment of 299–308; biographer's approach to 5; Bullock's assessment of 301; contribution to trade union movement 301–303; credit from historians 5; lack of recognition from Labour movement 3–4; no previous biographies 300; place in history 308–309

— **Formative Years (1887-1913)**: birth and birthplace 7; childhood employment 8; Christian influence 9; cultural development 14–15; electrical trade 10–17; engaged to Doris Slade (1912) 14; exposure to Marxism 11; Italian ancestry 8; learns electrical theory 13–14; marries Doris Slade (1913) 10; at Picton Reading Room (Liverpool) 14, *15*; school 8; seeks to start seagoing career 9–10; sickliness and recovery 8–9, 299; Socialist sympathies 11–12; trade unionism 16–17; unemployment 13, 14; witnesses Maypole Colliery disaster (1908) 271

— **Family And Personal Life**: aunt. *See* McLellan, Catherine; birth (1887) 7, 299; children. *See* Citrine, Norman; Citrine, Ronnie; death (1983) 10; dog. *See* Rex; family background 8; family homes 8, 10, 34, 198, 298; family incidence of TB 9, 299; father. *See* Citrine, Alfred; grandfather. *See* Cirtini, Francisco; married (1913) 10; mother. *See* Citrine, Isabella; seafaring tradition 10; siblings 7, 299; widowed (1973) 298; wife. *See* Citrine, Doris

— **Character and Attributes**: administrative capability 35; ambition 26; ankle weakness 25; approach to union activism 20–26;

assertiveness 12; Beatrice Webb's description 89–91; Bevan's jibes 4, 225–226; broad vision and perspective 3; Christian influence on 9; consistency 175; cultural interests 14–16, 32, 197; financial and legal skills 20–21; good health in later life 283, 298; health regime 299; idealism 26; illnesses 8–9, *136*, 142, 144, 147, 155, 238, 299, 303; interest in palmistry and phrenology 10; lexicography 14; memory 203; musicianship 16–17; negotiation skills 26–27; non-sectarianism 10; non-smoker 9; philosophy on life 270; physique 128; prescience 4; self-analysis and self-awareness 8–9; shorthand skill 43–44; his source of authority 134–135; speechmaking skill 2; stamina 238; tenor voice 17, 23, 24; trade union law expertise 110; work ethic 25

— **Political Views**: anti-communism. *See below* **Anti-Communism**; anti-dictatorship 166; anti-Fascism. *See below* **Anti-Fascism**; constitutional monarchy 167; industrial relations 121–123; opposition to World War I 27; political action secondary to industrial action 42, 80; pro-democracy 4, 166–168; syndicalism 19, 42

— **Labour Party**: addresses Parliamentary Labour Party (1924) 62–64; early activism 12; involvement in 157; joins Labour Party and ILP (1906) 11; not interested in joining 1945 Cabinet 266; parliamentary candidate for Wallasey (Cheshire) (1918) 9, 30–31, 42, 305; Socialist sympathies 11–12; wartime reputation 250

— **Trade Union Career** (1911-46): chooses union career 301; contribution to trade union movement 301; Electrical Trades Union (1911-23). *See* Electrical Trades Union; Federation of Engineering and Shipbuilding Trades (1919-24). *See* Federation of Engineering and Shipbuilding Trades; IFTU (1928-45). *See* International Federation of Trade Unions; Mond-Turner Talks. *See* Mond-Turner Talks; trade union law. *See* trade union law; TUC (1924-46). *See* TUC

— **World War 1 (1914-18)**: exemption from war service 27; opposes diluted labour 27–28; opposition to 27; union activities 27–29

— **General Strike (1926)**. *See* General Strike (1926)

— **Anti-Communism**: Anglo-Russian Joint Advisory Committee (ARJAC) joint secretary (1925) 93–94; asserts Communist responsibility for Nazism's rise 163; attitude to Communist trade unionists 104; characterises 'dictatorship of the proletariat' as denial of democracy and liberty 164; 'communistic' sympathies alleged by Beatrice Webb 53, 63; discontinues TUC Anglo-Russian Committee (1927) 96, 98; early enthusiasm for Russian Revolution 4, 92; early exposure to Marxism 11; greets USSR trade delegation (1924) 61–62, 92–93; highlights dictatorial similarity of Communist practices to Fascism 166; House of Lords maiden speech (1959) 289–291; likens USSR to State Capitalism 190; nuanced anti-communism 4; opposes National Minority Movement 99–109; Soviet's dislike of WMC 97; start of prolonged Communist attacks 108; visits USSR (1925) 94–96, 164, 183; visits USSR (1935) 183–196

— **Anti-Fascism**: analysis of fascism 167–168; anti-appeasement stance 178–182; contribution assessed

303–304, 305 International Federation of Trade Unions. *See* International Federation of Trade Unions; pro-Jewish stance 171–173; pro-rearmament stance 173–176; Spanish Civil War 176–177, 305; visits Austria (1934) 170

— **World War 2 (1939-45)**. *See* World War 2 (1939-45), WMC and

— **Postwar Career (1945-62)**: Atomic Energy Authority, part-time Board member (1958) 278; Central Electricity Authority (1947-57). *See* Central Electricity Authority; depression and recovery 266; National Coal Board (1946-47). *See* National Coal Board; not interested in Cabinet post (1945) 266

— **House Of Lords (1959-72)**. *See* House of Lords

— **Awards And Honours**: coat of arms 269–270; knighthood (1935) 173, 197–200; motto 270; peerage (1946) 268–270; Privy Councillor (1940) 202–203, 304, 306; refuses MacDonald's offer of peerage (1930) 142–143, 197; refuses offer of knighthood (1932) 197

— **Relationships**: Clement Attlee 226–230; Lord Beaverbrook 221–222; Aneurin Bevan 4, 168–169, 225; Ernest Bevin. *See* Bevin, Ernest; Alexander Bustamante 178; Neville Chamberlain 180; Winston Churchill. *See* Churchill, Winston; Arthur Cook 86–87; Hugh Gaitskell 277, 283–284; Herbert Morrison 229; A. A. Purcell 55; Franklin Roosevelt 231, 233; Sir Alan Smith 124; Philip Snowden 152–153; Richard Tawney 244–246; James H. Thomas 55; Mikhail Tomsky 99, 195

— **Speeches And Speechmaking**: American Federation of Labor (1940) 1, 2, 204, 206, 231, 233, 264; Bevin compliments 32, 128–129; Brighton TUC Congress (1933) 164, 167–168, 171; Glasgow TUC Congress (1919) 32, 129; House of Lords (1959) (maiden speech) 286, 287–291; House of Lords (1960) ('responsibilities of management') 291–292; House of Lords (1961) ('wage pause' policy) 292–293; Margate TUC Congress (1936) 199; Parliamentary Labour Party (1924) 62–63; speechmaking skill 2; Weymouth TUC Congress (1934) 170; World Federation of Trade Unions (1945) 249

Clark-Kerr, Sir Archibald 239

Clegg, Hugh 5, 44, 272

Clynes, J. R. 40, 57, 139, 148

Cold War 250, 308

Cole, G. D. H. 142, 145–146, 155, 166, 194, 218

Cole, Margaret 90

collective bargaining. *See* wage bargaining

colonial working conditions. *See* Moyne Commission

Comintern 56, 94, 98, 100, 106, 107, 163, 184, 195, 290

Common Market, WMC supports UK membership 295–296, 297

Communication Workers Union 40

Communist labour movement. *See also* **Anti-Communism**: Anglo-Russian Joint Advisory Committee. *See* TUC; TUC, WMC's career ; 'dictatorship of the proletariat' 164; dislike of WMC 97; General Strike (1926) 96; influence amongst British trade unionists 104; and International Federation of Trade Unions 55, 93; International Lenin School 106–107; National Minority Movement 65, 77, 98, 99–109, 118; power workers unofficial strikes (1949-50) 282; Red International of Labour Unions 56, 93, 96, 98, 100, 102, 105, 158, 192

Communist Party of Germany 163–165

Communist Party of Great Britain 73, 102, 105, 107, 109, 165, 194–195, 196, 200, 290

compulsory arbitration 27, 29

Congress of Industrial Organisations 233, 241–248, 243, 252, 257

Conservative Party: coalition government (1940-45) 201; Empire Free Trade policy 154; general election 1922 53; general election 1923 54; general election 1924 64; general election 1935 167; general election 1945 263–264; general election 1959 287General Strike (1926). *See* General Strike (1926) ; Orpington by-election (1962) 294; second Labour government (1929-31) 138, 141; and Spanish Civil War 176, 294; Trade Disputes and Trade Union (Amendment) Bill 1930 138; trade union law. *See* trade union law

Cook, Arthur 56, 65, 70, 73, 79, 80, 85, 86–87, 89, 103, 118, 124, 125, 126, 129, *136*, 271

Craven, William Craven, 6th Earl of 291

Cripps, Sir Stafford 146, 157, 163, 164–166, 172, 180, 221, 227, 234, 235–236

Crumpsall (Manchester) 34

cultural interests 14–16

Czechoslovakia, Sudetenland crisis (1938) 178–179

Daily Express 214

Daily Herald 42–43, 71, 97, 131, 134, 150, 155, 196, 213–214

Daily Mail 82, 141, 202

Daily Worker 109, 196, 207

Dalton, Hugh 175, 179, 181, 182, 203, 260, 262, 300

Davis, Jonathan 5

de Gaulle, General Charles *248*, 296

Deakin, Arthur 249, 252

Delacourt-Smith, Charles Delacourt-Smith, Baron 297

Democracy or Disruption? – An Examination of Communist Influences in the Trade Unions. See writings

democracy, WMC's pro-democratic stance 4, 166–168

Dickens, Charles 32

'dictatorship of the proletariat' 165

Dictatorships, and the Trade Union Movement. See writings

diluted labour 27–28

Dimitrov, Georgi 184

dockworkers' national strike (1924) 58

Dollfuss, Engelbert 170

Drumalbyn, Niall Macpherson, 1st Baron 297

Economic Advisory Council 141–142, 144

The Economic Consequences of Mr Churchill (Keynes) 69, 143

Eden, Anthony 177, 234, 237, 244, 246, 247, 250, 262, 263

Education Act 1944 266

Edward VIII, King 166, 172

Edwards, Ebby 223, 262, 270

EEC. *See* European Economic Community

Egremont, Wallasey (Wirral) 10

'Electric Republic.' *See* USSR

electrical trade 10–17, 271

Electrical Trades Union: banners *23*; Cammell Laird recognises 22; collective bargaining 21–22; compulsory arbitration 27, 29; and depression of 1920–22 46; diluted labour 27–28; *Electrical Trades Journal* 16, 26, 37, 39, 41, 92; Home Office warning about London District militancy (1918) 45; leaders *43*; London District 44–47, 100; membership card *23*; membership fall 33; membership growth 25, 33; national strike (1914) 20; national wage bargaining 29–30; World War 1 (1914-18) 27–29

Electrical Trades Union, WMC's career: *ABC of Chairmanship* (1939) 38; administrative work 34–35; admires C. H. Stavenhagen's technical writing 46; approach to activism 20–26; Assistant General Secretary (1920) 33, 33–47, *43*; branch autonomy 37; District Secretary (1914) 21, 25–26, 114; District Secretary (reelected) (1917) 28; early activism 16–17; financial and legal skills 20–21; governance 34; investigates London District financial irregularities (1921-22) 46–47; joins (1911) 16; Liverpool police strike (1919) 29; London District Committee problems 44–47; Merseyside District Committee (1912) 22; Merseyside District Committee Chair (1913) 23; militancy 18–25; move from London to Manchester (1907) 34; national miners' strike (1921) 69; negotiation skills 26–27; possibility of becoming General Secretary 48; re-elected Assistant General Secretary (1923) 37; reforms branch financial practices 35–37; relations with leadership 29; relations with shop stewards 30; salary 25, 32; supports Whitley Councils 29; unpopularity with branch officials 37; WMC leaves Liverpool (1919) 32; World War 1 (1914-18) 27–29

Electron (magazine of ETU LDC) 47

emergency powers, debate on taking 166

Emergency Powers Act 1920. *See* trade union law

employment. *See* **Formative Years**

Enfield Cable Company 46

engagement 14

Engineering Employers' Federation 57, 124, 127

Erle Royal Commission (1869) 112

Ernest Bevin, Labour's Churchill (Adonis) 134

Ernest Bevin: Portrait of a Great Englishman (Williams) 61, 134

Ethiopia, Italy invades (1936) 173

European Economic Community, WMC supports UK membership 295–296, 297

Evans, Myrddin 252

Evans, Trevor 262

Evening Standard 198, 214

Fabian Society 88

Feather, Victor 238

Federation of Engineering and Shipbuilding Trades: WMC becomes President (1917) 41; WMC becomes Secretary (1919) 41

Finland, WMC visits (1940) 236

Firth, Alec 66

Foot, Michael 176, 226

fortune telling 10

Foreign Office and Washington Embassy, 241–247, 262–265

Foulkes, Frank 282

France: Germany invades (1940) 162, 201, 207; and IFTU 56, 162; pact with USSR (1934) 185; 'Phoney War' (1939-40) 207; 'Popular Front' government (1934) 184–185; Spanish Civil War 176; Sudetenland crisis (1938) 179; syndicalism 18; vetoes UK's EEC membership 296; WMC evacuated from (1940) 201

Franco, Francisco 176, 294

Gaitskell, Hugh 272, *273*, 276, 277, 278, 280, 283, 287

Gallagher, Willie 99

general election 1918 9, 30–31, 42

general election 1922 53

general election 1923 54

general election 1924 62, 64

general election 1931 140, 155, 218, 228

general election 1935 167, 228

general election 1945 263–264

general election 1959 287

General Strike (1926). *See also*
  Samuel Commission and Report:
  aftermath and lessons learned
  86–88, 302, 303; background to
  61, 67–72; and Communist labour
  movement 96; events during 83–86;
  government legislation after 115;
  legality 115; negotiations between
  coal owners and miners' leaders
  81–83; Scarborough Trades Union
  Congress (1925) 77–79; TUC
  preparations for 72–77; views of
  WMC's role 88–91; WMC's Diary
  of 83; WMC's 'Memorandum'
  79–80, 86; WMC's positive response
  after 122
George II, King of Greece 259
George V, King 82, 147, 167
George VI, King 202, *273*
Germany. *See also* World War
  2: Allgemeiner Deutscher
  Gewerkschaftsbund 158, 161–161;
  Anglo-Russian Joint Advisory
  Committee meeting in Berlin (1927)
  97; Berlin Olympic Games (1936)
  172; causes of Nazism's rise 162;
  Churchill warns against Nazism 4,
  172; Communist defeat by Nazism
  163–165; Communist labour
  movement 107; IFTU moves to
  Berlin (1931) 158; Nazi takeover
  (1933-34) 158–161; Reichstag fire
  (1933) 184; Spanish Civil War
  support for Franco 177; WMC
  asserts Communist contribution to
  Nazism's rise 163
Gilbert, W. S. 14, 203
Gladstone, W. E. 111–112
Goering, Hermann 159, 161
Gold Standard 69, 143, 154
Gompers, Samuel 58, 254
Goodrich, Carter 255
Gordon, Archibald 250, 252, 253
Gosling, Harry 54, 59
Graham, Willie 149, 151
Greece, WMC visits (1945) 258–260

Green, William ('Bill') 171, 231, 248
Greenwood, Arthur 202, 211, 220, 225,
  227, 256
Gregg shorthand method 43–44
Gridley, Sir Arthur 276, 277, 282
Gromyko, Andrei 257
Guilty Men (Foot) 226
Gusev, Fyodor 262

Hacking, John 275
Hailsham, Lord. *See* Hogg, Sir Douglas
Halifax, Edward Wood, 1st Earl of 208,
  244, 245–246, 250, 251, 252, 256
Hands Off Russia campaign (1919–20)
  56, 99
Hannah, Leslie 273, 280, 284–285
Henderson, Arthur 53–54, 57, 88,
  116–117, 139, 141, 142, 143, 149,
  151–152, 156–157, 228
Hicks, George 55, 56, 65, 76, 85, 94,
  95, 96, 97, 98, 99, 117, 121, 126
Hill, John 48
Hillman, Sydney 252
Hindenburg, Field Marshall Paul von
  161
History of Trade Unionism 1666–1920
  (Sydney and Beatrice Webb) 88, 110
Hitler, Adolf 159, 161, 170, 172,
  178–179, 194, 204, 207, 227, 229,
  234, 263
Hobsbawm, Eric 163, 184
Hodges, Frank 54
Hogg, Sir Douglas 116
Holmes, Walter 204
Home Office 45
Home Secretary. *See* Shortt, Edward
Hopkins, Harry 242, 245, 261
Horner, Arthur 100, 102, 103–104,
  105, 169, 196, 222–223, 270, 275
House of Lords: Labour representation
  in 143; Life Peerages Act 1958 286;
  proposals to abolish 166; *Taff Vale*
  judgment 112–113
House of Lords, WMC in: attendance
  269; Common Market membership
  debate (1962) 295–296; excuses

absences due to advancing age 297–298; feels 'at home' 286; interventions and speeches (1962-72) 297–298; maiden speech (1959) 286, 287–291; non-attendance 268–269; opposes hereditary principle 286; responsibilities of management' speech (1960) 292; supports postal workers strikers (1971) 297; Transport Bill 1962 debate 294–295; 'wage pause' policy speech (1961) 292–293

Hyde Park (London) 117

Hyndley, John Hindley, 1st Viscount 272

I Search for Truth in Russia. *See* writings

ICFTU. *See* International Confederation of Free Trade Unions

IFTU. *See* International Federation of Trade Unions

illnesses 8–9, 142, 144, 147, 155

ILO. *See* International Labour Organisation

Imperial Chemical Industries (ICI) 123

Ince, Godfrey 217

Independent Labour Party. *See* Labour Party 125

Industrial Democracy (Sydney and Beatrice Webb) 20, 88

industrial relations law. *See* Mond-Turner Talks; trade union law

Industrial Syndicalist Education League 55

International Confederation of Free Trade Unions 250

International Federation of Trade Unions: and Anglo-Russian Joint Advisory Committee 93; anti-fascism 170; assists postwar recovery of European trade unions 258; Bevin's involvement in 252; Arthur Deakin as WFTU President 249; Executive Council *159*; headquarters 158; moves from Amsterdam to Berlin (1931) 158; moves to Paris (1933) 158, 162; A. A. Purcell as President

55; and Red International of Labour Unions 56, 93, 158; James H. Thomas as President 56; TUC leaves to join ICFTU (1948) 250; WFTU replaces (1945) 249; WMC as President 4, 158, 304–305; WMC persuades AFL to rejoin (1936) 244; WMC's last meeting 249; WMC's reports 160, 162, 165; World Trade Union Conference (1945) *248*, 249, 256–258; World War 2 201, 203, 204, 207–208

International Labour Organisation 51, 137, 158, 198, 252, 253–255, 261, 267

International Lenin School 106

Italy: invades Ethiopia (1936) 174; Mussolini's dictatorship 160, 165, 166, 172; Spanish Civil War support for Franco 177; WMCs Italian ancestry 8

Japan: attacks Pearl Harbor (1941) 236; competes with UK in world markets 124

Jenkins, Roy Jenkins, Lord 215, 300

Jewish Daily Forward 171

Jews, WMC supports against Fascism 171–173

Johnson, Alan 40

Joint Industrial Committees. *See* Whitley Councils

Jouhaux, Léon 185

Joynson-Hicks, Sir William 71

Keynes, John Maynard 69, 142, 143–144, 154

King, William Mackenzie 233

KPD. *See* Communist Party of Germany

Kuznetsov, Vasily *248*, 249

La Guardia, Fiorella 171

The Labour Chairman. *See* writings

labour law. *See* trade union law

Labour Magazine 74–77, 86, 101

Labour Party. *See also* **Labour Party**:
Bevan almost expelled (1944)
225–226; Bevan expelled (1939)
225–226; Bevin's suspicion of 61;
coalition government (1940-45)
201, 221, 304; Emergency Powers
Act proposal 166; and European
Economic Community 296; first
Labour government (1924) 53–64,
302; foundation (1906) 113; general
election 1922 53–54; general
election 1923 54; general election
1924 62–63; general election 1931
140, 218, 228; general election
1935 167, 228; general election
1945 263–264; general election
1959 287; headquarters 132;
Labour Magazine 74, 86; Labour
Representation Committee 113;
'landslide' government (1945-51)
120, 157, 264, 266–267, 302; main
opposition party (1922) 53–54;
nationalisation programme (1945-
51) 278–280, 304; 'Red Letter'
('Zinoviev Letter') affair 62, 63;
second Labour government (1929-
31) 98, 118, 119, 137–157, 302;
start of Attlee-Bevin ascendence
(1942) 222; TUC dominance 157,
180–182; weakness in House of
Lords 143
Labour Supply Board 209
*Labour's Final Weapon – Industrial
Unionism* (Stavenhagen) 45
Lane-Fox, George 71
Lansbury, George 157, 174, 175, 181
Laski, Harold 145, 166
law. *See* trade union law
League for Human Rights, Peace and
Democracy 233
League of Nations 174, 185
Lee, Jenny 195, 225
Leggett, Frederick 217, 251, 255
Leipart, Theodor 160, 161
Lenin, Vladimir 4, 92, 96, 98, 106, 107,
194

Leverhulme, William Hesketh Lever, 1st
Viscount 26
Lewis, John L. 231, 243, 245
lexicography 14
Liberal Party: coalition government
(1940-45) 201; general election
1922 53; general election 1924 64;
Orpington by-election (1962) 294;
second Labour government (1929-
31) 119, 138, 141, 148trade union
law. *See* trade union law
Life Peerages Act 1958 286
Liphook (Hampshire) 89
literature: WMC's interests 14, 32, 197;
WMC's writings. *See* writings
Liverpool: global city 7–8; Picton
Reading Room 14, *15*; police strike
(1919) 31–32, 41; Port of Liverpool
Employers' Association 21; religious
sectarianism 10; shipbuilding and
repair industries 21; transport
general strike (1911) 18; view of
(1907) *6*, 7; WMC leaves (1919)
32; WMC works as electrician 11;
WMC's birthplace 7, 299; WMC's
early political activism 12
Liverpool Echo 23
Lloyd, Geoffrey 277
Lloyd George, David 53, 137, 141
Lloyd, John 5, 38
Lloyd, Selwyn 292, 294
London: ETU District militancy 44–47,
100; Hyde Park TUC demonstration
(1927) 117–118; transport strike
(1924) 58, 59
Louis, Joe 172
Low, David 197–198
Lozovsky, Alexander 96, 192–193
Lubin, Isidor 255

MacDonald, Frances E. 66
MacDonald, James Ramsay 11, 40,
53–55, 57, 59–60, 63, 81–82, 88–89,
95, 137–157, 181, 197, 218, 300,
303
Macmillan, Harold 287, 288, 293, 294

Macpherson, Niall 297
Maisky, Ivan 195, 235
management responsibilities, WMC's
    speech on (1960) 291–292
Manchester: ETU HQ 33–34; WMC
    in 33–34
Manchester Guardian 107, 121
Mancroft, Stormont Mancroft, 2nd
    Baron 286
Marquand, David 300
marriage 10
Marshall Plan 249
Martin, Roderick 103
Marxism. *See* Communism
Maxton, James 125
May Committee and Report (1931)
    148–149
McLellan, Catherine (WMC's aunt)
    9
McLellan, Isabella. *See* Citrine, Isabella
memoirs. *See* writings
Men and Work (1964). *See* writings
Merry England and *Britain for the British*
    (Blatchford) 11
Merseyside. *See* Liverpool
Merseyside Shipbuilding Employers'
    Federation 21
militancy. *See* Electrical Trades Union;
    strikes
Milne-Bailey, Walter 66, 129, 144–145,
    147, 154
Miners' Federation of Great Britain:
    becomes National Union of
    Mineworkers 270; Black Friday 70;
    General Strike (1926) 67–91; Hull
    Trades Union Congress (1924) 65;
    miners' strikes (1942) 222–225;
    and National Minority Movement
    105; national strike (1921) 69; 'Red
    Friday' (1925) 61, 66, 71–72, 75, 88;
    Triple Alliance (miners, road and
    rail unions) negotiations (1921) 51,
    69, 115
Minkin, Lewis 302
Minority Movement. *See* Communist
    labour movement

Molotov, Vyacheslav 235–237, 305
monarchy: Abdication of Edward VIII
    (1936-37) 167, 172; WMC's view of
    167
Mond Moonshine (Cook and Maxton) 125
Mond, Sir Alfred (Lord Melchett) 123
Mond-Turner Talks (1927-29):
    background to 121–123;
    commencement of 123–124; legacy
    of 128; TUC agrees to participate
    124–125; WMC criticises Sir Alan
    Smith 124; WMC's reports 125–128
Morrison, Herbert 120, 179, 181, 182,
    200, 216, 227–228, 264, 279–280,
    287
Morton, Harold 45
Mosley, Oswald 154, 167
Moss Bank Brass Band 16–17
Moyne Commission (1938-40) 177–
    178, 305
Murphy, J. T. 30, 99
Murray, Philip 243, 245–246, 253
music 16–17
Mussolini, Benito 160, 172
My American Diary. See writings

National Coal Board, WMC's career:
    achievements 270–272; director of
    welfare and training (1945) 267;
    early experience of coalmines as
    electrician 271
National Confederation of Employers
    Organisations 124, 127
National Economic Development
    Council 294
National Joint Council/ National
    Council of Labour 156–157, 181,
    303–304
National Minority Movement. *See*
    Communist labour movement
National Union of Mineworkers 270
National Union of Police & Prison
    Officers 31–32
National Union of Railwaymen 39
nationalisation programme (1945-51):
    overview of 278–280; TUC input

304; WMC's approach at BEA 284–285

Nazism. *See* Germany

New Brighton Tower Company 10, 13

New Clarion 155

New Leader 195

'The Next Step in Industrial Relations.' *See* writings

Noel-Baker, Philip 276

Norway 180

nuclear power stations 278

Nutgrove Band (St Helens) 16–17

Oakdale Presbyterian Mission 9, 16

Olympic Games in Berlin (1936) 172

opera 14

oratory. *See* **Speeches and Speechmaking**

Orpington by-election (1962) 294

palmistry 10

Papandreou, Georgios 259

Parker, J. M. T. 180–181

Parliament: Bevin becomes MP for Central Wandsworth (1940) 202; Bevin stands for Gateshead (1931) 155, 218; WMC stands for Wallasey (1918) 9, 30–31, 42, 305

Parliamentary Committee (1906) 111–112

Passfield, Baron. *See* Webb, Sydney

Pearce, Robert 227

Perkins, Frances 255

Pétain, Marshal Philippe 207

phrenology 10

Picton Reading Room (Liverpool) 14, *15*

Pilkington's glass company 12, 13, 15

police strike in Liverpool (1919) 31–32, 41

politics. *See* **Labour Party**; **Political Views**

Pollitt, Harry 100, 104, 196

postal workers strike (1971), WMC presses for resolution of 297

Privy Council, WMC's membership 202–203, 304, 306

Public Order Act 1936 171

Pugh, Arthur 68, 78, 81, *81*, 82, 85, 97, 197

Punch 286

Purcell, A. A. 55–56, 57, 61–62, 64, 65, 71, 76, 83, 85, *93*, 94, 95, 97, 98, 99, 100, 117

railways: Beeching Report (1962) 294; General Strike (1926) 70; national strike (1919) 50, 114; Transport Bill 1962 294–295; Triple Alliance (miners, road and rail unions) negotiations (1921) 51, 69, 115

rearmament: Bevin's political positioning on 4; WMC's pro-rearmament stance 4, 175–176

rearmament, WMC supports 173–176

'Red Friday' (1925) 61, 66, 71–72, 75, 88

Red International of Labour Unions. *See* Communist labour movement

'Red Letter' ('Zinoviev Letter') affair 62, 63

Regulation 1AA. *See* trade union law

Reichstag fire (1933) 184

religion. *See* **Character and Attributes**

religious sectarianism 10

Rex (WMC's Alsatian dog) 270

Richards, Walter *6*, 7

Riddell, Neil 5, 28, 88

road transport: Triple Alliance (miners, road and rail unions) negotiations (1921) 51, 69, 115

Robens, Alf 276, 277

Roberts, Bryn 252

Rome, Treaty of (1957) 296

Roosevelt, Franklin 1–2, 134, 203, 206, 231, 232, 233, 242, 243, 245, 257–258, 261, 305, 308

Rothermere, Harold Harmsworth, 1st Viscount 154

Rowan, Jim 27, 29, 39, 41, 48

Royal Air Force 227
Royal Commission on unemployment
    insurance (1931) 147–148
Ruskin College conference (1927) 117
Russia. *See* USSR

Salisbury, Robert Gascoyne-Cecil, 5th
    Marquess of 294
Samuel, Herbert Samuel, 1st Viscount
    71, 84, 85
Samuel Commission and Report
    (1925-26) 71, 72, 73, 79, 80, 81,
    103
Sankey Commission (1919) 88
Schevenels, Walther 162–163, 207–208,
    249
Schmeling, Max 172
Seacombe, Wallasey (Wirral) 8
Seacombe Victoria Brass Band 16–17
seafaring tradition (Citrine Family) 9
Self, Sir Henry 275, 276
Shackleton, Edward Shackleton, Baron
    291
Shakespeare, William 14, 197
Shaw, George Bernard 14
Shaw, Tom 54
Shinwell, Emmanuel ('Manny') 59, 146,
    225, 247, 267, 268, 272, 275
shipbuilding and repair industries
    21–22
shop stewards. *See* wage bargaining
shorthand 43–44
Shortt, Edward (Home Secretary 1919-
    22) 31
Shvernik, Nicolai 189, 192, 235, 236
sickness 8–9
Simon, Sir John 170, 205
Simpson, Wallis 172
singing 17, 23, 24
Skidelsky, Robert 147–148, 154, 155
Slade, Doris. *See* Citrine, Doris
Slesser, Sir Henry 116, 138
Sloan, Pat 194–195
Smith, Sir Allan 57–58, 124, 127
Smith, Herbert 70, 80, 82, 85, 86, 105,
    125, 271

Snowden, Philip 11, 139, 142, 147,
    148–153, 155
Social Democratic Federation 11
Socialism. *See* **Labour Party**
Socialist League 146, 163, 164, 166,
    181, 218, 227, 235, 244
Society for Socialist Inquiry and
    Propaganda 145–146, 155, 218
Society of Railway Servants, Associated
    112–113
South Wales Miners' Federation 73,
    104
Soviet Union. *See* USSR
Spanish Civil War (1936-39): WMC
    debates with Marquess of Salisbury
    in House of Lords (1962) 294;
    WMC's support for Republican
    government 176–177, 305
St Helen's (Lancashire) 12, 15
Stalin, Joseph 95, 97, 98, 99, 195, 234,
    235, 249, 257, 259, 261
Stavenhagen, C. H. 45, 46
Steel-Maitland, Arthur 74
Stewart, Archie 46–47
strikes: General Strike (1926). *See*
    General Strike (1926) ; Liverpool
    police strike (1919) 31–32; Liverpool
    transport general strike (1911) 18;
    London transport strike (1924) 58,
    59; miners' strikes (1942) 222–225;
    national docks strike (1924) 58;
    national electricians' strike (1914)
    20; national miners' strike (1921)
    69; national railway strike (1919)
    50, 114; postal workers strike (1971)
    297; power workers unofficial strikes
    (1949-50) 282–283; and WMC's
    House of Lords maiden speech
    289–291
Sudetenland crisis (1938) 178–179
Sullivan, Arthur 203
Sunday Times 291
Swales, Alonso 56, 68, 70, 71, 76, 77,
    78, 82, 95, 97, 98, 117, 126, 138
syndicalism 19, 42, 44–45, 58, 61

Taff Vale judgment (1901) 112–113

'Talks with Our Officers' 37

Tanner, Jack 252

Tawney, Richard 142, 167, 244–246, 250, 251

Taylor, A. J. P. 219

Taylor, Robert 5, 75

Tewson, Vincent 66, 261, 293, 305

Thomas, James H. 39, 54, 55, 76, 78, 82, 84, 139

Thorpe, Andrew 181

Tillett, Ben 93, 117

Times, The 97, 197, 246, 291–292

Tomlinson, George 254

Tomsky, Mikhail 61–62, 93 *93*, 94, 95, 96, 97, 99, 165–166, 189, 195

Tracey, Herbert 66, 70, 145

trade union law: Emergency Powers Act 1920 59, 82, 114–115; Emergency Powers Act 1940 208, 212; Erle Royal Commission (1869) 112; Hyde Park TUC demonstration (1927) 117–118; Parliamentary Committee (1906) 111–112; Regulation 1AA (1944) 224–225, 255; Ruskin College conference (1927) 117; *Taff Vale* judgment (1901) 112–113; Trade Disputes Act 1906 113–114, 115, 120; Trade Disputes and Trade Union Act 1927 110, 115–120, 137, 146, 205, 224, 229; Trade Disputes and Trade Union (Amendment) Bill 1930 138–139; Trade Union Act 1871 111–112; Trade Union Defence Committee 117; TUC's lobbying effectiveness 111; WMC discusses with Attlee (1943) 120; WMC discusses with Churchill (1941-42) 119; WMC's expertise 110; WMC's opposition to restrictive laws 110–111, 116–120

Trade Unionism – its Rise, Development and Future. See writings

Trades Councils 100

Transport and General Workers' Union 58

Transport Bill 1962 294–295

Transport House 132

Transport Workers' Federation 70–71

Tribune 226

Triple Alliance (miners, road and rail unions) negotiations (1921) 51, 69, 115

Trotsky, Leon 96–98

Truman, Harry 249, 261

tuberculosis 9, 299

TUC: Anglo-Russian Joint Advisory Committee *93*, 93–94, 96, 98, 183; Assistant General Secretary 51; Colonial Advisory Committee 177congresses. *See* TUC congresses; dominance within Labour Party 157, 180–182; Economic Committee 144–145; and first Labour government (1924) 53–64; foundation (1868) 64; General Council 50–51, *68*; General Secretary 51; growth of trade union movement (1914-20) 50; headquarters 52; increase in General Council's power 64–66; influence on 1945 Labour government 266–267; International Committee 94; and International Federation of Trade Unions 56; *Labour Magazine* 74, 86, 101; move to Transport House (1928) 132; and nationalisation programme 304; official visit to USSR (1924) 93; Parliamentary Committee 50; and second Labour government (1929-31) 137–157; secretariat 66; Special Industrial Committee 70, 72, 78, 79, 81; and trade union law. *See* trade union law; Trades Councils 100; Trotsky's attack on (1927) 97–98; WMC's continued interest 274; WMC's reports on conferences 41–42; World War 2. *See* World War 2

TUC, congresses: Belfast (1929) 128; Blackpool (1942) 240–241, 243, 247, 253; Blackpool (1944) 258;

Blackpool (1945) 264; Bournemouth (1926) 86, 96; Brighton (1933) 162, 167–168, 173, *210*; Brighton (1946) 268; Edinburgh (1927) 32, 101, 121; Edinburgh (1941) 212–213, 216; Glasgow (1919) 32, 128; Hull (1924) 52, 65–66, 70; Margate (1936) 184, 198; Plymouth (1937) 193, 196; Scarborough (1925) 71, 77–79, 94; Swansea (1928) 101, 126; Weymouth (1934) 170–171

TUC, WMC's career: Acting General Secretary (1925) 53, 61, 78; addresses Parliamentary Labour Party (1924) 62–64; Anglo-Russian Joint Advisory Committee meeting in Berlin (1927) 93; Anglo-Russian Joint Advisory Committee secretary (1924) 62, 63; apolitical approach 302; ARJAC joint secretary (1925) 93–94; Assistant General Secretary (1924) 48–49, 52–66; attends Economic Advisory Council (1929-31) 142; beginning of decline in influence (1942) 222; Bevan's hostility 226; builds TUC secretariat 66; calls for overhaul of strike-calling procedures 74–77; contribution to trade union movement 301; discontinues Anglo-Russian Committee (1927) 96, 98; General Council member (1925) 129; General Secretary (1926) 86, 129–130; General Strike (1926) 67–91; greets USSR trade delegation (1924) 61–62, 92–93; Hull Congress (1924) 65–66; ideas for TUC reform 42–43, 53, 64; IFTU reports to General Council. *See* International Federation of Trade Unions ; illness (1929-30) 142, 144, 147, 155; leaves to join National Coal Board (1945) 267–268, 307; 'Memorandum' on preparations for General Strike (1925) 79–80, 86; Mond-Turner Talks (1927-29) 121–128; Moyne

Commission (1938-39) 177–178; National Joint Council secretary (1931) 156–157, 228; National Minority Movement 99–109; rebuffed at UN San Francisco founding conference 1945, 261–265; reluctance to leave 267–268; second Labour government (1929-31) 138–157; tours USA and Canada (1940) 1–2; Trade Disputes and Trade Union (Amendment) Bill 1930 138; Trade Union Defence Committee joint Secretary (1927) 117; *Tribune* cartoons 226; visits Austria (1934) 170; visits Moscow (1940) 3; visits USSR (1925) 94–96; visits USSR (1935) 183–196; World War 2. *See* World War 2 (1939-45), WMC and *The T.U.C. in Wartime* (TUC) 206

Turner, Ben 117, 123

Two Careers (1967). *See* writings

unemployment, WMC's time of 13, 14

United Nations 254–255, 261–263

United States. *See also* American Federation of Labor; World War 2: Congress of Industrial Organisations : assertiveness 137–138; Bevin visits (1916) 58; competes with UK in world markets 124; establishment of United Nations 255; League for Human Rights, Peace and Democracy 233; WMC visits (1934) 171–172; WMC visits (1936) 172

USSR. *See also* Comintern; Communist labour movement; World War 2: All-Union Central Council of Trade Unions 56, 95; Bolshevik Revolution (1917) 4, 92; civil war (1919–20) 56; Cold War 250, 308; 'dictatorship of the proletariat' 165; Five-Year Plans 186, 189, 190; joins League of Nations (1934) 185; Lenin's 'Electric Republic' vision 4, 92, 96, 194; Lenin's personality cult 95; map of WMC's 1935 tour

187; Moscow Trials (1937) 195; pact with France (1934) 185; Roosevelt's hopes for postwar relations with 257–258; trade relations with UK (1924) 61–62, 92–93, 140; trade unions lose independence 166; TUC official visit (1924) 93; UK recognises (1924) 61; 'United Front' policy against Fascism 184; WMC likens to State Capitalism 190; WMC visits (1925) 94–96, 165; WMC's six visits 4

Vladeck, Baruk Charney 171

wage bargaining: collective bargaining 21–22; compulsory arbitration 27, 29, 206; shop stewards 30; Whitley Councils 29, 123; World War 2 206
'wage pause' policy WMC opposes 292–294
Walkden, Alec *210*
Wallasey, Wirral (Cheshire) 8, 9, 10, 30–31, 42, 305
Webb, Beatrice 20, 46, 53, 63, 69–70, 88, 89–91, 110, 186, 194
Webb, Bill 45, 57
Webb, Sydney, 1st Baron Passfield 20, 57, 89, 91, 110, 152, 186, 194
Wembley Park (London) 198, 268
West Indies, working conditions in. *See* Moyne Commission
Westminster Central Hall (London) 208
WFTU. *See* World Federation of Trade Unions
Whitley Councils 29, 123
Wikipedia 207
Williams, Francis 61, 134
Wilson, Harold 276
Winant, John 252, 262
Woll, Matthew 233
Woodcock, George 145, 205, 256
Workers Press 108
Workers Publications Ltd 108
World Federation of Trade Unions 249–250

World Trade Union Conference (1945) *248*, 249, 256–258
World War 1. *See* **World War 1**
World War 2 (1939-45). *See also* Bevin, Ernest; Churchill, Winston: Advisory Committees (government/TUC) 204–208; aid to USSR 239; Allies' ascendency 257; Allies' plans for postwar Germany 239–240; Attlee downplays threat from Hitler (1934) 227; Beveridge Report (1942) 256, 266; Bevin Boys (1944) 222; Churchill delays Second Front (1941) 235, 237, 239; Citrine warns against Nazism 4, 172; coalition government (1940-45) 201, 221; D-Day (1944) 223, 257; demobilisation plans 255–256; disputes over manpower assignment policy (1941) 212–216, 219; Education Act 1944 266; Finland-USSR Winter War (1939-40) 236; German threat to invade UK (1940) 204; Germany ascendent (1941-42) 237; Germany invades Norway (1940) 180; Germany invades the West (1940) 161–162, 201, 207; Germany invades USSR (1941) 3, 194, 234–235; Hitler's suicide (1945) 263; Japan attacks Pearl Harbor (1941) 236; joint US/UK military mission to USSR (1941) 220; Marshall Plan 249; Nazi-Soviet non-aggression pact (1939) 179; 'Phoney War' (1939-40) 207; pro-USSR opinion 3, 234; Roosevelt's death (1945) 261; Roosevelt's hopes for postwar relations with USSR 257–258; Tehran Conference (1943) 257; TUC delegation excluded from first UN Conference (1945) 261–263; TUC involvement in war effort 204–208; US isolationism 231, 243, 264; victory in Europe (1945) 263
World War 2 (1939-45), WMC and: Anglo-French Trade Union Council meetings (1939-40)

207; Anglo-Soviet Trade Union Committee (ASTUC) 234, 238; anti-appeasement stance before 178–182; arranges evacuation of IFTU staff from France (1940) 208; attempts to extend ASTUC to US unions 236–237, 240–248; beginning of decline in influence (1942) 222; Bevan's hostility 225–226; criticises Michael Foot's *Guilty Men* book 226; diplomatic contribution during 4–5, 203–204, 232, 250, 264–265, 306; dispute with Bevan over skilled labour conscription policy (1941) 212–216; encourages 'one TUC' approach to consultations with government 206; evacuated from France (1940) 201; evacuates IFTU staff from France (1940) 208; in German 'Black Book' 204; hostile reception in USA (1942) 243; hostility from Bevin and Foreign Office 244–265; hosts Soviet trade union delegation (1941-42) 237–238; ILO Conference (1944) 253–255; leads TUC delegation to inaugural UN Conference (1945) 261–263; map of USA/Canada 1940 tour *232*; miners' strikes (1942) 222–225; negotiations with Chamberlain 204–206; postwar depression and recovery 266; Privy Councillor (1940) 202–203, 306; pro-rearmament stance before 4, 173–176; 'Quisling' incident and Bevin 213–215; relationship with Attlee 226–230; relationship with Bevin 208–230; relationship with Churchill 203–204; reputation within Labour Party 250; shocked by Roosevelt's death 261; supports Ministry of Production (1942) 207; supports postwar German reparations 239–240; Tawney briefs Eden against WMC 244–246, 251; tours USA and Canada (1940) 1–2, 204, 206, 231–234; visits Finland (1940) 236; visits Greece (1945) 258–260; visits Moscow (1941) 3, 234–237; visits Moscow (1943) 238–239; visits USA (1942) 222, 243; visits USA (1943) 248; visits USA (1944) 257; wartime travels summarised 264–265; Westminster Central Hall special conference (1940) 208

writings: *ABC of Chairmanship* (1939) 3, 38–41, 40; autobiography, vol 1. *Men and Work* (1964), 5, 300; vol 2. *Two Careers* (1967), 5, 300; *The Labour Chairman* 1920, 38, 39; 'The Next Step in Industrial Relations' (1927), 121–122; *Labour and the Community* (1928); *Democracy or Disruption? – An Examination of Communist; Influences in the Trade Unions* (1928) 101,104,107–8; *The Tolpuddle Martyrs centenary book* (1934); *Dictatorships, and the Trade Union Movement* (1933), 162, 305; *I Search for Truth in Russia* (1936 and 1938), 109, 185, 187, 194–6; *The ABC of Chairmanship* (1939), 3, 38–41; *My Finnish Diary* (1940); *Slavery under Hitler's New Order* (1941); *In Russia Now* (1942); *British Trade Unions* (1942); *My American Diary* (1943) 232

Yorkshire Electricity Board 279

Zinoviev, Grigory 62, 96, 195

Lightning Source UK Ltd.
Milton Keynes UK
UKHW011937060821
388460UK00008B/640/J